CAMBRIDGE GREEK AND LATIN CLASSICS

DEMOSTHENES
SELECTED PRIVATE SPEECHES

EDITED BY

C. CAREY

AND

R. A. REID

Lecturers in Greek
University of St Andrews

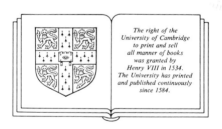

CAMBRIDGE UNIVERSITY PRESS

CAMBRIDGE
LONDON   NEW YORK   NEW ROCHELLE
MELBOURNE   SYDNEY

Published by the Press Syndicate of the University of Cambridge
The Pitt Building, Trumpington Street, Cambridge CB2 IRP
32 East 57th Street, New York, NY 10022, USA
10 Stamford Road, Oakleigh, Melbourne 3166, Australia

First published 1985

Printed in Great Britain by the
University Press, Cambridge

Library of Congress catalogue card number: 84-21356

British Library cataloguing in publication data

Demosthenes.
Selected private speeches.—(Cambridge
Greek and Latin classics)
I. Title   II. Carey, C.   III. Reid, R. A.
885′ 01   PA3949. A7

ISBN 0 521 23960 5 hard covers
ISBN 0 521 28373 6 paperback

CONTENTS

Preface   *page* vii

Abbreviations   viii

Introduction   I

   1   *The Athenian legal system*   I

   2   *Speechwriters*   13

Note on the text   20

DEMOSTHENES:
SELECTED PRIVATE SPEECHES

   54 Against Conon   23

   37 Against Pantaenetus   34

   39 Against Boeotus   47

   56 Against Dionysodorus   56

Commentary   69

Index   237

PREFACE

Little need be said in defence of a commentary on a selection of private speeches from the Demosthenic corpus. The last English-language commentary to cover any of the speeches contained in this book was that of Doherty in 1927. In general, Greek oratory has been sadly neglected in recent decades. Part of the reason is the general unpopularity of the art of rhetoric; like that of adultery it is publicly disavowed while privately practised (and perhaps practised the less well for being disavowed). A further reason perhaps is that Greek oratory has often in the past been approached primarily as a source of good prose style rather than as an art form as interesting and rewarding as any other Greek literary genre.

This book is intended principally for the use of undergraduates and students in the upper forms of schools. Though we have commented on linguistic matters of interest and textual matters where significant, we have sought above all to examine the speeches as functional artefacts, as attempts to persuade. Unless it is written as an exercise a speech is as much a functional artefact as a table or a chair, and it is legitimate to ask while reading how well it performs the function for which it was written. We have also sought to use the speeches to shed light on some aspects of Athenian society in the fourth century B.C. In the preparation of the text we have undertaken no independent collation of manuscripts but have relied on the reports of the Oxford and Budé editions of Rennie and Gernet. For reasons of space we have not included a critical apparatus. Places where we disagree with the Oxford text are listed in the Note on the Text. When referring to speeches in the Demosthenic corpus which are of doubtful authenticity we have not used square brackets, since the question of authenticity in such cases is irrelevant to the purposes of this book.

We wish to express our gratitude to Sir Kenneth Dover for stimulating ideas and encouragement, to the general editors of the series for their valuable assistance, to the staff of Cambridge University Press, especially the subeditor, Susan Moore, and the reader, Owen Kember, and finally to undergraduates in the Greek class at St Andrews, past and present, for their patience.

St Andrews, January 1984   C. C./R. A. R.

ABBREVIATIONS

Bonner–Smith	R. J. Bonner and G. Smith, *The administration of justice from Homer to Aristotle* (Chicago) I (1930), II (1938).
Cohen	E. E. Cohen, *Ancient Athenian maritime courts* (Princeton 1973).
Davies	J. K. Davies, *Athenian propertied families, 600–300 B.C.* (Oxford 1971).
Denniston *GP*	*J. D. Denniston, The Greek particles*² (Oxford 1954).
Doherty	F. C. Doherty, *Three private speeches of Demosthenes* (Oxford 1927).
Dover	K. J. Dover, *Greek popular morality in the time of Plato and Aristotle* (Oxford 1974).
Fine *Horoi*	J. V. A. Fine, *Horoi* (*Hesperia*: Suppl. IX, 1951).
Finley	M. I. Finley, *Studies in land and credit in ancient Athens, 500–200 B.C.* (New Brunswick 1951; repr. 1973).
Gernet	L. Gernet, *Démosthène, plaidoyers civils* (Paris) I (1954), II (1957), III (1959), IV (1960).
Goodwin *MT*	W. W. Goodwin, *Syntax of the moods and tenses of the Greek verb* (New York 1875; repr. London and New York 1965).
Harrison	A. R. W. Harrison, *The law of Athens* (Oxford) I (1968), II (1971).
IG	*Inscriptiones Graecae* (Berlin 1873–).
Isager–Hansen	S. Isager and M. H. Hansen, *Aspects of Athenian society in the fourth century B.C.* (Odense 1975).
Lipsius	J. H. Lipsius, *Das attische Recht und Rechtsverfahren* (Leipzig 1905–15).
MacDowell *AHL*	D. M. MacDowell, *Athenian homicide law in the age of the orators* (Manchester 1963).
MacDowell *Law*	D. M. MacDowell, *The law in classical Athens* (London 1978).
Paley–Sandys	F. A. Paley and J. E. Sandys, *Select private orations of Demosthenes* (Cambridge) I³ (1898), II (1875).

Rennie	W. Rennie, *Demosthenis orationes* (Oxford) II.2 (1921), III (1931).
Rhodes	P. J. Rhodes, *A commentary on the Aristotelian 'Athenaion politeia'* (Oxford 1981).
SEG	*Supplementum Epigraphicum Graecum* (Leiden 1923–).
Tod	M. N. Tod, *A selection of Greek historical inscriptions* II (Oxford 1948).
Westermann	A. Westermann, *Ausgewählte Reden des Demosthenes* III² (Berlin 1865).
Wyse	W. Wyse, *The speeches of Isaeus* (Cambridge 1904).

INTRODUCTION

1. THE ATHENIAN LEGAL SYSTEM[1]

i. *The juries*

The principle of Athenian justice, as of British, was trial by a panel of laymen. For service on juries there was no wealth qualification, and no legal knowledge was required. All that was necessary was to be over thirty years of age, male, and in possession of full citizen rights. To ensure an adequate supply of jurors for the growing number of cases in the fifth century, and to ensure that all classes were represented on juries, pay for jury service was introduced by Pericles in the middle of the century, at a rate of two obols per day. This was later raised by Cleon to three obols in the 420s. The attempt to make juries truly representative of Athenian society can have succeeded only for a short time. Since three obols was equivalent to the wage of an unskilled labourer in the last third of the fifth century, Aristophanes' picture (*Wasps* 300ff.) of poor citizens relying on the jury pay for their keep may be true for his time. But in the fourth century the jurors' pay failed to keep pace with inflation. In the latter half of the century an unskilled labourer could earn $1\frac{1}{2}$ drachmas (nine obols), but the juror still received his three obols. At this period the jurors' pay represented minimal compensation for loss of time rather than a living wage. The poor rate of pay will have attracted only the relatively well-to-do or those who could earn their living in no other way.[2]

Although in principle the Athenian court resembled ours, if a modern could somehow be transported back to witness an Athenian trial he would be struck by the differences more than by the similarities. In a modern court the burden of judgement is divided between judge and jury, each with a separate function. The jury concerns itself solely with questions of fact. The judge controls the procedure, decides questions

[1] This account is intended solely as a brief introduction to the subject. Those who desire more detailed information may consult the handbooks listed in the Abbreviations.

[2] The latter would include the elderly, the infirm, and those whose work was seasonal. On the composition of the juries see A. H. M. Jones, *Athenian democracy* (Oxford 1957) 36f., Dover 34f.

of law, sums up the issues before the jury votes, and in case of conviction fixes penalty. But the Athenian jury suffered no such restriction. The word *dikastes*, which we translate 'juror', embraces the functions of both judge and jury. Each court had a presiding magistrate who supervised the procedure and gave formal announcement of the verdict after the jurors had voted. But he did not advise the jury on points of law. Nor did he sum up the arguments of both sides before the vote. Each juror was his own arbiter on points of law, and each was left to retain in his head the salient points of both sides of the dispute. In the Athenian courts, moreover, it was the jury, not the presiding magistrate, who fixed the penalty. For many offences penalties were fixed by law (this type of trial was called an *agon atimetos*). But in cases where no penalty was laid down (*agon timetos*) it was left to the parties involved to propose alternative punishments or awards. The verb used is *timasthai*; the name for the proposal is *timema*. It was for the jury to decide between these alternatives.

Thus the Athenian jury exercised far more power than a modern jury. Furthermore, each jury sat as the representative of the Athenian demos. Speakers addressing Athenian courts often say 'you did this' or 'you decided that' when referring to decisions made by the assembly. Part of the community stands for the whole. And since the jury represented the sovereign demos, its decisions were final.

The Athenian jury also differed from the modern jury in size. The size of the jury varied according to the seriousness of the issue. In the fourth century we have evidence for juries ranging from two hundred to twenty-five hundred. A jury of six thousand is recorded for an important political trial in 415.[3]

Finally, our time-traveller would be struck by the absence of discussion. Neither the vote on the main issue nor the vote on the penalty was preceded by any discussion on the part of the jury.

Such a system has certain obvious advantages. The size of the juries, combined with the use of secret ballot, made bribery and intimidation difficult. There is in fact evidence of some corruption towards the end of the fifth century,[4] but the elaborate procedure for the allocation of

[3] For references see Harrison II 47. The numbers given in the text are rounded down, for juries usually consisted of odd numbers, 201, 2,501 etc., the purpose being to avoid a tie.

[4] *Ath. Pol.* 27.5.

jurors to different courts in the fourth century made it virtually impossible to bribe a jury. The absence of any property qualification or special training for jurors prevented the courts from serving a sectional interest, even though, as was noted above, it is unlikely that juries contained a full cross-section of the citizen population.

But the disadvantages are equally obvious. The absence of a legal expert to decide points of law meant that the layman had to answer such questions for himself. This was less of a drawback in ancient Athens than it would be today, for Athenian laws were drafted in the language of everyday (polite) speech, not in any specialist jargon. But obscurities there were. And since Athenian laws often simply named offences without defining them, it often fell to the jury to decide whether or not a given act fell within the scope of a given law.[5] This problem was at its most acute in cases (such as the occasion for which Dem. 37 was written) where the defendant lodges a formal plea that the case is not admissible on technical grounds.[6] The absence of a summing-up meant that each juror had to retain the salient points of each side in his head. The absence of discussion left little room for argument (other than between immediate neighbours) and reflection before voting. Above all, the size of the juries, combined with all these factors, allowed much more scope for emotion. Crowd behaviour is a recognizable phenomenon in all societies, and a body of two hundred or more is a potential crowd. It is easy for a crowd to be manipulated by a skilful speaker. Athenian juries were especially prone to emotional display; they tended to express their views of a speaker in unambiguous terms, with shouts of approval, derision or outrage.[7] Our time-traveller might find an Athenian courtroom on occasion more reminiscent of a football match than of a modern trial.

ii. Prosecutors

There was in Athens no equivalent to the Director of Public Prosecutions in England and Wales, the Procurator Fiscal in Scotland, or the District Attorney in the United States. Sometimes the assembly or the council appointed official prosecutors for particular cases.[8] But for most cases, both public and private, the Athenian legal system relied on volunteer

[5] See on 39.40.
[7] See on 54.1.
[6] See introduction to 37.
[8] See MacDowell *Law* 61f.

prosecutors. In public cases prosecution was open to any free adult male who wished to prosecute, though some public cases could not be brought by non-citizens, and no case (public or private) could be brought by a man who had been deprived of his citizen rights. Public cases (*demosiai dikai*) concerned offences which were believed to affect the whole community; this included not only wrongs done to the state but also certain types of wrong done to individuals which were held to damage the fabric of society, such as wrongs done to parents. In private cases (*idiai dikai*) only the alleged victim could sue. Anyone proposing to prosecute in either type of case initiated the proceedings himself. This is true not only of what we should call civil cases (such as disputes arising from contracts) but also what we should call criminal cases. Thus Ariston prosecutes Conon for battery himself (Dem. 54). The major distinction in Athenian law is between public and private actions, not civil and criminal.

It was up to the prosecutor to summons his opponent; he took with him summons-witnesses (*kleteres*) to witness that the summons had been duly served. The summons ordered the defendant to appear on a specific day before the magistrate under whose jurisdiction the case fell. In most types of private case, the defendant was summoned to appear before the tribal judges. This was a body of forty (in the fourth century), four from each tribe; each tribal division of four dealt with the cases in which the defendant was a member of their tribe. In matters up to ten drachmas these could decide the issue themselves. Other cases they pased on to a public arbitrator, who heard both sides and gave judgement.[9] If either party appealed, the tribal judges then brought the case to court. In public cases the stage of arbitration was omitted. In both types of case the next stage was the *anakrisis* (preliminary hearing), details of which are obscure. The magistrate perhaps satisfied himself about such details as the capacity of both parties to appear in court, and that the correct legal procedures had been adopted. The date was then set for the trial.

iii. Evidence

It was up to the litigant (both defendant and plaintiff) to assemble for himself the evidence needed to support his case. He would need to

[9] Cases which did not come before a public arbitrator could be decided by a private arbitrator appointed by both sides. See on 54.26–9 and cf. 56.16.

consult the relevant laws, and private documents such as wills and contracts, and assemble witnesses. Transcripts of laws and other documents were read out by the clerk of the court. From the end of the fifth century there was a state archive of laws in the Metroon (shrine of the Mother Goddess) which litigants could consult. But no written copy was circulated in court; so the jurors would have to rely on memory to determine whether the law had been quoted accurately. The procedure was probably policed quite effectively by the litigants themselves, since a misquotation, or at any rate a gross misquotation, by one party would be pounced upon by the opponent. The penalty for citing a non-existent law was death,[10] and again each litigant would presumably watch his opponent. It was, of course, always possible to quote selectively.

The basic procedure was the same for witnesses as for laws in the fourth century. In the fifth century witnesses gave evidence in person. In the fourth century the litigant drafted the testimony, which was read out in court by the clerk. The witness merely confirmed that the statement was correct. The practice obviously offers scope for abuse, since careful choice of wording by the litigant could distort the effect of a witness's testimony while remaining broadly true to the facts. No opportunity was allowed for cross-examination of witnesses for the opposition.[11] In order to be sure of friendly witnesses the sensible course was to take witnesses along in any action which might involve subsequent litigation.[12] In unexpected crises such as the case of Ariston in Dem. 54 a man would have to rely on accidental witnesses, or even hostile witnesses, as at Dem. 57.14.

iv. Timing

Although it was possible to delay the introduction of a case into court, once in court it was settled quickly. Any case which came into court had to be settled in a single day. Only one public case could be tried by any one jury on a single day, but a jury could try several private

[10] Dem. 26.24.

[11] If a witness gave false testimony it was open to the opponent to bring an action for perjury (*dike pseudomartyrion*), provided that he declared his intention to do so before the votes were cast.

[12] This is implied at Dem. 57.14 and stated at Isae. 3.19.

cases in one day. Speedy decisions were ensured by the use of the water clock (*klepsydra*). This was a crude but effective device, consisting of a water-filled pot with a hole in the base. The water was allowed to trickle away; the speaker had to finish when the water ran out. Different amounts of water were allowed for different kinds of trial. Each party was allowed the same amount of time to present his case, though he was not obliged to use up all of his allowance.[13] The hole was stopped with a bung while the clerk read out documents and depositions.

v. Speeches

Once he freed his ears from the clamour of the jury, the principal idiosyncrasy our time-traveller would notice in the Athenian court would be the method used for the presentation of the case. First and foremost, the modern system assigns a relatively insignificant role to the parties to a suit. Although an individual may elect to conduct his own case, it is almost invariable to engage the services of a lawyer, who will not only decide such issues as the kind of action to be brought or the most appropriate defence plea but will also conduct the case in court, including the extraction of evidence from friendly witnesses and the demolition of hostile witnesses. The plaintiff or defendant will speak only to give evidence, and his evidence is on a par with that of the witnesses. Secondly, all witnesses present their own testimony. Thirdly, the modern trial proceeds in a pedestrian manner. Each piece of evidence is tested by both sides before the next piece of evidence is introduced. Interruptions objecting to procedural breaches are tolerated.

This is a world away from the Athenian system, which placed the onus squarely on the shoulders of the parties to the suit. Litigants were expected to conduct their own case in court. It is unlikely that any law actually stated that a litigant had to speak for himself. But by tradition this was what happened and it would have been foolhardy for a litigant to depart from tradition. Anyone who failed to present his own case would risk creating the impression that he was too unsure of the justice of his case to speak on his own behalf. The method of presentation was continuous exegesis, that is, speeches. Instead of the slow, halting

---

[13] Hence at Dem. 36 fin., 38 fin., the speaker can say, with evident confidence in his case: 'pour out the water' (i.e. the unused residue).

procedure used in modern courts, each litigant delivered a speech, without interruption from his opponent. Prosecution preceded defence, as in modern courts. Information which in our system is obtained from witnesses was in Athenian courts given directly by the principals to the suit. The role of the witness was simply to give objective corroboration of the statements made by the litigant.

The only exception to the above procedure was that it was possible for an acquaintance or relative of a litigant to speak on his behalf after the conclusion of the litigant's speech. Such a helper was called a *synegoros*, and his speech counted against the time-allowance of his protégé. On occasion speakers ask the jurors' permission to introduce such supporters,[14] but if there was ever any rule that permission must be sought it was a dead letter in the fourth century, for such requests are by no means invariable. The role played by the *synegoros* varied. Often he would merely draw conclusions from evidence already presented in the main speech. But sometimes the *synegoros* handled the whole case. The litigant in such cases merely delivered a brief introduction. Thus the banker Phormion, an ex-slave whose command of Greek was limited, only uttered a few sentences in his defence against his stepson, while a *synegoros* delivered the main speech (Dem. 36). Likewise, in the prosecution of the ex-courtesan Neaira, Theomnestus, the supposed prosecutor, delivers the introduction, while the prosecution is handled by the *synegoros* Apollodorus (Dem. 59). Here the probable reason is that Apollodorus wishes to avoid the penalties attending failure to obtain one-fifth of the votes,[15] which would damage his political career. But cases such as these two are unusual.

In theory at least the *synegoros* was not professional. Usually he took pains to represent himself as friend or relative of his protégé, as a dispassionate defender of the innocent or at least an enemy of the opponent. It was in fact illegal for a *synegoros* to take a fee.[16] But the law was unenforceable, since only the parties to the transaction would know the facts, and neither had reason to expose himself. There is evidence that the services of a *synegoros* could be engaged for money.[17] But the law had one important effect. It made it unsafe for a man to appear too often as *synegoros*. If any institution was likely to develop into

[14] E.g. Dem. 34.52, Hyp. *Lyc.* 20.   [15] See on 54.1, 56.4.
[16] Dem. 46.26.
[17] Dem. 21.112, 51.16, Lycurg. *Leocr.* 138.

the Athenian equivalent of the modern barrister it was the role of *synegoros*, and the restrictions, legal and conventional, on its use prevented any such evolution.

The advantage of this system is that recourse to law is relatively cheap, unlike today when anybody who is not wealthy thinks twice about resorting to legal action. The disadvantage is that the result will depend at least in part on the skill of the litigant as a public speaker, which in turn depends on education and experience and therefore on income.[18] The scales of justice were loaded in favour of wealth and influence. But it is difficult to imagine a society in which they are not.

Not only the form but also the content of surviving forensic speeches testifies to the gulf between ancient Athenian practice and our own. The modern jury is expected to make its decision on the basis of the facts. So too was the Athenian jury. But in addition to the facts of the case the jury was expected to take account of other factors which we would consider irrelevant.

1. The general character of the litigant was considered relevant. Speakers frequently offer evidence of their own good character by citing particular good deeds, or describing their general conduct, in public and sometimes in private life. This is true not only of cases such as scrutiny for public office (as e.g. Lys. 16.10ff.), where even we should concede the relevance of the speaker's character, for we ourselves expect higher standards from politicians than from e.g. businessmen. But such information is equally common in suits about wrongs, property or debts. Thus we find speakers listing liturgies and war-taxes to which they have contributed (as e.g. Lys. 19.57ff., 21.1ff., 25.12)[19] or donations (*epidoseis*) which they have made to the state (as Dem. 34.38f.). Military services may be cited (as Lys. 20.24ff.), or success in athletics (Lys. 19.63). Not only do speakers expect gratitude from the jury for such services, but it is clearly acceptable for a man to admit that his aim in serving the state was to lay up credit to serve him in the event of a future trial (Lys. 16.17, 20.31, 25.13). In view of the solidarity of the family in archaic and classical Greece, one is not surprised to see litigants claiming credit for the deeds of ancestors (Andoc. 1.141, Lys. 14.24, 30.1, Isae. 5.46). In addition, the litigant seeks to benefit from the prestige of his witnesses

---

[18] Likewise, the rich could hire *synegoroi* (preceding note) or underlings to harass an opponent (see on 39.2).

[19] See on 54.44.

and *synegoroi* and the goodwill which they have earned from the public (Dem. 51.16ff., Lys. 12.86, 14.21f., 30.31). The following passage from Lycurgus (*Leocr.* 139f.) illustrates both the effect such supporters could have and the range of benefactions they could call upon:

'But some of them, not content with attempting to mislead you with arguments, will actually claim the right to beg off defendants on the strength of their own public services. These are the ones *I* most resent. Though they have used these services for the advantage of their own family they ask public gratitude from you. For a man does not deserve such gratitude from you simply because he has had brilliant success in keeping horses [i.e. for the panhellenic games] or in performing the office of choregus [i.e. in defraying the cost of providing, training and dressing a chorus for the dramatic festivals at Athens] or has spent money on some other such thing (for such achievements win a crown for the individual alone but do not help others), but because he has had great success as trierarch [i.e. in fitting out a warship and keeping it in repair for a year] or has built walls around his country or has contributed to the safety of all from his private means...But in my opinion nobody has performed services of sufficient magnitude for the city that he can claim as a special favour [the remission of] the punishment of traitors...'

What is clear is that when a man went to court he threw his whole life, his family, and his friends into the balance against his opponent.

2. As well as presenting himself as a decent citizen, the speaker will seek to blacken his opponent's character. If the speaker is a man who pays his taxes and performs his public duties, his opponent is quite the reverse (Isae. 5.36, Dem. 42.22f., 21.154ff.). In addition, the opponent may be credited with a variety of offences ranging from the petty to the monstrous (as Andoc. 1.124, Lys. 13.66, Isae. 8.40ff., Dem. 21. 128ff., 40.32f., 53.17).[20] All manner of prejudices are appealed to. The opponent may be associated by the speaker with men whom the jury has reason to disapprove of or even hate.[21] It may be claimed that his origins are base, alien or servile (as Lys. 30.2, 6, 27, Dem. 21.149).[22] Such accusations may be true or false. The point is that they are, in

[20] See on 54.37.   [21] See on 54.39, 56.7, 39.2.
[22] See also the passages collected by Dover, 30ff.

our eyes, irrelevant to the matter in hand. Just as a man may claim credit for the good deeds of his ancestors, so he may hold his opponent responsible for any crimes in his family history (as Lys. 13.67f., 14.33ff.).

Character (good or bad) is a factor taken into account in a modern court, but usually after the verdict and before sentence is passed.

3. In addition to 'irrelevant' character evidence, we find equally 'irrelevant' appeals to emotion. The jury is often requested to show its indignation (as Lys. 6.17, 14.8, 28.2, Dem. 21.34, 21.98, 45.65) or its pity (as Lys. 4.20, 19.53, Dem. 58.69); usually the former request comes from the prosecution, the latter from the defendant. In particular, it was common for defendants to bring their children into court to excite the jurors' pity (cf. e.g. Hyp. *Eux.* 41). The practice was common enough to be satirized by Aristophanes (*Wasps* 568ff., 976ff.). It is criticized by Plato's Socrates, *Ap.* 34c–d. The speaker in Lys. 20.34 complains: 'Yet we see, jurors, that if someone brings his children on to the rostrum and weeps and wails, you pity the children if they are to be disfranchised for his sake, and you dismiss the father's crimes for the children's sake, though you do not know whether they will grow up to be good or bad.'

4. Greek litigants often introduce prudential arguments. The jury is asked to consider the bad precedent they will establish if they make the wrong decision and find for the opponent. For instance, plaintiffs are at pains to point out that a conviction in the present instance will serve as a deterrent and so protect society (Lys. 1.47, 14.12, Dem. 50.66); plaintiffs argue that the acquittal of the guilty will discourage decent conduct in future (Dem. 50.64) or encourage criminals (as Lys. 1.36, 27.7, 30.23, Dem. 59.112),[23] defendants that conviction will discourage decent conduct (Lys. 20.32, 21.12). In suits involving trade the jurors are advised that the wrong decision will adversely affect them all by discouraging trade with Athens (Lys. 22.21, Dem. 34.51f.).[24] They are intimidated with reminders that the gods can see how they vote, even though the voting is secret (Lys. 6.53, Dem. 19.239, 59.126, Lycurg. *Leocr.* 146), or with suggestions that either the victims or mankind in general will take the acquittal of the guilty as an indication that the jurors approve of the crime (Lys. 12.100, 13.93ff., 28.17, Lycurg. *Leocr.* 149), or that the jurors are under suspicion of having been bribed (Lys. 28.9, 29.13), or a warning that if they vote amiss they

[23] Cf. 54.43.   [24] See on 56.48ff.

will not be able to face their families (Dem. 59.111, cf. Lycurg. *Leocr.* 141). Many of the arguments used are weak, if examined objectively in the study. Thus, the argument that the court will set a precedent, which would have some weight under our legal system, was only at best partially true in Athens, where no court was bound by the decisions of another; for Athens it was valid only to the extent that a spate of convictions or acquittals would create an atmosphere of insecurity or security in a particular area of conduct, and the latter might result in some abuses. All such arguments have weight only in so far as the jury accepts the speaker's unshakeable assumption that his opponent is in the wrong.

Questions of this sort are in fact raised in modern courts; but only after the verdict, and before sentence is passed, i.e. once the issue of guilt or innocence, which Athenian litigants take as a foregone conclusion, has been decided. The Athenian jury is being asked, in these and a host of similar passages, to consider not just the facts but also the effect of their vote on themselves, collectively or individually, before they decide innocence or guilt.

To a greater or lesser extent these elements impede objective judgement. Their presence is readily explained. The character of a man on trial is not now considered relevant to the facts of the case. But one of the mainstays of Greek oratory from the fifth century onward was argument from probability, that is argument from general trends in human behaviour to the particular instance. Against this background character is of vital importance. The general behaviour of a man, good or bad, enables us to imagine his conduct in a particular situation and assess the truth or falsehood of an allegation against him. This is a principle most of us accept in our everyday lives. It would no doubt have shocked an ancient Athenian to learn that in Britain today a man's past convictions may not be cited as evidence against him; it would in fact be difficult to determine whether our courts acquit more guilty men than the Athenian courts convicted innocents. A further reason for the inclusion of personalities is credibility. If a man can demonstrate that his general conduct is virtuous, we are prone to credit him with honesty, and vice versa. If I can convince a third party that I am a decent man and my opponent is a villain, the third party will be inclined to believe me and disbelieve my opponent.

The inclusion of personalities, and likewise appeals to emotion, were also inevitable in view of the severe limitations of the Athenian system. It is always possible for an intelligent criminal to escape punishment even when those around him are convinced of his guilt. The role of the volunteer prosecutor and the difficulty of obtaining evidence in many cases in the absence of an effective police force will have made it easier in Athens for a wrongdoer either to escape detection or to intimidate an accuser. Even if it were not convinced of his guilt in the case before it, a jury might still feel inclined to convict in order to punish the accused for past wrongs which had never been brought to trial. We should also remember that the Athenian jury had only limited alternatives open to it. It could acquit or convict, and it could decide between proposed penalties; even the latter course was closed in cases where the law prescribed a fixed penalty. It could not (as a modern judge can) use the sentencing to soften the harshness of the factual verdict. It is possible, for instance, for a modern judge (in a civil case) to find for the plaintiff but award derisory damages, or (in a criminal case) to take into account mitigating circumstances and impose a light sentence. If an Athenian jury believed a man guilty but wished to temper justice with mercy they could only acquit or (and only in a *timetos agon*) vote for the lighter sentence. Hence evidence of a man's general character becomes relevant both to prosecution and defence, as do considerations of the hardship which conviction may cause.

A more severe limitation conducive to such 'irrelevancies' was the size of the jury. Athenian juries were voluble and volatile, as is any large body. It is easier before such a body to arouse prejudice by blackening a man's character or to summon up pity by displaying one's children than to establish one's case with a cool demonstration of the facts. The insistence that the litigant represent himself further favoured an emotional display, since the speaker is compelled to register the emotions proper to his situation or appear a fraud. To abolish such arguments it would have been necessary to change the jury system fundamentally by introducing small juries and presidents with a knowledge of the law and powers to impose order and reason. But any wholesale change along these lines would have weakened Athenian democracy. The courts were important for Athenian politics. The constant political trials were the overflow from the business of the assembly. They enabled the people to choose between rival individuals, caucuses and policies, and, equally important, to keep politicians under their control.[25] For this purpose large and unfettered juries were essential. It would have been a rash politician who proposed sweeping changes. Procedural change was theoretically possible but in practice difficult. The use of inflammatory and insubstantial argument is closely connected with the use of uninterrupted speech, and speechmaking was so much a part of all Greek administration that lawcourts without speeches were inconceivable. Even had these obstacles not existed, innate Greek conservatism would have prevented any tampering with a system which had been found serviceable. Plato might despise the behaviour of the juries, Aristophanes might mock them, individual litigants might object to practices of which they disapproved, but the average Athenian must have been satisfied with the system. In several respects he was right. The size of the juries, together with the elaborate method of allocating jurors to courts, protected weak and poor litigants from corruption by the rich and powerful; it also underpinned the political power of the ordinary man. The dogged amateurism of the whole system prevented the growth of a legal profession and so both kept the laws free from jargon and made recourse to the law cheap. For all its faults, and they were many, the Athenian system was not devoid of virtues.

2. SPEECHWRITERS

i. *The role of the logographer*

While the tradition of self-representation prevented the emergence of the professional pleader, the importance of oratory in Athenian litigation fostered the growth of another profession, that of the speechwriter.

---

[25] Athenian juries were in many respects an extension of the assembly. They heard appeals from candidates for office who were rejected at their *dokimasia*; they tried officials against whom complaints were made, either at the first assembly meeting in each prytany, where the conduct of officials was put to the vote, or at the εὔθυνα on expiry of office. Proposers of new laws or decrees could be attacked by the *graphe paranomon* (indictment for illegal legislation) up to a year after the measure was passed; even after this period, this action could be brought against the law or decree and its annulment procured. And of course it was possible for political opponents to bring other public or private suits against each other.

The practice of providing friendly witnesses, the use of *synegoroi*, and the solidarity of the family in Athens tend to turn the Athenian trial into a confrontation between two groups rather than two individuals.[26] It must always have been customary for anyone who had been involved in the courts as litigant, witness or juror to advise any friend about to become involved in litigation. But in the second half of the fifth century a new service evolved. In Aristophanes' *Clouds* 466ff. Strepsiades is told that if he acquires the New Education people will flock to him and pay vast sums for legal aid. The connection which Aristophanes makes between professional legal aid and the New Education is quite correct. The fifth century saw an attempt to impose on man and his world a thoroughgoing set of rules. One aspect, and a major aspect, of this scientific spirit was the growth of rhetoric, the art of finding the most appropriate means of persuasion in any given case. The importance of the lawcourts in Athenian public life, and the importance of speech-making in the courts, offered an obvious source of income and influence to an intelligent man properly trained. It is not clear whether Aristophanes envisages this legal expert as merely giving *advice* on the prescriptions of the law, on possible ambiguities and serviceable lines of argument, or as actually writing the speech. Certainly it is at about this time that the professional speechwriter appeared. The oligarch Antiphon is reputed to have been the first practitioner.[27]

The term 'speechwriter', or the Greek *logographos*,[28] is a somewhat inadequate description of a role which, far more than that of the *synegoros*, was the nearest approximation in ancient Athens to the modern lawyer. The oligarch Antiphon, Thucydides tells us (8.61.1), was held in great esteem for the good advice which he gave to litigants. He did more than merely write the speech. There is an interesting passage in the Demosthenic corpus (Dem. 58.19f.), where a logographer is described as arranging a settlement between his client and the opposing side. Clearly the logographer is to be imagined here as handling his client's case from start to finish, with the exception that

[26] M. Lavency, *Aspects de la logographie judiciaire attique* (Louvain 1964) 80.

[27] Plut. *Mor.* 832c.

[28] The word is discussed by Lavency, op. cit. 36ff. It denotes a writer of *logoi*, and is used of writers of prose narrative (*logoi* in the sense 'stories') and writers of speeches (*logoi* in the sense 'speeches'). It is in the latter sense that we use the words *logographos* and logographer.

the client has to speak in court. A scene in Theophrastus (*Characters* 17.8) shows us a client complaining after the trial that his logographer has missed out many useful arguments. Here again the logographer is in complete control. Clearly we should imagine the logographer not as a man who gives stylistic polish to his client's views but as a legal consultant.

When first approached by a potential client, the logographer will have ascertained the latter's version of the facts of the case. The next step would be to decide on the chances of success in court. When consulted by a defendant with a weak case, the logographer had three choices. He could urge compromise (if this was possible); he could accept the brief and pocket the fee; he could refuse to associate himself with a lost cause. If the client was a prosecutor the logographer would have to bear in mind the penalties in both public and private suits for failure to obtain one-fifth of the votes cast.[29] If there was a real danger of such failure, the same three choices were open. To assess the chances of success the logographer would draw upon his knowledge of the law, of the behaviour of Athenian juries and of recent decisions in similar cases. He would also take into account the mood of the city. Thus, at a time of grain shortage a weak mercantile suit such as Dem. 56 might stand some chance of success. The mood of the people would be a very important factor in political cases. An important factor in weak cases, and one which might perhaps override all negative considerations, might be the size of the fee. Even if the chances of success were moderate or good, the logographer might still perhaps decline it for personal or political considerations connected with the individuals or groups on either or both sides, just as he might accept a weak case if it enabled him to score a point against an enemy or help a friend.

Once he had decided to accept the case, the logographer had to give detailed consideration to the strengths and weaknesses of his client's position. Weaknesses would either have to be met head on or, if possible, evaded or trivialized. Strengths would have to be stressed. Of considerable importance for such decisions was an adequate knowledge of the opponent's case. For he would have to refute the opponent as well as prove his client's claims. Where there had been arbitration, that is in most private suits, each party would know all the evidence which the other proposed to introduce in court.[30] Even where there had been

---

[29] See on 54.1, 56.4.   [30] See on 54.27.

no arbitration, most suits involved some sort of preliminary confrontation, if only a bitter quarrel, and this would reveal much. Besides this, there were many ways in which a man might learn in advance what his opponent proposed to say, by listening to gossip and enlisting the services of his friends and relatives or the opponent's enemies. In addition, since by training and experience the logographer was able to exploit the contradictory arguments and conclusions which can be drawn from a single set of facts, he would know how *he* would have presented the opponent's case.[31] In addition to the 'facts', the logographer would collect examples of similar events to those under discussion or judicial decisions in similar cases which, though not binding on the jury, might be expected to influence it.[32] He would also consider what crimes, real or fictitious, he could attribute to the opponent, what prejudices he could manipulate against him. With all this raw material gathered he could write the speech.[33] The logographer's role did not need to end with the writing of the speech. We may imagine that he would remain close to his client in court to give final advice. He might even perhaps, if he were acting for the defence, make final alterations in court to meet any unforeseen points made by the prosecution; that is, if this could be done surreptitiously. The client's task was to memorize the speech and practise it until it sounded like an extempore performance. Even in this we may imagine some coaching from the logographer. The success of this exercise depended on the theatrical instincts, the nerve, and the speaking experience of the client, and will have varied from case to case. We have no way of knowing how often the fraud was transparent.

There was nothing illegal in the writing of speeches for pay, nor in hiring a speechwriter. But there is good evidence that public opinion

[31] Some items could be anticipated with little effort. References to public services undertaken in the past, attempts at character assassination, appeals for pity etc. could be taken for granted. See in general A. P. Dorjahn, *TAPA* 66 (1935) 274–95 on the sources of information open to a Greek litigant.

[32] Demosthenes 21.36 describes his opponent as collecting cases in just this way.

[33] K. J. Dover, *Lysias and the corpus Lysiacum* (Berkeley and Los Angeles 1968) 150ff. suggests that many speeches delivered in court were the product of collaboration between the logographer and the client rather than the exclusive work of the logographer. The arguments of S. Usher, *GRBS* 17 (1976) 31–40 to the contrary are convincing.

disapproved of the logographer's trade. Plato (*Phaedrus* 257c) speaks of the term *logographos* as an insult hurled at Lysias. Dinarchus (5.3) describes a man as 'a *logographos* and good-for-nothing'. Aeschines (2.80) when prosecuted by Demosthenes says: 'I beg you to rescue me and not to hand me over to the *logographos*, the Scythian [viz. Demosthenes].' The oligarch Antiphon says (fr. III, I Gernet): 'My accusers claim that I wrote speeches for others and that I made money from this practice.'[34]

That the trade should be unpopular is hardly surprising. The speechwriter broke no law, but he contravened the spirit of Athenian justice. The system was based on the assumption that each litigant told the truth to the best of his ability. As has been noted, this offers an advantage to the naturally articulate. But the use of a professional speechwriter creates a further imbalance, for the man with a bought speech has an obvious advantage over the untutored speaker. Rhetoric, not justice, may carry the day. And since speechwriters cost money, the principle of equality before the law is patently weakened, for the advantage is with wealth. The extent of the popular distrust of professionalism may be seen in Dem. 32.31f, where Demon, a relative of Demosthenes, tries with evident discomfort to meet the accusation of his opponents that Demosthenes is helping. But although logographers were unpopular with the general public, they were evidently popular with litigants, though of course nobody would admit, before judgement at least, that he had paid money for a speech.

One result of the strange half-light in which the transaction between logographer and client was conducted was the existence of speeches whose authorship was uncertain. In the classical period the question whether a man had or had not written certain speeches could be raised within a few years of his death. Dionysius of Halicarnassus (*Isoc.* 18) tells us that whereas an adopted son of Isocrates, Aphareus, maintained that Isocrates wrote no speeches for the lawcourt, Aristotle said that the booksellers carried many bundles of Isocrates' forensic speeches.[35] When the library at Alexandria was acquiring Greek literary texts, many speeches must have arrived bearing no name. It was natural for these to be attributed to known logographers where possible, and

---

[34] See further Lavency, op. cit. 42, 64f.

[35] See K. J. Dover, op. cit. 25. Compare what Isocrates himself wrote in 354/3 at 15.36ff.

indeed such attribution was sometimes made where it is impossible. Thus the speech which appears as number 58 in the Demosthenic corpus was clearly written by an enemy of Demosthenes (58.35f., 39–44); yet this fact has not prevented its attribution to Demosthenes. In antiquity doubts were entertained about the authenticity of many speeches attributed to major Attic orators of the fourth century, and modern scholars are equally suspicious. Of the speeches in the present collection, serious doubts have been raised about the authorship of Dem. 56.[36]

ii. Demosthenes

Demosthenes was born in 385/4,[37] the son of a wealthy Athenian businessman,[38] also called Demosthenes. The elder Demosthenes died in 376/5, and for the next ten years the guardians whom he had appointed mismanaged the estate to their own profit. Immediately upon coming of age in the summer of 366, Demosthenes successfully prosecuted his guardians, but the sums he recovered, while still leaving him in the liturgical class, were only a fraction of his father's wealth. The success of the speeches concerning his inheritance probably laid the foundations for Demosthenes' career as a speechwriter. Since the logographer worked behind the scenes, recommendation to prospective clients will have come mainly by word of mouth, from satisfied customers and general gossip. Though this was no doubt effective enough when a logographer was established in his career, it must have been a difficult career to begin. The precocious personal success of Demosthenes must have been an excellent advertisement to prospective clients.

It is easy to see what attracted Demosthenes to a career as a logographer. Obviously artistic ambition is one factor. Demosthenes had proved that he had a talent for oratory, and he had been well trained, by Isaeus according to tradition. Each new case offered a challenge to his skill, and an opportunity to increase his reputation as

[36] See the introduction to that speech. If Dover's hypothesis of collaboration between logographer and client is accepted the situation is complicated further, since many speeches would be *partly* the work of a logographer. But see n. 33 above.

[37] The date is controversial (384/3 is also possible), but the issue is immaterial for our purposes. See Davies 123–6.

[38] For the estate of the elder Demosthenes, and the amount which his son eventually recovered, see Davies 127–33.

a verbal craftsman. Oratory is not now prized as an art, but it was not only a useful skill, indeed the most useful skill, in Athenian public life, it was an art in which the average Greek took immense delight, as the influence of oratory on fifth-century tragedy amply demonstrates. We should not underrate the artistic motive. But more important, probably, was the financial motive. Though far from destitute, Demosthenes was only moderately wealthy. An increase in his wealth was both desirable in itself and necessary for the political career to which he aspired. To perform with commendable lavishness the liturgies necessary to establish a good reputation, to be able to bribe and hire agents, to have resources of money to cover possible fines resulting from political trials, all this required considerable wealth. Besides serving as a source of income, the logographic speeches furthered Demosthenes' ambitions in two ways. First, they offered an opportunity to develop further his considerable rhetorical skill. It was possible to discover by experience the sort of exaggeration, omission, evasion, flattery and vilification which would work in practice and to develop his style without facing any personal risk. Secondly, this period enabled Demosthenes to establish political contacts. Among the speeches written for others as Demosthenes began his career as a public speaker were the speeches against Androtion (Dem. 22), Timocrates (Dem. 24) and Aristocrates (Dem. 23), all in political trials, in the years 355–352.

In approaching a forensic speech it is necessary to bear in mind the purpose for which it was written. The function of judicial oratory is to persuade the jury for or against a particular verdict. Rhetoric is an amoral tool. Its end is persuasion; this need not rule out, but it does not necessitate, truth. The Greek litigant is not an objective narrator of truth but a man with something at stake. Anything he says must be treated with caution. A man who is in the wrong may distort the truth wholesale; but equally a man who is in the right may distort the truth to strengthen his case. Such distortion may consist of downright lies, or minute alterations of detail, even omissions. It is necessary to approach a forensic speech in a spirit of scepticism, to look for weaknesses in the argument, to ascertain what the opponent may have said in reply. There is always a danger that we shall do the speaker less than justice. And we can never be certain that we have arrived at the truth. But since the speaker has had twenty-four centuries to present his case unopposed, he cannot reasonably complain.

NOTE ON THE TEXT

In the preparation of this text much reliance has been placed on the editions of others, especially those of W. Rennie (Oxford Classical Texts) and L. Gernet (Budé). For critical apparatus the reader is referred to these two editions. There follows a list of the readings adopted in this text which differ from those of Rennie.

Dem. 54

§ 1   ὧν SA: περὶ ὧν Rauchenstein: ἢν ἔχων FQD
§ 7   Διότιμος Mensching, cf. §§ 31, 34: Θεότιμος codd.
§ 26 τοῦτο καὶ codd.: καὶ τοῦτο Robertson
§ 40 εὔορκον μηδὲν codd.: εὔορκον ⟨ἑκὼν⟩ μηδὲν Rennie   ὡς νόμιμον, ἀξιοπιστότερος codd.: ὡς νόμιμον, ⟨κατ' ἐξωλείας αὐτοῦ καὶ γένους καὶ οἰκίας⟩, ἀξιοπιστότερος Blass

Dem. 37

§ 18 οὗτος codd.: secl. Blass
§ 25 Θρασύμωι Hopper: Θρασύλλωι Harpocr.: Θρασύλλου codd.
§ 31 ἀπεδόμεθα SA: ἐωνήμεθα FQD
§ 32 τότε AFQD: το S in fine versus
§ 55 λυσιτελούντων codd.: λυσιτελούντως Naber

Dem. 56

§ 30 γὰρ SFQD: γε A   ἀκαριαῖος A: ἀεὶ ὡραῖος Sandys: ἀκέραιος SFQD

DEMOSTHENES
SELECTED PRIVATE SPEECHES

54 ΚΑΤΑ ΚΟΝΩΝΟΣ ΑΙΚΕΙΑΣ

Ὑβρισθείς, ὦ ἄνδρες δικασταί, καὶ παθὼν ὑπὸ Κόνωνος τουτουὶ τοιαῦτα, ὥστε πολὺν χρόνον πάνυ μήτε τοὺς οἰκείους μήτε τῶν ἰατρῶν μηδένα προσδοκᾶν περιφεύξεσθαί με, ὑγιάνας καὶ σωθεὶς ἀπροσδοκήτως ἔλαχον αὐτῶι τὴν δίκην τῆς αἰκείας ταυτηνί. πάντων δὲ τῶν φίλων καὶ τῶν οἰκείων, οἷς συνεβουλευόμην, ἔνοχον μὲν φασκόντων αὐτὸν ἐκ τῶν πεπραγμένων εἶναι καὶ τῆι τῶν λωποδυτῶν ἀπαγωγῆι καὶ ταῖς τῆς ὕβρεως γραφαῖς, συνβουλευόντων δέ μοι καὶ παραινούντων μὴ μείζω πράγματ' ἢ δυνήσομαι φέρειν ἐπάγεσθαι, μηδ' ὑπὲρ τὴν ἡλικίαν ὧν ἐπεπόνθειν ἐγκαλοῦντα φαίνεσθαι, οὕτως ἐποίησα καὶ δι' ἐκείνους ἰδίαν ἔλαχον δίκην, ἥδιστ' ἄν, ὦ ἄνδρες Ἀθηναῖοι, θανάτου κρίνας τουτονί. καὶ τούτου συγγνώμην ἕξετε, εὖ 2 οἶδ' ὅτι, πάντες, ἐπειδὰν ἃ πέπονθ' ἀκούσητε· δεινῆς γὰρ οὔσης τῆς τότε συμβάσης ὕβρεως οὐκ ἐλάττων ἡ μετὰ ταῦτ' ἀσέλγει' ἐστὶ τουτουί. ἀξιῶ δὴ καὶ δέομαι πάντων ὁμοίως ὑμῶν πρῶτον μὲν εὐνοϊκῶς ἀκοῦσαί μου περὶ ὧν πέπονθα λέγοντος, εἶτα, ἐὰν ἠδικῆσθαι καὶ παρανενομῆσθαι δοκῶ, βοηθῆσαί μοι τὰ δίκαια. ἐξ ἀρχῆς δ' ὡς ἕκαστα πέπρακται διηγήσομαι πρὸς ὑμᾶς, ὡς ἂν οἷός τ' ὦ διὰ βραχυτάτων.

Ἐξῆλθον ἔτος τουτὶ τρίτον εἰς Πάνακτον φρουρᾶς ἡμῖν 3 προγραφείσης. ἐσκήνωσαν οὖν οἱ υἱεῖς οἱ Κόνωνος τουτουὶ ἐγγὺς ἡμῶν, ὡς οὐκ ἂν ἐβουλόμην· ἡ γὰρ ἐξ ἀρχῆς ἔχθρα καὶ τὰ προσκρούματ' ἐκεῖθεν ἡμῖν συνέβη· ἐξ ὧν δέ, ἀκούσεσθε. ἔπινον ἑκάστοθ' οὗτοι τὴν ἡμέραν, ἐπειδὴ τάχιστ' ἀριστήσαιεν, ὅλην, καὶ τοῦθ', ἕως περ ἦμεν ἐν τῆι φρουρᾶι, διετέλουν ποιοῦντες. ἡμεῖς δ' ὥσπερ ἐνθάδ' εἰώθειμεν, οὕτω διήγομεν καὶ ἔξω. ἣν οὖν δειπνοποιεῖσθαι τοῖς ἄλλοις ὥραν συμβαίνοι, 4 ταύτην ἂν ἤδη ἐπαρώινουν οὗτοι, τὰ μὲν πόλλ' εἰς τοὺς παῖδας ἡμῶν τοὺς ἀκολούθους, τελευτῶντες δὲ καὶ εἰς ἡμᾶς αὐτούς. φήσαντες γὰρ καπνίζειν αὐτοὺς ὀψοποιουμένους τοὺς παῖδας ἢ κακῶς λέγειν, ὅ τι τύχοιεν, ἔτυπτον καὶ τὰς ἀμίδας κατεσκεδάννυον καὶ προσεούρουν, καὶ ἀσελγείας καὶ ὕβρεως

οὐδ' ότιοῦν ἀπέλειπον. όρῶντες δ' ἡμεῖς ταῦτα καὶ λυπούμενοι
τὸ μὲν πρῶτον ἀπεπεμψάμεθα, ὡς δ' ἐχλεύαζον ἡμᾶς καὶ οὐκ
ἐπαύοντο, τῶι στρατηγῶι τὸ πρᾶγμ' εἴπομεν κοινῇι πάντες
5 οἱ σύσσιτοι προσελθόντες, οὐκ ἐγὼ τῶν ἄλλων ἔξω. λοιδορη-
θέντος δ' αὐτοῖς ἐκείνου καὶ κακίσαντος αὐτοὺς οὐ μόνον περὶ
ὧν εἰς ἡμᾶς ἠσέλγαινον, ἀλλὰ καὶ περὶ ὧν ὅλως ἐποίουν ἐν
τῶι στρατοπέδωι, τοσούτου ἐδέησαν παύσασθαι ἢ αἰσχυνθῆναι,
ὥστ' ἐπειδὴ θᾶττον συνεσκότασεν, εὐθὺς ὡς ἡμᾶς εἰσεπήδησαν
ταύτηι τῆι ἑσπέραι, καὶ τὸ μὲν πρῶτον κακῶς ἔλεγον,
τελευτῶντες δὲ καὶ πληγὰς ἐνέτειναν ἐμοί, καὶ τοσαύτην
κραυγὴν καὶ θόρυβον περὶ τὴν σκηνὴν ἐποίησαν ὥστε καὶ
τὸν στρατηγὸν καὶ τοὺς ταξιάρχους ἐλθεῖν καὶ τῶν ἄλλων
στρατιωτῶν τινάς, οἵπερ ἐκώλυσαν μηδὲν ἡμᾶς ἀνήκεστον
παθεῖν μηδ' αὐτοὺς ποιῆσαι παροινουμένους ὑπὸ τουτωνί.
6 τοῦ δὲ πράγματος εἰς τοῦτο προελθόντος, ὡς δεῦρ' ἐπανήλθομεν,
ἦν ἡμῖν, οἷον εἰκός, ἐκ τούτων ὀργὴ καὶ ἔχθρα πρὸς ἀλλήλους.
μὰ τοὺς θεοὺς οὐ μὴν ἔγωγ' ὠιόμην δεῖν οὔτε δίκην λαχεῖν
αὐτοῖς οὔτε λόγον ποιεῖσθαι τῶν συμβάντων οὐδένα, ἀλλ'
ἐκεῖν' ἁπλῶς ἐγνώκειν τὸ λοιπὸν εὐλαβεῖσθαι καὶ φυλάττεσθαι
μὴ πλησιάζειν τοῖς τοιούτοις. πρῶτον μὲν οὖν τούτων ὧν
εἴρηκα βούλομαι τὰς μαρτυρίας παρασχόμενος, μετὰ ταῦθ' οἷ'
ὑπ' αὐτοῦ τούτου πέπονθ' ἐπιδεῖξαι, ἵν' εἰδῆθ' ὅτι ὧι προσῆκεν
τοῖς τὸ πρῶτον ἁμαρτηθεῖσιν ἐπιτιμᾶν, οὗτος αὐτὸς πρότερος
πολλῶι δεινότερ' εἴργασται.

ΜΑΡΤΥΡΙΑΙ

7 Ὧν μὲν τοίνυν οὐδέν' ὠιμην δεῖν λόγον ποιεῖσθαι, ταῦτ'
ἐστίν. χρόνωι δ' ὕστερον οὐ πολλῶι περιπατοῦντος, ὥσπερ
εἰώθειν, ἑσπέρας ἐν ἀγορᾶι μου μετὰ Φανοστράτου τοῦ
Κηφισιέως, τῶν ἡλικιωτῶν τινός, παρέρχεται Κτησίας ὁ υἱὸς
ὁ τούτου, μεθύων, κατὰ τὸ Λεωκόριον, ἐγγὺς τῶν Πυθοδώρου.
κατιδὼν δ' ἡμᾶς καὶ κραυγάσας, καὶ διαλεχθείς τι πρὸς αὐτὸν
οὕτως ὡς ἂν μεθύων, ὥστε μὴ μαθεῖν ὅ τι λέγοι, παρῆλθε
πρὸς Μελίτην ἄνω. ἔπινον δ' ἄρ' ἐνταῦθα (ταῦτα γὰρ ὕστερον
ἐπυθόμεθα) παρὰ Παμφίλωι τῶι γναφεῖ Κόνων οὑτοσί, Διότιμός

τις, Ἀρχεβιάδης, Σπίνθαρος ὁ Εὐβούλου, Θεογένης ὁ Ἀνδρομένους, πολλοί τινες, οὓς ἐξαναστήσας ὁ Κτησίας ἐπορεύετ'
εἰς τὴν ἀγοράν. καὶ ἡμῖν συμβαίνει ἀναστρέφουσιν ἀπὸ τοῦ 8
Φερρεφαττίου καὶ περιπατοῦσιν πάλιν κατ' αὐτό πως τὸ
Λεωκόριον εἶναι, καὶ τούτοις περιτυγχάνομεν. ὡς δ' ἀνεμείχθημεν, εἷς μὲν αὐτῶν, ἀγνώς τις, Φανοστράτωι προσπίπτει
καὶ κατεῖχεν ἐκεῖνον, Κόνων δ' οὑτοσὶ καὶ ὁ υἱὸς αὐτοῦ καὶ
ὁ Ἀνδρομένους υἱὸς ἐμοὶ προσπεσόντες τὸ μὲν πρῶτον ἐξέδυσαν,
εἶθ' ὑποσκελίσαντες καὶ ῥάξαντες εἰς τὸν βόρβορον οὕτω
διέθηκαν ἐναλλόμενοι καὶ ὑβρίζοντες, ὥστε τὸ μὲν χεῖλος
διακόψαι, τοὺς δ' ὀφθαλμοὺς συγκλεῖσαι· οὕτω δὲ κακῶς ἔχοντα
κατέλιπον, ὥστε μήτ' ἀναστῆναι μήτε φθέγξασθαι δύνασθαι.
κείμενος δ' αὐτῶν ἤκουον πολλὰ καὶ δεινὰ λεγόντων. καὶ 9
τὰ μὲν ἄλλα καὶ βλασφημίαν ἔχει τινὰ καὶ ὀνομάζειν ὀκνήσαιμ'
ἂν ἐν ὑμῖν ἔνια, ὃ δὲ τῆς ὕβρεώς ἐστι τῆς τούτου σημεῖον
καὶ τεκμήριον τοῦ πᾶν τὸ πρᾶγμ' ὑπὸ τούτου γεγενῆσθαι,
τοῦθ' ὑμῖν ἐρῶ· ᾖδε γὰρ τοὺς ἀλεκτρυόνας μιμούμενος τοὺς
νενικηκότας, οἱ δὲ κροτεῖν τοῖς ἀγκῶσιν αὐτὸν ἠξίουν ἀντὶ
πτερύγων τὰς πλευράς. καὶ μετὰ ταῦτ' ἐγὼ μὲν ἀπεκομίσθην
ὑπὸ τῶν παρατυχόντων γυμνός, οὗτοι δ' ᾤχοντο θοἰμάτιον
λαβόντες μου. ὡς δ' ἐπὶ τὴν θύραν ἦλθον, κραυγὴ καὶ βοὴ
τῆς μητρὸς καὶ τῶν θεραπαινίδων ἦν, καὶ μόγις ποτ' εἰς
βαλανεῖον ἐνεγκόντες με καὶ περιπλύναντες ἔδειξαν τοῖς ἰατροῖς.
ὡς οὖν ταῦτ' ἀληθῆ λέγω, τούτων ὑμῖν τοὺς μάρτυρας
παρέξομαι.

MΑΡΤΥΡΕΣ

Συνέβη τοίνυν, ὦ ἄνδρες δικασταί, καὶ Εὐξίθεον τουτονὶ τὸν 10
Χολλήιδην, ὄνθ' ἡμῖν συγγενῆ, καὶ Μειδίαν μετὰ τούτου ἀπὸ
δείπνου ποθὲν ἀπιόντας περιτυχεῖν πλησίον ὄντι μοι τῆς οἰκίας
ἤδη, καὶ εἴς τε τὸ βαλανεῖον φερομένωι παρακολουθῆσαι, καὶ
ἰατρὸν ἄγουσιν παραγενέσθαι. οὕτω δ' εἶχον ἀσθενῶς ὥστε,
ἵνα μὴ μακρὰν φεροίμην οἴκαδ' ἐκ τοῦ βαλανείου, ἐδόκει τοῖς
παροῦσιν ὡς τὸν Μειδίαν ἐκείνην τὴν ἑσπέραν κομίσαι, καὶ
ἐποίησαν οὕτω. λάβ' οὖν καὶ τὰς τούτων μαρτυρίας, ἵν' εἰδῆθ'
ὅτι πολλοὶ συνίσασιν ὡς ὑπὸ τούτων ὑβρίσθην.

ΜΑΡΤΥΡΙΑΙ

Λαβὲ δὴ καὶ τὴν τοῦ ἰατροῦ μαρτυρίαν.

ΜΑΡΤΥΡΙΑ

11 Τότε μὲν τοίνυν παραχρῆμ' ὑπὸ τῶν πληγῶν ἃς ἔλαβον καὶ τῆς ὕβρεως οὕτω διετέθην, ὡς ἀκούετε καὶ μεμαρτύρηται παρὰ πάντων ὑμῖν τῶν εὐθὺς ἰδόντων. μετὰ δὲ ταῦτα τῶν μὲν οἰδημάτων τῶν ἐν τῶι προσώπωι καὶ τῶν ἑλκῶν οὐδὲν ἔφη φοβεῖσθαι λίαν ὁ ἰατρός, πυρετοὶ δὲ παρηκολούθουν μοι συνεχεῖς καὶ ἀλγήματα, ὅλου μὲν τοῦ σώματος πάνυ σφοδρὰ καὶ δεινά, μάλιστα δὲ τῶν πλευρῶν καὶ τοῦ ἤτρου, καὶ τῶν 12 σιτίων ἀπεκεκλείμην. καὶ ὡς μὲν ὁ ἰατρὸς ἔφη, εἰ μὴ κάθαρσις αἵματος αὐτομάτη μοι πάνυ πολλὴ συνέβη περιωδύνωι ὄντι καὶ ἀπορουμένωι ἤδη, κἂν ἔμπυος γενόμενος διεφθάρην· νῦν δὲ τοῦτ' ἔσωισεν τὸ αἷμ' ἀποχωρῆσαν. ὡς οὖν καὶ ταῦτ' ἀληθῆ λέγω, καὶ παρηκολούθησέ μοι τοιαύτη νόσος ἐξ ἧς εἰς τοὔσχατον ἦλθον, ἐξ ὧν ὑπὸ τούτων ἔλαβον πληγῶν, λέγε τὴν τοῦ ἰατροῦ μαρτυρίαν καὶ τὴν τῶν ἐπισκοπούντων.

ΜΑΡΤΥΡΙΑΙ

13 Ὅτι μὲν τοίνυν οὐ μετρίας τινὰς καὶ φαύλας λαβὼν πληγάς, ἀλλ' εἰς πᾶν ἐλθὼν διὰ τὴν ὕβριν καὶ τὴν ἀσέλγειαν τὴν τούτων πολὺ τῆς προσηκούσης ἐλάττω δίκην εἴληχα, πολλαχόθεν νομίζω δῆλον ὑμῖν γεγενῆσθαι. οἶμαι δ' ὑμῶν ἐνίους θαυμάζειν, τί ποτ' ἐστὶν ἃ πρὸς ταῦτα τολμήσει Κόνων λέγειν. βούλομαι δὴ προειπεῖν ὑμῖν ἁγὼ πέπυσμαι λέγειν αὐτὸν παρεσκευάσθαι, ἀπὸ τῆς ὕβρεως καὶ τῶν πεπραγμένων τὸ πρᾶγμ' ἄγοντ' εἰς γέλωτα καὶ σκώμματ' ἐμβαλεῖν πειράσεσθαι, 14 καὶ ἐρεῖν ὡς εἰσὶν ἐν τῆι πόλει πολλοί, καλῶν κἀγαθῶν ἀνδρῶν υἱεῖς, οἳ παίζοντες οἷ' ἄνθρωποι νέοι σφίσιν αὐτοῖς ἐπωνυμίας πεποίηνται, καὶ καλοῦσι τοὺς μὲν ἰθυφάλλους, τοὺς δ' αὐτοληκύθους, ἐρῶσι δ' ἐκ τούτων ἑταιρῶν τινές, καὶ δὴ καὶ τὸν υἱὸν τὸν ἑαυτοῦ εἶναι τούτων ἕνα, καὶ πολλάκις περὶ

ἑταίρας καὶ εἰληφέναι καὶ δεδωκέναι πληγάς, καὶ ταῦτ' εἶναι
νέων ἀνθρώπων. ἡμᾶς δὲ πάντας τοὺς ἀδελφοὺς παροίνους
μέν τινας καὶ ὑβριστὰς κατασκευάσει, ἀγνώμονας δὲ καὶ πικρούς.
ἐγὼ δ', ὦ ἄνδρες δικασταί, χαλεπῶς ἐφ' οἷς πέπονθα ἐνηνοχώς, 15
οὐχ ἧττον τοῦτ' ἀγανακτήσαιμ' ἂν καὶ ὑβρίσθαι νομίσαιμι,
εἰ οἷόν τ' εἰπεῖν, εἰ ταῦτ' ἀληθῆ δόξει Κόνων οὑτοσὶ λέγειν
περὶ ἡμῶν, καὶ τοσαύτη τις ἄγνοια παρ' ὑμῖν ἐστιν, ὥσθ',
ὁποῖός ἄν τις ἕκαστος εἶναι φῇ ἢ ὁ πλησίον αὐτὸν αἰτιάσηται,
τοιοῦτος νομισθήσεται, τοῦ δὲ καθ' ἡμέραν βίου καὶ τῶν
ἐπιτηδευμάτων μηδ' ὁτιοῦν ἔσται τοῖς μετρίοις ὄφελος. ἡμεῖς 16
γὰρ οὔτε παροινοῦντες οὔθ' ὑβρίζοντες ὑπ' οὐδενὸς ἀνθρώπων
ἑωράμεθα, οὐδ' ἄγνωμον οὐδὲν ἡγούμεθα ποιεῖν, εἰ περὶ ὧν
ἠδικήμεθ' ἀξιοῦμεν κατὰ τοὺς νόμους δίκην λαβεῖν. ἰθυφάλλοις
δὲ καὶ αὐτοληκύθοις συγχωροῦμεν εἶναι τοῖς υἱέσι τοῖς τούτου,
καὶ ἔγωγ' εὔχομαι τοῖς θεοῖς εἰς Κόνωνα καὶ τοὺς υἱεῖς τοὺς
τούτου καὶ ταῦτα καὶ τὰ τοιαῦθ' ἅπαντα τρέπεσθαι. οὗτοι 17
γάρ εἰσιν οἱ τελοῦντες ἀλλήλους τῶι Ἰθυφάλλωι, καὶ τοιαῦτα
ποιοῦντες ἃ πολλὴν αἰσχύνην ἔχει καὶ λέγειν, μή τί γε δὴ
ποιεῖν ἀνθρώπους μετρίους. ἀλλὰ τί ταῦτ' ἐμοί; θαυμάζω γὰρ
ἔγωγε, εἴ τίς ἐστιν πρόφασις παρ' ὑμῖν ἢ σκῆψις ηὑρημένη
δι' ἥν, ἂν ὑβρίζων τις ἐξελέγχηται καὶ τύπτων, δίκην οὐ
δώσει. οἱ μὲν γὰρ νόμοι πολὺ τἀναντία καὶ τὰς ἀναγκαίας
προφάσεις, ὅπως μὴ μείζους γίγνωνται, προείδοντο, οἷον
(ἀνάγκη γάρ μοι ταῦτα καὶ ζητεῖν καὶ πυνθάνεσθαι διὰ τοῦτον
γέγονεν) εἰσὶ κακηγορίας δίκαι· φασὶ τοίνυν ταύτας διὰ τοῦτο 18
γίγνεσθαι, ἵνα μὴ λοιδορούμενοι τύπτειν ἀλλήλους προάγωνται. πάλιν αἰκείας εἰσί· καὶ ταύτας ἀκούω διὰ τοῦτ' εἶναι
τὰς δίκας, ἵνα μηδείς, ὅταν ἥττων ᾖ, λίθῳ μηδὲ τῶν τοιούτων
ἀμύνηται μηδενί, ἀλλὰ τὴν ἐκ τοῦ νόμου δίκην ἀναμένῃ.
τραύματος πάλιν εἰσὶν γραφαὶ τοῦ μὴ τιτρωσκομένων τινῶν
φόνους γίγνεσθαι. τὸ φαυλότατον, οἶμαι, τὸ τῆς λοιδορίας, 19
πρὸ τοῦ τελευταίου καὶ δεινοτάτου προεώραται, τοῦ μὴ φόνον
γίγνεσθαι, μηδὲ κατὰ μικρὸν ὑπάγεσθαι ἐκ μὲν λοιδορίας εἰς
πληγάς, ἐκ δὲ πληγῶν εἰς τραύματα, ἐκ δὲ τραυμάτων εἰς
θάνατον, ἀλλ' ἐν τοῖς νόμοις εἶναι τούτων ἑκάστου τὴν δίκην,

μὴ τῆι τοῦ προστυχόντος ὀργῆι μηδὲ βουλήσει ταῦτα
20 κρίνεσθαι. εἶτ' ἐν μὲν τοῖς νόμοις οὕτως· ἂν δ' εἴπηι Κόνων
'ἰθύφαλλοί τινές ἐσμεν ἡμεῖς συνειλεγμένοι, καὶ ἐρῶντες οὓς ἂν
ἡμῖν δόξηι παίομεν καὶ ἄγχομεν', εἶτα γελάσαντες ὑμεῖς ἀφήσετε;
οὐκ οἴομαί γε. οὐ γὰρ ἂν γέλως ὑμῶν ἔλαβεν οὐδένα, εἰ παρὼν
ἐτύγχανεν ἡνίχ' εἱλκόμην καὶ ἐξεδυόμην καὶ ὑβριζόμην, καὶ
ὑγιὴς ἐξελθὼν φοράδην ἦλθον οἴκαδε, ἐξεπεπηδήκει δὲ μετὰ
ταῦθ' ἡ μήτηρ, καὶ κραυγὴ καὶ βοὴ τῶν γυναικῶν τοσαύτη
παρ' ἡμῖν ἦν ὡσπερανεὶ τεθνεῶτός τινος, ὥστε τῶν γειτόνων
τινὰς πέμψαι πρὸς ἡμᾶς ἐρησομένους ὅ τι ἐστὶν τὸ συμβεβηκός.
21 ὅλως δ', ὦ ἄνδρες δικασταί, δίκαιον μὲν οὐδενὶ δήπου σκῆψιν
οὐδεμίαν τοιαύτην οὐδ' ἄδειαν ὑπάρχειν παρ' ὑμῖν, δι' ἣν
ὑβρίζειν ἐξέσται· εἰ δ' ἄρ' ἐστίν τωι, τοῖς δι' ἡλικίαν τούτων
τι πράττουσιν, τούτοις ἀποκεῖσθαι προσήκει τὰς τοιαύτας
καταφυγάς, κἀκείνοις οὐκ εἰς τὸ μὴ δοῦναι δίκην, ἀλλ' εἰς
22 τὸ τῆς προσηκούσης ἐλάττω. ὅστις δ' ἐτῶν μέν ἐστιν πλειόνων
ἢ πεντήκοντα, παρὼν δὲ νεωτέροις ἀνθρώποις καὶ τούτοις
υἱέσιν, οὐχ ὅπως ἀπέτρεψεν ἢ διεκώλυσεν, ἀλλ' αὐτὸς ἡγεμὼν
καὶ πρῶτος καὶ πάντων βδελυρώτατος γεγένηται, τίν' ἂν
οὗτος ἀξίαν τῶν πεπραγμένων ὑπόσχοι δίκην; ἐγὼ μὲν γὰρ
οὐδ' ἀποθανόντ' οἴομαι. καὶ γὰρ εἰ μηδὲν αὐτὸς εἴργαστο
τῶν πεπραγμένων, ἀλλ' εἰ παρεστηκότος τούτου Κτησίας ὁ
υἱὸς ὁ τούτου ταῦθ' ἅπερ νυνὶ πεποιηκὼς ἐφαίνετο, τοῦτον
23 ἐμισεῖτ' ἂν δικαίως. εἰ γὰρ οὕτω τοὺς αὑτοῦ προῆκται παῖδας
ὥστ' ἐναντίον ἐξαμαρτάνοντας ἑαυτοῦ, καὶ ταῦτ' ἐφ' ὧν ἐνίοις
θάνατος ἢ ζημία κεῖται, μήτε φοβεῖσθαι μήτ' αἰσχύνεσθαι, τί
τοῦτον οὐκ ἂν εἰκότως παθεῖν οἴεσθε; ἐγὼ μὲν γὰρ ἡγοῦμαι
ταῦτ' εἶναι σημεῖα τοῦ μηδὲ τοῦτον τὸν ἑαυτοῦ πατέρ'
αἰσχύνεσθαι· εἰ γὰρ ἐκεῖνον αὐτὸς ἐτίμα καὶ ἐδεδίει, κἂν τούτους
αὐτὸν ἠξίου.
24   Λαβὲ δή μοι καὶ τοὺς νόμους, τόν τε τῆς ὕβρεως καὶ
τὸν περὶ τῶν λωποδυτῶν· καὶ γὰρ τούτοις ἀμφοτέροις ἐνόχους
τούτους ὄψεσθε. λέγε.

ΝΟΜΟΙ

Τούτοις τοῖς νόμοις ἀμφοτέροις ἐκ τῶν πεπραγμένων ἔνοχος Κόνων ἐστὶν οὑτοσί· καὶ γὰρ ὕβριζεν καὶ ἐλωποδύτει. εἰ δὲ μὴ κατὰ τούτους προειλόμεθ' ἡμεῖς δίκην λαμβάνειν, ἡμεῖς μὲν ἀπράγμονες καὶ μέτριοι φαινοίμεθ' ἂν εἰκότως, οὗτος δ' ὁμοίως πονηρός. καὶ μὴν εἰ παθεῖν τί μοι συνέβη, φόνου καὶ τῶν 25 δεινοτάτων ἂν ἦν ὑπόδικος. τὸν γοῦν τῆς Βραυρωνόθεν ἱερείας πατέρ' ὁμολογουμένως οὐχ ἁψάμενον τοῦ τελευτήσαντος, ὅτι τῶι πατάξαντι τύπτειν παρεκελεύσατο, ἐξέβαλεν ἡ βουλὴ ἡ ἐξ Ἀρείου πάγου, δικαίως· εἰ γὰρ οἱ παρόντες ἀντὶ τοῦ κωλύειν τοὺς ἢ δι' οἶνον ἢ δι' ὀργὴν ἢ τιν' ἄλλην αἰτίαν ἐξαμαρτάνειν ἐπιχειροῦντας αὐτοὶ παροξυνοῦσιν, οὐδεμί' ἐστὶν ἐλπὶς σωτηρίας τῶι περιπίπτοντι τοῖς ἀσελγαίνουσιν, ἀλλ' ἕως ἂν ἀπείπωσιν, ὑβρίζεσθαι ὑπάρξει· ὅπερ ἐμοὶ συνέβη.

Ἃ τοίνυν, ὅθ' ἡ δίαιτα ἐγίγνετο, ἐποίουν, βούλομαι πρὸς 26 ὑμᾶς εἰπεῖν· καὶ γὰρ ἐκ τούτων τὴν ἀσέλγειαν θεάσεσθ' αὐτῶν. ἐποίησαν μὲν γὰρ ἔξω μέσων νυκτῶν τὴν ὥραν, οὔτε τὰς μαρτυρίας ἀναγιγνώσκειν ἐθέλοντες οὔτ' ἀντίγραφα διδόναι, τῶν τε παρόντων ἡμῖν καθ' ἕν' οὑτωσὶ πρὸς τὸν λίθον ἄγοντες καὶ ἐξορκοῦντες, καὶ γράφοντες μαρτυρίας οὐδὲν πρὸς τὸ πρᾶγμα, ἀλλ' ἐξ ἑταίρας εἶναι παιδίον αὐτῶι τοῦτο καὶ πεπονθέναι τὰ καὶ τά, ἃ μὰ τοὺς θεούς, ἄνδρες δικασταί, οὐδεὶς ὅστις οὐκ ἐπετίμα τῶν παρόντων καὶ ἐμίσει, τελευτῶντες δὲ καὶ αὐτοὶ οὗτοι ἑαυτούς. ἐπειδὴ δ' οὖν ποτ' ἀπεῖπον καὶ 27 ἐνεπλήσθησαν ταῦτα ποιοῦντες, προκαλοῦνται ἐπὶ διακρούσει καὶ τῶι μὴ σημανθῆναι τοὺς ἐχίνους ἐθέλειν ἐκδοῦναι περὶ τῶν πληγῶν παῖδας, ὀνόματα γράψαντες. καὶ νῦν οἶμαι περὶ τοῦτ' ἔσεσθαι τοὺς πολλοὺς τῶν λόγων αὐτοῖς. ἐγὼ δ' οἶμαι δεῖν πάντας ὑμᾶς ἐκεῖνο σκοπεῖν, ὅτι οὗτοι, εἰ τοῦ γενέσθαι τὴν βάσανον ἕνεκα προὐκαλοῦντο καὶ ἐπίστευον τῶι δικαίωι τούτωι, οὐκ ἂν ἤδη τῆς διαίτης ἀποφαινομένης, νυκτός, οὐδεμιᾶς ὑπολοίπου σκήψεως οὔσης, προὐκαλοῦντο, ἀλλὰ πρῶτον 28 μὲν πρὸ τοῦ τὴν δίκην ληχθῆναι, ἡνίκ' ἀσθενῶν ἐγὼ κατεκείμην, καὶ οὐκ εἰδὼς εἰ περιφεύξομαι, πρὸς ἅπαντας τοὺς εἰσιόντας

τοῦτον ἀπέφαινον τὸν πρῶτον πατάξαντα καὶ τὰ πλεῖσθ᾽
ὧν ὕβρισμην διαπεπραγμένον, τότ᾽ ἂν εὐθέως ἧκεν ἔχων
μάρτυρας πολλοὺς ἐπὶ τὴν οἰκίαν, τότ᾽ ἂν τοὺς οἰκέτας
παρεδίδου καὶ τῶν ἐξ Ἀρείου πάγου τινὰς παρεκάλει· εἰ γὰρ
29 ἀπέθανον, παρ᾽ ἐκείνοις ἂν ἦν ἡ δίκη. εἰ δ᾽ ἄρ᾽ ἠγνόησε
ταῦτα, καὶ τοῦτο τὸ δίκαιον ἔχων, ὡς νῦν φήσει, οὐ
παρεσκευάσατ᾽ ὑπὲρ τηλικούτου κινδύνου, ἐπειδή γ᾽ ἀνεστηκὼς
ἤδη προσεκαλεσάμην αὐτόν, ἐν τῆι πρώτηι συνόδωι πρὸς
τῶι διαιτητῆι παραδιδοὺς ἐφαίνετ᾽ ἄν· ὧν οὐδὲν πέπρακται
τούτωι. ὅτι δ᾽ ἀληθῆ λέγω καὶ διακρούσεως ἕνεχ᾽ ἡ πρόκλησις
ἦν, λέγε ταύτην τὴν μαρτυρίαν· ἔσται γὰρ ἐκ ταύτης φανερόν.

MΑΡΤΥΡΙΑ

30 Περὶ μὲν τοίνυν τῆς βασάνου ταῦτα μέμνησθε, τὴν ὥραν
ἡνίκα προὐκαλεῖτο, ὧν ἕνεκ᾽ ἐκκρούων ταῦτ᾽ ἐποίει, τοὺς
χρόνους τοὺς πρώτους, ἐν οἷς οὐδαμοῦ τοῦτο βουληθεὶς τὸ
δίκαιον αὑτῶι γενέσθαι φαίνεται, οὐδὲ προκαλεσάμενος, οὐδ᾽
ἀξιώσας. ἐπειδὴ τοίνυν ταὐτὰ πάντ᾽ ἠλέγχεθ᾽ ἅπερ καὶ νῦν,
πρὸς τῶι διαιτητῆι, καὶ φανερῶς ἐδείκνυτο πᾶσιν ὧν ἔνοχος
31 τοῖς ἐγκεκλημένοις, ἐμβάλλεται μαρτυρίαν ψευδῆ καὶ ἐπι-
γράφεται μάρτυρας ἀνθρώπους οὓς οὐδ᾽ ὑμᾶς ἀγνοήσειν οἴομαι,
ἐὰν ἀκούσητε, ᾽Διότιμος Διοτίμου Ἰκαριεύς, Ἀρχεβιάδης
Δημοτέλους Ἁλαιεύς, Χαιρήτιος Χαιριμένους Πιθεὺς μαρτυροῦσιν ἀπιέναι ἀπὸ δείπνου μετὰ Κόνωνος, καὶ προσελθεῖν
ἐν ἀγορᾶι μαχομένοις Ἀρίστωνι καὶ τῶι υἱεῖ τῶι Κόνωνος,
32 καὶ μὴ πατάξαι Κόνωνα ᾽Ἀρίστωνα᾽, ὡς ὑμᾶς εὐθέως
πιστεύσοντας, τὸ δ᾽ ἀληθὲς οὐ λογιουμένους, ὅτι πρῶτον μὲν
οὐδέποτ᾽ ἂν οὔθ᾽ ὁ Λυσίστρατος οὔθ᾽ ὁ Πασέας οὔθ᾽ ὁ Νικήρατος
οὔθ᾽ ὁ Διόδωρος, οἳ διαρρήδην μεμαρτυρήκασιν ὁρᾶν ὑπὸ
Κόνωνος τυπτόμενον ἐμὲ καὶ θοἰμάτιον ἐκδυόμενον καὶ τἆλλ᾽
ὅσ᾽ ἔπασχον ὑβριζόμενον, ἀγνῶτες ὄντες κἀπὸ ταὐτομάτου
παραγενόμενοι τῶι πράγματι τὰ ψευδῆ μαρτυρεῖν ἠθέλησαν,
εἰ μὴ ταῦθ᾽ ἑώρων πεπονθότα· ἔπειτ᾽ αὐτὸς ἐγὼ οὐδέποτ᾽
ἄν, μὴ παθὼν ὑπὸ τούτου ταῦτα, ἀφεὶς τοὺς καὶ παρ᾽ αὐτῶν
τούτων ὁμολογουμένους τύπτειν ἐμὲ πρὸς τὸν οὐδ᾽ ἀψάμενον

πρῶτον εἰσιέναι προειλόμην. τί γὰρ ἄν; ἀλλ' ὑφ' οὖ γε 33
πρώτου ἐπλήγην καὶ μάλισθ' ὑβρίσθην, τούτωι καὶ δικάζομαι
καὶ μισῶ καὶ ἐπεξέρχομαι. καὶ τὰ μὲν παρ' ἐμοῦ πάνθ' οὕτως
ἐστὶν ἀληθῆ καὶ φαίνεται· τούτωι δὲ μὴ παρασχομένωι τούτους
μάρτυρας ἦν δήπου λόγος οὐδείς, ἀλλ' ἑαλωκέναι παραχρῆμ'
ὑπῆρχε σιωπῆι. συμπόται δ' ὄντες τούτου καὶ πολλῶν
τοιούτων ἔργων κοινωνοὶ εἰκότως τὰ ψευδῆ μεμαρτυρήκασιν.
εἰ δ' ἔσται τὸ πρᾶγμα τοιοῦτον, ἐὰν ἅπαξ ἀπαναισχυντήσωσίν
τινες καὶ τὰ ψευδῆ φανερῶς τολμήσωσι μαρτυρεῖν, οὐδὲν δὲ
τῆς ἀληθείας ὄφελος, πάνδεινον ἔσται πρᾶγμα. ἀλλὰ νὴ Δί' 34
οὐκ εἰσὶ τοιοῦτοι. ἀλλ' ἴσασιν ὑμῶν, ὡς ἐγὼ νομίζω, πολλοὶ
καὶ τὸν Διότιμον καὶ τὸν Ἀρχεβιάδην καὶ τὸν Χαιρήτιον
τὸν ἐπιπόλιον τουτονί, οἳ μεθ' ἡμέραν μὲν ἐσκυθρωπάκασιν καὶ
λακωνίζειν φασὶ καὶ τρίβωνας ἔχουσιν καὶ ἁπλᾶς ὑποδέδενται,
ἐπειδὰν δὲ συλλεγῶσιν καὶ μετ' ἀλλήλων γένωνται, κακῶν
καὶ αἰσχρῶν οὐδὲν ἐλλείπουσι. καὶ ταῦτα τὰ λαμπρὰ καὶ 35
νεανικά ἐστιν αὐτῶν 'οὐ γὰρ ἡμεῖς μαρτυρήσομεν ἀλλήλοις;
οὐ γὰρ ταῦθ' ἑταίρων ἐστὶ καὶ φίλων; τί δὲ καὶ δεινόν ἐστιν
ὧν παρέξεται κατὰ σοῦ; τυπτόμενόν φασί τινες ὁρᾶν; ἡμεῖς δὲ
μηδ' ἦφθαι τὸ παράπαν μαρτυρήσομεν. ἐκδεδύσθαι θοἰμάτιον;
τοῦτ' ἐκείνους προτέρους πεποιηκέναι ἡμεῖς μαρτυρήσομεν. τὸ
χεῖλος ἐρρᾶφθαι; τὴν κεφαλὴν δέ γ' ἡμεῖς ἢ ἕτερόν τι κατεαγέναι
φήσομεν.' ἀλλὰ καὶ μάρτυρας ἰατροὺς παρέχομαι. τοῦτ' οὐκ 36
ἔστιν, ὦ ἄνδρες δικασταί, παρὰ τούτοις· ὅσα γὰρ μὴ δι' αὐτῶν,
οὐδενὸς μάρτυρος καθ' ἡμῶν εὐπορήσουσιν. ἡ δ' ἀπ' αὐτῶν
ἑτοιμότης οὐδ' ἂν εἰπεῖν μὰ τοὺς θεοὺς δυναίμην ὅση καὶ
οἵα πρὸς τὸ ποιεῖν ὁτιοῦν ὑπάρχει. ἵνα δ' εἰδῆθ' οἵα καὶ
διαπραττόμενοι περιέρχονται, λέγ' αὐτοῖς ταυτασὶ τὰς μαρτυρίας, σὺ δ' ἐπίλαβε τὸ ὕδωρ.

MAPTYPIAI

Τοίχους τοίνυν διορύττοντες καὶ παίοντες τοὺς ἀπαντῶντας, 37
ἆρ' ἂν ὑμῖν ὀκνῆσαι δοκοῦσιν ἐν γραμματειδίωι τὰ ψευδῆ
μαρτυρεῖν ἀλλήλοις οἱ κεκοινωνηκότες τοσαύτης καὶ τοιαύτης
φιλαπεχθημοσύνης καὶ πονηρίας καὶ ἀναιδείας καὶ ὕβρεως;

πάντα γὰρ ταῦτ' ἔμοιγ' ἐν τοῖς ὑπὸ τούτων πραττομένοις
ἐνεῖναι δοκεῖ. καίτοι καὶ τούτων ἕτερ' ἐστὶν πεπραγμένα τούτοις
δεινότερα, ἀλλ' ἡμεῖς οὐχ οἷοί τε γενοίμεθ' ἂν πάντας ἐξευρεῖν
τοὺς ἠδικημένους.

38 Ὃ τοίνυν πάντων ἀναιδέστατον μέλλειν αὐτὸν ἀκούω
ποιεῖν, βέλτιον νομίζω προειπεῖν ὑμῖν εἶναι. φασὶ γὰρ
παραστησάμενον τοὺς παῖδας αὐτὸν κατὰ τούτων ὁμεῖσθαι,
καὶ ἀράς τινας δεινὰς καὶ χαλεπὰς ἐπαράσεσθαι καὶ τοιαύτας
οἵας ἀκηκοώς γέ τις θαυμάσας ἀπήγγελλεν ἡμῖν. ἔστι δ', ὦ
ἄνδρες δικασταί, ἀνυπόστατα μὲν τὰ τοιαῦτα τολμήματα· οἱ
γὰρ οἶμαι βέλτιστοι καὶ ἥκιστ' ἂν αὐτοί τι ψευσάμενοι μάλισθ'
ὑπὸ τῶν τοιούτων ἐξαπατῶνται· οὐ μὴν ἀλλὰ δεῖ πρὸς τὸν
39 βίον καὶ τὸν τρόπον ἀποβλέποντας πιστεύειν. τὴν δὲ τούτου
πρὸς τὰ τοιαῦτ' ὀλιγωρίαν ἐγὼ πρὸς ὑμᾶς ἐρῶ· πέπυσμαι
γὰρ ἐξ ἀνάγκης. ἀκούω γάρ, ὦ ἄνδρες δικασταί, Βάκχιόν
τέ τινα, ὃς παρ' ὑμῖν ἀπέθανε, καὶ Ἀριστοκράτην τὸν τοὺς
ὀφθαλμοὺς διεφθαρμένον καὶ τοιούτους ἑτέρους καὶ Κόνωνα
τουτονὶ ἑταίρους εἶναι μειράκι' ὄντας καὶ Τριβαλλοὺς ἐπωνυμίαν
ἔχειν· τούτους τά θ' Ἑκαταῖα [κατεσθίειν,] καὶ τοὺς ὄρχεις
τοὺς ἐκ τῶν χοίρων, οἷς καθαίρουσιν ὅταν εἰσιέναι μέλλωσιν,
συλλέγοντας ἑκάστοτε συνδειπνεῖν ἀλλήλοις, καὶ ῥᾷον ὀμνύναι
40 καὶ ἐπιορκεῖν ἢ ὁτιοῦν. οὐ δὴ Κόνων ὁ τοιοῦτος πιστός
ἐστιν ὀμνύων, οὐδὲ πολλοῦ δεῖ, ἀλλ' ὁ μηδ' εὔορκον μηδὲν
ἂν ὀμόσας, κατὰ δὲ δὴ παίδων ὧν μὴ νομίζετε μηδ' ἂν μελλήσας,
ἀλλὰ κἂν ὁτιοῦν παθὼν πρότερον, εἰ δ' ἄρ' ἀναγκαῖον, ὀμνύων
ὡς νόμιμον, ἀξιοπιστότερος τοῦ κατὰ τῶν παίδων ὀμνύοντος
καὶ διὰ τοῦ πυρός. ἐγὼ τοίνυν ὁ δικαιότερόν σου πιστευθεὶς
ἂν κατὰ πάντ', ὦ Κόνων, ἠθέλησ' ὀμόσαι ταυτί, οὐχ ὑπὲρ
τοῦ μὴ δοῦναι δίκην ὧν ἠδίκηκα, καὶ ὁτιοῦν ποιῶν, ὥσπερ
σύ, ἀλλ' ὑπὲρ τῆς ἀληθείας καὶ ὑπὲρ τοῦ μὴ προσυβρισθῆναι,
ὡς οὐ κατεπιορκησόμενος τὸ πρᾶγμα. λέγε τὴν πρόκλησιν.

ΠΡΟΚΛΗΣΙΣ

41 Ταῦτ' ἐγὼ καὶ τότ' ἠθέλησ' ὀμόσαι, καὶ νῦν ὀμνύω τοὺς
θεοὺς καὶ τὰς θεὰς ἅπαντας καὶ πάσας ὑμῶν ἕνεκ', ὦ ἄνδρες

δικασταί, καὶ τῶν περιεστηκότων, ἦ μὴν παθὼν ὑπὸ Κόνωνος ταῦθ' ὧν δικάζομαι, καὶ λαβὼν πληγάς, καὶ τὸ χεῖλος διακοπεὶς οὕτως ὥστε καὶ ῥαφῆναι, καὶ ὑβρισθεὶς τὴν δίκην διώκειν. καὶ εἰ μὲν εὐορκῶ, πολλά μοι ἀγαθὰ γένοιτο καὶ μηδέποτ' αὖθις τοιοῦτο μηδὲν πάθοιμι, εἰ δ' ἐπιορκῶ, ἐξώλης ἀπολοίμην αὐτὸς καὶ εἴ τί μοι ἔστιν ἢ μέλλει ἔσεσθαι. ἀλλ' οὐκ ἐπιορκῶ, οὐδ' ἂν Κόνων διαρραγῇ. ἀξιῶ τοίνυν ὑμᾶς, ὦ ἄνδρες 42 δικασταί, πάνθ' ὅσ' ἐστὶν δίκαι' ἐπιδείξαντος ἐμοῦ καὶ πίστιν προσθέντος ὑμῖν, ὥσπερ ἂν αὐτὸς ἕκαστος παθὼν τὸν πεποιηκότ' ἐμίσει, οὕτως ὑπὲρ ἐμοῦ πρὸς Κόνωνα τουτονὶ τὴν ὀργὴν ἔχειν, καὶ μὴ νομίζειν ἴδιον τῶν τοιούτων μηδὲν ὃ κἂν ἄλλωι τυχὸν συμβαίη, ἀλλ' ἐφ' ὅτου ποτ' ἂν συμβῇ, βοηθεῖν καὶ τὰ δίκαι' ἀποδιδόναι, καὶ μισεῖν τοὺς πρὸ μὲν τῶν ἁμαρτημάτων θρασεῖς καὶ προπετεῖς, ἐν δὲ τῶι δίκην ὑπέχειν ἀναισχύντους καὶ πονηροὺς καὶ μήτε δόξης μήτ' ἔθους μήτ' ἄλλου μηδενὸς φροντίζοντας πρὸς τὸ μὴ δοῦναι δίκην. ἀλλὰ δεήσεται Κόνων καὶ κλαήσει. σκοπεῖτε δὴ πότερός ἐστιν 43 ἐλεινότερος, ὁ πεπονθὼς οἷ' ἐγὼ πέπονθ' ὑπὸ τούτου, εἰ προσυβρισθεὶς ἄπειμι καὶ δίκης μὴ τυχών, ἢ Κόνων, εἰ δώσει δίκην; πότερον δ' ὑμῶν ἑκάστωι συμφέρει ἐξεῖναι τύπτειν καὶ ὑβρίζειν ἢ μή; ἐγὼ μὲν οἴομαι μή. οὐκοῦν, ἂν μὲν ἀφιῆτε, ἔσονται πολλοί, ἐὰν δὲ κολάζητε, ἐλάττους.

Πόλλ' ἂν εἰπεῖν ἔχοιμ', ὦ ἄνδρες δικασταί, καὶ ὡς ἡμεῖς 44 χρήσιμοι, καὶ αὐτοὶ καὶ ὁ πατήρ, ἕως ἔζη, καὶ τριηραρχοῦντες καὶ στρατευόμενοι καὶ τὸ προσταττόμενον ποιοῦντες, καὶ ὡς οὐδὲν οὔθ' οὗτος οὔτε τῶν τούτου οὐδείς· ἀλλ' οὔτε τὸ ὕδωρ ἱκανὸν οὔτε νῦν περὶ τούτων ὁ λόγος ἐστίν. εἰ γὰρ δὴ ὁμολογουμένως ἔτι τούτων καὶ ἀχρηστοτέροις καὶ πονηρο- τέροις ἡμῖν εἶναι συνέβαινεν, οὐ τυπτητέοι, οὐδ' ὑβριστέοι δήπου ἐσμέν.

Οὐκ οἶδ' ὅ τι δεῖ πλείω λέγειν· οἶμαι γὰρ ὑμᾶς οὐδὲν ἀγνοεῖν τῶν εἰρημένων.

37 ΠΑΡΑΓΡΑΦΗ ΠΡΟΣ ΠΑΝΤΑΙΝΕΤΟΝ

Δεδωκότων, ὦ ἄνδρες δικασταί, τῶν νόμων παραγράψασθαι
περὶ ὧν ἄν τις ἀφεὶς καὶ ἀπαλλάξας δικάζηται, γεγενημένων
ἀμφοτέρων μοι τούτων πρὸς Πανταίνετον τουτονί, παρεγραψάμην, ὡς ἠκούσατ' ἀρτίως, μὴ εἰσαγώγιμον εἶναι τὴν
δίκην, οὐκ οἰόμενος δεῖν ἀφεῖσθαι τοῦ δικαίου τούτου, οὐδ',
ἐπειδὰν ἐξελέγξω πρὸς ἅπασι τοῖς ἄλλοις καὶ ἀφεικότα τοῦτον
ἐμαυτὸν καὶ ἀπηλλαγμένον, ἐγγενέσθαι τούτωι μὴ φάσκειν
ἀληθῆ με λέγειν, καὶ ποιεῖσθαι τεκμήριον ὡς, εἴπερ ἐπράχθη
τι τοιοῦτον, παρεγραψάμην ἄν αὐτόν, ἀλλ' ἐπὶ ταύτης τῆς
σκήψεως εἰσελθὼν ἀμφότερ' ὑμῖν ἐπιδεῖξαι, καὶ ὡς οὐδὲν
2 ἠδίκηκα τοῦτον καὶ ὡς παρὰ τὸν νόμον μοι δικάζεται. εἰ μὲν
οὖν ἐπεπόνθει τι τούτων Πανταίνετος ὧν νῦν ἐγκαλεῖ, κατ'
ἐκείνους ἄν τοὺς χρόνους εὐθὺς ἐφαίνετό μοι δικαζόμενος, ἐν
οἷς τὸ συμβόλαιον ἡμῖν πρὸς ἀλλήλους ἐγένετο, οὐσῶν μὲν
ἐμμήνων τούτων τῶν δικῶν, ἐπιδημούντων δ' ἡμῶν ἀμφοτέρων,
ἁπάντων δ' ἀνθρώπων εἰωθότων παρ' αὐτὰ τἀδικήματα
μᾶλλον ἢ χρόνων ἐγγεγενημένων ἀγανακτεῖν. ἐπειδὴ δ' οὐδὲν
ἠδικημένος, ὡς καὶ ὑμεῖς οἶδ' ὅτι φήσετε, ἐπειδὰν τὰ πεπραγμέν'
ἀκούσητε, τῶι κατορθῶσαι τὴν πρὸς Εὔεργον δίκην ἐπηρμένος
συκοφαντεῖ, ὑπόλοιπόν ἐστι παρ' ὑμῖν, ὦ ἄνδρες δικασταί,
ἐπιδείξανθ' ὡς οὐδ' ὁτιοῦν ἀδικῶ, καὶ μάρτυρας ὧν ἄν λέγω
3 παρασχόμενον, πειρᾶσθαι σώιζειν ἐμαυτόν. δεήσομαι δὲ καὶ
μέτρια καὶ δίκαι' ὑμῶν ἁπάντων, ἀκοῦσαί τέ μου περὶ ὧν
παρεγραψάμην εὐνοϊκῶς, καὶ προσέχειν ὅλωι τῶι πράγματι
τὸν νοῦν· πολλῶν γὰρ δικῶν ἐν τῆι πόλει γεγενημένων, οὐδένα
πω δίκην οὔτ' ἀναιδεστέραν οὔτε συκοφαντικωτέραν οἶμαι
φανήσεσθαι δεδικασμένον ἧς νῦν οὑτοσὶ λαχὼν εἰσελθεῖν
τετόλμηκεν. ἐξ ἀρχῆς δ', ὡς ἄν οἷός τ' ὦ διὰ βραχυτάτων,
ἅπαντα τὰ πραχθέντα διηγήσομαι πρὸς ὑμᾶς.

4　　　Ἐδανείσαμεν πέντε καὶ ἑκατὸν μνᾶς ἐγὼ καὶ Εὔεργος, ὦ
ἄνδρες δικασταί, Πανταινέτωι τουτωί, ἐπ' ἐργαστηρίωι τ'
ἐν τοῖς ἔργοις ἐν Μαρωνείαι καὶ τριάκοντ' ἀνδραπόδοις. ἦν
δὲ τοῦ δανείσματος τετταράκοντα μὲν καὶ πέντε μναῖ ἐμαί,

τάλαντον δ' Εὐέργου. συνέβαινε δὲ τοῦτον ὀφείλειν Μνησικλεῖ
μὲν Κολλυτεῖ τάλαντον, Φιλέαι δ' Ἐλευσινίωι καὶ Πλείστορι
πέντε καὶ τετταράκοντα μνᾶς. πρατὴρ μὲν δὴ τοῦ ἐργαστηρίου 5
καὶ τῶν ἀνδραπόδων ὁ Μνησικλῆς ἡμῖν γίγνεται (καὶ γὰρ
ἐώνητ' ἐκεῖνος αὐτὰ τούτωι παρὰ Τηλεμάχου τοῦ πρότερον
κεκτημένου)· μισθοῦται δ' οὗτος παρ' ἡμῶν τοῦ γιγνομένου
τόκου τῶι ἀργυρίωι, πέντε καὶ ἑκατὸν δραχμῶν τοῦ μηνὸς
ἑκάστου. καὶ τιθέμεθα συνθήκας, ἐν αἷς ἥ τε μίσθωσις ἦν
γεγραμμένη καὶ λύσις τούτωι παρ' ἡμῶν ἔν τινι ῥητῶι χρόνωι.
πραχθέντων δὲ τούτων ἐλαφηβολιῶνος μηνὸς ἐπὶ Θεοφίλου 6
ἄρχοντος, ἐγὼ μὲν ἐκπλέων εἰς τὸν Πόντον εὐθὺς ὠιχόμην,
οὗτος δ' ἐνθάδ' ἦν καὶ Εὔεργος. τὰ μὲν δὴ πραχθέντα τούτοις
πρὸς αὐτούς, ἕως ἀπεδήμουν ἐγώ, οὐκ ἂν ἔχοιμ' εἰπεῖν. οὔτε
γὰρ ταὐτὰ λέγουσιν οὔτ' ἀεὶ ταῦθ' οὗτός γε, ἀλλὰ τοτὲ
μὲν ἐκπεσεῖν ὑπ' ἐκείνου βίαι παρὰ τὰς συνθήκας ἐκ τῆς
μισθώσεως, τοτὲ δ' αὐτὸν αἴτιον αὑτῶι πρὸς τὸ δημόσιον
γενέσθαι τῆς ἐγγραφῆς, τοτὲ δ' ἄλλ' ὅ τι ἂν βούληται. ἐκεῖνος 7
δ' ἁπλῶς οὔτε τοὺς τόκους ἀπολαμβάνων οὔτε τῶν ἄλλων
τῶν ἐν ταῖς συνθήκαις ποιοῦντος οὐδὲν τούτου, ἐλθὼν παρ'
ἑκόντος τούτου λαβὼν ἔχειν τὰ ἑαυτοῦ· μετὰ δὲ ταῦτ' ἀπελθόντα
τοῦτον ἥκειν τοὺς ἀμφισβητήσοντας ἄγοντα, αὐτὸς δ' οὐχ
ὑπεξελθεῖν ἐκείνοις, τοῦτον δ' οὐχὶ κωλύειν ἔχειν ὅσαπερ
ἐμισθώσατο, εἰ ποιοίη τὰ συγκείμενα. τούτων μὲν δὴ τοιούτους
ἀκούω λόγους. ἐκεῖνο δ' οἶδ' ὅτι, εἰ μὲν οὗτος ἀληθῆ λέγει 8
καὶ δεινὰ πέπονθεν, ὥσπερ φησίν, ὑπὸ τοῦ Εὐέργου, ἔχει
δίκην ἧς ἐτιμήσατ' αὐτός· εἷλεν γὰρ εἰσελθὼν αὐτὸν ὡς ὑμᾶς,
καὶ οὐ δήπου τῶν αὐτῶν παρά τε τοῦ πεποιηκότος δίκαιός
ἐστιν δίκην λαβεῖν καὶ παρ' ἐμοῦ τοῦ μηδ' ἐπιδημοῦντος· εἰ
δ' ὁ Εὔεργος ἀληθῆ λέγει, σεσυκοφάντηται μὲν ὡς ἔοικεν ἐκεῖνος,
ἐγὼ δ' οὐδ' οὕτως τῶν αὐτῶν φεύγοιμ' ἂν δίκην εἰκότως.
ὡς οὖν ταῦτα πρῶτον ἀληθῆ λέγω, τούτων τοὺς μάρτυρας
ὑμῖν παρέξομαι.

ΜΑΡΤΥΡΕΣ

Ὅτι μὲν τοίνυν καὶ πρατὴρ ἦν ἡμῖν τῶν κτημάτων ὅσπερ 9
ἐξ ἀρχῆς αὐτὸς ἐώνητο, καὶ κατὰ τὰς συνθήκας οὗτος ἐμισθώσαθ'

ἡμέτερον ὂν τὸ ἐργαστήριον καὶ τἀνδράποδα, καὶ οὔτε παρῆν
ἐγὼ τοῖς μετὰ ταῦτα πρὸς Εὔεργον τούτωι πραχθεῖσιν οὔτ'
ἐπεδήμουν ὅλως, ἔλαχέν τε δίκην ἐκείνωι καὶ οὐδὲν πώποθ'
ἡμῖν ἐνεκάλει, ἀκούετε τῶν μαρτύρων, ὦ ἄνδρες δικασταί.

10 ἐπειδὴ τοίνυν ἀφικόμην σχεδόν τι πάντ' ἀπολωλεκὼς ὅσ'
ἔχων ἐξέπλευσα, ἀκούσας καὶ καταλαβὼν τοῦτον μὲν
ἀφεστηκότα, τὸν δ' Εὔεργον ἔχοντα καὶ κρατοῦνθ' ὧν ἐωνήμεθα,
θαυμαστῶς ὡς ἐλυπήθην, ὁρῶν τὸ πρᾶγμά μοι περιεστηκὸς
εἰς ἄτοπον· ἢ γὰρ κοινωνεῖν ἔδει τῆς ἐργασίας καὶ τῶν ἐπιμελειῶν
τῶι Εὐέργωι, ἢ χρήστην ἀντὶ τούτου τὸν Εὔεργον ἔχειν,
καὶ πρὸς ἐκεῖνον πάλιν μίσθωσιν γράφειν καὶ συμβόλαιον
11 ποιεῖσθαι· τούτων δ' οὐδέτερον προηιρούμην. ἀηδῶς δ' ἔχων
οἷς λέγω τούτοις, ἰδὼν τὸν Μνησικλέα τὸν πρατῆρα τούτων
ἡμῖν γεγενημένον, προσελθὼν ἐμεμφόμην αὐτῶι, λέγων οἷον
ἄνθρωπον προὔξένησέ μοι, καὶ τοὺς ἀμφισβητοῦντας καὶ τί
ταῦτ' ἐστὶν ἠρώτων. ἀκούσας δ' ἐκεῖνος τῶν μὲν ἀμφισβητούντων κατεγέλα, συνελθεῖν δ' ἔφη τούτους βούλεσθαι πρὸς
ἡμᾶς, καὶ συνάξειν αὐτὸς ἡμᾶς, καὶ παραινέσειν τούτωι πάντα
12 ποιεῖν τὰ δίκαι' ἐμοί, καὶ οἴεσθαι πείσειν. ὡς δὲ συνήλθομεν,
τὰ μὲν πολλὰ τί δεῖ λέγειν; ἧκον δ' οἱ δεδανεικέναι φάσκοντες
τούτωι ἐπὶ τῶι ἐργαστηρίωι καὶ τοῖς ἀνδραπόδοις ἃ ἡμεῖς
ἐπριάμεθα παρὰ Μνησικλέους, καὶ οὐδὲν ἦν ἁπλοῦν οὐδ' ὑγιὲς
τούτων. πάντα δ' ἐξελεγχόμενοι ψευδῆ λέγοντες, καὶ τοῦ
Μνησικλέους βεβαιοῦντος ἡμῖν, προκαλοῦνται πρόκλησιν ἡμᾶς
ὡς οὐ δεξομένους, ἢ κομίσασθαι πάντα τὰ χρήματα παρ'
αὐτῶν καὶ ἀπελθεῖν, ἢ διαλῦσαι σφᾶς ὑπὲρ ὧν ἐνεκάλουν,
αἰτιώμενοι πολλῶι πλείονος ἄξι' ἔχειν ὧν ἐδεδώκεμεν χρημάτων.
13 ἀκούσας δ' ἐγώ, παραχρῆμα, οὐδὲ βουλευσάμενος, κομίσασθαι
συνεχώρησα, καὶ τὸν Εὔεργον ἔπεισα. ἐπειδὴ δ' ἔδει τὰ χρήμαθ'
ἡμᾶς ἀπολαμβάνειν καὶ τὸ πρᾶγμ' εἰς τοῦτο προῆκτο, οὐκ
ἔφασαν μετὰ ταῦτα δώσειν οἱ τότ' ἐκεῖν' ἐπαγγειλάμενοι, εἰ
μὴ πρατῆρες γιγνοίμεθ' ἡμεῖς τῶν κτημάτων αὐτοῖς, νοῦν
ἔχοντες, ὦ ἄνδρες Ἀθηναῖοι, κατ' αὐτό γε τοῦτο· ἑώρων γὰρ
ἡμᾶς οἷ' ἐσυκοφαντούμεθ' ὑπὸ τούτου. ὡς οὖν καὶ ταῦτ' ἀληθῆ
λέγω, λαβέ μοι καὶ ταύτας τὰς μαρτυρίας.

ΜΑΡΤΥΡΙΑΙ

Ἐπειδὴ τοίνυν τὸ πρᾶγμ' ἐνταῦθ' εἰστήκει, καὶ τὰ μὲν χρήματ' 14
οὐ προίενθ' οὓς ἐπήγαγεν οὗτος, ἡμεῖς δ' εἰκότως ἐφαινόμεθ'
ὧν ἐωνήμεθα κρατεῖν, ἱκέτευεν, ἐδεῖτο, ἠντεβόλει πρατῆρας
ἡμᾶς γενέσθαι. ἀξιοῦντος δὲ τούτου καὶ πολλὰ δεηθέντος ἐμοῦ
καὶ τί οὐ ποιήσαντος; καὶ τοῦθ' ὑπέμεινα. ὁρῶν δ' αὐτόν, 15
ὦ ἄνδρες Ἀθηναῖοι, κακοήθη, καὶ τὸ μὲν ἐξ ἀρχῆς τοῦ
Μνησικλέους κατηγοροῦντα πρὸς ἡμᾶς, πάλιν δ' ὧι φίλος
ἦν τὰ μάλιστα, τῶι Εὐέργωι, τούτωι προσκεκρουκότα, καὶ
τὸ μὲν πρῶτον ὡς ἐγὼ κατέπλευσα, ἄσμενον φάσκονθ' ἑορακέναι
με, ἐπειδὴ δ' ἔδει τὰ δίκαια ποιεῖν, ἐμοὶ πάλιν δυσκολαίνοντα,
καὶ ἅπασι μέχρι τοῦ προλαβεῖν καὶ τυχεῖν ὧν δέοιτο φίλον
ὄντα, μετὰ ταῦτα δ' ἐχθρὸν καὶ διάφορον γιγνόμενον, ἠξίουν 16
ἀπαλλαττόμενος καὶ πρατὴρ ὑπὲρ τούτου γιγνόμενος, πάντων
ἀφεθεὶς τῶν ἐγκλημάτων καὶ ἀπαλλαγείς, οὕτω διαλύεσθαι.
τούτων δὲ συγχωρηθέντων οὗτος μὲν ἀφῆκεν ἁπάντων ἐμέ,
ἐγὼ δὲ πρατήρ, ὥσπερ ἐδεῖθ' οὗτος, τῶν κτημάτων ἐγιγνόμην,
καθάπερ αὐτὸς ἐπριάμην παρὰ Μνησικλέους. κομισάμενος δὲ
τἀμαυτοῦ καὶ τοῦτον οὐδ' ὁτιοῦν ἀδικῶν, μὰ τοὺς θεούς, οὐδ'
ἂν εἴ τι γένοιτο, ὠιήθην ἂν δίκην μοι λαχεῖν ποτὲ τουτουί.

Τὰ μὲν δὴ γεγενημένα, καὶ περὶ ὧν οἴσετε τὴν ψῆφον, 17
καὶ δι' ἃ τὴν δίκην συκοφαντούμενος παρεγραψάμην μὴ
εἰσαγώγιμον εἶναι, ταῦτ' ἐστιν, ὦ ἄνδρες δικασταί. παρασχόμενος δὲ μάρτυρας οἳ παρῆσαν ἡνίκ' ἀφείμην ὑπὸ τούτου
καὶ ἀπηλλαττόμην, ὡς οὐκ εἰσαγώγιμος ἐκ τῶν νόμων ἐστὶν
ἡ δίκη, μετὰ ταῦτ' ἐπιδείξω. καί μοι λέγε ταύτην τὴν μαρτυρίαν.

ΜΑΡΤΥΡΙΑ

Λέγε δή μοι καὶ τὴν τῶν ἐωνημένων μαρτυρίαν, ἵν' εἰδῆθ'
ὅτι τούτου κελεύοντος αὖτ' ἀπεδόμην οἷς οὗτος ἐκέλευσεν.

ΜΑΡΤΥΡΙΑ

Οὐ τοίνυν μόνον ἡμῖν εἰσιν οὗτοι μάρτυρες, ὡς ἀφείμεθα 18
καὶ νῦν συκοφαντούμεθα, ἀλλὰ καὶ Πανταίνετος αὐτός. ὅτε

γὰρ λαγχάνων Εὐέργωι τὴν δίκην εἴασεν ἐμέ, τότ' ἐμαρτύρει
οὗτος πρὸς ἔμ' αὐτῶι μηδὲν ἔγκλημ' ὑπόλοιπον εἶναι· οὐ γὰρ
ἂν δήπου, τῶν αὐτῶν ἀδικημάτων παρόντων, ἀμφοῖν δ' ὁμοίως
ἐγκαλῶν, τὸν μὲν εἴασεν τῶι δ' ἐδικάζετο. ἀλλὰ μὴν ὅτι γ'
οὐκ ἐῶσιν οἱ νόμοι περὶ τῶν οὕτω πραχθέντων πάλιν
λαγχάνειν, οἶμαι μὲν ὑμᾶς καὶ μηδὲν εἰπόντος ἐμοῦ γιγνώσκειν·
ὅμως δὲ λέγ' αὐτοῖς καὶ τὸν νόμον τουτονί.

ΝΟΜΟΣ

19 'Ακούετ', ὦ ἄνδρες δικασταί, τοῦ νόμου λέγοντος ἄντικρυς,
ὦν ἂν ἀφῆι καὶ ἀπαλλάξηι τις, μηκέτι τὰς δίκας εἶναι. καὶ
μὴν ὅτι γ' ἀμφότερ' ἐστὶ πεπραγμένα ταῦτα τούτωι πρὸς
ἡμᾶς, ἠκούσατε τῶν μαρτυριῶν. ἁπάντων μὲν τοίνυν τῶν
ἐν τοῖς νόμοις ἀπειρημένων οὐ προσήκει δικάζεσθαι, ἥκιστα
δὲ τούτων. ἃ μὲν γὰρ τὸ δημόσιον πέπρακεν, ἔχοι τις ἂν
20 εἰπεῖν ὡς ἀδίκως οὐ προσήκοντα πέπρακεν· καὶ περὶ ὧν
ἔγνω τὸ δικαστήριον, ἔστιν εἰπεῖν ὡς ἐξαπατηθὲν τοῦτ'
ἐποίησεν, καὶ περὶ τῶν ἄλλων τῶν ἐν τῶι νόμωι καθ' ἑκάστου
γένοιτ' ἄν τις εἰκότως λόγος. ἃ δ' αὐτὸς ἐπείσθη καὶ ἀφῆκεν,
οὐκ ἔνι δήπουθεν εἰπεῖν οὐδ' αὐτὸν αἰτιάσασθαι, ὡς οὐ δικαίως
ταῦτ' ἐποίησεν. οἱ μὲν οὖν παρά τι τῶν ἄλλων τούτων
δικαζόμενοι τοῖς ὑφ' ἑτέρων δικαίοις ὡρισμένοις οὐκ ἐμμένουσιν,
ὁ δ' ὧν ἂν ἀφῆι πάλιν λαγχάνων τοῖς ὑφ' ἑαυτοῦ. διὸ πάντων
μάλιστ' ἄξιον τούτοις χαλεπαίνειν.

21 Οὐκοῦν ὡς μὲν ἀφῆκέ με πάντων, ὅτ' ἐγιγνόμην τῶν
ἀνδραπόδων πρατήρ, ἐπέδειξα· ὅτι δ' οὐκ ἐῶσιν οἱ νόμοι
τούτων εἶναι δίκας, ἀκηκόατ' ἀρτίως ἀναγιγνωσκομένου τοῦ
νόμου. ἵνα δ', ὦ ἄνδρες 'Αθηναῖοι, μή τις οἴηται τοῖς περὶ
τῶν πραγμάτων αὐτῶν δικαίοις ἁλισκόμενόν μ' ἐπὶ τοῦτ'
ἀποχωρεῖν, καὶ καθ' ἕκαστον ὧν ἐγκαλεῖ βούλομαι δεῖξαι αὐτὸν
22 ψευδόμενον. λέγε δ' αὐτὸ τὸ ἔγκλημα, ὅ μοι δικάζεται.

ΕΓΚΛΗΜΑ

Ἔβλαψέ με Νικόβουλος ἐπιβουλεύσας ἐμοὶ καὶ τῆι οὐσίαι τῆι ἐμῆι,
ἀφελέσθαι κελεύσας 'Αντιγένην τὸν ἑαυτοῦ οἰκέτην τὸ ἀργύριον τοῦ

ἐμοῦ οἰκέτου, ὃ ἔφερεν καταβολὴν τῆι πόλει τοῦ μετάλλου, ὃ ἐγὼ
ἐπριάμην ἐνενήκοντα μνῶν, καὶ αἴτιος ἐμοὶ γενόμενος ἐγγραφῆναι
τὸ διπλοῦν τῶι δημοσίωι.

Ἐπίσχες. ταυτὶ πάντα, ἃ νῦν ἐγκέκληκεν ἐμοί, πρότερον 23
τὸν Εὔεργον αἰτιασάμενος τὴν δίκην εἷλε. μεμαρτύρηται μὲν
δὴ καὶ ἐν ἀρχῆι μοι τοῦ λόγου πρὸς ὑμᾶς ὡς ἀπεδήμουν,
ὅτε τούτοις αἱ πρὸς ἀλλήλους ἐγίγνοντο διαφοραί· οὐ μὴν
ἀλλὰ καὶ ἐκ τοῦ ἐγκλήματος τούτου δῆλόν ἐστιν. οὐδαμοῦ
γὰρ ὡς ἐγώ τι πεποίηκα τούτων ἔγραψεν, ἀλλ' ὑπογράψας
ἐπιβουλεῦσαί με αὐτῶι καὶ τῆι οὐσίαι, προστάξαι φησὶ τῶι
παιδὶ ταῦτα ποιεῖν, ψευδόμενος· πῶς γὰρ ἐγὼ προσέταξα,
ὃς ὅτ' ἐξέπλεον τῶν γενησομένων ἐνταῦθ' οὐδ' ὁτιοῦν δήπουθεν
ἤιδειν; εἶτα καὶ πόση μωρία, λέγονθ' ὡς ἐπεβούλευον ἀτιμῶσαι 24
καὶ τὰ ἔσχατα πρᾶξαι, οἰκέτηι με ταῦτα προστάξαι γεγραφέναι,
ἃ οὐδὲ πολίτης πολίτην δύναιτ' ἂν ποιῆσαι; τί οὖν ἐστι
τοῦτο; οὐκ ἔχων οἶμαι κατ' οὐδὲν διὰ τὴν ἀποδημίαν εἰς
ἐμὲ τούτων ἀνενεγκεῖν τι, συκοφαντεῖν δὲ βουλόμενος, ὡς
προσέταξα, ἐνέγραψεν· οὐδὲ γὰρ λόγος ἦν, εἰ μὴ τοῦτ' ἐποίησε.
λέγε τἀκόλουθον.   25

ΕΓΚΛΗΜΑ

Καὶ ἐπειδὴ ὦφλον ἐγὼ τῶι δημοσίωι, καταστήσας Ἀντιγένην τὸν
ἑαυτοῦ οἰκέτην εἰς τὸ ἐργαστήριον τὸ ἐμὸν τὸ ἐπὶ Θρασύμωι κύριον
τῶν ἐμῶν, ἀπαγορεύοντος ἐμοῦ.

Ἐπίσχες. πάλιν ταυτὶ πάνθ' ὑπ' αὐτοῦ τοῦ πράγματος
ἐξελεγχθήσεται ψευδόμενος. γέγραφεν γὰρ καταστῆσαι μὲν ἐμέ,
ἀπαγορεύειν δ' αὐτόν. ταῦτα δ' οὐχ οἷόν τε τὸν μὴ παρόντα.
οὔτε γὰρ καθίστην ἐγώ, ὅ γ' ὢν ἐν τῶι Πόντωι, οὔτ' ἀπηγόρευεν
οὗτος τῶι μὴ παρόντι· πῶς γάρ; πῶς οὖν εἰς ἀνάγκην ἦλθεν 26
ταῦθ' οὕτω γράψαι; ὁ Εὔεργος τότ' οἶμαι πλημμελῶν ὢν
δέδωκε δίκην, συνήθως ἔχων ἐμοὶ καὶ γνώριμος ὢν κατέστησεν
τὸν οἰκέτην οἴκοθεν λαβὼν παρ' ἐμοῦ φυλάττειν ὡς αὑτόν.
εἰ μὲν οὖν ἔγραψε τἀληθές, γέλως ἂν ἦν· τί γάρ, εἰ κατέστησεν
Εὔεργος, ἐγώ σ' ἀδικῶ; φεύγων δὲ τοῦτο τοιαῦτ' ἠνάγκασται
γράφειν, ἵν' ἦι πρὸς ἔμ' αὐτῶι τὸ ἔγκλημα. λέγε τὰ ἐφεξῆς.

ΕΓΚΛΗΜΑ

Κἄπειτα πείσας τοὺς οἰκέτας τοὺς ἐμοὺς καθέζεσθαι εἰς τὸν κεγχρεῶνα ἐπὶ βλάβηι τῆι ἐμῆι.

27 Τουτὶ παντελῶς ἤδη καὶ ἀναιδές ἐστιν· οὐ γὰρ μόνον ἐκ τοῦ προκαλεῖσθαι τούτους παραδοῦναι, τοῦτον δὲ μὴ 'θέλειν, ἀλλὰ καὶ ἐκ πάντων δῆλόν ἐστιν ψεῦδος ὄν. τίνος γὰρ εἵνεκ' ἔπειθον; ἵνα νὴ Δί' αὐτοὺς κτήσωμαι. ἀλλ' αἱρέσεώς μοι δοθείσης ἢ ἔχειν ἢ κομίσασθαι τὰ ἐμαυτοῦ, εἱλόμην κομίσασθαι, καὶ ταῦτα μεμαρτύρηται. λέγε δὴ τὴν πρόκλησιν ὅμως.

ΠΡΟΚΛΗΣΙΣ

28 Ταύτην τοίνυν οὐχὶ δεξάμενος τὴν πρόκλησιν, ἀλλὰ φυγών, σκέψασθ' οἷον εὐθέως μετὰ ταῦτ' ἐγκαλεῖ. λέγε τοὐχόμενον.

ΕΓΚΛΗΜΑ

Καὶ κατεργασάμενος τὴν ἀργυρῖτιν, ἣν οἱ ἐμοὶ οἰκέται ἠργάσαντο, καὶ ἔχων τὸ ἀργύριον τὸ ἐκ ταύτης τῆς ἀργυρίτιδος.

Πάλιν ταῦτα πῶς ἔνεστ' ἐμοὶ πεπρᾶχθαι τῶι μὴ παρόντι, 29 καὶ περὶ ὧν Εὐέργου κατεδικάσω; λέγε δ' αὐτοῖς τὸ ἐφεξῆς.

ΕΓΚΛΗΜΑ

Καὶ ἀποδόμενος τὸ ἐργαστήριον τὸ ἐμὸν καὶ τοὺς οἰκέτας παρὰ τὰς συνθήκας, ἃς ἔθετο πρός με.

Ἐπίσχες. τουτὶ πολὺ πάνθ' ὑπερβέβληκεν τἄλλα. πρῶτον μὲν γὰρ 'παρὰ τὰς συνθήκας', φησίν, 'ἃς ἔθετο πρὸς ἐμέ.' αὗται δ' εἰσὶ τίνες; ἐμισθώσαμεν τῶν τόκων τῶν γιγνομένων τούτωι τὰ ἡμέτερ' ἡμεῖς, καὶ ἄλλ' οὐδέν· πρατὴρ μὲν γὰρ ὁ Μνησικλῆς ἡμῖν ἐγεγόνει τούτου παρόντος καὶ κελεύοντος. 30 μετὰ ταῦτα δὲ τὸν αὐτὸν τρόπον ἡμεῖς ἑτέροις ἀπεδόμεθα, ἐφ' οἷσπερ αὐτοὶ ἐπριάμεθα, οὐ μόνον κελεύοντος ἔτι τούτου, ἀλλὰ καὶ ἱκετεύοντος· οὐδεὶς γὰρ ἤθελεν δέχεσθαι τοῦτον πρατῆρα. τί οὖν αἱ τῆς μισθώσεως ἐνταῦθα συνθῆκαι; τί

τοῦτ', ὦ φαυλότατ' ἀνθρώπων, ἐνέγραψας; ἀλλὰ μὴν ὅτι
σοῦ κελεύοντος καὶ ἐφ' οἷσπερ ἐωνήμεθ' αὐτοὶ πάλιν ἀπεδόμεθα,
λέγε τὴν μαρτυρίαν.

ΜΑΡΤΥΡΙΑ

Μαρτυρεῖς τοίνυν καὶ σύ· ἃ γὰρ ἡμεῖς πέντε καὶ ἑκατὸν μνῶν   31
ἀπεδόμεθα, ταῦθ' ὕστερον τριῶν ταλάντων καὶ δισχιλίων καὶ
ἑξακοσίων ἀπέδου σύ· καίτοι τίς ἂν καθάπαξ πρατῆρά σ'
ἔχων σοὶ δραχμὴν ἔδωκε μίαν; ἀλλὰ μὴν ὅτι ταῦτ' ἀληθῆ
λέγω, κάλει μοι τούτων τοὺς μάρτυρας.

ΜΑΡΤΥΡΕΣ

Ἔχων μὲν τοίνυν ἦν ἐπείσθη τῶν αὐτοῦ τιμήν, δεηθεὶς δ'   32
ἐμοῦ τότε γενέσθαι πρατῆρα καθ' ὃ συνέβαλον ἀργύριον, αὐτὸς
δυοῖν ταλάντοιν προσδικάζεται. καὶ τὰ λοιπὰ τῶν ἐγκλημάτων
ἔτ' ἐστὶ δεινότερα. λέγε δή μοι τὸ λοιπὸν τοῦ ἐγκλήματος.

ΕΓΚΛΗΜΑ

Ἐνταυθὶ πόλλ' ἄττα καὶ δεινά μοι ἅμ' ἐγκαλεῖ· καὶ γὰρ   33
αἴκειαν καὶ ὕβριν καὶ βιαίων καὶ πρὸς ἐπικλήρους ἀδικήματα.
τούτων δ' εἰσὶν ἑκάστου χωρὶς αἱ δίκαι καὶ οὔτε πρὸς ἀρχὴν
τὴν αὐτὴν οὔθ' ὑπὲρ τιμημάτων τῶν αὐτῶν, ἀλλ' ἡ μὲν
αἴκεια καὶ τὰ τῶν βιαίων πρὸς τοὺς τετταράκοντα, αἱ δὲ
τῆς ὕβρεως πρὸς τοὺς θεσμοθέτας, ὅσα δ' εἰς ἐπικλήρους, πρὸς
τὸν ἄρχοντα. οἱ δὲ νόμοι καὶ τούτων διδόασι τὰς παραγραφὰς
ἀντιλαγχάνειν, περὶ ὧν οὐκ εἰσὶν εἰσαγωγεῖς. λέγε δ' αὐτοῖς
τουτονὶ τὸν νόμον.

ΝΟΜΟΣ

Τοῦτο τοίνυν ἐμοῦ παραγεγραμμένου πρὸς τῆι ἄλληι παρα-   34
γραφῆι, καὶ οὐκ ὄντων εἰσαγωγέων τῶν θεσμοθετῶν ὑπὲρ
ὧν λαγχάνει Πανταίνετος, ἐξαλήλιπται καὶ οὐ πρόσεστι τῆι
παραγραφῆι. τὸ δ' ὅπως, ὑμεῖς σκοπεῖτε· ἐμοὶ μὲν γάρ, ἕως
ἂν ἔχω τὸν νόμον αὐτὸν δεικνύναι, οὐδ' ὁτιοῦν διαφέρει· οὐ
γὰρ τὸ γιγνώσκειν καὶ συνιέναι τὰ δίκαι' ὑμῶν ἐξαλεῖψαι
δυνήσεται.

35 Λαβὲ δὴ καὶ τὸν μεταλλικὸν νόμον· καὶ γὰρ ἐκ τούτου δείξειν οἴομαι, οὔτ' οὖσαν εἰσαγώγιμον τὴν δίκην, χάριτός τ' ὢν μᾶλλον ἄξιος ἢ τοῦ συκοφαντεῖσθαι. λέγε.

ΝΟΜΟΣ

Οὗτος σαφῶς ὁ νόμος διείρηκεν ὧν εἶναι δίκας προσήκει μεταλλικάς. οὐκοῦν ὁ μὲν νόμος, ἐάν τις ἐξίλληι τινὰ τῆς ἐργασίας, ὑπόδικον ποιεῖ· ἐγὼ δ' οὐχ ὅπως αὐτὸς ἐξίλλω, ἀλλ' ὧν τοῦτον ἄλλος ἀπεστέρει, τούτων ἐγκρατῆ κατέστησα 36 καὶ παρέδωκα, καὶ πρατὴρ τούτου δεηθέντος ἐγενόμην. ναί, φησίν· ἀλλὰ κἂν ἄλλο τι ἀδικῆι τις περὶ τὰ μέταλλα, καὶ τούτων εἰσὶν δίκαι. ὀρθῶς γ', ὦ Πανταίνετε· ἀλλὰ ταῦτα τί ἐστιν; ἂν τύφηι τις, ἂν ὅπλ' ἐπιφέρηι, ἂν ἐπικατατέμνηι τῶν μέτρων ἐντός. ταῦτ' ἐστὶν τἄλλα, ὧν οὐδὲν δήπου πέπρακται πρὸς ὑμᾶς ἐμοί, πλὴν εἰ τοὺς κομιζομένους ἃ προεῖντό σοι, μεθ' ὅπλων ἥκειν νομίζεις. εἰ δὲ ταῦθ' ἡγεῖ, πρὸς ἅπαντας τοὺς προϊεμένους τὰ ἑαυτῶν εἰσί σοι δίκαι μεταλλικαί. ἀλλ' 37 οὐ δίκαιον. φέρε γάρ, ὅστις ἂν μέταλλον παρὰ τῆς πόλεως πρίηται, τοὺς κοινοὺς παρελθὼν νόμους, καθ' οὓς καὶ διδόναι καὶ λαμβάνειν πᾶσι προσήκει δίκας, ἐν ταῖς μεταλλικαῖς δικάσεται, ἐὰν δανείσηται παρά του; τί δ', ἂν κακῶς ἀκούσηι; ἂν πληγὰς λάβηι; ἂν κλοπὴν ἐγκαλῆι; ἂν προεισφορὰν μὴ 38 κομίζηται; ἂν ὅλως ἄλλο τι; ἐγὼ μὲν οὐκ οἴομαι, ἀλλὰ τὰς μεταλλικὰς εἶναι δίκας τοῖς κοινωνοῦσι μετάλλου καὶ τοῖς ἕτερον συντρήσασιν εἰς τὰ τῶν πλησίον καὶ ὅλως τοῖς ἐργαζομένοις τὰ μέταλλα καὶ τῶν ἐν τῶι νόμωι τι ποιοῦσιν· τῶι δὲ δανείσαντι Πανταινέτωι, καὶ ταῦτ' ἀπειληφότι γλίσχρως καὶ μόλις παρὰ τούτου, οὐκ εἶναι δίκην μεταλλικὴν πρὸς φευκτέον, οὐδ' ἐγγύς.

39 Ὡς μὲν οὖν οὔτ' ἠδίκηκα τοῦτον οὐδὲν οὔτ' εἰσαγώγιμος ἐκ τῶν νόμων ἐστὶν ἡ δίκη, ταῦτ' ἄν τις σκοπῶν ῥαιδίως γνοίη. οὐδὲν τοίνυν δίκαιον ἔχων οὐδὲ καθ' ἓν λέγειν ὑπὲρ ὧν ἐγκαλεῖ, ἀλλὰ καὶ ψευδῆ γεγραφὼς εἰς τὸ ἔγκλημα καὶ περὶ ὧν ἀφῆκε δικαζόμενος, τοῦ ἐξελθόντος μηνός, ὦ ἄνδρες Ἀθηναῖοι, ἐπειδὴ ἔμελλον εἰσιέναι τὴν δίκην, ἤδη τῶν

δικαστηρίων ἐπικεκληρωμένων, προσελθὼν καὶ περιστήσας τοὺς
μεθ' ἑαυτοῦ, τὸ ἐργαστήριον τῶν συνεστώτων, πρᾶγμα ποιεῖ
πάνδεινον· ἀναγιγνώσκει μοι πρόκλησιν μακράν, ἀξιῶν, ὃν 40
φησιν οἰκέτην ταῦτα συνειδέναι, βασανίζεσθαι, κἂν μὲν ἦι
ταῦτ' ἀληθῆ, τὴν δίκην ἀτίμητον ὀφλεῖν αὐτῶι, ἐὰν δὲ ψευδῆ,
τὸν βασανιστὴν Μνησικλέα ἐπιγνώμον' εἶναι τῆς τιμῆς τῆς
τοῦ παιδός. λαβὼν δ' ἐγγυητὰς τούτων παρ' ἐμοῦ, καὶ
σημηναμένου τὴν πρόκλησιν ἐμοῦ, οὐχ ὡς δίκαιον ὄν (ποῦ 41
γάρ ἐστι δίκαιον, ἐν οἰκέτου σώματι καὶ ψυχῆι ἢ δύ' ὠφληκέναι
τάλαντα, ἢ μηδὲν τὸν συκοφαντοῦντα ζημιοῦσθαι;) ἀλλ' ἐγὼ
πολλῶι τῶι δικαίωι περιεῖναι βουλόμενος συνεχώρουν. καὶ
μετὰ ταῦτα προσκαλεῖταί μέν με τὴν δίκην πάλιν, ἐπειδὴ θᾶττον
ἀνείλετο τὰς παρακαταβολάς (οὕτως εὐθὺς ἦν δῆλος οὐδ' οἷς
αὐτὸς ὡρίσατ' ἐμμένων δικαίοις)· ἐπειδὴ δ' ἥκομεν πρὸς τὸν 42
βασανιστήν, ἀντὶ τοῦ τὴν πρόκλησιν ἀνοίξας δεῖξαι τὰ
γεγραμμένα καὶ κατὰ ταῦτα πράττειν ὅ τι δόξαι (διὰ γὰρ
τὸν θόρυβον τότε καὶ τὸ μέλλειν καλεῖσθαι τὴν δίκην τοιοῦτον
ἦν· προκαλοῦμαί σε ταυτί· δέχομαι· φέρε δὴ τὸν δακτύλιον·
λαβέ· τίς δ' ἐγγυητής; οὑτοσί· οὐδὲν οὔτ' ἀντίγραφον οὔτ'
ἄλλ' οὐδὲν ἐποιησάμην τοιοῦτον) ἀντὶ δὲ τοῦ ταῦθ' οὕτως
ὥσπερ λέγω πράττειν ἑτέραν ἧκεν ἔχων πρόκλησιν, ἀξιῶν
αὐτὸς βασανίζειν τὸν ἄνθρωπον, καὶ ἐπιλαβόμενος εἷλκεν, καὶ
ἐνέλειπεν οὐδὲν ἀσελγείας. καὶ ἔγωγ' ἐνεθυμήθην, ὦ ἄνδρες 43
δικασταί, ἡλίκον ἐστὶ πλεονέκτημα τὸ καταπεπλάσθαι τὸν
βίον. ἐγὼ γὰρ ἐμαυτῶι ταῦτα πάσχειν ἐδόκουν καταφρονούμενος τῶι ἁπλῶς καὶ ὡς πέφυκα ζῆν, καὶ δίκην διδόναι
παμμεγέθη ταῦτ' ἀνεχόμενος. ὅτι δ' οὖν ἠναγκαζόμην, παρ'
ἃ ἡγούμην δίκαι' εἶναι, ἀντιπροκαλεῖσθαι, καὶ τὸν οἰκέτην
παρεδίδουν, καὶ ὅτι ταῦτ' ἀληθῆ λέγω, λέγε τὴν πρόκλησιν.

ΠΡΟΚΛΗΣΙΣ

Φυγὼν μὲν τοίνυν ταῦτα, φυγὼν δ' ἃ τὸ πρῶτον αὐτὸς 44
προὐκαλέσατο, ἔγωγ', ὅ τι ποτ' ἐρεῖ πρὸς ὑμᾶς, θαυμάζω.
ἵνα δ' εἰδῆθ' ὑφ' οὗ φησὶ καὶ τὰ δεινὰ πεπονθέναι, θεάσασθε.
οὗτός ἐστιν ὁ Πανταίνετον ἐκβαλών, οὗτός ἐσθ' ὁ κρείττων

τῶν φίλων τῶν Πανταινέτου καὶ τῶν νόμων. οὐ γὰρ ἔγωγ᾽ ἐπεδήμουν, οὐδ᾽ αὐτὸς ἐγκαλεῖ.

45 Βούλομαι δ᾽ ὑμῖν καὶ δι᾽ ὧν τοὺς πρότερον δικαστὰς ἐξαπατήσας εἷλε τὸν Εὔεργον εἰπεῖν, ἵν᾽ εἰδῆθ᾽ ὅτι καὶ νῦν οὐδὲν οὔτ᾽ ἀναιδείας οὔτε τοῦ ψεύδεσθαι παραλείψει. πρὸς δὲ τούτοις καὶ περὶ ὧν ἐμοὶ δικάζεται νυνί, τὰς αὐτὰς οὔσας ἀπολογίας εὑρήσετε· ὅσπερ ἔλεγχος ἀκριβέστατός ἐστιν ὑπὲρ τοῦ τότ᾽ ἐκεῖνον σεσυκοφαντῆσθαι. οὗτος γὰρ ᾐτιάσατ᾽ ἐκεῖνον πρὸς ἅπασι τοῖς ἄλλοις ἐλθόντ᾽ εἰς ἀγρὸν ὡς αὐτὸν ἐπὶ τὰς ἐπικλήρους εἰσελθεῖν καὶ τὴν μητέρα τὴν αὐτοῦ, καὶ τοὺς νόμους 46 ἧκεν ἔχων τοὺς τῶν ἐπικλήρων πρὸς τὸ δικαστήριον. καὶ πρὸς μὲν τὸν ἄρχοντα, ὃν τῶν τοιούτων οἱ νόμοι κελεύουσιν ἐπιμελεῖσθαι, καὶ παρ᾽ ὧι τῶι μὲν ἠδικηκότι κίνδυνος περὶ τοῦ τί χρὴ παθεῖν ἢ ἀποτεῖσαι, τῶι δ᾽ ἐπεξιόντι μετ᾽ οὐδεμιᾶς ζημίας ἡ βοήθεια, οὐδέπω καὶ τήμερον ἐξήτασται, οὐδ᾽ εἰσήγγειλεν οὔτ᾽ ἔμ᾽ οὔτε τὸν Εὔεργον ὡς ἀδικοῦντας, ἐν δὲ τῶι δικαστηρίωι ταῦτα κατηγόρει καὶ δυοῖν ταλάντοιν εἷλε 47 δίκην. ἦν γὰρ οἶμαι κατὰ μὲν τοὺς νόμους προειδότα τὴν αἰτίαν, ἐφ᾽ ἧι κρίνεται, ῥάιδιον τἀληθῆ καὶ τὰ δίκαι᾽ ἐπιδείξαντ᾽ ἀποφεύγειν, ἐν δὲ μεταλλικῆι δίκηι, περὶ ὧν οὐδ᾽ ἂν ἤλπισεν αὐτοῦ κατηγορηθήσεσθαι, χαλεπὸν παραχρῆμ᾽ ἔχειν ἀπολύσασθαι τὴν διαβολήν· ἡ δ᾽ ὀργὴ ⟨ἡ⟩ παρὰ τῶν ἐξηπατημένων ὑπὸ τούτου δικαστῶν, ἐφ᾽ ὧι τὴν ψῆφον εἶχον πράγματι, 48 τούτου κατεψηφίσατο. καίτοι τὸν ἐκείνους ἐξηπατηκότα τοὺς δικαστάς, ἆρ᾽ ὀκνήσειν ὑμᾶς ἐξαπατᾶν οἴεσθε; ἢ πεπιστευκότ᾽ εἰσιέναι τοῖς πράγμασιν, ἀλλ᾽ οὐ τοῖς λόγοις καὶ τοῖς συνεστῶσιν μεθ᾽ αὑτοῦ μάρτυσιν, τῶι τ᾽ ἀκαθάρτωι καὶ μιαρῶι Προκλεῖ, τῶι μεγάλωι τούτωι, καὶ Στρατοκλεῖ τῶι πιθανωτάτωι πάντων ἀνθρώπων καὶ πονηροτάτωι, καὶ τῶι μηδὲν ὑποστελλόμενον 49 μηδ᾽ αἰσχυνόμενον κλάησειν καὶ ὀδυρεῖσθαι; καίτοι τοσούτου δεῖς ἐλέου τινὸς ἄξιος εἶναι, ὥστε μισηθείης ἂν δικαιότατ᾽ ἀνθρώπων ἐξ ὧν πεπραγμάτευσαι· ὅς γ᾽ ὀφείλων μνᾶς ἑκατὸν καὶ πέντε καὶ οὐχ οἷός τ᾽ ὢν διαλῦσαι, τοὺς ταῦτα συνευπορήσαντας καὶ γενομένους αἰτίους σοι τοῦ τὰ δίκαια ποιῆσαι τοῖς συμβαλοῦσιν ἐξ ἀρχῆς, χωρὶς ὧν περὶ αὐτὰ τὰ συμβόλαι᾽

ἠδίκεις, καὶ πρὸς ἀτιμῶσαι ζητεῖς. καὶ τοὺς μὲν ἄλλους τοὺς δανειζομένους ἴδοι τις ἂν ἐξισταμένους τῶν ὄντων· σοὶ δ' ὁ συμβεβληκὼς τοῦτο πέπονθεν, καὶ δανείσας τάλαντον δύ' ὤφληκεν συκοφαντηθείς. ἐγὼ δὲ τετταράκοντα μνᾶς δανείσας 50 δυοῖν ταλάντοιν ταυτηνὶ φεύγω δίκην. καὶ ἐφ' οἷς δανείσασθαι μὲν οὐδεπώποτ' ἐδυνήθης ἑκατὸν μνῶν πλέον, πέπρακας δὲ καθάπαξ τριῶν ταλάντων καὶ δισχιλίων, εἰς ταῦτα τέτταρ' ὡς ἔοικεν ἠδίκησαι τάλαντα. ὑπὸ τοῦ ταῦτα; ὑπὸ τοῦ οἰκέτου νὴ Δία τοῦ ἐμοῦ. τίς δ' ἂν οἰκέτηι παραχωρήσειε πολίτης τῶν αὑτοῦ; ἢ τίς ἂν φήσειεν, ὧν δίκην λαχὼν ἥιρηκεν οὗτος Εὔεργον, τούτων καὶ τὸν ἐμὸν παῖδ' ὑπεύθυνον εἶναι προσήκειν; χωρὶς δὲ τούτων αὐτὸς αὐτὸν οὗτος ἀφῆκε τῶν 51 τοιούτων αἰτιῶν ἁπασῶν. οὐ γὰρ νῦν ἔδει λέγειν, οὐδ' εἰς τὴν πρόκλησιν γράφειν ἐν ἧι βασανίζειν ἐξήιτει, ἀλλὰ λαχόντ' ἐκείνωι τὴν δίκην τὸν κύριον διώκειν ἐμέ. νῦν δ' εἴληχεν μὲν ἐμοί, κατηγορεῖ δ' ἐκείνου. ταῦτα δ' οὐκ ἐῶσιν οἱ νόμοι· τίς γὰρ πώποτε τῶι δεσπότηι λαχών, τοῦ δούλου τὰ πράγματα, ὥσπερ κυρίου, κατηγόρησεν;

Ἐπειδὰν τοίνυν τις αὐτὸν ἔρηται 'καὶ τί δίκαιον ἕξεις 52 λέγειν πρὸς Νικόβουλον;' μισοῦσι, φησίν, Ἀθηναῖοι τοὺς δανείζοντας· Νικόβουλος δ' ἐπίφθονός ἐστι, καὶ ταχέως βαδίζει, καὶ μέγα φθέγγεται, καὶ βακτηρίαν φορεῖ· ταῦτα δ' ἐστὶν ἅπαντα, φησίν, πρὸς ἐμοῦ. καὶ ταῦτ' οὐκ αἰσχύνεται λέγων, οὐδὲ τοὺς ἀκούοντας οἴεται μανθάνειν ὅτι συκοφαντοῦντός ἐστι λογισμὸς οὗτος, οὐκ ἀδικουμένου. ἐγὼ δ' ἀδικεῖν μὲν οὐδένα 53 τῶν δανειζόντων οἴομαι, μισεῖσθαι μέντοι τινὰς ἂν εἰκότως ὑφ' ὑμῶν, οἳ τέχνην τὸ πρᾶγμα πεποιημένοι μήτε συγγνώμης μήτ' ἄλλου μηδενός εἰσιν ἀλλ' ἢ τοῦ πλείονος. διὰ γὰρ τὸ καὶ δεδανεῖσθαι πολλάκις, μὴ μόνον αὐτὸς τούτωι δανεῖσαι, οὐδ' ἐγὼ τούτους ἀγνοῶ, οὐδὲ φιλῶ, οὐ μέντοι γ' ἀποστερῶ μὰ Δία, οὐδὲ συκοφαντῶ. ὅστις δ' εἴργασται μὲν ὥσπερ ἐγὼ 54 πλέων καὶ κινδυνεύων, εὐπορήσας δὲ μικρῶν ἐδάνεισεν ταῦτα, καὶ χαρίσασθαι βουλόμενος καὶ μὴ λαθεῖν διαρρυὲν αὐτὸν τἀργύριον, τί τις ἂν τοῦτον εἰς ἐκείνους τιθείη; εἰ μὴ τοῦτο λέγεις, ὡς ὃς ἂν σοὶ δανείσηι, τοῦτον δημοσίαι μισεῖσθαι προσήκει. λέγε δή μοι τὰς μαρτυρίας, τίς ἐγὼ πρὸς τοὺς συμβάλλοντας ἄνθρωπος καὶ πρὸς τοὺς δεομένους εἰμί.

MΑΡΤΥΡΙΑΙ

55 Τοιοῦτος, ὦ Πανταίνετε, ἐγώ, ὁ ταχὺ βαδίζων, καὶ τοιοῦτος σύ, ὁ ἀτρέμας. ἀλλὰ μὴν περὶ τοῦ ἐμοῦ γε βαδίσματος ἢ τῆς διαλέκτου, τἀληθῆ πάντ' ἐρῶ πρὸς ὑμᾶς, ὦ ἄνδρες δικασταί, μετὰ παρρησίας. ἐγὼ γὰρ οὐχὶ λέληθ' ἐμαυτόν, οὐδ' ἀγνοῶ, οὐ τῶν εὖ πεφυκότων κατὰ ταῦτ' ὢν ἀνθρώπων, οὐδὲ τῶν λυσιτελούντων ἑαυτοῖς. εἰ γὰρ ἐν οἷς μηδὲν ὠφελοῦμαι ποιῶν, 56 λυπῶ τινάς, πῶς οὐκ ἀτυχῶ κατὰ τοῦτο τὸ μέρος; ἀλλὰ τί χρὴ παθεῖν; ἂν τῶι δεῖνι δανείσω, διὰ ταῦτα δίκην προσοφλεῖν; μηδαμῶς. κακίαν γὰρ ἐμοὶ καὶ πονηρίαν οὔθ' οὗτος προσοῦσαν οὐδεμίαν δείξει, οὔθ' ὑμῶν τοσούτων ὄντων οὐδὲ εἷς σύνοιδεν. τἆλλα δὲ ταῦθ' ἕκαστος ἡμῶν, ὅπως ἔτυχεν, πέφυκεν οἶμαι. καὶ φύσει μάχεσθαι μὲν ἔχοντ' οὐκ εὔπορόν ἐστιν (οὐ γὰρ ἂν ἀλλήλων διεφέρομεν οὐδέν), γνῶναι δ' ἰδόνθ' 57 ἕτερον καὶ ἐπιπλῆξαι ῥάιδιον. ἀλλὰ τί τούτων ἐμοὶ πρὸς σέ, Πανταίνετε; πολλὰ καὶ δεινὰ πέπονθας; οὐκοῦν εἴληφας δίκην. οὐ παρ' ἐμοῦ γε; οὐδὲ γὰρ ἠδικήθης οὐδὲν ὑπ' ἐμοῦ. οὐ γὰρ ἄν ποτ' ἀφῆκας, οὐδ', ὅτ' Εὐέργωι προηιροῦ λαγχάνειν, εἴασας ἐμέ, οὐδὲ πρατῆρ' ἠξίωσας ὑποστῆναι τόν γε δεινά σε καὶ πόλλ' εἰργασμένον. εἶτα καὶ πῶς ἂν ὁ μὴ παρὼν 58 μηδ' ἐπιδημῶν ἐγὼ τί σ' ἠδίκησα; εἰ τοίνυν ὡς οἷόν τε μέγιστ' ἠδικῆσθαι δοίη τις αὐτῶι καὶ ἐρεῖν ἅπαντ' ἀληθῆ περὶ τούτων νυνί, ἐκεῖνό γ' οἶμαι πάντας ἂν ὑμᾶς ὁμολογῆσαι, ὅτι πολλὰ συμβέβηκεν ἠδικῆσθαί τισιν ἤδη μείζω τῶν εἰς χρήματα γιγνομένων ἀδικημάτων· καὶ γὰρ ἀκούσιοι φόνοι καὶ ὕβρεις εἰς ἃ μὴ δεῖ καὶ πόλλ' ἄλλα τοιαῦτα γίγνεται. ἀλλ' ὅμως ἁπάντων τούτων ὅρος καὶ λύσις τοῖς παθοῦσι τέτακται τὸ 59 πεισθέντας ἀφεῖναι. καὶ τοῦθ' οὕτω τὸ δίκαιον ἐν πᾶσιν ἰσχύει, ὥστ' ἐὰν ἑλών τις ἀκουσίου φόνου καὶ σαφῶς ἐπιδείξας μὴ καθαρόν, μετὰ ταῦτ' αἰδέσηται καὶ ἀφῆι, οὐκέτ' ἐκβαλεῖν κύριος τὸν αὐτόν ἐστιν. οὐδέ γ', ἂν ὁ παθὼν αὐτὸς ἀφῆι τοῦ φόνου, πρὶν τελευτῆσαι, τὸν δράσαντα, οὐδενὶ τῶν λοιπῶν συγγενῶν

ἔξεστ' ἐπεξιέναι, ἀλλ' οὓς ἐκπίπτειν καὶ φεύγειν, ἂν ἁλίσκωνται,
καὶ τεθνάναι προστάττουσιν οἱ νόμοι, τούτους, ἐὰν ἀφεθῶσιν
ἅπαξ, ἁπάντων ἐκλύει τῶν δεινῶν τοῦτο τὸ ῥῆμα. εἶθ' ὑπὲρ 60
μὲν ψυχῆς καὶ τῶν μεγίστων οὕτως ἰσχύει καὶ μένει τὸ ἀφεῖναι,
ὑπὲρ δὲ χρημάτων καὶ ἐλαττόνων ἐγκλημάτων ἄκυρον ἔσται;
μηδαμῶς. οὐ γὰρ εἰ μὴ τῶν δικαίων ἐγὼ παρ' ὑμῖν τεύξομαι,
τοῦτ' ἔστι δεινότατον, ἀλλ' εἰ πρᾶγμα δίκαιον ὡρισμένον ἐκ
παντὸς τοῦ χρόνου νῦν καταλύσετ' ἐφ' ἡμῶν.

39 ΠΡΟΣ ΒΟΙΩΤΟΝ ΠΕΡΙ ΤΟΥ ΟΝΟΜΑΤΟΣ

Οὐδεμιᾶι φιλοπραγμοσύνηι μὰ τοὺς θεούς, ὦ ἄνδρες δικασταί,
τὴν δίκην ταύτην ἔλαχον Βοιωτῶι, οὐδ' ἠγνόουν ὅτι πολλοῖς
ἄτοπον δόξει τὸ δίκην ἐμὲ λαγχάνειν, εἴ τις ἐμοὶ ταὐτὸν ὄνομ'
οἴεται δεῖν ἔχειν· ἀλλ' ἀναγκαῖον ἦν ἐκ τῶν συμβησομένων,
εἰ μὴ τοῦτο διορθώσομαι, ἐν ὑμῖν κριθῆναι. εἰ μὲν οὖν ἑτέρου 2
τινὸς οὗτος ἔφη πατρὸς εἶναι καὶ μὴ τοῦ ἐμοῦ, περίεργος
ἂν εἰκότως ἐδόκουν εἶναι φροντίζων ὅ τι βούλεται καλεῖν οὗτος
ἑαυτόν. νῦν δὲ λαχὼν δίκην τῶι πατρὶ τῶι ἐμῶι καὶ μεθ'
ἑαυτοῦ κατασκευάσας ἐργαστήριον συκοφαντῶν, Μνησικλέα
τε, ὃν ἴσως γιγνώσκετε πάντες, καὶ Μενεκλέα τὸν τὴν Νῖνον
ἑλόντ' ἐκεῖνον, καὶ τοιούτους τινάς, ἐδικάζεθ' υἱὸς εἶναι φάσκων
ἐκ τῆς Παμφίλου θυγατρὸς καὶ δεινὰ πάσχειν καὶ τῆς πατρίδος
ἀποστερεῖσθαι. ὁ πατὴρ δέ (πᾶσα γὰρ εἰρήσεται ἡ ἀλήθει', 3
ὦ ἄνδρες δικασταί) ἅμα μὲν φοβούμενος εἰς δικαστήριον εἰσιέναι,
μή τις, οἷ' ὑπὸ πολιτευομένου, ἑτέρωθί που λελυπημένος
ἐνταυθοῖ ἀπαντήσειεν αὐτῶι, ἅμα δ' ἐξαπατηθεὶς ὑπὸ τῆς
τουτουὶ μητρός, ὀμοσάσης αὐτῆς ἦ μήν, ἐὰν ὅρκον αὐτῆι
διδῶι περὶ τούτων, μὴ ὀμεῖσθαι, τούτων δὲ πραχθέντων οὐδὲν
ἔτ' ἔσεσθαι αὐτοῖς, καὶ μεσεγγυησαμένης ἀργύριον, ἐπὶ τούτοις
δίδωσι τὸν ὅρκον. ἡ δὲ δεξαμένη, οὐ μόνον τοῦτον, ἀλλὰ 4
καὶ τὸν ἀδελφὸν τὸν ἕτερον πρὸς τούτωι κατωμόσατ' ἐκ τοῦ
πατρὸς εἶναι τοῦ ἐμοῦ. ὡς δὲ τοῦτ' ἐποίησεν, εἰσάγειν εἰς
τοὺς φράτερας ἦν ἀνάγκη τούτους καὶ λόγος οὐδεὶς ὑπελείπετο.
εἰσήγαγεν, ἐποιήσατο, ἵνα τἀν μέσωι συντέμω, ἐγγράφει τοῖς

Ἀπατουρίοις τουτονὶ μὲν Βοιωτὸν εἰς τοὺς φράτερας, τὸν
5 δ᾽ ἕτερον Πάμφιλον· Μαντίθεος δ᾽ ἐνεγεγράμμην ἐγώ. συμβάσης
δὲ τῶι πατρὶ τῆς τελευτῆς πρὶν τὰς εἰς τοὺς δημότας ἐγγραφὰς
γενέσθαι, ἐλθὼν εἰς τοὺς δημότας οὑτοσὶ ἀντὶ Βοιωτοῦ
Μαντίθεον ἐνέγραψεν ἑαυτόν, τοῦτο δ᾽ ὅσα βλάπτει ποιῶν
πρῶτον μὲν ἐμέ, εἶτα δὲ καὶ ὑμᾶς, ἐγὼ διδάξω, ἐπειδὰν ὧν
λέγω παράσχωμαι μάρτυρας.

MΑΡΤΥΡΕΣ

6 Ὃν μὲν τοίνυν τρόπον ἡμᾶς ἐνέγραψεν ὁ πατήρ, ἀκηκόατε
τῶν μαρτύρων· ὅτι δ᾽ οὐκ οἰομένου τούτου δεῖν ἐμμένειν,
δικαίως καὶ ἀναγκαίως ἔλαχον τὴν δίκην, τοῦτ᾽ ἤδη δείξω. ἐγὼ
γὰρ οὐχ οὕτω δήπου σκαιός εἰμ᾽ ἄνθρωπος οὐδ᾽ ἀλόγιστος,
ὥστε τῶν μὲν πατρώιων, ἃ πάντ᾽ ἐμὰ ἐγίγνετο, ἐπειδήπερ
ἐποιήσατο τούτους ὁ πατήρ, συγκεχωρηκέναι τὸ τρίτον
νείμασθαι μέρος καὶ στέργειν ἐπὶ τούτωι, περὶ δ᾽ ὀνόματος
ζυγομαχεῖν, εἰ μὴ τὸ μὲν ἡμᾶς μεταθέσθαι μεγάλην ἀτιμίαν
ἔφερε καὶ ἀνανδρίαν, τὸ δὲ ταὐτὸν ἔχειν τοῦτον ἡμῖν ὄνομα
διὰ πόλλ᾽ ἀδύνατον ἦν.

7 Πρῶτον μὲν γάρ, εἰ δεῖ τὰ κοινὰ τῶν ἰδίων εἰπεῖν πρότερον,
τίν᾽ ἡμῖν ἡ πόλις ἐπιτάξει τρόπον, ἄν τι δέηι ποιεῖν; οἴσουσι
νὴ Δί᾽ οἱ φυλέται τὸν αὐτὸν τρόπον ὅνπερ καὶ τοὺς ἄλλους.
οὐκοῦν Μαντίθεον Μαντίου Θορίκιον οἴσουσιν, ἐὰν χορηγὸν
ἢ γυμνασίαρχον ἢ ἑστιάτορ᾽ ἢ ἐάν τι τῶν ἄλλων φέρωσιν.
τῶι δῆλον οὖν ἔσται πότερον σὲ φέρουσιν ἢ ἐμέ; σὺ μὲν
8 γὰρ φήσεις ἐμέ, ἐγὼ δὲ σέ. καὶ δὴ καλεῖ μετὰ τοῦθ᾽ ὁ ἄρχων
ἢ πρὸς ὅντιν᾽ ἂν ἦι ἡ δίκη. οὐχ ὑπακούομεν, οὐ λειτουργοῦμεν.
πότερος ταῖς ἐκ τῶν νόμων ἔσται ζημίαις ἔνοχος; τίνα δ᾽
οἱ στρατηγοὶ τρόπον ἐγγράψουσιν, ἂν εἰς συμμορίαν
ἐγγράφωσιν, ἢ ἂν τριήραρχον καθιστῶσιν; ἢ ἂν στρατεία
9 τις ἦι, τῶι δῆλον ἔσται πότερός ἐσθ᾽ ὁ κατειλεγμένος; τί
δ᾽, ἂν ἄλλη τις ἀρχὴ καθιστῆι λειτουργεῖν, οἷον ἄρχων,
βασιλεύς, ἀθλοθέται, τί σημεῖον ἔσται πότερον καθιστᾶσιν;
προσπαραγράψουσι νὴ Δία τὸν ἐκ Πλαγγόνος, ἂν σὲ
ἐγγράφωσιν, ἂν δ᾽ ἐμέ, τῆς ἐμῆς μητρὸς τοὔνομα. καὶ τίς

ἤκουσε πώποτε, ἢ κατὰ ποῖον νόμον προσπαραγράφοιτ' ἂν
τοῦτο τὸ παράγραμμα ἢ ἄλλο τι πλὴν ὁ πατὴρ καὶ ὁ δῆμος;
ὧν ὄντων ἀμφοῖν τῶν αὐτῶν πολλὴ ταραχὴ συμβαίνει. φέρε, 10
εἰ δὲ κριτὴς καλοῖτο Μαντίθεος Μαντίου Θορίκιος, τί ἂν
ποιοῖμεν; ἢ βαδίζοιμεν ἂν ἄμφω; τῶι γὰρ ἔσται δῆλον πότερον
σὲ κέκληκεν ἢ ἐμέ; πρὸς Διός, ἂν δ' ἀρχὴν ἡντινοῦν ἡ πόλις
κληροῖ, οἷον βουλῆς, θεσμοθέτου, τῶν ἄλλων, τῶι δῆλος ὁ
λαχὼν ἡμῶν ἔσται; πλὴν εἰ σημεῖον, ὥσπερ ⟨ἂν⟩ ἄλλωι
τινί, τῶι χαλκίωι προσέσται· καὶ οὐδὲ τοῦθ' ὁποτέρου ἐστὶν
οἱ πολλοὶ γνώσονται. οὐκοῦν ὁ μὲν ἑαυτόν, ἐγὼ δ' ἐμαυτὸν
φήσω τὸν εἰληχότ' εἶναι. λοιπὸν εἰς τὸ δικαστήριον [ἡμᾶς] 11
εἰσιέναι. οὐκοῦν ἐφ' ἑκάστωι τούτων δικαστήριον ἡμῖν ἡ πόλις
καθιεῖ, καὶ τοῦ μὲν κοινοῦ καὶ ἴσου, τοῦ τὸν λαχόντ' ἄρχειν,
ἀποστερησόμεθα, ἀλλήλους δὲ πλυνοῦμεν, καὶ ὁ τῶι λόγωι
κρατήσας ἄρξει. καὶ πότερ' ἂν βελτίους εἴημεν τῶν ὑπαρχουσῶν
δυσκολιῶν ἀπαλλαττόμενοι, ἢ καινὰς ἔχθρας καὶ βλασφημίας
ποιούμενοι; ἃς πᾶσ' ἀνάγκη συμβαίνειν, ὅταν ἀρχῆς ἤ τινος
ἄλλου πρὸς ἡμᾶς αὐτοὺς ἀμφισβητῶμεν. τί δ', ἂν ἄρα (δεῖ 12
γὰρ ἅπαντα [ἡμᾶς] ἐξετάσαι) ἅτερος ἡμῶν πείσας τὸν ἕτερον,
ἐὰν λάχηι, παραδοῦναι αὐτῶι τὴν ἀρχήν, οὕτω κληρῶται,
τὸ δυοῖν πινακίοιν τὸν ἕνα κληροῦσθαι τί ἄλλ' ἐστίν; εἶτ'
ἐφ' ὧι θάνατον ζημίαν ὁ νόμος λέγει, τοῦθ' ἡμῖν ἀδεῶς ἐξέσται
πράττειν; 'πάνυ γε· οὐ γὰρ ἂν αὐτὸ ποιήσαιμεν.' οἶδα κἀγώ,
τὸ γοῦν κατ' ἐμέ· ἀλλ' οὐδ' αἰτίαν τοιαύτης ζημίας ἐνίους
ἔχειν καλόν, ἐξὸν μή.

Εἶεν. ἀλλὰ ταῦτα μὲν ἡ πόλις βλάπτεται· ἐγὼ δ' ἰδίαι 13
τί; θεάσασθ' ἡλίκα, καὶ σκοπεῖτ' ἄν τι δοκῶ λέγειν· πολὺ
γὰρ χαλεπώτερα ταῦθ' ὧν ἀκηκόατ' ἐστίν. ὁρᾶτε μὲν γὰρ
ἅπαντες αὐτὸν χρώμενον, ἕως μὲν ἔζη, Μενεκλεῖ καὶ τοῖς περὶ
ἐκεῖνον ἀνθρώποις, νῦν δ' ἑτέροις ἐκείνου βελτίοσιν οὐδέν,
καὶ τὰ τοιαῦτ' ἐζηλωκότα καὶ δεινὸν δοκεῖν εἶναι βουλόμενον·
καὶ νὴ Δί' ἴσως ἔστιν. ἂν οὖν προϊόντος τοῦ χρόνου τῶν 14
αὐτῶν τι ποιεῖν τούτοις ἐπιχειρῆι (ἔστι δὲ ταῦτα γραφαί,
φάσεις, ἐνδείξεις, ἀπαγωγαί), εἶτ' ἐπὶ τούτων τινί (πολλὰ
γὰρ ἐστι τἀνθρώπινα, καὶ τοὺς πάνυ δεινοὺς ἑκάστοτε, ὅταν

πλεονάζωσιν, ἐπίστασθ᾽ ὑμεῖς κοσμίους ποιεῖν) ὄφληι τῶι
δημοσίωι, τί μᾶλλον οὗτος ἐγγεγραμμένος ἔσται ἐμοῦ; ὅτι
15 νὴ Δί᾽ εἴσονται πάντες πότερός ποτ᾽ ὤφλεν. καλῶς. ἂν δέ,
ὃ τυχὸν γένοιτ᾽ ἄν, χρόνος διέλθηι καὶ μὴ ἐκτεισθῆι τὸ
ὄφλημα, τί μᾶλλον οἱ τούτου παῖδες ἔσονται τῶν ἐμῶν
ἐγγεγραμμένοι, ὅταν τοὔνομα καὶ ὁ πατὴρ καὶ ἡ φυλὴ καὶ
πάντ᾽ ἦι ταὐτά; τί δ᾽, εἴ τις δίκην ἐξούλης αὐτῶι λαχὼν
μηδὲν ἐμοὶ φαίη πρὸς αὐτὸν εἶναι, κυρίαν δὲ ποιησάμενος
ἐγγράψαι, τί μᾶλλον ἂν εἴη τοῦτον ἢ ἔμ᾽ ἐγγεγραφώς; τί
16 δ᾽, εἴ τινας εἰσφορὰς μὴ θείη; τί δ᾽, εἴ τις ἄλλη περὶ τοὔνομα
γίγνοιτ᾽ ἢ λῆξις δίκης ἢ δόξ᾽ ὅλως ἀηδής; τίς εἴσεται τῶν
πολλῶν πότερός ποθ᾽ οὗτός ἐστιν, δυοῖν Μαντιθέοιν ταὐτοῦ
πατρὸς ὄντοιν; φέρε, εἰ δὲ δίκην ἀστρατείας φεύγοι, χορεύοι
δ᾽ ὅταν στρατεύεσθαι δέηι; καὶ γὰρ νῦν, ὅτ᾽ εἰς Ταμύνας
παρῆλθον οἱ ἄλλοι, ἐνθάδε τοὺς Χοᾶς ἄγων ἀπελείφθη καὶ
τοῖς Διονυσίοις καταμείνας ἐχόρευεν, ὡς ἅπαντες ἑωρᾶθ᾽ οἱ
17 ἐπιδημοῦντες. ἀπελθόντων δ᾽ ἐξ Εὐβοίας τῶν στρατιωτῶν
λιποταξίου προσεκλήθη, κἀγὼ ταξιαρχῶν τῆς φυλῆς ἠναγκαζόμην κατὰ τοὐνόματος τοῦ ἐμαυτοῦ πατρόθεν δέχεσθαι τὴν
λῆξιν· καὶ εἰ μισθὸς ἐπορίσθη τοῖς δικαστηρίοις, εἰσῆγον ἂν
δῆλον ὅτι. ταῦτα δ᾽ εἰ μὴ σεσημασμένων ἤδη συνέβη τῶν
18 ἐχίνων, κἂν μάρτυρας ὑμῖν παρεσχόμην. εἶεν. εἰ δὲ ξενίας
προσκληθείη; πολλοῖς δὲ προσκρούει, καὶ ὃν ἠναγκάσθη τρόπον
ὁ πατὴρ ποιήσασθαι αὐτόν, οὐ λέληθεν. ὑμεῖς δ᾽, ὅτε μὲν
τοῦτον οὐκ ἐποιεῖθ᾽ ὁ πατήρ, τὴν μητέρ᾽ ἀληθῆ λέγειν ἡγεῖσθ᾽
αὐτοῦ· ἐπειδὰν δ᾽ οὕτως γεγονὼς οὗτος ὀχληρὸς ἦι, πάλιν
ὑμῖν ποτε δόξει ᾽κεῖνος ἀληθῆ λέγειν. τί δ᾽, εἰ ψευδομαρτυρίων
ἁλώσεσθαι προσδοκῶν ἐφ᾽ οἷς ἐρανίζει τούτοις τοῖς περὶ αὐτόν,
ἐρήμην ἐάσειεν τελεσθῆναι τὴν δίκην; ἆρά γε μικρὰν ἡγεῖσθε
βλάβην, ὦ ἄνδρες Ἀθηναῖοι, ἐν κοινωνίαι τὸν ἅπαντα βίον
τῆς τούτου δόξης καὶ τῶν ἔργων εἶναι;
19 Ὅτι τοίνυν οὐδ᾽ ἃ διεξελήλυθ᾽ ὑμῖν μάτην φοβοῦμαι, θεω-
ρήσατε. οὗτος γὰρ ἤδη καὶ γραφάς τινας, ὦ ἄνδρες Ἀθηναῖοι,
πέφευγεν, ἐφ᾽ αἷς οὐδὲν αἴτιος ὢν ἐγὼ συνδιαβάλλομαι, καὶ
τῆς ἀρχῆς ἠμφεσβήτει, ἣν ὑμεῖς ἔμ᾽ ἐχειροτονήσατε, καὶ πολλὰ

καὶ δυσχερῆ διὰ τοὔνομα συμβέβηκεν ἡμῖν, ὧν, ἵν' εἰδῆτε,
ἑκάστων μάρτυρας ὑμῖν παρέξομαι.

ΜΑΡΤΥΡΕΣ

Ὁρᾶτ', ὦ ἄνδρες Ἀθηναῖοι, τὰ συμβαίνοντα, καὶ τὴν ἀηδίαν 20
τὴν ἐκ τοῦ πράγματος. εἰ τοίνυν μηδὲν ἀηδὲς ἦν ἐκ τούτων,
μηδ' ὅλως ἀδύνατον ταὐτὸν ἔχειν ὄνομ' ἡμῖν συνέβαινεν, οὐ
δήπου τοῦτον μὲν δίκαιον τὸ μέρος τῶν [ἐμῶν] χρημάτων
ἔχειν κατὰ τὴν ποίησιν, ἣν ὁ πατὴρ αὐτὸν ἀναγκασθεὶς
ἐποιήσατο, ἐμὲ δ' ἀφαιρεθῆναι τοὔνομα, ὃ βουλόμενος καὶ οὐδ'
ὑφ' ἑνὸς βιασθεὶς ἔθετο. οὐκ ἔγωγ' ἡγοῦμαι. ἵνα τοίνυν εἰδῆτε,
ὅτι οὐ μόνον εἰς τοὺς φράτερας οὕτως, ὡς μεμαρτύρηται, ὁ
πατὴρ τὴν ἐγγραφὴν ἐποιήσατο, ἀλλὰ καὶ τὴν δεκάτην ἐμοὶ
ποιῶν τοὔνομα τοῦτ' ἔθετο, λαβέ μοι καὶ ταύτην τὴν μαρτυρίαν.

ΜΑΡΤΥΡΙΑ

Ἀκούετ', ἄνδρες Ἀθηναῖοι, ὅτι ἐγὼ μέν εἰμ' ἐπὶ τοὐνόματος 21
τούτου πάντα τὸν χρόνον, τουτονὶ δὲ Βοιωτὸν εἰς τοὺς
φράτερας, ἡνίκ' ἠναγκάσθη, ἐνέγραψεν ὁ πατήρ. ἡδέως τοίνυν
ἐροίμην ἂν αὐτὸν ἐναντίον ὑμῶν· εἰ μὴ ἐτελεύτησεν ὁ πατήρ,
τί ἂν ποτ' ἐποίεις πρὸς τοῖς δημόταις; οὐκ ἂν εἴας σεαυτὸν
ἐγγράφειν Βοιωτόν; ἀλλ' ἄτοπον δίκην μὲν λαγχάνειν τούτου,
κωλύειν δὲ πάλιν. καὶ μὴν εἴ γ' εἴας αὐτόν, ἐνέγραψεν ἂν
σ' εἰς τοὺς δημότας, ὅπερ εἰς τοὺς φράτερας. οὐκοῦν δεινόν,
ὦ γῆ καὶ θεοί, φάσκειν μὲν ἐκεῖνον αὐτοῦ πατέρ' εἶναι, τολμᾶν
δ' ἄκυρα ποιεῖν ἃ ἐκεῖνος ἔπραξεν ζῶν.

Ἐτόλμα τοίνυν πρὸς τῶι διαιτητῆι πρᾶγμ' ἀναιδέστατον 22
λέγειν, ὡς ὁ πατὴρ αὐτοῦ δεκάτην ἐποίησεν ὥσπερ ἐμοῦ καὶ
τοὔνομα τοῦτ' ἔθετ' αὐτῶι, καὶ μάρτυράς τινας παρείχετο,
οἷς ἐκεῖνος οὐδεπώποτ' ὤφθη χρώμενος. ἐγὼ δ' οὐδέν' ὑμῶν
ἀγνοεῖν οἴομαι, ὅτι οὔτ' ἂν ἐποίησε δεκάτην οὐδεὶς παιδίου
μὴ νομίζων αὑτοῦ δικαίως εἶναι, οὔτε ποιήσας καὶ στέρξας,
ὡς ἂν υἱόν τις στέρξαι, πάλιν ἔξαρνος ἐτόλμησε γενέσθαι. οὐδὲ 23
γὰρ εἴ τι τῆι μητρὶ πρὸς ὀργὴν ἦλθεν τῆι τούτων, τούτους ἂν

ἐμίσει, νομίζων αὐτοῦ εἶναι· πολὺ γὰρ μᾶλλον εἰώθασιν, ὧν
ἂν ἑαυτοῖς διενεχθῶσιν ἀνὴρ καὶ γυνή, διὰ τοὺς παῖδας
καταλλάττεσθαι ἢ δι' ἂν ἀδικηθῶσιν ὑφ' αὐτῶν, τοὺς κοινοὺς
παῖδας πρὸς μισεῖν. οὐ τοίνυν ἐκ τούτων ἔστιν ἰδεῖν μόνον
ὅτι ψεύσεται, ταῦτ' ἂν λέγηι, ἀλλὰ πρὶν ἡμέτερος φάσκειν
συγγενὴς εἶναι, εἰς Ἱπποθωντίδ' ἐφοίτα φυλὴν εἰς παῖδας
24 χορεύσων. καίτοι τίς ἂν ὑμῶν οἴεται τὴν μητέρα πέμψαι τοῦτον
εἰς ταύτην τὴν φυλήν, δεινὰ μέν, ὥς φησιν, ὑπὸ τοῦ πατρὸς
πεπονθυῖαν, δεκάτην δ' εἰδυῖαν πεποιηκότ' ἐκεῖνον καὶ πάλιν
ἔξαρνον ὄντα; ἐγὼ μὲν οὐδέν' ἂν οἶμαι. εἰς γὰρ τὴν Ἀκαμαντίδ'
ὁμοίως ἐξῆν σοι φοιτᾶν, καὶ ἐφαίνετ' ἂν οὖσ' ἀκόλουθος ἡ
φυλὴ τῆι θέσει τοὐνόματος. ὡς τοίνυν ταῦτ' ἀληθῆ λέγω,
τούτων μάρτυρας ὑμῖν τοὺς συμφοιτῶντας καὶ τοὺς εἰδότας
παρέξομαι.

ΜΑΡΤΥΡΕΣ

25 Οὕτω τοίνυν φανερῶς παρὰ τὸν τῆς αὐτοῦ μητρὸς ὅρκον καὶ
τὴν τοῦ δόντος ἐκείνηι τὸν ὅρκον εὐήθειαν πατρὸς τετυχηκὼς
καὶ ἀνθ' Ἱπποθωντίδος ἐν Ἀκαμαντίδι φυλῆι γεγονώς, οὐκ
ἀγαπᾶι Βοιωτὸς οὑτοσί, ἀλλὰ καὶ δίκας ἐμοὶ δύ' ἢ τρεῖς εἴληχεν
ἀργυρίου πρὸς αἷς καὶ πρότερόν μ' ἐσυκοφάντει. καίτοι πάντας
26 οἶμαι τοῦθ' ὑμᾶς εἰδέναι, τίς ἦν χρηματιστὴς ὁ πατήρ. ἐγὼ
δ' ἐάσω ταῦτα. ἀλλ' εἰ δίκαι' ὀμώμοκεν ἡ μήτηρ ἡ τούτων,
ἐπ' αὐτοφώρωι συκοφάντην ἐπιδεικνύει τοῦτον ταῖς δίκαις
ταύταις. εἰ γὰρ οὕτω δαπανηρὸς ἦν, ὥστε γάμωι γεγαμηκὼς
τὴν ἐμὴν μητέρα, ἑτέραν εἶχε γυναῖκα, ἧς ὑμεῖς ἐστέ, καὶ δύ'
οἰκίας ὤικει, πῶς ἂν ἀργύριον τοιοῦτος ὢν κατέλιπεν;
27 Οὐκ ἀγνοῶ τοίνυν, ὦ ἄνδρες Ἀθηναῖοι, ὅτι Βοιωτὸς οὑτοσὶ
δίκαιον μὲν οὐδὲν ἕξει λέγειν, ἥξει δ' ἐπὶ ταῦθ' ἅπερ ἀεὶ λέγει,
ὡς ἐπηρέαζεν ὁ πατὴρ αὐτῶι πειθόμενος ὑπ' ἐμοῦ, ἀξιοῖ δ'
αὐτὸς ὡς δὴ πρεσβύτερος ὢν τοὔνομ' ἔχειν τὸ τοῦ πρὸς πατρὸς
πάππου. πρὸς δὴ ταῦτ' ἀκοῦσαι βέλτιον ὑμᾶς βραχέα. ἐγὼ
γὰρ οἶδα τοῦτον, ὅτ' οὔπω συγγενὴς ἦν ἐμοί, ὁρῶν ὥσπερ
ἂν ἄλλον τιν' οὑτωσί, νεώτερον ὄντ' ἐμοῦ καὶ συχνῶι, ὅσ'
28 ἐξ ὄψεως, οὐ μὴν ἰσχυρίζομαι τούτωι (καὶ γὰρ εὔηθες)· ἀλλ'

εἴ τις ἔροιτο Βοιωτὸν τουτονί, ὅτ' ἐν Ἱπποθωντίδι φυλῆι ἠξίους χορεύειν, οὔπω τοῦ πατρὸς εἶναι φάσκων τοῦ ἐμοῦ υἱός, τί σαυτὸν ἔχειν δικαίως ἂν θείης ὄνομα; εἰ γὰρ Μαντίθεον, οὐκ ἂν διὰ τοῦτό γε φαίης ὅτι πρεσβύτερος εἶ ἐμοῦ. ὃς γὰρ οὐδὲ τῆς φυλῆς τότε σοι προσήκειν ἡγοῦ τῆς ἐμῆς, πῶς ἂν τοῦ γε πάππου τοῦ ἐμοῦ ἠμφεσβήτεις; ἔτι δ', ὦ ἄνδρες 29 Ἀθηναῖοι, τὸν μὲν τῶν ἐτῶν χρόνον οὐδεῖς οἶδεν ὑμῶν (ἐγὼ μὲν γὰρ ἐμοὶ πλείονα, οὗτος δ' ἑαυτῶι φήσει), τὸν δὲ τοῦ δικαίου λόγον ἅπαντες ἐπίστασθε. ἔστι δ' οὗτος τίς; ἀφ' οὗ παῖδας ἐποιήσατο τούτους ὁ πατήρ, ἀπὸ τούτου καὶ νομίζεσθαι. πρότερον τοίνυν ἔμ' εἰς τοὺς δημότας ἐνέγραψε Μαντίθεον, πρὶν εἰσαγαγεῖν τοῦτον εἰς τοὺς φράτερας. ὥστ' οὐ τῶι χρόνωι μόνον, ἀλλὰ καὶ τῶι δικαίωι πρεσβεῖον ἔχοιμ' ἂν ἐγὼ τοὔνομα τοῦτ' εἰκότως. εἶεν. εἰ δέ τίς σ' ἔροιτο, 30 'εἰπέ μοι, Βοιωτέ, πόθεν νῦν Ἀκαμαντίδος φυλῆς γέγονας καὶ τῶν δήμων Θορίκιος καὶ υἱὸς Μαντίου, καὶ τὸ μέρος τῶν ὑπ' ἐκείνου καταλειφθέντων ἔχεις;' οὐδὲν ἂν ἄλλ' ἔχοις εἰπεῖν, πλὴν ὅτι κἀμὲ ζῶν ἐποιήσατο Μαντίας. τί τεκμήριον, εἴ τίς σ' ἔροιτο, ἢ μαρτύριόν ἐστί σοι τούτου; εἰς τοὺς φράτερας μ' εἰσήγαγε, φήσειας ἄν. τί οὖν σ' ἐνέγραψεν ὄνομα, εἴ τις ἔροιτο, Βοιωτὸν ἂν εἴποις· τοῦτο γὰρ εἰσήχθης. οὐκοῦν δεινὸν 31 εἰ τῆς μὲν πόλεως καὶ τῶν ὑπ' ἐκείνου καταλειφθέντων διὰ τοὔνομα τοῦτο μέτεστί σοι, τοῦτο δ' ἀξιοῖς ἀφεὶς ἕτερον μεταθέσθαι σαυτῶι. φέρ', εἴ σ' ὁ πατὴρ ἀξιώσειεν ἀναστάς, ἢ μένειν ἐφ' οὗ σ' αὐτὸς ἐποιήσατ' ὀνόματος, ἢ πατέρ' ἄλλον σαυτοῦ φάσκειν εἶναι, ἆρ' οὐκ ἂν μέτρι' ἀξιοῦν δοκοίη; ταὐτὰ τοίνυν ταῦτ' ἐγώ σ' ἀξιῶ, ἢ πατρὸς ἄλλου σεαυτὸν παρα- γράφειν, ἢ τοὔνομ' ἔχειν ὃ 'κεῖνος ἔδωκέ σοι. νὴ Δί', ἀλλ' 32 ὕβρει καὶ ἐπηρείαι τινὶ τοῦτ' ἐτέθη σοι. ἀλλὰ πολλάκις μέν, ὅτ' οὐκ ἐποιεῖθ' ὁ πατὴρ τούτους, ἔλεγον οὗτοι ὡς οὐδὲν χείρους εἰσὶν οἱ τῆς μητρὸς τῆς τούτου συγγενεῖς τῶν τοῦ πατρὸς τοῦ ἐμοῦ. ἔστι δ' ὁ Βοιωτὸς ἀδελφοῦ τῆς τούτου μητρὸς ὄνομα. ἐπειδὴ δ' εἰσάγειν ὁ πατὴρ τούτους ἠναγκάζετο, ἐμοῦ προεισηγμένου Μαντιθέου, οὕτω τοῦτον εἰσάγει Βοιωτόν, τὸν ἀδελφὸν δ' αὐτοῦ Πάμφιλον. ἐπεὶ σὺ δεῖξον, ὅστις Ἀθηναίων

ταὐτὸν ὄνομα τοῖς αὑτοῦ παισὶν ἔθετο δυοῖν· κἂν δείξῃς,
ἐγὼ συγχωρήσω δι' ἐπήρειάν σοι τοῦτο τοὔνομα θέσθαι τὸν
33 πατέρα. καίτοι εἴ γε τοιοῦτος ἦσθα, ὥστε ποιήσασθαι μὲν
σαυτὸν ἀναγκάσαι, ἐξ ὅτου δ' ἀρέσεις ἐκείνωι τρόπου μὴ
σκοπεῖν, οὐκ ἦσθ' οἷον δεῖ τὸν προσήκοντ' εἶναι περὶ τοὺς
γονέας, οὐκ ὢν δ' οὐκ ἐπηρέαζου δικαίως ἄν, ἀλλ' ἀπωλώλεις.
ἢ δεινόν γ' ἂν εἴη, εἰ κατὰ μὲν τῶν ὑπὸ τοῦ πατρὸς αὑτοῦ
νομιζομένων παίδων οἱ περὶ τῶν γονέων ἰσχύσουσιν νόμοι,
κατὰ δὲ τῶν αὑτοὺς εἰσβιαζομένων ἄκοντας ποιεῖσθαι ἄκυροι
γενήσονται.
34 Ἀλλ', ὦ χαλεπώτατε Βοιωτέ, μάλιστα μὲν ὧν πράττεις
πάντων παῦσαι, εἰ δ' ἄρα μὴ βούλει, ἐκεῖνό γε πρὸς Διὸς
πείθου· παῦσαι μὲν σαυτῶι παρέχων πράγματα, παῦσαι
δ' ἐμὲ συκοφαντῶν, ἀγάπα δ' ὅτι σοι πόλις, οὐσία, πατὴρ
γέγονεν. οὐδεὶς ἀπελαύνει σ' ἀπὸ τούτων, οὔκουν ἔγωγε. ἀλλ'
ἂν μέν, ὥσπερ εἶναι φὴς ἀδελφός, καὶ τὰ ἔργ' ἀδελφοῦ ποιῇς,
δόξεις εἶναι συγγενής, ἂν δ' ἐπιβουλεύῃς, δικάζῃι, φθονῇς,
βλασφημῇς, δόξεις εἰς ἀλλότρι' ἐμπεσὼν ὡς οὐ προσήκουσιν
35 οὕτω χρῆσθαι. ἐπεὶ ἔγωγ' οὐδ' εἰ τὰ μάλισθ' ὁ πατὴρ ὄντα σ'
ἑαυτοῦ μὴ ἐποιεῖτ' ἀδικῶ. οὐ γὰρ ἐμοὶ προσῆκεν εἰδέναι, τίνες
εἰσὶν υἱεῖς ἐκείνου, ἀλλ' ἐκείνωι δεῖξαι, τίν' ἐμοὶ νομιστέον
ἔστ' ἀδελφόν. ὃν μὲν τοίνυν οὐκ ἐποιεῖτό σε χρόνον, οὐδ'
ἐγὼ προσήκονθ' ἡγούμην, ἐπειδὴ δ' ἐποιήσατο, κἀγὼ νομίζω.
τί τούτου σημεῖον; τῶν πατρώιων ἔχεις τὸ μέρος μετὰ τὴν
τοῦ πατρὸς τελευτήν· ἱερῶν, ὁσίων μετέχεις· ἀπάγει σ' οὐδεὶς
ἀπὸ τούτων. τί βούλει; ἂν δὲ φῇι δεινὰ πάσχειν καὶ κλάῃι
καὶ ὀδύρηται καὶ κατηγορῇι ἐμοῦ, ἃ μὲν ἂν λέγῃι, μὴ πιστεύετε
(οὐ γὰρ δίκαιον μὴ περὶ τούτων ὄντος τοῦ λόγου νυνί),
ἐκεῖνο δ' ὑπολαμβάνετε, ὅτι οὐδὲν ἔστ' αὐτῶι ἧττον δίκην
36 λαμβάνειν Βοιωτῶι κληθέντι. τί οὖν φιλονικεῖς; μηδαμῶς· μὴ
ἔχ' οὕτω πρὸς ἡμᾶς ἐθελέχθρως· οὐδὲ γὰρ ἐγὼ πρὸς σέ, ἐπεὶ
καὶ νῦν, ἵνα μηδὲ τοῦτο λάθῃ σε, ὑπὲρ σοῦ λέγω μᾶλλον,
ἀξιῶν μὴ ταὐτὸν ἔχειν ὄνομ' ἡμᾶς. εἰ γὰρ μηδὲν ἄλλο, ἀνάγκη
τὸν ἀκούσαντ' ἐρέσθαι πότερος, δύ' ἂν ὦσι Μαντίθεοι
Μαντίου. οὐκοῦν, ὃν ἠναγκάσθη ποιήσασθαι, σὲ ἂν λέγῃι, ἐρεῖ.

τί οὖν ἐπιθυμεῖς τούτων; ἀνάγνωθι δέ μοι λαβὼν δύο ταυτασὶ
μαρτυρίας, ὡς ἐμοὶ Μαντίθεον καὶ τούτωι Βοιωτὸν ὁ πατὴρ
ὄνομ' ἔθετο.

ΜΑΡΤΥΡΙΑΙ

Λοιπὸν ἡγοῦμαι τοῦθ' ὑμῖν ἐπιδεῖξαι, ὦ ἄνδρες Ἀθηναῖοι, ὡς 37
οὐ μόνον εὐορκήσετε, ἂν ἁγὼ λέγω ψηφίσησθε, ἀλλὰ καὶ ὡς
οὗτος [αὐτὸς] αὑτοῦ κατέγνω Βοιωτόν, ἀλλ' οὐ Μαντίθεον
ὄνομα δικαίως ἂν ἔχειν. λαχόντος γὰρ ἐμοῦ τὴν δίκην ταύτην
Βοιωτῶι Μαντίου Θορικίωι, ἐξ ἀρχῆς τ' ἠντεδίκει καὶ ὑπώμνυθ'
ὡς ὢν Βοιωτός, καὶ τὸ τελευταῖον, ἐπεὶ οὐκέτ' ἐνῆν αὐτῶι
διακρούσασθαι, ἐρήμην ἐάσας καταδιαιτῆσαι, σκέψασθε πρὸς
θεῶν τί ἐποίησεν· ἀντιλαγχάνει μοι τὴν μὴ οὖσαν Βοιωτὸν 38
αὑτὸν προσαγορεύσας. καίτοι ἐξ ἀρχῆς τ' ἔδει ἐᾶν αὐτὸν
τελέσασθαι τὴν δίκην κατὰ Βοιωτοῦ, εἴπερ μηδὲν προσῆκεν
αὐτῶι τοὐνόματος, ὕστερόν τε μὴ αὐτὸν φαίνεσθαι ἐπὶ τῶι
ὀνόματι τούτωι ἀντιλαγχάνοντα τὴν μὴ οὖσαν. ὃς οὖν αὐτὸς
αὑτοῦ κατέγνω δικαίως ⟨ἂν⟩ εἶναι Βοιωτός, τί ὑμᾶς ἀξιώσει
τοὺς ὀμωμοκότας ψηφίζεσθαι; ὡς δὲ ταῦτ' ἀληθῆ λέγω, λαβέ
μοι τὴν ἀντίληξιν καὶ τὸ ἔγκλημα τουτί.

ΑΝΤΙΛΗΞΙΣ, ΕΓΚΛΗΜΑ

Εἰ μὲν τοίνυν οὗτος ἔχει δεῖξαι νόμον ὃς ποιεῖ κυρίους εἶναι 39
τοὺς παῖδας τοῦ ἑαυτῶν ὀνόματος, ἃ λέγει νῦν οὗτος ὀρθῶς
ἂν ψηφίζοισθε. εἰ δ' ὁ μὲν νόμος, ὃν πάντες ἐπίστασθ' ὁμοίως
ἐμοί, τοὺς γονέας ποιεῖ κυρίους οὐ μόνον θέσθαι τοὔνομ' ἐξ
ἀρχῆς, ἀλλὰ κἂν πάλιν ἐξαλεῖψαι βούλωνται καὶ ἀποκηρῦξαι,
ἐπέδειξα δ' ἐγὼ τὸν πατέρα, ὃς κύριος ἦν ἐκ τοῦ νόμου, τούτωι
μὲν Βοιωτόν, ἐμοὶ δὲ Μαντίθεον θέμενον, πῶς ὑμῖν ἔστιν
ἄλλο τι πλὴν ἁγὼ λέγω ψηφίσασθαι; ἀλλὰ μὴν ὧν γ' ἂν μὴ 40
ὦσι νόμοι, γνώμηι τῆι δικαιοτάτηι δικάσειν ὀμωμόκατε, ὥστ'
εἰ μηδεὶς ἦν περὶ τούτων κείμενος νόμος, κἂν οὕτω δικαίως
πρὸς ἐμοῦ τὴν ψῆφον ἔθεσθε. τίς γάρ ἐστιν ὑμῶν ὅστις ταὐτὸν
ὄνομα τοῖς αὑτοῦ παισὶν τέθειται δυοῖν; τίς δ', ὧι μήπω
παῖδες εἰσί, θήσεται; οὐδεὶς δήπου. οὐκοῦν ὃ δίκαιον τῆι γνώμηι 41

τοῖς ὑμετέροις αὐτῶν παισὶν ὑπειλήφατε, τοῦτο καὶ περὶ ἡμῶν εὐσεβὲς γνῶναι. ὥστε καὶ κατὰ τὴν δικαιοτάτην γνώμην καὶ κατὰ τοὺς νόμους καὶ κατὰ τοὺς ὅρκους καὶ κατὰ τὴν τούτου προσομολογίαν ἐγὼ μὲν μέτρι᾽ ὑμῶν, ὦ ἄνδρες Ἀθηναῖοι, δέομαι καὶ δίκαι᾽ ἀξιῶ, οὗτος δ᾽ οὐ μόνον οὐ μέτρια, ἀλλ᾽ οὐδ᾽ εἰωθότα γίγνεσθαι.

56 ΚΑΤΑ ΔΙΟΝΥΣΟΔΩΡΟΥ ΒΛΑΒΗΣ

Κοινωνός εἰμι τοῦ δανείσματος τούτου, ἄνδρες δικασταί. συμβαίνει δ᾽ ἡμῖν τοῖς τὴν κατὰ θάλατταν ἐργασίαν προηιρημένοις καὶ τὰ ἡμέτερ᾽ αὐτῶν ἐγχειρίζουσιν ἑτέροις ἐκεῖνο μὲν σαφῶς εἰδέναι, ὅτι ὁ δανειζόμενος ἐν παντὶ προέχει ἡμῶν. λαβὼν γὰρ ἀργύριον φανερὸν καὶ ὁμολογούμενον, ἐν γραμματειδίωι δυοῖν χαλκοῖν ἐωνημένωι καὶ βυβλιδίωι μικρῶι πάνυ τὴν ὁμολογίαν καταλέλοιπε τοῦ ποιήσειν τὰ δίκαια. ἡμεῖς δ᾽ οὐ φαμὲν δώσειν, ἀλλ᾽ εὐθὺς τῶι δανειζομένωι δίδομεν

2 τὸ ἀργύριον. τῶι οὖν ποτὲ πιστεύοντες καὶ τί λαβόντες τὸ βέβαιον, προϊέμεθα; ὑμῖν, ὦ ἄνδρες δικασταί, καὶ τοῖς νόμοις τοῖς ὑμετέροις, οἳ κελεύουσιν, ὅσα ἄν τις ἑκὼν ἕτερος ἑτέρωι ὁμολογήσηι, κύρια εἶναι. ἀλλά μοι δοκεῖ οὔτε τῶν νόμων οὔτε συγγραφῆς οὐδεμιᾶς ὄφελος εἶναι οὐδέν, ἂν ὁ λαμβάνων τὰ χρήματα μὴ πάνυ δίκαιος ἦι τὸν τρόπον, καὶ δυοῖν θάτερον,

3 ἢ ὑμᾶς δεδιὼς ἢ τὸν συμβαλόντα αἰσχυνόμενος. ὧν οὐδέτερον πρόσεστι Διονυσοδώρωι τουτωί, ἀλλ᾽ εἰς τοσοῦτον ἥκει τόλμης, ὥστε δανεισάμενος παρ᾽ ἡμῶν ἐπὶ τῆι νηὶ τρισχιλίας δραχμὰς ἐφ᾽ ὧι τε τὴν ναῦν καταπλεῖν Ἀθήναζε, καὶ δέον ἡμᾶς ἐν τῆι πέρυσιν ὥραι κεκομίσθαι τὰ χρήματα, τὴν μὲν ναῦν εἰς Ῥόδον κατεκόμισε καὶ τὸν γόμον ἐκεῖσε ἐξελόμενος ἀπέδοτο παρὰ τὴν συγγραφὴν καὶ τοὺς νόμους τοὺς ὑμετέρους, ἐκ δὲ τῆς Ῥόδου πάλιν ἀπέστειλε τὴν ναῦν εἰς Αἴγυπτον κἀκεῖθεν εἰς Ῥόδον, ἡμῖν δὲ τοῖς Ἀθήνησι δανείσασιν οὐδέπω καὶ νῦν οὔτε τὰ χρήματα ἀποδίδωσιν οὔτε τὸ ἐνέχυρον καθίστησιν

4 εἰς τὸ ἐμφανές, ἀλλὰ δεύτερον ἔτος τουτὶ καρπούμενος τὰ ἡμέτερα, καὶ ἔχων τό τε δάνειον καὶ τὴν ἐργασίαν καὶ τὴν

ναῦν τὴν ὑποκειμένην ἡμῖν, οὐδὲν ἧττον εἰσελήλυθεν πρὸς
ὑμᾶς, δῆλον ὡς ζημιώσων ἡμᾶς τῇι ἐπωβελίαι καὶ κατα-
θησόμενος εἰς τὸ οἴκημα πρὸς τῶι ἀποστερεῖν τὰ χρήματα.
ὑμῶν οὖν, ὦ ἄνδρες Ἀθηναῖοι, ὁμοίως ἁπάντων δεόμεθα
καὶ ἱκετεύομεν βοηθῆσαι ἡμῖν, ἂν δοκῶμεν ἀδικεῖσθαι. τὴν
δὲ ἀρχὴν τοῦ συμβολαίου διεξελθεῖν ὑμῖν πρῶτον βούλομαι·
οὕτως γὰρ καὶ ὑμεῖς ῥᾶιστα παρακολουθήσετε.

Διονυσόδωρος γὰρ οὑτοσί, ὦ ἄνδρες Ἀθηναῖοι, καὶ ὁ 5
κοινωνὸς αὐτοῦ Παρμενίσκος προσελθόντες ἡμῖν πέρυσιν τοῦ
μεταγειτνιῶνος μηνὸς ἔλεγον ὅτι βούλονται δανείσασθαι ἐπὶ
τῆι νηί, ἐφ' ὧι τε πλεῦσαι εἰς Αἴγυπτον καὶ ἐξ Αἰγύπτου εἰς
Ῥόδον ἢ εἰς Ἀθήνας, διομολογησάμενοι τοὺς τόκους ⟨τοὺς⟩
εἰς ἑκάτερον τῶν ἐμπορίων τούτων. ἀποκριναμένων δ' ἡμῶν, 6
ὦ ἄνδρες δικασταί, ὅτι οὐκ ἂν δανείσαιμεν εἰς ἕτερον ἐμπόριον
οὐδὲν ἀλλ' ἢ εἰς Ἀθήνας, οὕτω προσομολογοῦσι πλεύσεσθαι
δεῦρο, καὶ ἐπὶ ταύταις ταῖς ὁμολογίαις δανείζονται παρ' ἡμῶν
ἐπὶ τῇι νηὶ τρισχιλίας δραχμὰς ἀμφοτερόπλουν, καὶ συγγραφὴν
ἐγράψαντο ὑπὲρ τούτων. ἐν μὲν οὖν ταῖς συνθήκαις δανειστὴς
ἐγράφη Πάμφιλος οὑτοσί· ἐγὼ δ' ἔξωθεν μετεῖχον αὐτῶι τοῦ
δανείσματος. καὶ πρῶτον ὑμῖν ἀναγνώσεται αὐτὴν τὴν
συγγραφήν.

ΣΥΓΓΡΑΦΗ

Κατὰ ταύτην τὴν συγγραφήν, ὦ ἄνδρες δικασταί, λαβόντες 7
παρ' ἡμῶν τὰ χρήματα Διονυσόδωρός τε οὑτοσὶ καὶ ὁ κοινωνὸς
αὐτοῦ Παρμενίσκος ἀπέστελλον τὴν ναῦν εἰς τὴν Αἴγυπτον
ἐνθένδε. καὶ ὁ μὲν Παρμενίσκος ἐπέπλει ἐπὶ τῆς νεώς, οὑτοσὶ
δὲ αὐτοῦ κατέμενεν. ἦσαν γάρ, ὦ ἄνδρες δικασταί, ἵνα μηδὲ
τοῦτο ἀγνοῆτε, ὑπηρέται καὶ συνεργοὶ πάντες οὗτοι Κλεομένους
τοῦ ἐν τῇι Αἰγύπτωι ἄρξαντος, ὃς ἐξ οὗ τὴν ἀρχὴν παρέλαβεν
οὐκ ὀλίγα κακὰ ἠργάσατο τὴν πόλιν τὴν ὑμετέραν, μᾶλλον
δὲ καὶ τοὺς ἄλλους Ἕλληνας, παλιγκαπηλεύων καὶ συνιστὰς
τὰς τιμὰς τοῦ σίτου καὶ αὐτὸς καὶ οὗτοι μετ' αὐτοῦ. οἱ μὲν 8
γὰρ αὐτῶν ἀπέστελλον ἐκ τῆς Αἰγύπτου τὰ χρήματα, οἱ
δ' ἐπέπλεον ταῖς ἐμπορίαις, οἱ δ' ἐνθάδε μένοντες διετίθεντο

τὰ ἀποστελλόμενα· εἶτα πρὸς τὰς καθεστηκυίας τιμὰς ἔπεμπον
γράμματα οἱ ἐπιδημοῦντες τοῖς ἀποδημοῦσιν, ἵνα ἐὰν μὲν παρ'
ὑμῖν τίμιος ἦι ὁ σῖτος, δεῦρο αὐτὸν κομίσωσιν, ἐὰν δ' εὐωνότερος
γένηται, εἰς ἄλλο τι καταπλεύσωσιν ἐμπόριον. ὅθεν περ οὐχ
ἥκιστα, ὦ ἄνδρες δικασταί, συνετιμήθη τὰ περὶ τὸν σῖτον
9 ἐκ τῶν τοιούτων ἐπιστολῶν καὶ συνεργιῶν. ὅτε μὲν οὖν
ἐνθένδε ἀπέστελλον οὗτοι τὴν ναῦν, ἐπιεικῶς ἔντιμον κατέλιπον
τὸν σῖτον· διὸ καὶ ὑπέμειναν ἐν τῆι συγγραφῆι γράψασθαι
εἰς ᾿Αθήνας πλεῖν, εἰς δ' ἄλλο μηδὲν ἐμπόριον. μετὰ δὲ ταῦτα,
ὦ ἄνδρες δικασταί, ἐπειδὴ ὁ Σικελικὸς κατάπλους ἐγένετο καὶ
αἱ τιμαὶ τοῦ σίτου ἐπ' ἔλαττον ἐβάδιζον καὶ ἡ ναῦς ἡ τούτων
ἀνῆκτο εἰς Αἴγυπτον, εὐθέως οὗτος ἀποστέλλει τινὰ εἰς τὴν
῾Ρόδον ἀπαγγελοῦντα τῶι Παρμενίσκωι τῶι κοινωνῶι τὰ
ἐνθένδε καθεστηκότα, ἀκριβῶς εἰδὼς ὅτι ἀναγκαῖον εἴη τῆι
10 νηὶ προσσχεῖν εἰς ῾Ρόδον. πέρας δ' οὖν, λαβὼν γὰρ ὁ
Παρμενίσκος ὁ τουτουὶ κοινωνὸς τὰ γράμματα τὰ παρὰ τούτου
ἀποσταλέντα, καὶ πυθόμενος τὰς τιμὰς τὰς ἐνθάδε [τοῦ σίτου]
καθεστηκυίας, ἐξαιρεῖται τὸν σῖτον ἐν τῆι ῾Ρόδωι κἀκεῖ
ἀποδίδοται, καταφρονήσαντες μὲν τῆς συγγραφῆς, ὦ ἄνδρες
δικασταί, καὶ τῶν ἐπιτιμίων, ἃ συνεγράψαντο αὐτοὶ οὗτοι
καθ' αὐτῶν, ἐάν τι παραβαίνωσιν, καταφρονήσαντες δὲ τῶν
νόμων τῶν ὑμετέρων, οἳ κελεύουσι τοὺς ναυκλήρους καὶ τοὺς
ἐπιβάτας πλεῖν εἰς ὅ τι ἂν συνθῶνται ἐμπόριον, εἰ δὲ μή,
11 ταῖς μεγίσταις ζημίαις εἶναι ἐνόχους. καὶ ἡμεῖς ἐπειδὴ τάχιστα
ἐπυθόμεθα τὸ γεγονός, ἐκπεπληγμένοι τῶι πράγματι προσῆιμεν
τούτωι τῶι ἀρχιτέκτονι τῆς ὅλης ἐπιβουλῆς, ἀγανακτοῦντες,
οἷον εἰκός, καὶ ἐγκαλοῦντες ὅτι διαρρήδην ἡμῶν διορισαμένων
ἐν ταῖς συνθήκαις ὅπως ἡ ναῦς μηδαμόσε καταπλεύσεται ἀλλ'
ἢ εἰς ᾿Αθήνας, καὶ ἐπὶ ταύταις ταῖς ὁμολογίαις δανεισάντων
τὸ ἀργύριον, ἡμᾶς μὲν ἐν ὑποψίαι καταλέλοιπεν τοῖς βουλομένοις
αἰτιᾶσθαι καὶ λέγειν, ὡς ἄρα καὶ ἡμεῖς κεκοινωνήκαμεν τῆς
σιτηγίας τῆς εἰς τὴν ῾Ρόδον, αὐτοὶ δὲ οὐδὲν μᾶλλον τὴν ναῦν
ἥκουσι κατακομίζοντες εἰς τὸ ὑμέτερον ἐμπόριον εἰς ὃ συνεγράψ-
12 αντο. ἐπειδὴ δὲ οὐδὲν ἐπεραίνομεν ὑπὲρ τῆς συγγραφῆς καὶ
τῶν δικαίων διαλεγόμενοι, ἀλλὰ τό γε δάνειον καὶ τοὺς τόκους

ἠξιοῦμεν ἀπολαβεῖν τοὺς ἐξ ἀρχῆς ὁμολογηθέντας. οὗτος δὲ
οὕτως ὑβριστικῶς ἐχρήσατο ἡμῖν, ὥστε τοὺς μὲν τόκους τοὺς
ἐν τῆι συγγραφῆι γεγραμμένους οὐκ ἔφη δώσειν· 'εἰ δὲ βούλεσθε,'
ἔφη, 'κομίζεσθαι τὸ πρὸς μέρος τοῦ πλοῦ τοῦ πεπλευσμένου,
δώσω ὑμῖν' φησὶν 'τοὺς εἰς Ῥόδον τόκους· πλείους δ' οὐκ
ἂν δοίην', αὐτὸς ἑαυτῶι νομοθετῶν καὶ οὐχὶ τοῖς ἐκ τῆς
συγγραφῆς δικαίοις πειθόμενος. ὡς δ' ἡμεῖς οὐκ ἂν ἔφαμεν 13
συγχωρῆσαι οὐδὲν τούτων, λογιζόμενοι ὅτι, ὁπότε τοῦτο
πράξομεν, ὁμολογοῦμεν καὶ αὐτοὶ εἰς Ῥόδον σεσιτηγηκέναι,
ἔτι μᾶλλον ἐπέτεινεν οὗτος καὶ μάρτυρας πολλοὺς παραλαβὼν
προσήιει, φάσκων ἕτοιμος εἶναι ἀποδιδόναι τὸ δάνειον καὶ
τοὺς τόκους τοὺς εἰς Ῥόδον, οὐδὲν μᾶλλον, ὦ ἄνδρες δικασταί,
ἀποδοῦναι διανοούμενος, ἀλλ' ἡμᾶς ὑπολαμβάνων οὐκ ἂν
ἐθελῆσαι λαβεῖν τὸ ἀργύριον διὰ τὰς ὑπούσας αἰτίας. ἐδήλωσε
δὲ αὐτὸ τὸ ἔργον. ἐπειδὴ γάρ, ὦ ἄνδρες Ἀθηναῖοι, τῶν ὑμετέρων 14
πολιτῶν τινὲς παραγενόμενοι ἀπὸ ταὐτομάτου συνεβούλευον
ἡμῖν τὸ μὲν διδόμενον λαμβάνειν, περὶ δὲ τῶν ἀντιλεγομένων
κρίνεσθαι, τοὺς δὲ εἰς Ῥόδον τόκους μὴ καθομολογεῖν τέως
ἂν κριθῶμεν, ἡμεῖς μὲν ταῦτα συνεχωροῦμεν, οὐκ ἀγνοοῦντες,
ὦ ἄνδρες δικασταί, τὸ ἐκ τῆς συγγραφῆς δίκαιον, ἀλλ' ἡγούμενοι
δεῖν ἐλαττοῦσθαί τι καὶ συγχωρεῖν ὥστε μὴ δοκεῖν φιλόδικοι
εἶναι, οὗτος δ' ὡς ἑώρα ἡμᾶς ὁμόσε πορευομένους, 'ἀναιρεῖσθε'
φησὶ 'τοίνυν τὴν συγγραφήν.' 'ἡμεῖς ἀναιρώμεθα; οὐδέν γε 15
μᾶλλον ἢ ὁτιοῦν· ἀλλὰ κατὰ μὲν τἀργύριον ὃ ἂν ἀποδῶις,
ὁμολογήσομεν ἐναντίον τοῦ τραπεζίτου ἄκυρον ποιεῖν τὴν
συγγραφήν, τὸ μέντοι σύνολον οὐκ ἂν ἀνελοίμεθα, ἕως ἂν
περὶ τῶν ἀντιλεγομένων κριθῶμεν. τί γὰρ ἔχοντες δίκαιον
ἢ τί τὸ ἰσχυρὸν ἀντιδικήσομεν, ἐάν τε πρὸς διαιτητὴν ἐάν
τε εἰς δικαστήριον δέηι βαδίζειν, ἀνελόμενοι τὴν συγγραφήν,
ἐν ἧι τὴν ὑπὲρ τῶν δικαίων βοήθειαν ἔχομεν;' ταῦτα δὲ 16
ἡμῶν λεγόντων, ὦ ἄνδρες δικασταί, καὶ ἀξιούντων Διονυσόδωρον τουτονὶ τὴν μὲν συγγραφὴν μὴ κινεῖν μηδὲ ἄκυρον
ποιεῖν τὴν ὁμολογουμένην καὶ ὑπ' αὐτῶν τούτων κυρίαν
εἶναι, τῶν δὲ χρημάτων ὅσα μὲν αὐτὸς ὁμολογεῖ, ἀποδοῦναι
ἡμῖν, περὶ δὲ τῶν ἀντιλεγομένων [ὡς] ἑτοίμων ὄντων κριθῆναι,

εἴτε βούλοιντο ἐφ' ἑνὸς εἴτε κἂν πλείοσι τῶν ἐκ τοῦ ἐμπορίου, οὐκ ἔφη προσέχειν Διονυσόδωρος τούτων οὐδενί, ἀλλ' ὅτι τὴν συγγραφὴν ὅλως οὐκ ἀνηιρούμεθα ἀπολαμβάνοντες ἃ οὗτος ἐπέταττεν, ἔχει δεύτερον ἔτος τὰ ἡμέτερα καὶ χρῆται

17 τοῖς χρήμασιν· καὶ ὃ πάντων ἐστὶ δεινότατον, ὦ ἄνδρες δικασταί, ὅτι αὐτὸς μὲν οὗτος παρ' ἑτέρων εἰσπράττει ναυτικοὺς τόκους ἀπὸ τῶν ἡμετέρων χρημάτων, οὐκ 'Αθήνησι δανείσας οὐδ' εἰς 'Αθήνας, ἀλλ' εἰς 'Ρόδον καὶ Αἴγυπτον, ἡμῖν δὲ τοῖς δανείσασιν εἰς τὸ ὑμέτερον ἐμπόριον οὐκ οἴεται δεῖν τῶν δικαίων οὐδὲν ποιεῖν. ὅτι δ' ἀληθῆ λέγω, ἀναγνώσεται ὑμῖν τὴν πρόκλησιν ἣν ὑπὲρ τούτων προὐκαλεσάμεθ' αὐτόν.

ΠΡΟΚΛΗΣΙΣ

18 Ταῦτα τοίνυν, ὦ ἄνδρες δικασταί, προκαλεσαμένων ἡμῶν Διονυσόδωρον τουτονὶ πολλάκις, καὶ ἐπὶ πολλὰς ἡμέρας ἐκτιθέντων τὴν πρόκλησιν, εὐήθεις ἔφη παντελῶς ἡμᾶς εἶναι, εἰ ὑπολαμβάνομεν αὐτὸν οὕτως ἀλογίστως ἔχειν ὥστ' ἐπὶ διαιτητὴν βαδίζειν, προδήλου ὄντος ὅτι καταγνώσεται αὐτοῦ ἀποτεῖσαι τὰ χρήματα, ἐξὸν αὐτῶι ἐπὶ τὸ δικαστήριον ἥκειν φέροντα τὸ ἀργύριον, εἶτ' ἐὰν μὲν δύνηται ὑμᾶς παρακρούσασθαι, ἀπιέναι τἀλλότρια ἔχοντα, εἰ δὲ μή, τηνικαῦτα καταθεῖναι τὰ χρήματα, ὡς ⟨ἂν⟩ ἄνθρωπος οὐ τῶι δικαίωι πιστεύων, ἀλλὰ διάπειραν ὑμῶν λαμβάνειν βουλόμενος.

19 Τὰ μὲν τοίνυν πεπραγμένα Διονυσοδώρωι ἀκηκόατε, ὦ ἄνδρες δικασταί· οἶμαι δ' ὑμᾶς θαυμάζειν ἀκούοντας πάλαι τὴν τόλμαν αὐτοῦ, καὶ τῶι ποτε πιστεύων εἰσελήλυθεν δευρί. πῶς γὰρ οὐ τολμηρόν, εἴ τις ἄνθρωπος δανεισάμενος χρήματα

20 ἐκ τοῦ ἐμπορίου τοῦ 'Αθηναίων, καὶ συγγραφὴν διαρρήδην γραψάμενος ἐφ' ὧι τε καταπλεῖν τὴν ναῦν εἰς τὸ ὑμέτερον ἐμπόριον, εἰ δὲ μή, ἀποτίνειν διπλάσια τὰ χρήματα, μήτε τὴν ναῦν κατακεκόμικεν εἰς τὸν Πειραιᾶ μήτε τὰ χρήματα ἀποδίδωσι τοῖς δανείσασιν, τόν τε σῖτον ἐξελόμενος ἐν 'Ρόδωι ἀπέδοτο, καὶ ταῦτα διαπεπραγμένος μηδὲν ἧττον τολμᾶι

21 βλέπειν εἰς τὰ ὑμέτερα πρόσωπα; ἃ δὴ λέγει πρὸς ταῦτα ἀκούσατε. φησὶ γὰρ τὴν ναῦν πλέουσαν ἐξ Αἰγύπτου ῥαγῆναι,

καὶ διὰ ταῦτα ἀναγκασθῆναι καὶ προσσχεῖν εἰς τὴν Ῥόδον
κἀκεῖ ἐξελέσθαι τὸν σῖτον. καὶ τούτου τεκμήριον λέγει, ὡς
ἄρα ἐκ τῆς Ῥόδου μισθώσαιτο πλοῖα καὶ δεῦρο ἀποστείλειε
τῶν χρημάτων ἔνια. ἓν μὲν τοῦτό ἐστιν αὐτῶι μέρος τῆς
ἀπολογίας, δεύτερον δ᾽ ἐκεῖνο· φησὶ γὰρ ἑτέρους τινὰς δανειστὰς 22
συγκεχωρηκέναι αὐτῶι τοὺς τόκους τοὺς εἰς Ῥόδον· δεινὸν
οὖν, εἰ ἡμεῖς μὴ συγχωρήσομεν ταὐτὰ ἐκείνοις. τρίτον πρὸς
τούτοις τὴν συγγραφὴν κελεύειν φησὶν αὐτὸν σωθείσης τῆς
νεὼς ἀποδοῦναι τὰ χρήματα, τὴν δὲ ναῦν οὐ σεσῶισθαι εἰς
τὸν Πειραιᾶ. πρὸς ἕκαστον δὴ τούτων, ὦ ἄνδρες δικασταί,
ἀκούσατε ἃ λέγομεν δίκαια.

Πρῶτον μὲν τὸ ῥαγῆναι τὴν ναῦν ὅταν λέγηι, οἶμαι πᾶσιν 23
ὑμῖν φανερὸν εἶναι ὅτι ψεύδεται. εἰ γὰρ τοῦτο συνέβη παθεῖν
τῆι νηί, οὔτ᾽ ἂν εἰς τὴν Ῥόδον ἐσώθη οὔτ᾽ ἂν ὕστερον πλόϊμος
ἦν. νῦν δὲ φαίνεται εἰς τὴν Ῥόδον σωθεῖσα καὶ πάλιν ἐκεῖθεν
ἀποσταλεῖσα εἰς Αἴγυπτον καὶ ἔτι καὶ νῦν πλέουσα πανταχόσε,
πλὴν οὐκ εἰς Ἀθήνας. καίτοι πῶς οὐκ ἄτοπον, ὅταν μὲν
εἰς τὸ Ἀθηναίων ἐμπόριον δεήσηι κατάγειν τὴν ναῦν, ῥαγῆναι
φάσκειν, ὅταν δὲ εἰς τὴν Ῥόδον τὸν σῖτον ἐξελέσθαι, τηνικαῦτα
δὲ πλόϊμον οὖσαν φαίνεσθαι τὴν αὐτὴν ναῦν;

Διὰ τί οὖν, φησίν, ἐμισθωσάμην ἕτερα πλοῖα καὶ μετεξειλόμην 24
τὸν γόμον καὶ δεῦρ᾽ ἀπέστειλα; ὅτι, ὦ ἄνδρες Ἀθηναῖοι,
οὐ τῶν ἁπάντων ἀγωγίμων οὔθ᾽ οὗτος ἦν κύριος οὔθ᾽ ὁ
κοινωνὸς αὐτοῦ, ἀλλ᾽ οἱ ἐπιβάται τὰ ἑαυτῶν χρήματα
ἀπέστελλον οἶμαι δεῦρο ἐν ἑτέροις πλοίοις ἐξ ἀνάγκης, ἐπειδὴ
προκατέλυσαν οὗτοι τὸν πλοῦν· ὧν μέντοι αὐτοὶ ἦσαν κύριοι,
οὐδὲ ταῦτα ἀπέστελλον πάντα δεῦρο, ἀλλ᾽ ἐκλεγόμενοι τίνων
αἱ τιμαὶ ἐπετέταντο. ἐπεὶ τί δήποτε μισθούμενοι ἕτερα πλοῖα, 25
ὥς φατε, οὐχ ἅπαντα τὸν γόμον τῆς νεὼς μετενέθεσθε, ἀλλὰ
τὸν σῖτον αὐτοῦ ἐν τῆι Ῥόδωι κατελίπετε; ὅτι, ὦ ἄνδρες
δικασταί, τοῦτον μὲν συνέφερεν αὐτοῖς ἐκεῖσε πωλεῖν (τὰς γὰρ
τιμὰς τὰς ἐνθάδε ἀνεικέναι ἤκουον)· τὰ δ᾽ ἄλλ᾽ ἀγώγιμα ὡς
ὑμᾶς ἀπέστελλον, ἀφ᾽ ὧν κερδανεῖν ἤλπιζον. ὥστε τὴν μίσθωσιν
τῶν πλοίων ὅταν λέγηις, οὐ τοῦ ῥαγῆναι τὴν ναῦν τεκμήριον
λέγεις, ἀλλὰ τοῦ συμφέροντος ὑμῖν.

26　Περὶ μὲν οὖν τούτων ἱκανά μοι τὰ εἰρημένα· περὶ δὲ τῶν δανειστῶν, οὓς φασι συγκεχωρηκέναι λαβεῖν παρ' αὐτῶν τοὺς εἰς Ῥόδον τόκους, ἔστι μὲν οὐδὲν πρὸς ἡμᾶς τοῦτο. εἰ γάρ τις ὑμῖν ἀφῆκέν τι τῶν αὑτοῦ, οὐδὲν ἀδικεῖται οὔθ' ὁ δοὺς οὔθ' ὁ πείσας· ἀλλ' ἡμεῖς οὔτ' ἀφείκαμέν σοι οὐδὲν οὔτε συγκεχωρήκαμεν τῶι πλῶι τῶι εἰς Ῥόδον, οὐδ' ἐστὶν ἡμῖν

27　οὐδὲν κυριώτερον τῆς συγγραφῆς. αὕτη δὲ τί λέγει καὶ ποῖ προστάττει τὸν πλοῦν ποιεῖσθαι; Ἀθήνηθεν εἰς Αἴγυπτον καὶ ἐξ Αἰγύπτου εἰς Ἀθήνας· εἰ δὲ μή, ἀποτίνειν κελεύει διπλάσια τὰ χρήματα. ταῦτα εἰ μὲν πεποίηκας, οὐδὲν ἀδικεῖς, εἰ δὲ μὴ πεποίηκας μηδὲ κατακεκόμικας τὴν ναῦν Ἀθήναζε, προσήκει σε ζημιοῦσθαι τῶι ἐπιτιμίωι τῶι ἐκ τῆς συγγραφῆς· τοῦτο γὰρ τὸ δίκαιον οὐκ ἄλλος οὐδείς, ἀλλ' αὐτὸς σὺ σαυτῶι ὥρισας. δεῖξον οὖν τοῖς δικασταῖς δυοῖν θάτερον, ἢ τὴν συγγραφήν, ὡς οὐκ ἔστιν ἡμῖν κυρία, ἢ ὡς οὐ δίκαιος εἶ πάντα κατὰ

28　ταύτην πράττειν. εἰ δέ τινες ἀφείκασίν τί σοι καὶ συγκεχωρήκασιν τοὺς εἰς Ῥόδον τόκους ὁτωιδήποτε τρόπωι πεισθέντες, διὰ ταῦτα οὐδὲν ἀδικεῖς ἡμᾶς, οὓς παρασυγγεγράφηκας εἰς Ῥόδον καταγαγὼν τὴν ναῦν; οὐκ οἶμαί γε· οὐ γὰρ τὰ ὑφ' ἑτέρων συγκεχωρημένα δικάζουσιν οὗτοι νῦν, ἀλλὰ τὰ ὑπ' αὐτοῦ σοῦ πρὸς ἡμᾶς συγγεγραμμένα. ἐπεὶ ὅτι γε καὶ τὸ περὶ τὴν ἄφεσιν τῶν τόκων, εἰ ἄρα γέγονεν ὡς οὗτοι λέγουσιν, μετὰ τοῦ συμφέροντος τοῦ τῶν δανειστῶν γέγονε,

29　πᾶσιν ὑμῖν φανερόν ἐστιν. οἱ γὰρ ἐκ τῆς Αἰγύπτου δανείσαντες τούτοις ἑτερόπλουν τἀργύριον εἰς Ἀθήνας, ὡς ἀφίκοντο εἰς τὴν Ῥόδον καὶ τὴν ναῦν ἐκεῖσε οὗτοι κατεκόμισαν, οὐδὲν οἶμαι διέφερεν αὐτοῖς ἀφεμένοις τῶν τόκων καὶ κομισαμένοις τὸ δάνειον ἐν τῆι Ῥόδωι πάλιν ἐνεργὸν ποιεῖν εἰς τὴν Αἴγυπτον, ἀλλ' ἐλυσιτέλει πολλῶι μᾶλλον τοῦτ' ἢ δεῦρ' ἐπαναπλεῖν.

30　ἐκεῖσε μὲν γὰρ ἀκαριαῖος ὁ πλοῦς, καὶ δὶς ἢ τρὶς ὑπῆρχεν αὐτοῖς ἐργάσασθαι τῶι αὐτῶι ἀργυρίωι· ἐνταῦθα δ' ἐπιδημήσαντας παραχειμάζειν ἔδει καὶ περιμένειν τὴν ὡραίαν. ὥστ' ἐκεῖνοι μὲν οἱ δανεισταὶ προσκεκερδήκασιν καὶ οὐκ ἀφείκασι τούτοις οὐδέν· ἡμῖν δ' οὐχ ὅπως περὶ τοῦ τόκου ὁ λόγος ἐστίν, ἀλλ' οὐδὲ τἀρχαῖα ἀπολαβεῖν δυνάμεθα.

Μὴ οὖν ἀποδέχεσθε τούτου φενακίζοντος ὑμᾶς καὶ τὰ πρὸς 31 τοὺς ἄλλους δανειστὰς πεπραγμένα παραβάλλοντος, ἀλλ' ἐπὶ τὴν συγγραφὴν ἀνάγετ' αὐτὸν καὶ τὰ ἐκ τῆς συγγραφῆς δίκαια. ἔστι γὰρ ἐμοί τε λοιπὸν διδάξαι ὑμᾶς τοῦτο, καὶ οὗτος ἰσχυρίζεται τῶι αὐτῶι τούτωι, φάσκων τὴν συγγραφὴν κελεύειν σωθείσης τῆς νεὼς ἀποδιδόναι τὸ δάνειον. καὶ ἡμεῖς 32 ταῦτα οὕτω φαμὲν δεῖν ἔχειν. ἡδέως δ' ἂν πυθοίμην αὐτοῦ σοῦ, πότερον ὡς ὑπὲρ διεφθαρμένης τῆς νεὼς διαλέγει, ἢ ὡς ὑπὲρ σεσωισμένης. εἰ μὲν γὰρ διέφθαρται ἡ ναῦς καὶ ἀπόλωλεν, τί περὶ τῶν τόκων διαφέρει καὶ ἀξιοῖς ἡμᾶς κομίζεσθαι τοὺς εἰς Ῥόδον τόκους; οὔτε γὰρ τοὺς τόκους οὔτε τἀρχαῖα προσήκει ἡμᾶς ἀπολαβεῖν. εἰ δ' ἐστὶν ἡ ναῦς σῶς καὶ μὴ διέφθαρται, διὰ τί ἡμῖν οὐκ ἀποδίδως τὰ χρήματα ἃ συνεγράψω; πόθεν 33 οὖν ἀκριβέστατα ἂν μάθοιτε, ἄνδρες Ἀθηναῖοι, ὅτι σέσωισται ἡ ναῦς; μάλιστα μὲν ἐξ αὐτοῦ τοῦ εἶναι τὴν ναῦν ἐν πλῶι, οὐχ ἧττον δὲ καὶ ἐξ ὧν αὐτοὶ οὗτοι λέγουσιν. ἀξιοῦσιν γὰρ ἡμᾶς τά τε ἀρχαῖα ἀπολαβεῖν καὶ μέρος τι τῶν τόκων, ὡς σεσωισμένης μὲν τῆς νεώς, οὐ πεπλευκυίας δὲ πάντα τὸν πλοῦν. σκοπεῖτε δέ, ὦ ἄνδρες Ἀθηναῖοι, πότερον ἡμεῖς τοῖς ἐκ 34 τῆς συγγραφῆς δικαίοις χρώμεθα ἢ οὗτοι, οἳ οὔτε εἰς τὸ συγκείμενον ἐμπόριον πεπλεύκασιν, ἀλλ' εἰς Ῥόδον καὶ Αἴγυπτον, σωθείσης τε τῆς νεὼς καὶ οὐ διεφθαρμένης ἄφεσιν οἴονται δεῖν εὑρίσκεσθαι τῶν τόκων παρασυγγεγραφηκότες, καὶ αὐτοὶ μὲν πολλὰ χρήματα εἰργασμένοι παρὰ τὴν σιτηγίαν τὴν εἰς Ῥόδον, τὰ δ' ἡμέτερα χρήματα ἔχοντες καὶ καρπούμενοι δεύτερον ἔτος τουτί. καινότατον δ' ἐστὶ πάντων τὸ 35 γιγνόμενον· τὸ μὲν γὰρ δάνειον τὸ ἀρχαῖον ἀποδιδόασιν ἡμῖν ὡς σεσωισμένης τῆς νεώς, τοὺς τόκους δ' ἀποστερῆσαι οἴονται δεῖν ὡς διεφθαρμένης. καίτοι ἡ συγγραφὴ οὐχ ἕτερα μὲν λέγει περὶ τῶν τόκων, ἕτερα δὲ περὶ τοῦ ἀρχαίου δανείσματος, ἀλλὰ τὰ δίκαια ταὐτὰ περὶ ἀμφοῖν ἐστιν καὶ ἡ πρᾶξις ἡ αὐτή. ἀνάγνωθι δέ μοι πάλιν τὴν συγγραφήν.   36

ΣΥΓΓΡΑΦΗ

...Ἀθήνηθεν εἰς Αἴγυπτον καὶ ἐξ Αἰγύπτου Ἀθήναζε.

Ἀκούετε, ὦ ἄνδρες Ἀθηναῖοι· ''Ἀθήνηθεν,' φησίν, 'εἰς Αἴγυπτον καὶ ἐξ Αἰγύπτου Ἀθήναζε.' λέγε τὰ λοιπά.

ΣΥΓΓΡΑΦΗ

Σωθείσης δὲ τῆς νεὼς εἰς Πειραιᾶ...

37 Ἄνδρες Ἀθηναῖοι, πάνυ ἁπλοῦν ἐστιν διαγνῶναι ὑμῖν ὑπὲρ ταύτης τῆς δίκης, καὶ οὐδὲν δεῖ λόγων πολλῶν. ἡ ναῦς ὅτι μὲν σέσωισται καὶ ἔστιν σῶς, καὶ παρ' αὐτῶν τούτων ὁμολογεῖται (οὐ γὰρ ἂν ἀπεδίδοσαν τό τε ἀρχαῖον δάνειον καὶ τῶν τόκων μέρος τι), οὐ κατακεκόμισται δ' εἰς τὸν Πειραιᾶ. διὰ τοῦτο ἡμεῖς μὲν οἱ δανείσαντες ἀδικεῖσθαί φαμεν, καὶ ὑπὲρ τούτου δικαζόμεθα, ὅτι οὐ κατέπλευσεν εἰς τὸ συγκείμενον 38 ἐμπόριον. Διονυσόδωρος δὲ οὔ φησιν ἀδικεῖν δι' αὐτὸ τοῦτο· οὐ γὰρ δεῖν αὐτὸν ἀποδοῦναι πάντας τοὺς τόκους, ἐπειδὴ ἡ ναῦς οὐ κατέπλευσεν εἰς τὸν Πειραιᾶ. ἡ δὲ συγγραφὴ τί λέγει; οὐ μὰ Δί' οὐ ταῦτα ἃ σὺ λέγεις, ὦ Διονυσόδωρε· ἀλλ' ἐὰν μὴ ἀποδῶις τὸ δάνειον καὶ τοὺς τόκους ἢ μὴ παράσχηις τὰ ὑποκείμενα ἐμφανῆ καὶ ἀνέπαφα, ἢ ἄλλο τι παρὰ τὴν συγγραφὴν ποιήσηις, ἀποτίνειν κελεύει σε διπλάσια τὰ χρήματα. καί μοι λέγε αὐτὸ τοῦτο τῆς συγγραφῆς.

ΣΥΓΓΡΑΦΗ

Ἐὰν δὲ...μὴ παράσχωσι τὰ ὑποκείμενα ἐμφανῆ καὶ ἀνέπαφα, ἢ ποιήσωσίν τι παρὰ τὴν συγγραφήν, ἀποδιδότωσαν διπλάσια τὰ χρήματα.

39 Ἔστιν οὖν ὅποι παρέσχηκας ἐμφανῆ τὴν ναῦν, ἀφ' οὗ τὰ χρήματα ἔλαβες παρ' ἡμῶν, ὁμολογῶν σῶν εἶναι αὐτός; ἢ καταπέπλευκας ἐξ ἐκείνου τοῦ χρόνου εἰς τὸ Ἀθηναίων ἐμπόριον, τῆς συγγραφῆς διαρρήδην λεγούσης εἰς τὸν Πειραιᾶ κατάγειν τὴν ναῦν καὶ ἐμφανῆ παρέχειν τοῖς δανείσασιν; 40 καὶ γὰρ τοῦτο, ἄνδρες Ἀθηναῖοι. θεάσασθε τὴν ὑπερβολήν.

ἐρράγη ἡ ναῦς, ὥς φησιν οὗτος, καὶ διὰ τοῦτ' εἰς Ῥόδον
κατήγαγεν αὐτήν. οὐκοῦν τὸ μετὰ τοῦτο ἐπεσκευάσθη καὶ
πλόϊμος ἐγένετο. διὰ τί οὖν, ὦ βέλτιστε, εἰς μὲν τὴν Αἴγυπτον
καὶ τἆλλα ἐμπόρια ἀπέστελλες αὐτήν, Ἀθήναζε δὲ οὐκ
ἀπέσταλκας οὐδέπω καὶ νῦν πρὸς ἡμᾶς τοὺς δανείσαντας,
οἷς ἡ συγγραφὴ κελεύει σε ἐμφανῆ καὶ ἀνέπαφον τὴν ναῦν
παρέχειν, καὶ ταῦτ' ἀξιούντων ἡμῶν καὶ προκαλεσαμένων
σε πολλάκις; ἀλλ' οὕτως ἀνδρεῖος εἶ, μᾶλλον δὲ ἀναίσχυντος, 41
ὥστ' ἐκ τῆς συγγραφῆς ὀφείλων ἡμῖν διπλάσια τὰ χρήματα,
οὐκ οἴει δεῖν οὐδὲ τοὺς τόκους τοὺς γιγνομένους ἀποδοῦναι,
ἀλλὰ τοὺς εἰς Ῥόδον προστάττεις ἀπολαβεῖν, ὥσπερ τὸ σὸν
πρόσταγμα τῆς συγγραφῆς δέον κυριώτερον γενέσθαι, καὶ
τολμᾷς λέγειν ὡς οὐκ ἐσώθη ἡ ναῦς εἰς τὸν Πειραιᾶ· ἐφ'
ὧι δικαίως ἂν ἀποθάνοις ὑπὸ τῶν δικαστῶν. διὰ τίνα γὰρ 42
μᾶλλον, ὦ ἄνδρες δικασταί, οὐ σέσωισται ἡ ναῦς εἰς τὸν
Πειραιᾶ; πότερον δι' ἡμᾶς τοὺς διαρρήδην δανείσαντας εἰς
Αἴγυπτον καὶ εἰς Ἀθήνας, ἢ διὰ τοῦτον καὶ τὸν κοινωνὸν
αὐτοῦ, οἳ ἐπὶ ταύταις ταῖς ὁμολογίαις δανεισάμενοι, ἐφ' ὧι
τε καταπλεῖν Ἀθήναζε, εἰς Ῥόδον κατήγαγον τὴν ναῦν; ὅτι
δὲ ἑκόντες καὶ οὐκ ἐξ ἀνάγκης ταῦτ' ἔπραξαν, ἐκ πολλῶν
δῆλον. εἰ γὰρ ὡς ἀληθῶς ἀκούσιον τὸ συμβὰν ἐγένετο καὶ 43
ἡ ναῦς ἐρράγη, τὸ μετὰ τοῦτ' ἐπειδὴ ἐπεσκεύασαν τὴν ναῦν,
οὐκ ἂν εἰς ἕτερα δήπου ἐμπόρια ἐμίσθωσαν αὐτήν, ἀλλ' ὡς
ὑμᾶς ἀπέστελλον, ἐπανορθούμενοι τὸ ἀκούσιον σύμπτωμα. νῦν
δ' οὐχ ὅπως ἐπηνωρθώσαντο, ἀλλὰ πρὸς τοῖς ἐξ ἀρχῆς
ἀδικήμασι πολλῶι μείζω προσεξημαρτήκασιν, καὶ ὥσπερ
ἐπὶ καταγέλωτι ἀντιδικοῦντες εἰσεληλύθασιν, ὡς ἐπ' αὐτοῖς
ἐσόμενον, ἐὰν καταψηφίσησθε αὐτῶν, τὰ ἀρχαῖα μόνον
ἀποδοῦναι καὶ τοὺς τόκους. ὑμεῖς οὖν, ὦ ἄνδρες Ἀθηναῖοι, 44
μὴ ἐπιτρέπετε τούτοις οὕτως ἔχουσιν, μηδ' ἐπὶ δυοῖν ἀγκύραιν
ὁρμεῖν αὐτοὺς ἐᾶτε, ὡς, ἐὰν μὲν κατορθώσωσι, τἀλλότρια
ἕξοντας, ἐὰν δὲ μὴ δύνωνται ἐξαπατῆσαι ὑμᾶς, αὐτὰ τὰ
ὀφειλόμενα ἀποδώσοντας· ἀλλὰ τοῖς ἐπιτιμίοις ζημιοῦτε τοῖς
ἐκ τῆς συγγραφῆς. καὶ γὰρ ἂν δεινὸν εἴη, αὐτοὺς μὲν τούτους
διπλασίαν καθ' αὑτῶν τὴν ζημίαν γράψασθαι, ἐάν τι παρα-

βαίνωσι τῶν ἐν τῆι συγγραφῆι, ὑμᾶς δ' ἠπιωτέρως ἔχειν πρὸς αὐτούς, καὶ ταῦτα οὐχ ἧττον ἡμῶν συνηδικημένους.

45 Τὰ μὲν οὖν περὶ τοῦ πράγματος δίκαια βραχέα ἐστὶ καὶ εὐμνημόνευτα. ἐδανείσαμεν Διονυσοδώρωι τουτωὶ καὶ τῶι κοινωνῶι αὐτοῦ τρισχιλίας δραχμὰς Ἀθήνηθεν εἰς Αἴγυπτον καὶ ἐξ Αἰγύπτου Ἀθήναζε· οὐκ ἀπειλήφαμεν τὰ χρήματα οὐδὲ τοὺς τόκους, ἀλλ' ἔχουσι τὰ ἡμέτερα καὶ χρῶνται δεύτερον ἔτος· οὐ κατακεκομίκασιν τὴν ναῦν εἰς τὸ ὑμέτερον ἐμπόριον οὐδέπω καὶ νῦν, οὐδ' ἡμῖν παρεσχήκασιν ἐμφανῆ· ἡ δὲ συγγραφὴ κελεύει, ἐὰν μὴ παρέχωσιν ἐμφανῆ τὴν ναῦν, ἀποτίνειν αὐτοὺς διπλάσια τὰ χρήματα, τὴν δὲ πρᾶξιν εἶναι καὶ ἐξ ἑνὸς καὶ 46 ἐξ ἀμφοῖν. ταῦτ' ἔχοντες τὰ δίκαια εἰσεληλύθαμεν πρὸς ὑμᾶς, ἀξιοῦντες τὰ ἡμέτερα αὐτῶν ἀπολαβεῖν δι' ὑμῶν, ἐπειδὴ παρ' αὐτῶν τούτων οὐ δυνάμεθα. ὁ μὲν παρ' ἡμῶν λόγος οὗτός ἐστιν. οὗτοι δὲ δανείσασθαι μὲν ὁμολογοῦσιν καὶ μὴ ἀπο-δεδωκέναι, διαφέρονται δὲ ὡς οὐ δεῖ τελεῖν αὐτοὺς τοὺς τόκους τοὺς ἐν τῆι συγγραφῆι, ἀλλὰ τοὺς εἰς Ῥόδον, οὓς οὔτε 47 συνεγράψαντο οὔτε ἔπεισαν ἡμᾶς. εἰ μὲν οὖν, ὦ ἄνδρες Ἀθηναῖοι, ἐν τῶι Ῥοδίων δικαστηρίωι ἐκρινόμεθα, ἴσως ἂν οὗτοι ἐπλεονέκτουν ἡμῶν, σεσιτηγηκότες πρὸς αὐτοὺς καὶ καταπεπλευκότες τῆι νηὶ εἰς τὸ ἐκείνων ἐμπόριον· νῦν δὲ εἰς Ἀθηναίους εἰσεληλυθότες καὶ συγγραψάμενοι εἰς τὸ ὑμέτερον ἐμπόριον, οὐκ ἀξιοῦμεν ἐλαττωθῆναι ὑπὸ τῶν καὶ ἡμᾶς καὶ ὑμᾶς ἠδικηκότων.

48 Χωρὶς δὲ τούτων, ἄνδρες Ἀθηναῖοι, μὴ ἀγνοεῖτε, ὅτι νυνὶ μίαν δίκην δικάζοντες νομοθετεῖτε ὑπὲρ ὅλου τοῦ ἐμπορίου, καὶ παρεστᾶσι πολλοὶ τῶν κατὰ θάλατταν ἐργάζεσθαι προ-αιρουμένων ὑμᾶς θεωροῦντες, πῶς τὸ πρᾶγμα τουτὶ κρίνετε. εἰ μὲν γὰρ ὑμεῖς τὰς συγγραφὰς καὶ τὰς ὁμολογίας τὰς πρὸς ἀλλήλους γιγνομένας ἰσχυρὰς οἴεσθε δεῖν εἶναι καὶ τοῖς παραβαίνουσιν αὐτὰς μηδεμίαν συγγνώμην ἕξετε, ἑτοιμότερον προήσονται τὰ ἑαυτῶν οἱ ἐπὶ τοῦ δανείζειν ὄντες, ἐκ δὲ 49 τούτων αὐξηθήσεται ὑμῖν τὸ ἐμπόριον. εἰ μέντοι ἐξέσται τοῖς ναυκλήροις, συγγραφὴν γραψαμένοις ἐφ' ὧι τε καταπλεῖν εἰς Ἀθήνας, ἔπειτα κατάγειν τὴν ναῦν εἰς ἕτερα ἐμπόρια, φάσκοντας

ῥαγῆναι καὶ τοιαύτας προφάσεις ποριζομένους οἵαισπερ καὶ Διονυσόδωρος οὑτοσὶ χρῆται, καὶ τοὺς τόκους μερίζειν πρὸς τὸν πλοῦν ὃν ἂν φήσωσιν πεπλευκέναι, καὶ μὴ πρὸς τὴν συγγραφήν, οὐδὲν κωλύσει ἅπαντα τὰ συμβόλαια διαλύεσθαι. τίς γὰρ ἐθελήσει τὰ ἑαυτοῦ προέσθαι, ὅταν ὁρᾶι τὰς μὲν 50 συγγραφὰς ἀκύρους, ἰσχύοντας δὲ τοὺς τοιούτους λόγους, καὶ τὰς αἰτίας τῶν ἠδικηκότων ἔμπροσθεν οὔσας τοῦ δικαίου; μηδαμῶς, ὦ ἄνδρες δικασταί· οὔτε γὰρ τῶι πλήθει τῶι ὑμετέρωι συμφέρει τοῦτο οὔτε τοῖς ἐργάζεσθαι προηιρημένοις, οἵπερ χρησιμώτατοί εἰσιν καὶ κοινῆι πᾶσιν ὑμῖν καὶ ἰδίαι τῶι ἐντυγχάνοντι. διόπερ δεῖ ὑμᾶς αὐτῶν ἐπιμέλειαν ποιεῖσθαι.

Ἐγὼ μὲν οὖν ὅσαπερ οἷός τ᾽ ἦν, εἴρηκα· ἀξιῶ δὲ καὶ τῶν φίλων μοί τινα συνειπεῖν. δεῦρο Δημόσθενες.

COMMENTARY

54 Against Conon

Date

Possible evidence for dating is furnished by §3, where Ariston speaks of garrison duty at Panactum on the border between Athens and Boeotia; this took place two years before the present trial. Demosthenes (19.326) speaks of an expedition to Panactum in 343; he also tells us that no such expedition had taken place during the Sacred War (355–346). However, all the forts on the border with Boeotia seem to have been manned in 357 (schol. ad Dem. 21.193). This suggests 357 or 343 as the date of the garrison duty in §3, and 355 or 341 as the date of the speech. Both dates rest on the assumption that the φρουρά mentioned in the text was part of a formal expedition for a specific military purpose. However, it is possible that the garrison was made up of ephebes undergoing their training (Arist. *Ath. Pol.* 42.4, Thuc. 2.13.7, Aeschin. 2.167), i.e. that the φρουρά mentioned is quite distinct from the type of expedition referred to in Dem. 19.[1] If so, the passage is of no value for dating. But the phrase φρουρᾶς ἡμῖν προγραφείσης (see on §3) suggests a selection from the roll of adult citizens, not the obligatory φρουρά of the ephebe. Sandys finds further evidence for the 340s in the name adopted by the club to which Conon belonged as a young man (§39), Triballi. Conon was now in his fifties (§22). The Triballi were in the news in 376 when they ravaged the coast of Thrace (Diod. 15.36), and this could have prompted the club to choose the name. If Conon was approximately twenty in 376 he would be in his fifties in the late 340s. But, as Gernet notes (III, 101 n. 1) the Triballi were already known in Athens in the fifth century. The only honest conclusion is: *non liquet*.

Ariston's action

Ariston has brought an action for battery (αἰκείας δίκη) against Conon. His account of his dealings with Conon's family is as follows.

Two years ago, Conon's sons were camped near Ariston on garrison

---

[1] This might explain the slack discipline.

duty at Panactum. Conon's sons, who were permanently drunk, abused
Ariston's slaves and finally assaulted Ariston himself. Ariston took no
action on his return to Athens, and was content to avoid Conon's sons.
But one evening some time afterwards, as Ariston and his friend
Phanostratus were walking in the agora, they encountered one of
Conon's sons, Ctesias. The latter, drunk, shouted and muttered
something unintelligible. Ariston and Phanostratus continued with
their walk, while Ctesias went to fetch Conon and Conon's friends, who
were drinking nearby. This gang met Ariston and Phanostratus as they
were walking back, and set upon them. One of them held Phanostratus
while Conon, Ctesias and another attacked Ariston, stripped him of his
cloak, tripped him in the mud, and beat and jumped on him, uttering
abusive language. Ariston nearly died from his injuries. The plaintiff
claims that he could have brought a more serious action for outrage
(ὕβρεως γραφή; see on §1) or arrested him as a λωποδύτης (for
removing his cloak); either of these courses could have resulted in
Conon's death. But nervous of undertaking so ambitious a prosecution,
Ariston has succumbed to the advice of friends and brought a suit for
battery (αἰκείας δίκη), to extract damages for his ill-treatment.

Conon in his defence argues as follows.

1. It was not he but his son who beat Ariston (§31f.). Conon adduces
witnesses who attest that they were coming home from dinner, together
with Conon, when they found Ariston and Conon's son fighting in the
agora. Clearly Conon is rejecting Ariston's account of two meetings
with Ctesias (the first with Ctesias alone, the second with Ctesias
accompanied by Conon and friends) and arguing that only one meeting
took place, which resulted in a fight which was witnessed by Conon.

2. Ariston like Ctesias is a member of a street-gang (§13ff.). Harmless
fights often take place between high-spirited youths, and A. has taken
an insignificant scuffle too seriously. His injuries were minor.[2]

Ariston's case looks at first sight impregnable. However, closer
inspection reveals a problem. According to A. (§32), the passers-by who
carried him home on the night in question depose 'that they saw me
being struck by Conon and stripped of my robe and subjected to all

---

[2] E. Mensching, *RhM* 106 (1963) 307–12, 309 concludes, from the digression
on self-defence which interrupts Ariston's reply to Conon's claim that A. belongs
to a street-gang (§§17–19), that Conon further claims that Ariston, not Ctesias,
started the fight. This is possible but unprovable.

the other outrage which I suffered'; the actual deposition was given in §9. There is however some reason to doubt that A. is paraphrasing his witnesses accurately.[3] In §9 Ariston says: ἐγὼ μὲν ἀπεκομίσθην ὑπὸ τῶν παρατυχόντων γυμνός, οὗτοι δ' ὤιχοντο θοἰμάτιον λαβόντες μου. If ὤιχοντο is given its normal pluperfect sense the natural conclusion is that Conon and friends *had left the scene* before the arrival of these passers-by. Since the verb might be aoristic or even imperfective the evidence of this passage is ambiguous. But §32 is less so. There A. says that his witnesses would not have given their evidence εἰ μὴ ταῦθ' ἑώρων πεπονθότα. The tense of the participle ('in this condition'; contrast τυπτόμενον, ἐκδυόμενον, ὑβριζόμενον in Ariston's paraphrase of their deposition, quoted above in translation) suggests again that the passers-by reached the spot *after* the departure of Conon, that they found A. already beaten and stripped. This is of course as one would expect; whether Conon attacked Ariston, or was drawn into a fight between A. and Ctesias, or was simply cheering Ctesias on from the sidelines, we should not expect him to await the arrival of witnesses who might testify against him in a subsequent lawsuit.[4] With the suggested distortion of the witnesses' testimony we may compare §10 where A. introduces the testimony of Midias and Euxitheus with the words λάβ' οὖν καὶ τὰς τούτων μαρτυρίας, ἵν' εἰδῆθ' ὅτι πολλοὶ συνίσασιν ὡς ὑπὸ τούτων ὑβρίσθην. But in fact these witnesses can only attest Ariston's condition after the incident; they cannot identify the perpetrators, for it is nowhere suggested that they witnessed the fight. It is striking that although A. *quotes* Conon's witnesses verbatim in §31 he *paraphrases* his own. Moreover, if the evidence of his witnesses is as decisive as A. suggests in §32 it is odd that he devotes so little attention to them and spends so much time attacking Conon's witnesses. A. insists that his witnesses, being strangers to him (§32), are reliable. But if the passers-by did not witness the fight, it is likely that the only witness to identify Conon was Phanostratus,[5] who as Ariston's friend is not impartial.

[3] Mensching likewise suggests that A. is misquoting his witnesses, because of (1) the long interval between the depositions (§9) and Ariston's paraphrase (§32), (2) the brief and evasive (he does not quote but paraphrases) treatment of evidence which should be decisive.

[4] We should remember that it was evening, and visibility may have been poor; Athenian streets were unlit.

[5] Mensching, op. cit. 312 n. 17 doubts that Phanostratus testified. The text does not allow us to decide. His testimony could be included with that of οἱ

Conon's version of the events is supported by three witnesses. Ariston maintains that they are lying; although his attempt to represent them as habitual criminals (§37) is unconvincing, they are certainly not impartial. Thus Conon has, it appears, more support from eyewitnesses than Ariston (it is possible that the arbitrator found for Conon – see on §33). This does not mean that we should accept Conon's version. But it seems that the oratorical strength of the speech masks a weakness in Ariston's factual evidence.

We must now attempt to arrive at the facts. It is most unlikely that Conon is telling the truth when he claims that he was no more than a passive spectator. Against this view is the extreme improbability that A. would sue Conon if Ctesias alone was responsible, as A. himself observes (§32). A. would of course find it easier to stir up resentment against an older man who behaved like a juvenile thug than against a youth like Ctesias, who could retort that such battles were normal nocturnal sport for young Athenians. But against this advantage must be set the obvious disadvantage that A. would be allowing the real culprit to escape. Also, there appears to be no doubt that Ariston was stripped; it takes more than one to strip a man. It is possible to accept Conon's claim that he came upon Ariston and Ctesias fighting in the agora, but reject his claim that he merely watched; we might suppose that he somehow became embroiled in the fight. But it is difficult to see why Ariston should complicate his story unnecessarily by inventing the first meeting with Ctesias instead of simply claiming that he met Conon and friends and was attacked.

Thus it seems likely that Ariston's account is broadly true. But whether Ariston has told the *whole* truth is uncertain. One cannot but be struck by the brevity of Ariston's account of his first meeting with Ctesias (§7). Since Ariston is arguing that the attack was completely unprovoked, it is important for him to prove that the first meeting passed without incident. But the meeting is passed over very quickly.

παρατυχόντες at the end of §9. At §32, where A. sets his own witnesses against Conon's, Phanostratus is not mentioned. But since the context is an argument from probability that his own witnesses as strangers are impartial while Conon's as friends and fellow-criminals are unreliable, it is not surprising that Phanostratus is ignored. It would be rash to conclude that Phanostratus did not testify from the absence of an explicit statement to the contrary. On the other hand, it is difficult to see why Phanostratus is mentioned by name in §7 unless A. proposes to introduce a deposition from him.

One is inclined to suspect that A. may be concealing something. It may be, as Paoli has suggested,[6] that when Ariston and Phanostratus met Ctesias alone they attacked or insulted him; Ctesias escaped and returned with reinforcements, including his father, flushed with wine and paternal affection. If this was what happened, Conon could hardly use anything which happened at the first meeting in his defence; his duty as a mature man was to remonstrate with Ariston, if necessary to sue him, but not to set out looking for revenge and attack him. Conon's best line of defence would be to deny any part in the incident. But although Conon might still be guilty of *aikeia*, if Ariston at the first encounter did something which, while not justifying the assault, prompted it, he would be wise to suppress it, for he might forfeit some of the jury's sympathy.

The speech against Conon is a splendid example of skilled *ethopoiia*, the adaptation of speech to character, a faculty associated more with Lysias than with Demosthenes. *Ethopoiia* does not consist in reflecting accurately the personality of the speaker but in adapting the speech to such factors as age, social position and way of life, and in ensuring that a consistent image is created of the personality which the writer wishes to project. This contributes to the persuasiveness of the speech in two ways. (1) If the speaker projects a personality which is consistent in itself and also agrees with such obvious factors as age, the impression is created that the speech is a natural and unrehearsed statement of the truth by a simple man. (2) Moral character is as important as dramatic character. The speaker must project himself as a trustworthy personality as well as a plausible personality. This may be done crudely; the speaker may detail his services to the state or the like. But the same effect may be achieved more subtly, if the speaker consistently presents a respectable character in the moral judgements which he makes. In the present speech both aspects are handled with consummate skill. Ariston is presented throughout as a simple, decent youth. His modest disinclination to undertake a more serious prosecution, his tolerance on garrison duty, his embarrassment at the offensive language attributed to Conon, his unwillingness to swear oaths lightly, all combine to create that πίστις which is the goal of rhetoric. There is of course a danger; tolerance can be confused with cowardice, upright morals with priggishness. But the character delineation is handled deftly, never over-

[6] U. E. Paoli, *Uomini e cose del mondo antico* (Florence 1947) 10.

done. The success of the characterization of Ariston in this speech may be judged from the fact that without ever offering a shred of solid evidence to his own good character Ariston emerges as an excellent young man.

1–2 προοίμιον. All Greek literature tends towards stylization, not least oratory. But it is in the προοίμιον (introduction) and its counterpart the ἐπίλογος (conclusion) that we find the greatest accumulation of obvious commonplaces.

1 ὑβρισθείς: this brief and lucid opening sentence, giving the plaintiff's case in a nutshell, is ideally suited to Ariston's persona. The clarity and directness suit the simple candour of youth. The dominant aspect of Conon's behaviour as presented by Ariston is stressed in the very first word; cf. 45.1. The participles, as often in Greek, bear the main idea of the sentence. **πάνυ:** with πολὺν χρόνον. For the emphatic postponement cf. 56.1 ἐν βυβλιδίωι μικρῶι πάνυ. **μήτε τῶν ἰατρῶν μηδένα:** perhaps an exaggeration. In §§9 and 36 he speaks of doctors, in §§10, 11 and 12 of a doctor (singular). Cf. on § 10. **ἔλαχον . . . δίκην** 'brought the action/suit' (lit. 'obtained by lot'). The next procedural step after the summons to the defendant (see on 37.41) was the acceptance of the case by the appropriate magistrate, when a plaintiff presented a statement of his charge or claim (cf. 37.22). On acceptance of the complaint the magistrate set a date for the preliminary hearing (ἀνάκρισις). Since the dates were assigned by lot, the magistrate was said κληροῦν τὰς δίκας and the plaintiff λαγχάνειν δίκην (βλάβης, φόνου etc.). Cf. Lys. 6.11. Although in origin the phrase denotes passivity, it is frequently used with an active meaning, and is best translated 'bring an action', 'prosecute'. Hence the cognate noun λῆξις is used to describe the written complaint presented to a magistrate. Cf. Harrison II 88f. **ἔνοχον μὲν φασκόντων αὐτόν:** the μέν clause, as often, has a concessive force: 'though all my friends and acquaintances said...', they advised me...' συμβουλεύεσθαι = 'consult', συμβουλεύειν = 'advise'. **τῆι τῶν λωποδυτῶν ἀπαγωγῆι καὶ ταῖς τῆς ὕβρεως γραφαῖς:** these are the more serious charges which Ariston could have brought. λωποδύται ('cloak-strippers', i.e. footpads who set upon and strip the unwary; cf. e.g. Lys. 10.10, Dem. 24.204) belonged, together with thieves, burglars, kidnappers and cutpurses, to those criminals classed as κακοῦργοι; these offences fell under the jurisdiction of the Eleven (for the functions of the Eleven see Arist. *Ath. Pol.* 52.1); the penalty was death. Since Ariston claims that he was beaten and stripped, it was technically possible to prosecute Conon as a λωποδύτης, even though the intention was not to steal but to humiliate. ἀπαγωγή is summary arrest; it was used especially against felons caught in the act (ἐπ' αὐτοφώρωι), but (at least in the fourth century) arrests could also be made afterwards; see Harrison II 221ff., Andoc. 1.91 with MacDowell ad loc. *Hybris* is given detailed treatment by MacDowell, *G&R* 23 (1976) 14ff. *Hybris* is a protean word which defies translation. The essential notion is of lack of restraint, 'wantonness'. ὕβρις and its cognates denote arrogance, violence or unrestrained behaviour, essentially irreligious or unprincipled self-assertion. As well as describing a pattern of behaviour *hybris* was the name of an offence under Athenian law. Since the law on *hybris* did not define the offence (Dem. 21.47 ἐάν τις ὑβρίζηι εἴς τινα..., cf. Aeschin. 1.15) we may suppose that litigants and juries gave much thought at the trial to the definition, and that the definition varied. Partly because of the vagueness of the law, partly because no speech delivered in a γραφὴ ὕβρεως has survived, there is still no universally accepted definition; see in general Lipsius 520ff., MacDowell *Law* 129ff., E. Ruschenbusch, *ZSSR* 82 (1965) 302–9, M. Gagarin, *Arktouros* (Berlin 1979) 229–36. Both *hybris* and *aikeia* covered assault (Dem. 21.32 is decisive against the view that *hybris* might include slander). The difference was threefold. (1) *Hybris* was a more serious offence. *Hybris* was covered by a γραφή, *aikeia* by a δίκη (see on § 18 for the difference between δίκη and γραφή). In cases of *aikeia* the plaintiff received such financial compensation as the court approved, but for *hybris* the penalty in extreme cases could be death (Lys. fr. 44). (2) The range of *hybris* was wider, since it appears to have been applicable in cases of rape (Aeschin. 1.15ff.), which was also covered by the δίκη βιαίων, and forcible confinement (Isae. 8.41). Thus (a) the law on *hybris* overlapped other laws protecting the person, (b) *hybris* covered other physical abuse, not only blows. (3) From Arist. *Rhet.* 1373b 38 it appears that it was possible to admit to *aikeia* without admitting to *hybris*. What converted *aikeia* into *hybris* was the motive. *Aikeia* can be unpremeditated; *hybris* is deliberate (Arist. *Rhet.* 1374a 13–15 οὐ γὰρ εἰ ἐπάταξεν πάντως ὕβρισεν, ἀλλ' εἰ ἕνεκά του, οἷον τοῦ ἀτιμάσαι ἐκεῖνον ἢ αὐτὸς ἡσθῆναι). *Hybris* is wilful or malicious or deliberate physical abuse. It is more serious than *aikeia* since it implies an assumption of one's own superiority (*Rhet.* 1378b 23–9) and involves a contempt for the rights of fellow-citizens intolerable in a democracy. Broadly similar in British law is the difference between the infliction of grievous bodily harm and assault with intent to commit grievous bodily harm, in that assault with intent and *hybris* embrace the subjective as well as the objective aspect of the offence. **ἐπάγεσθαι** 'not to take upon myself a greater task than I could bear'. Ariston suggests that a public indictment (γραφή) would be a laborious task for a young man inexperienced in litigation (as he claims to be); he may also be suggesting the physical difficulty of arresting Conon (ἀπαγωγή), who on Ariston's account has beaten him within an inch of his life. In fact it is the danger (see below) not the difficulty of the task which acts as a deterrent. **ὑπὲρ τὴν ἡλικίαν** 'beyond [the capacity of a man of] my age', i.e. beyond the natural forensic abilities and acceptable ambitions of a young man. What Ariston fears is the resentment of the jurors at excessive ambition in a young man; cf. Lys. 16.20 ἤδη δέ τινων ἠισθόμην, ὦ βουλή, καὶ διὰ ταῦτ' ἀχθομένων μοι, ὅτι νεώτερος ὢν ἐπεχείρησα λέγειν ἐν τῶι δήμωι, Lys. 9.14. However, Ariston understandably suppresses three other deterrents. (1) If a person after using his right to ἀπαγωγή or instituting a γραφή failed to obtain one-fifth of the votes cast, he was fined 1,000 drachmas, and lost the right to bring the same type of action in the future. (2) The chances of successful prosecution were greater in an αἰκείας δίκη than in a ὕβρεως γραφή. In the former the plaintiff had only to prove the fact of assault; in the latter he had to convince the jury of the motives of the offender, for which the only evidence might be small subjective details such as gesture and tone of voice (cf. Dem. 21.72). (3) In an αἰκείας δίκη the plaintiff was awarded damages; in a ὕβρεως γραφή any fine was paid to the state. **ὦν ἐπεπόνθειν:** ἐκείνων ἅ ἐπεπόνθειν. περί is unnecessary; for the rare (causal) genitive with ἐγκαλεῖν cf. 36.9 and 37.33. **ἥδιστ' ἂν κτλ.** 'though I should have preferred most of all to bring him to trial on a capital charge'. For θανάτου cf. Xen. *Cyr.* 1.2.14 θανάτου κρίνουσι 'they try capital cases', Thuc. 3.57.3 θανάτου κρίνεσθαι 'to be on trial for our lives', Dem. 21.64 κρίσις θανάτου. The genitive may be explained either as an extension of the genitive of price found with τιμᾶν, τιμᾶσθαι, in the fixing of penalties, or as an extension of the genitive found with verbs of accusing etc. Had A. used either of the alternatives mentioned above he could have pressed for the death penalty.

2 τούτου: the passionate desire for Conon's blood indicated in the participial clause. Since this vehement hatred jars with the mild and tolerant character assumed by Ariston, he hastens to excuse himself. **ὕβρεως:** either genitive of comparison or genitive absolute. Though A. has brought an αἰκείας δίκη against Conon, he treats the incident throughout as a case of ὕβρις; the word αἴκεια is used only twice, §§ 1, 18 (in the latter passage without reference to the present action). A. thus imparts greater emotive power to his case, and also, perhaps, offers an implicit argument *a fortiori* – if Conon is guilty of ὕβρις, he must be guilty of the lesser crime of αἴκεια. **εὐνοϊκῶς ἀκοῦσαί μου:** *captatio benevolentiae*, a regular motif. Arist. *Rhet.* 1415a 35 lists τὸ εὔνουν ποιῆσαι (sc. τὸν ἀκροατήν) as one of the functions of the *prooimion*. Cf. e.g. Plat. *Ap.* 17c, Andoc. 1.9, Dem. 3.3, 9.3, 27.3 and esp. 45.1 ἱκετεύω καὶ ἀντιβολῶ πρῶτον μὲν εὐνοϊκῶς ἀκοῦσαί μου. This formula is not an empty artifice. Greek juries were vociferous in their approval or disapproval of a speaker. See Plat. *Rep.* 492b, *Leg.* 876b, Dem. 45.6 and cf. e.g. 57.1, 50. **εἶτα, ἐὰν κτλ.:** cf. 27.3, 45.1 εἶτ' ἐὰν ἀδικεῖσθαι δοκῶ, βοηθῆσαί μοι τὰ δίκαια. Such appeals for βοήθεια are common. τὰ δίκαια is internal object of βοηθῆσαι. The internal object is used to define more closely the action of intransitive verbs; so here, 'give me just aid'. **διὰ βραχυτάτων:** another formula. Cf. e.g. Lys. 24.4, Dem. 45.2 ἐξ ἀρχῆς δ' ὡς ἂν οἷός τ' ὦ διὰ βραχυτάτων εἰπεῖν πειράσομαι τὰ πεπραγμένα μοι πρὸς Φορμίωνα. Cf. on 39.27.

3–12 The second major subdivision of the speech, διήγησις, the account of the 'factual' details which form the basis of the speaker's case. Ariston's narrative is in two parts, §§ 3–6 prehistory of the alleged attack, §§ 7–12 the attack and its consequences. Aristotle (*Rhet.* 1356a) recognizes πάθος (emotion) as a form of proof. πάθος consists in inducing in the audience the emotional state necessary for persuasion, i.e. (in judicial oratory) sympathy for the speaker and resentment against his opponent. The account of events in Panactum (§§ 3–6) achieves the double aim of creating the desired emotion in the jury and offering a yardstick by which to judge the plausibility of the subsequent account of the attack in the agora. §§ 3–9 are quoted by Dion. Hal. *Dem.* 12 with enthusiastic approval.

3 ἔτος τουτὶ τρίτον: an extension of the use of the accusative to express duration of time; 'two years ago'. The more usual order would be τρίτον ἔτος τουτί. **εἰς Πάνακτον:** see speech intro., *Date.* **προγραφείσης:** used of the public posting of those required for military service; see Arist. *Ath. Pol.* 53.7, Ar. *Birds* 450. The phrasing of the sentence suggests that the φρουρά was a formal expedition, not part of ephebe training, for it implies that A. and Conon's sons could have found themselves posted for other types of service, whereas garrison duty was obligatory for ephebes. **ὡς οὐκ ἂν ἐβουλόμην:** sc. αὐτοὺς σκηνῶσαι. ἐβουλόμην (usually with ἄν) is often used to express an unrealized possibility which the speaker regards as preferable to the actual state of affairs. Trans.: 'and I wish it had been otherwise'. Cf. 21.78 τοῦτον οὐδ' εἰ γέγον' εἰδὼς οὐδὲ γιγνώσκων, ὡς μηδὲ νῦν ὤφελον. **ἀριστήσαιεν:** optative of indefinite frequency. **ὅλην:** emphasized by postponement. The behaviour of Conon's sons is clearly expected to horrify decent Athenian opinion. The normal time for such heavy drinking would be at a symposium after the evening meal; Conon's sons begin drinking after lunch, and drink all day every day. Worst of all, they are treating their guard duty as though it were a holiday. Drunkenness in ancient as in modern times could be viewed with indulgence or severity according to individual attitudes; see A. P. McKay, *Stud. D. M. Robinson* (St Louis 1953) 863–5. In oratory the attitude taken will depend upon the needs of the writer (cf. on 37.41 and 54.38). At 21.73f. (cf. 21.38, 180) Demosthenes judges drunken offences less culpable than those committed when sober. There it suits his purpose to stress by contrast the heinousness of Midias' actions; here, writing for the victim of (alleged) drunken behaviour, he not unnaturally takes a dim view of riotous drinking. Cf. further Arist. *Rhet.* 1402b 10f. **ὥσπερ ἐνθάδ' εἰώθειμεν:** i.e. μετρίως. A brief (and suitably modest) but effective parenthesis contrasting the virtuous Ariston with these models of depravity. We have only Ariston's statement (allusive at that) that his behaviour was commendable; no witnesses are called. For the vagueness cf. 36.42 (ὁρᾶν) τοῦτον δ' ὑβρίζοντα καὶ εἰς ἅπερ εἴωθεν ἀναλίσκοντα.

4 δειπνοποιεῖσθαι: the time when the average man might relax with wine. **ἦν . . . ὥραν , . . . ταύτην:** the accusative *may* imply duration (for ὥρα is 'time' not 'hour' in classical Greek), but is better explained as adverbial accusative, common with ὥρα (as with καιρός); cf. Eur. *Bacch.* 724 with Dodds' note. **συμβαίνοι:** optative again expressing indefinite frequency. The regularity of the misbehaviour of Conon's sons is expressed repeatedly through a variety of means which reinforce the speaker's point without inducing boredom; ἑκάστοτε, ὅλην, the indefinite temporal clauses ἐπειδὴ...ἀριστήσαιεν, ἦν...συμβαίνοι, the ἕως clause, the imperfect with ἄν expressing habit (ἄν...ἐπαρ-ῴνουν), the simple imperfects διετέλουν, ἔπινον, ἔτυπτον, κατεσκεδάν-νυον, προσεούρουν, ἀπέλειπον. **ὅ τι τύχοιεν:** sc. λέγοντες. 'They claimed that our slaves annoyed them with smoke when cooking and they took every remark as an insult' (lit. 'and claimed they were insulting them, whatever they said'). Doherty takes ὅ τι τύχοιεν with φήσαντες, explaining: 'any excuse was good enough'; i.e. φήσαντες ὅ τι τύχοιεν means 'uttering any excuse which came into their heads'. But we should expect καὶ ὅ τι τύχοιεν. **κατεσκεδάννυον . . . προσεούρ-ουν:** sc. on the slaves. **ἀπεπεμψάμεθα:** Sandys supplies ταῦτα – 'we dismissed [ignored] the matter'. Paley compares Eur. *Hec.* 72 ἀπο-πέμπομαι ἔννυχον ὄψιν; but there the verb means 'I seek to avert from myself' (Latin *abominor*), not 'dismiss'. It is better to supply αὐτούς – 'we sent them away' (How? With reasoned argument? Appeals? Threats? Blows?). Herschig's ἐμεμψάμεθα is attractive; 'we remonstrated with them' (better ἀπ- or ἐπεμεμψάμεθα). **οὐκ ἐγὼ τῶν ἄλλων ἔξω:** added to emphasize πάντες, κοινῆι. The words stress that Ariston was no prig unwilling to tolerate high spirits; others took the actions of Conon's sons seriously.

5 περὶ ὧν ὅλως ἐποίουν: broadens the scope of the misdemeanours – the offences against Ariston's mess belong to a general pattern of mis-behaviour. **εἰσεπήδησαν** 'burst in'; used of violent irruption as here 21.22, 78. **ταξιάρχους:** ten in all, commanders of the tribal hoplite contingents. We deduce that Ariston and Conon's sons were hoplites. **μηδ' αὐτοὺς ποιῆσαι:** sc. μηδὲν ἀνήκεστον. Ariston claims only sufficient spirit to distinguish his forbearance from cowardice. He allows that under this final provocation, insulted and struck, he might have retaliated with physical violence. αὐτούς is subject of ποιῆσαι. The addition of the negative with κωλύω is rare in Attic prose.

6 οὔτε λόγον ποιεῖσθαι 'to attach no weight / pay no attention to the incidents'. On Ariston's account, Conon's sons had exposed themselves either to a ὕβρεως γραφή, both for their assault on A. and their treatment of the slaves (the ὕβρεως γραφή covered offences against slaves, Aeschin. 1.16, Dem. 21.46–8, [Xen.] *Ath. Pol.* 1.10; probably this covered only offences against other people's slaves, since owners were in the habit of beating their slaves, e.g. Ar. *Clouds* 7, 58; the inclusion of slaves perhaps represents a protection of owners' rights rather than a concern for human rights), or an αἰκείας δίκη. As the law on *hybris* shows, the Athenians were acutely sensitive to affronts to personal dignity, and Ariston's tolerance is surprising (and suspicious – see below, *The story so far*). **ἐκεῖν'**: object of ἐγνώκειν, with εὐλαβεῖσθαι καὶ φυλάττεσθαι in apposition. **μετὰ ταῦθ'**: simply reinforces the temporal function of the participle παρασχόμενος. Circumstantial participles are often reinforced by adverbs and particles in this way. **τοῖς . . . ἁμαρτηθεῖσιν:** neuter; 'that the very man who should have criticized the original offences has himself taken the lead in committing far more serious crimes'. τὸ πρῶτον refers to the acts of Conon's sons on garrison duty; Conon as their father should have rebuked them, but instead he has taken the lead (πρότερος) in the assault on Ariston.

The story so far. There is no good reason to doubt A.'s statement that the ill-will between himself and Conon's sons dates back to their shared military service. The incident recorded in §§ 7–9 is therefore a continuation of hostilities. But is Ariston telling the truth about the behaviour of Conon's sons? The strategus could on his own authority imprison, fine or dismiss anyone guilty of a breach of discipline; see Arist. *Ath. Pol.* 61.2. We are nowhere told exactly what constituted a breach of discipline; Arist. says only τὸν ἀτακτοῦντα (one Simon was dismissed – ἐξεκηρύχθη – for arriving too late for the battle of Corinth and for striking a taxiarch, Lys. 3.45). Presumably the definition (and the punishment) varied with the character of the individual general and the demands of the situation in which he found himself. According to Ariston, Conon's sons were guilty of general misbehaviour in the camp; they were also permanently drunk on duty, and despite being censured by the general for their conduct they went on to insult and assault Ariston. Yet no action was taken against them. If the misdemeanours of Conon's sons were as blatant as A. claims, the strategus need not have been deterred from severity by the unpopularity of the decision, for he would have had many witnesses to the offences to support him should Conon's sons attack him when his conduct was examined at the εὔθυνα on the expiry of his command. It is of course possible that the strategus lacked the courage to punish them; but his failure to act looks suspicious. Also suspicious is Ariston's inaction on his return home. He had many witnesses, including the general and the taxiarchs, to verify his account of the actions of Conon's sons, in particular the blows he received. Yet he decided to let sleeping malefactors lie, though he could have brought an action for *aikeia* or even *hybris*. It is possible that Ariston's actions in camp were less virtuous than he claims, that what took place at Panactum was not the malicious persecution of a harmless young man by a group of thugs but a series of incidents between two groups of high-spirited youths. This suspicion could be laid to rest if we could be sure that among the depositions produced in support of the allegations there was a statement by the strategus. If there was, it is surprising that Ariston does not stress the fact.

7 ἑσπέρας: we are not told precisely the time of year or the time of night. The question is important, since it has a bearing on the range of vision and consequently on the reliability of all witnesses to the incident. We are told that the incident took place 'not long' after the return to Athens, but this could refer to any time from spring to winter depending on the time and duration of the garrison duty and the speaker's definition of 'not long'. Since Ariston wishes to stress the causal connection between the events at Panactum and the incident in Athens, he could describe an interval of six months as 'not long'. If the expedition to Panactum took place in the spring or summer of 357/343, the incident in the agora could belong to the spring, summer, autumn or winter of 357/343, or even early 356/342. See speech intro., *Date*.
Λεωκόριον: in the agora, but precise location uncertain. R. E. Wycherley, *The stones of Athens* (Princeton 1978) 63f., would identify this landmark with a small enclosure in the north-west corner of the agora where various offerings have been found which were clearly dedicated to one or more female deities or heroines. The Λεωκόριον was

said to be the monument or shrine of the daughters of Leos, who sacrificed themselves to save their country. It was near this spot that Hipparchus was slain by Harmodius and Aristogiton (Thuc. 1.20, 6.57). From later writers it appears to have become a popular spot (no doubt as a recognizable landmark) with prostitutes (Alciphr. 3.5.1, Theophylact. *Ep.* 12). **τῶν Πυθοδώρου** 'Pythodorus' premises'. Pythodorus ὁ σκηνίτης (presumably the same tradesman) is mentioned in Isoc. 17.33. The plural suggests a collection of booths (σκηναί). **ὡς ἂν μεθύων:** sc. διαλεχθείη. μεθύων = μεθύων τις, 'a drunkard'. For the substantival use of the participle without article or τις see Goodwin *MT* 330f.

Ariston's account of this meeting is surprisingly brief. He claims that the alleged assault was completely unprovoked. It is therefore important for him to demonstrate that this initial meeting passed without incident. Since Conon, as is clear from §31, is alleging that this meeting was the *only* encounter between Ariston and Ctesias, that the fight took place at this time, and that he (Conon) came upon Ctesias fighting with Ariston, it is important for Ariston to prove that this meeting actually took place. We may assume that Phanostratus at the end of §9 upheld Ariston's version (see speech intro. n. 5). But a more circumstantial account might be expected. Ariston gives cursory and evasive treatment to an important point, and we may suspect that he is concealing something, perhaps some act of provocation which would explain the subsequent attack.

Μελίτην: on the high ground to the south-west of the agora. **δ' ἄρ':** preferable to γάρ (SFQ) as *lectio difficilior*; inferential – 'as it turned out'. **ἔπινον . . . παρὰ Παμφίλωι τῶι γναφεῖ:** Athenians were in the habit of passing their spare time in the various shops (Lys. 24.20, Dem. 25.52). Ariston may mean that Conon and his friends were lounging in the fuller's shop, or that they were his guests at a formal symposium. It is noteworthy that Ariston says only ἔπινον (the characteristic failing of Conon's family according to Ariston), whereas Conon claims he was at dinner (§31). Idlers tended to pass much of their time in the agora, and the shops in this area probably attracted more than their share of ne'er-do-wells; if Pamphilus' shop attracted this element, there may be a particular point in the mention of his name. **Διότιμός τις:** the MSS offer Θεότιμός τις; but in §31 one of Conon's witnesses is called Διότιμος, and Mensching 308 n. 4 (see p. 70 n. 2) plausibly suggests that the same man is meant here and that Θεότιμος is a scribal error (influenced by Θεογένης below); cf. §§31 and 34, where Χαιρήτιος is corrupted in A to Χαιρέτιμος after Διότιμος. **Ἀρχεβιάδης:** see on §31. **Σπίνθαρος ὁ Εὐβούλου:** probably the son of the celebrated politician Eubulus. Eubulus' father was named Spintharus, and male offspring frequently bore the name of the paternal grandfather. **ἐξαναστήσας:** the passive, with the intransitive tenses of the active, is sometimes used of troops rushing from ambush (Thuc. 3.107, Xen. *Hell.* 4.8.37, Eur. *El.* 217); the aorist active may be so used here, of the one who signals for the attack from ambush (Sandys). The military metaphor suits a young man, and perhaps implies that the attack was premeditated.

8 τοῦ Φερρεφαττίου: temple of Persephone; Hesychius says Φερρε-φάττιον τόπος ἐν ἀγορᾷ, a note which may be drawn from the present passage. Wycherley, *The stones of Athens* 98 suggests a location close to the Eleusinion, which was south-east of the agora, on the Acropolis slope. If his location of the Pherrephattion and the Leokorion is correct, Ariston followed the route through the agora taken by the Panathenaic procession on its way from the Dipylon gate to the Acropolis. **πως** 'I suppose', 'roughly'. αὐτό perhaps implies that it was no coincidence that Ctesias and his comrades met them at the very spot where he had passed them earlier; i.e. they were waiting for Ariston to pass that way as he returned home. **ἀνεμείχθημεν:** another military metaphor; μείγνυμι and προσμείγνυμι are often used of troops joining battle. **ἐξέδυσαν:** presumably two of them held him while the third stripped him.

9 ὀνομάζειν ὀκνήσαιμ' ἄν: Arist. *Rhet.* 1408a 16–18, speaking of the need to adopt the correct tone for the subject matter in order to establish the plausibility of the narrative, observes: παθητικὴ δέ, ἐὰν μὲν ᾖ ὕβρις, ὀργιζομένου λέξις, ἐὰν δὲ ἀσεβῆ καὶ αἰσχρά, δυσχεραίνοντος καὶ εὐλαβουμένου καὶ λέγειν. The device creates a bond of sympathy between speaker and audience, the former a man too decent to utter filth and the latter too decent to hear it; it also exaggerates the grossness of what was said or done by allowing free play to the imagination; cf. 21.79 εἶτα τῆς ἀδελφῆς, ἔτ' ἔνδον τότε καὶ παιδὸς οὔσης κόρης, ἐναντίον ἐφθέγγοντ' αἰσχρὰ καὶ τοιαῦθ' οἷ' ἂν ἄνθρωποι τοιοῦτοι φθέγξαιντο (οὐ γὰρ ἔγωγε προαχθείην ἂν εἰπεῖν πρὸς ὑμᾶς τῶν τότε ῥηθέντων οὐδέν), Aeschin. 1.55. ὕβρεως . . . σημεῖον: as showing delight in the offence (MacDowell *Law* 132). τεκμήριον κτλ.: Conon's cock impersonation shows that he saw the victory as *his* and amounts (so Ariston concludes) to an admission that he was the ringleader. ἀλεκτρυόνας: cock-fighting was popular at Athens. According to Aelian (*VH* 2.28) it was institutionalized, fights taking place once yearly in the theatre of Dionysus. But the sport was not restricted to official contests; private meetings could be held at any time (Aeschin. 1.53). The victory chant described here is consistent with Ariston's account of the attack. Cocks fought with their feet, to which spurs (πλῆκτρα) were attached; Ariston has just been trampled into the mud. γυμνός: μονοχίτων (not literally naked); cf. Plat. *Rep.* 474a, Ar. *Clouds* 498. ᾤχοντο: this verb is regularly pluperfect in sense (i.e. ʻ *had* gone off'); if this is the sense here, it is natural to suppose that Conon and his friends had gone *before* these passers-by reached Ariston; certainly Ariston nowhere suggests that the passers-by intervened *to stop* the fight. See speech intro., *Ariston's action* and cf. on § 32. θοἰμάτιον λαβόντες μου: a not unusual occurrence; cf. Alexis fr. 107 καὶ γὰρ ἐπὶ κῶμον ⟨πλεῖστον⟩ ἀνθρώπων ὁρῶ | πλῆθος προσιόν, ὡς τῶν καλῶν τε κἀγαθῶν | ἐνθάδε συνόντων· μὴ γένοιτό μοι μόνωι | νύκτωρ ἀπαντῆσαι καλῶς πεπραγόσιν | ὑμῖν περὶ τὸν βαλλισμόν· οὐ γὰρ ἄν ποτε | θοἰμάτιον ἀπενέγκαιμι μὴ φύσας πτερά. βαλανεῖον: from § 10 it is clear that this refers to the public baths. It is surprising that a man who had been beaten should be taken to a public bath instead of being washed at home. The move argues a desire to procure witnesses to support a legal action; cf. Lys fr. 75.6, Dem. 47.67.

10 Εὐξίθεον τουτονί: indicates that Euxitheus was present in court. ἰατρόν: there is a surprising fluctuation in the number of doctors attending Ariston. The plural is used in §§ 1, 9, 36, the singular is used twice in § 10, once in § 11, twice in § 12, and nothing is said to indicate that a different doctor is intended in each case. It would seem that either only one doctor attended him, and he seeks to strengthen his case by exaggerating the number of expert judgements on the seriousness of his condition, or several doctors attended him, only one of whom was convinced that Ariston was close to death. ὑπὸ τούτων: Midias and Euxitheus could testify only to Ariston's condition, not to the perpetrator.

11 The generous space devoted to the medical evidence and Ariston's return to it in §36 indicate its importance to his case and its probable effect on the jury. The jurors may not have understood all that A. says, but they will have been impressed by his terminology, especially as it is supported by medical evidence. τῶν ἐν τῶι προσώπωι: probably to be taken with οἰδημάτων only; there is no good reason to supply with τῶν ἑλκῶν; A. suffered from swelling round his eyes and mouth (§8) and cuts and bruises elsewhere on his body. πυρετοὶ... συνεχεῖς 'continuous fever'. ἀλγήματα 'pains'. ἦτρου: the pit of the stomach. τῶν σιτίων ἀπεκεκλείμην 'was cut off from food', i.e. 'had lost my appetite'. Cf. Hipp. Int. 1, Vict. 3.81.

12 κάθαρσις αἵματος 'evacuation/discharge of blood', presumably by expectoration. αὐτομάτη 'spontaneous', as against 'induced'. ἀπορουμένωι: could be middle ('despairing') or passive ('despaired of'). κἂν ἔμπυος γενόμενος διεφθάρην 'I should have died from suppuration [of the lungs]'. Ariston's description suggests either a pneumonic infection resulting indirectly from beating or exposure (depending on the time of year at which the incident took place) or direct injury to a lung resulting from the blows, such as a broken rib puncturing and collapsing a lung. A.'s doctor may have connected his illness with the cold (the lungs are especially sensitive to cold, Hipp. Morb. 1.26), with the beating in general (physical strain can cause suppuration of the lungs, Morb. 1.14 and 15), or even with the blows to the head (D. Irmer, Medizin-Historisches Journal 2 (1967) 54–62 notes that wounds to the head can affect other parts of the body, Epid. 3.4). The text does not say. At Morb. 1.12 the symptoms of περιπλευμονίη are pains, fever, cough, loss of appetite. Irmer notes that at Progn. 17 the symptoms of ἐμπύημα are continuing fever, failure to expectorate, loss of appetite. A.'s account is thus at least consistent with contemporary medical experience. It is a great pity that the deposition is lost, for we should like to know whether the doctor regarded ἐμπύημα as a probable, possible or remote contingency. τὸ αἷμ' ἀποχωρῆσαν: the 'ab urbe condita' construction, 'the discharge of blood'; in apposition with τοῦτο. τῶν ἐπισκοπούντων 'my visitors'.

13 The sentence ὅτι... γεγενῆσθαι sums up all that has been said so far, and returns to the thoughts of the opening (this device whereby the end returns to the beginning, is known as 'ring-composition'; it creates a satisfying impression of completeness). Then begins the third major section of the speech, πίστεις (proof). **εἰς πᾶν ἐλθών** 'find oneself in gravest danger'; cf. εἰς τοὔσχατον ἦλθον §12. **ἀσέλγειαν:** denotes unbridled behaviour, here violence; the word in this context is virtually synonymous with ὕβρις. **ἀπὸ τῆς ὕβρεως κτλ.:** πειράσεσθαι and ἐρεῖν are in apposition to παρεσκευάσθαι, where we should expect a new sentence (ἀπὸ γὰρ τῆς ὕβρεως...πειράσεται, καὶ ἐρεῖ...). 'He will attempt to divert the issue from the outrage which was committed and reduce it to laughter and ridicule.' Cf. 10.75 τὸ πρᾶγμα εἰς γελῶτα καὶ λοιδορίαν ἐμβαλόντες. Arist. *Rhet.* 1419b cites the sophist Gorgias to the effect that serious arguments must be destroyed with humour and jokes with seriousness. Conon tries to make light of the incident, and A. stresses its seriousness.

14 Conon argues that the incident was merely a fight between members of rival street-gangs. **καλῶν κἀγαθῶν:** can be both a social and moral term; see Dover 41–5. Probably both senses are present here. Such youths (including presumably Conon's sons) belong to upright and well-to-do families. Conon's social position can be gauged from the company he keeps. Among his companions on the night in question (§7) were Spintharus, son of a successful politician, and Archebiades, who belonged to a propertied family, and himself took part in politics (see on §31). **ἰθυφάλλους:** lit. 'with erect penis', but the Greek word has a resonance absent from the translation. ἰθύφαλλος is used of (1) the phallus pole carried in fertility ritual, (2) a song and dance performed in such ritual, (3) those who participate in the ritual. From its use as a title below §17 we may infer that it was also the name of the fertility god embodied in the phallus pole. See in general Crat. fr. 14, Hyp. fr. 50, Semus of Rhodes ap. Athen. 622c, and the entries of Hesych. and Suda. The word later occurs as a title of the phallic god Priapus (Diod. 4.6), whose worship spread to Greece from Asia after Alexander. The word thus has connotations of sexual potency, of unrestrained language and behaviour, and perhaps verbal abuse such as we often find in fertility ritual. Trans. 'satyrs'. The choice of the name (implying the transfer into everyday life of the licence found in fertility ritual) indicates a desire to shock. Cf. the club mentioned in Lys. fr. 53, whose members, calling themselves κακοδαιμονισταί, made a point of dining on days of ill-omen. Cf. the Hell-fire clubs in England early in the eighteenth century. **αὐτοληκύθους:** a strange idea (first suggested by Zink in the last century) has gained ground in recent years, that this word has an obscene meaning ('all-penis'), primarily because of its proximity to ἰθυφάλλους. But in its only other fourth-century occurrence, αὐτολήκυθος has connotations not of obscenity but of poverty (Antiphanes, *Athamas* fr. 16 ἀξυνακόλουθος ξηρὸς αὐτολήκυθος); this is borne out by the glosses in Hesychius and Bekker's *Anecdota* 465, 17, and the use of the word by Plut. *Mor.* 2.50c and Lucian, *Lex.* 10 of a parasite. The suggested obscene nuance receives no support from Ar. *Frogs* 1200ff., where an obscene meaning has been suggested for ληκύθιον, wrongly; see J. Henderson, *HSCP* 76 (1972) 133ff. αὐτολήκυθος (for the formation cf. αὐτόδαιτος) means lit. 'carrying one's own oil-flask' (to the baths), a task normally performed by a slave (cf. the use of βαλανεύω, Ar. *Peace* 1103). The title again expresses contempt for social norms. Despite the democratic political system, the Athenians retained their respect for wealth and position; it would offend against this prejudice for wealthy youths to ape the behaviour of the poor. The absence of servants would also mean the absence of the restraint occasioned by witnesses (Sandys). Trans.: 'down-and-outs', 'tramps', (American) 'bums'. **ἐκ τούτων:** with τινες. **ἑταιρῶν:** from ἑταίρα, not ἑταῖρος, as the accent makes clear. **νέων ἀνθρώπων:** characterizing genitive (a specialized use of the possessive genitive); 'this belongs to [i.e. is characteristic of / typical of / is what we expect from] young men'. **ἡμᾶς δὲ πάντας τοὺς ἀδελφούς** 'all us brothers', 'myself and all my brothers'. Ariston's brothers reappear briefly in §44. If they were present at Panactum, and if they deposed in §6, the reference to them here will have been less abrupt for the jury than it is for us. The alternative interpretation here, 'he will represent all of us as the Brothers...', i.e. a gang name, is unlikely in view of §44. **παροίνους:** denotes not merely drunkenness but riotous behaviour while drunk (cf. ἐπαρῴνουν §4). With παροίνους καὶ ὑβριστάς Conon may mean simply that Ariston indulges in such behaviour, or that Ariston started the fight (see on §17); Ariston is unclear on this point, perhaps deliberately so. **κατασκευάσει:** pejorative; the word often connotes fabrication. **ἀγνώμονας . . . καὶ πικρούς** 'unreasonable and vindictive'. They can inflict violence but not suffer it; they lack the spirit of give-and-take needed for such behaviour.

15–25 Ariston's reply. Only §§ 15–17 directly answer Conon's claim.

15 οὐχ ἧττον . . .ὑβρίσθαι νομίσαιμι: Ariston has been subjected to physical ὕβρις from Conon; he would regard it as a fresh outrage if Conon were allowed to prejudice the jury by blackening Ariston's character. **εἰ οἷόν τ' εἰπεῖν** apologizes for the use of such strong terms to describe the jury's behaviour. **ὥσθ' . . .ὄφελος:** Ariston makes a reasonable point, that the jury should not accept unsubstantiated assertions, especially where decent men (the μέτριοι) are at risk. Ariston clearly regards himself as one of the μέτριοι. However, he offers no proof of his μετριότης. His indignant assertion here is a skilful use of the moral attitudes of the jury to mask a complete lack of objective evidence. **ὁ πλησίον:** sc. ὤν, 'my neighbour'. **τοῦ . . .καθ' ἡμέραν βίου καὶ τῶν ἐπιτηδευμάτων** 'their daily life and character'.

16 οὔτε παροινοῦντες οὔθ' ὑβρίζοντες: the reply echoes the allegation. Ariston in fact simply counters assertion with assertion. **οὐδ' ἄγνωμον κτλ.:** neatly twists Conon's point that Ariston is ἀγνώμων in taking part in fights without being prepared to accept the risks; 'nor do we think we are behaving at all unreasonably, if we expect to receive lawful satisfaction for the wrongs we have suffered'. **περὶ ὧν ἠδικήμεθ'** 'concerning the wrongs we have suffered' (περὶ ἐκείνων ἃ ἠδικήμεθα). **ἰθυφάλλοις . . .καὶ αὐτοληκύθοις:** predicate. Conon argues that Ariston and Conon's sons belong to street-gangs. Ariston however accepts only that Conon's sons belong to such gangs; Conon has offered Ariston an excellent tool for character assassination. **εἰς Κόνωνα . . . τρέπεσθαι:** of the recoiling of ill-omened words or unholy acts upon the person responsible (more usually εἰς κεφαλήν τινι), as Ar. *Peace* 1063, *Lys.* 915, Dem. 19.130.

17 γάρ: explains the pious prayer which precedes. **οἱ τελοῦντες ἀλλήλους τῶι Ἰθυφάλλωι** 'these are the ones who initiate each other into the worship of Ithyphallus'. For the dative of the god or power involved see LSJ s.v. τελέω III. From what follows we are meant to conclude that these rites were indecent. A. envisages a mock-religious ceremony. This flouting of religion seems to have been typical of high-spirited young men in Athens; cf. the κακοδαιμονισταί (above

§14), the profanation of the mysteries in which Alcibiades was impli-
cated (Thuc. 6.27), and the alleged behaviour of Conon as a youth
(below §39). Ariston in contrast adopts (and thereby manipulates) the
piety of the average man. **ἃ . . . λέγειν:** for this device see on §9. **μή τί
γε δή:** μή τί γε and μή τί γε δή mean 'let alone', 'not to mention';
in origin the phrase is elliptical (a verb of saying is omitted). MSS have
μή ὅτι γε δή, but μή ὅτι / οὐχ ὅτι...ἀλλά is a stereotyped phrase
meaning 'not only...but...'. **ἀνθρώπους μετρίους:** such as A. and
the jury; the position is emphatic.

17–19 A. proceeds to show that there is no excuse in law for Conon's
crime. Conon is not in fact seeking to justify his own conduct but
arguing (a) that he was not involved, (b) that the whole incident was
just a case of youthful high spirits. The long account of legal remedies
is offered as an argument *a fortiori* – if the law does not allow pleas of
necessity (ἀναγκαῖαι προφάσεις), i.e. defence on the grounds of
mitigating circumstances, there can be no excuse for Conon's crime. But
one suspects that one purpose of the digression is to obscure the fact
that A. has no adequate reply to the allegation that he is a young roué.

17 οἱ μὲν γὰρ νόμοι: resumed in §20 ἐν μὲν τοῖς νόμοις. **ἀνάγκη γὰρ
κτλ.:** Aristophanes based a whole comedy (*Wasps*) on the lawcourts,
and he clearly expected an audience of average Athenians to understand
references to, and parodies of, court procedures, speechmaking, and
legal actions. Any Athenian who had served on a jury would have some
knowledge of the law, as would the relatives of such men from private
conversation (cf. 59.110). Equally, one supposes that litigants told their
friends about actions in which they were involved. But the Athenian
approach to the law remained essentially amateurish. Obvious experience in speaking and familiarity with the law were viewed with
suspicion, as suggesting a litigious nature. Ariston therefore prefaces his
account with the disclaimer that he was forced to research into the laws
because of Conon, and he introduces into his account words which
suggest unfamiliarity with the subject, φασί, ἀκούω, οἶμαι. Cf. 56.14 and
on 39.1. **κακηγορίας δίκαι:** actions for slander. Slander in Athens
covered not only defamation in general but specific accusations which
were forbidden, such as murder, desertion in battle, assault on parents;

see in general Lys. 10. The penalty was 500 drachmas (Lys. 10.12);
no offence was committed if the accusation was true (Lys. 10.23, 30,
Dem. 23.50).

18 λοιδορούμενοι τύπτειν ἀλλήλους προάγωνται: cf. 40.32 ἐξ ἀντι-
λογίας καὶ λοιδορίας πληγὰς συναψάμενος. **πάλιν αἰκείας εἰσί:** sc.
δίκαι. **ὅταν ἥττων ᾖ** 'when he is losing'. **τραύματος . . .γραφαί:** cases
of deliberate wounding were tried by the Areopagus. Wounding was a
γραφή (public suit), slander and assault were δίκαι (private suits). In
private suits only the person wronged could sue; offences covered by
γραφαί were deemed to affect the community, and prosecution was
open to ὁ βουλόμενος, any individual not barred by specific laws (some
actions could only be brought by citizens) or general disability (such
as *atimia*) who chose to initiate proceedings. **τοῦ μὴ . . .φόνους γίγνεσθαι:** the gen. of the articular inf. is used to express purpose (esp.
common in Thuc.); 'so that wounds may not lead to murder'. Cf. τοῦ
μὴ φόνον γίγνεσθαι κτλ. below.

19 προεώραται: προ- = 'before', 'rather than'. 'The least of these
offences…has been provided for, to avoid the ultimate and most
serious offence.' Cf. Isoc. 20.8. **τοῦ προστυχόντος** 'anybody at all', i.e.
'the individual'; 'that these crimes should not be judged by individual
anger or whim'. This claim that access to judicial redress prevents an
escalation of violence by removing the right (and the onus) to punish
from the individual has much in common with Aeschylus' depiction of
the creation of homicide courts in *Eumenides*.

20 ἰθύφαλλοι κτλ. 'we are a band of satyrs [lit. 'satyrs banded
together'] and in our love affairs [or 'because we are in love'] we beat
and throttle anyone we choose'. Ariston skilfully distorts Conon's
argument while retaining most of the individual elements. (1) The fights
between rival lovers (§14) have disappeared; Conon is represented as
claiming the right as a lover to assault at random. (2) Conon's
statement that *his son* belongs to such a gang has become an admission
that *Conon* too is a member. (3) Ariston here omits Conon's allegation
that Ariston is a libertine; A. is now a random victim of irrational
violence. **εἶτα:** expresses indignation, as often.

To counteract Conon's lighthearted approach, A. juxtaposes his own version of events. In contrast to the earlier narrative the present passage is more obviously emotive; we have the tricolon crescendo εἱλκόμην – ἐξεδυόμην – ὑβριζόμην, the pointed contrast ὑγιὴς ἐξελθὼν φοράδην ἦλθον οἴκαδε, the verb ἐξεπεπηδήκει ('rushed out', much stronger than ἐξέρχομαι), the comment ὡσπερανεὶ τεθνεῶτός τινος (contrast §9 where no comment was offered). In the narrative Ariston was stating 'facts'; here he is interpreting them; and the more serious he can make them appear the stronger his case.

εἱλκόμην κτλ.: the aorist represents an event as completed, the imperfect as in progress. The imperfect in narrative is thus more vivid.
ὥστε κτλ.: since this was not mentioned in the διήγησις, nor were any neighbours called to testify, we may perhaps dismiss this as invention.

21 δίκαιον: the strict letter of the law, as against equity. Strict justice recognizes no plea in defence of *hybris*, though leniency might be shown in certain cases. **εἰ δ' ἄρ'** 'if indeed', 'if at all'; see Denniston *GP* 37f.
δι' ἡλικίαν 'those who are prompted by youth to commit any such offence'. Cf. Lys. 24.17 καὶ οἱ μὲν νέοι συγγνώμης ἀξιοῦνται τυχεῖν παρὰ τῶν πρεσβυτέρων, τοῖς δὲ πρεσβυτέροις ἐξαμαρτάνουσιν ὁμοίως ἐπιτιμῶσιν ἀμφότεροι. **τούτοις**: resumes τοῖς πράττουσιν; not redundant but emphatic ('it is for *these*...'). **ἀποκεῖσθαι** 'be reserved'. **ἀλλ' εἰς τὸ τῆς προσηκούσης ἐλάττω**: sc. δίκην δοῦναι. Conon in fact is not claiming leniency for himself; he is stressing his son's youth (cf. §14) and claiming for *Ctesias* the indulgence granted to the young.

22 νεωτέροις ἀνθρώποις καὶ τούτοις υἱέσιν: Ariston is thinking solely of Ctesias, but uses the plural to generalize Conon's actions. **οὐχ ὅπως...ἀλλ'** 'not only did he not...but', a common idiom, in origin elliptical (οὐ λέγω ὅπως). **ἡγεμὼν καὶ πρῶτος καὶ πάντων βδελυρώτατος**: Demosthenes often arranges adjectives and substantives in a series of three. **οὐδ' ἀποθανόντ'**: sc. ἀξίαν ἂν δίκην τοῦτον ὑποσχεῖν. It is a regular practice of Demosthenes to answer his own rhetorical questions. For the desire for Conon's death cf. §1. It would be naive to suppose that A. seriously believes that Conon should die; if he did, he would have brought an action for *hybris*. A. is seeking to arouse indignation in the jury (πάθος), in order to induce them to vote first for conviction and then for the heavier of the proposed penalties. Cf. e.g. 21.21 δείξω πολλῶν θανάτων, οὐχ ἑνὸς ὄντ' ἄξιον (though we know that Demosthenes dropped the case). **παρεστηκότος τούτου**: this is Conon's claim; A. counters that Conon is guilty even on his own version of the facts, since he was responsible for Ctesias' upbringing.

23 προῆκται: middle, 'has trained them', 'has disposed them' (lit. 'has led them to such a point that...'; cf. 6.2); if change were needed, προεῖται 'has neglected/abandoned' would serve. **ἐφ' ὧν ἐνίοις** = ἐπὶ τούτων ὧν ἐνίοις, 'in the case of acts for some of which the penalty prescribed is death'. **ἐγὼ μὲν γὰρ κτλ.**: Ariston works on the simple principle 'like father like son'. If Conon's sons do not respect their father that shows that Conon did not respect *his* father. This is illogical, but effective; A. attempts to create prejudice by suggesting that Conon lacks filial piety; see on 39.31. **εἰ γὰρ κτλ**. 'for if Conon (αὐτός) had honoured and feared his father (ἐκεῖνον), he would have demanded that his sons (τούτους) too honour and fear him (αὐτόν)'.

24 ἀπράγμονες 'unassuming', 'retiring', 'inoffensive'. The ἀπράγμων minds his own business and avoids trouble (a common meaning of πράγματα), including litigation. Contrast 39.1 φιλοπραγμοσύνη (see note ad loc.). Aristophanes (*Wasps* 1040f.) contrasts οἱ ἀπράγμονες with sycophants. A. anticipates a possible objection; if the case is so serious, why has he brought an αἰκείας δίκη?

25 παθεῖν τι: a common euphemism for death; cf. e.g. 45.75, Ar. *Wasps* 385. **φόνου**: the penalty for unintentional homicide, which was tried at the Palladium, was exile; the penalty for intentional homicide, which was tried by the Areopagus, was death. Since A. speaks only of the Areopagus here and in § 28, he clearly envisages his relatives prosecuting Conon for intentional homicide. The definition of intentional homicide was broader in Athenian than in modern law (J. H. Loomis, *JHS* 92 (1972) 86ff.; cf. on 37.58); it included cases where the perpetrator intended only to injure but in fact kills, cases which we would class as manslaughter. **τὸν γοῦν κτλ.**: the precedent cited by Ariston offers an argument *a fortiori*, for according to Ariston the defendant was 'admittedly' guilty only of incitement, not personal participation as in Conon's case. According to Ariston the offence consisted solely in encouraging the assailant to strike. It is difficult to know what charge the priestess's father faced. McDowell *AHL* 67f. suggests τραῦμα ἐκ προνοίας (intentional wounding), since for this offence the penalty was exile (cf. ἐξέβαλεν). But it is difficult to see why a charge of wounding was brought if the victim died. Loomis suggests that the charge was βούλευσις of intentional homicide (incitement or conspiracy); ἐξέβαλεν would not be literally true, but would mean that the accused availed himself of the right granted to defendants in homicide trials to go into exile after the first speech, instead of waiting for the second speech on each side and the jury's verdict. But there is no good evidence that the Areopagus tried cases of βούλευσις. The answer may be that A. is not telling the whole truth. The priestess's father was charged with intentional homicide; it was only the defendant and his friends who 'admitted' that he did not touch the dead man; again ἐξέβαλεν is a succinct way of saying that the defendant fled after his first speech. Precedents in Greek trials are cited from memory, not from law-books, and by people with a vested interest. Cf. the distortion of Aeschin. 1.173 ὑμεῖς, ὦ Ἀθηναῖοι, Σωκράτην μὲν τὸν σοφιστὴν ἀπεκτείνατε, ὅτι Κριτίαν ἐφάνη πεπαιδευκώς. γοῦν 'at least', 'at any rate'. τὸν . . . τῆς Βραυρωνόθεν ἱερείας πατέρ': it is not unusual, when precedents are cited, for attention to be drawn to circumstances, attributes or achievements (offices held, birth etc.) which might have offered the convicted man a claim on the mercy of the court, the aim being to strengthen the argument a fortiori; cf. 59.117, 34.50. 'The priestess at [lit. 'from'] Brauron' was the priestess of Artemis Brauronia. The Brauronia, held every four years, was primarily a women's festival; its distinctive feature was the ceremony in which young girls danced the part of bears.

26–9 Conon's behaviour at the arbitration. It is common for the litigant to use his opponent's behaviour during the early stages of litigation as evidence that the opponent has no confidence in the strength of his own case. With Conon's attempts at delay cf. 21.84, 27.49ff., 28.1, 40.43. Since this is a common device, and one which it suited the litigant's interests to employ, we cannot always be sure that he is telling the truth. Ariston does however have one or more witnesses (§29).

Arbitration in Athens took two forms, public (a state-appointed arbitrator; all Athenians had to serve as public arbitrators during their fifty-ninth year, Arist. *Ath. Pol.* 53.4) and private (that is, privately agreed on by both parties). In the case of public arbitrators the litigant could appeal, and the case would be tried by jury. The decision of the private arbitrator was final. In the present passage we have a public arbitrator.

26 ἔξω μέσων νυκτῶν 'beyond midnight'; the plural used of a single night is common from Homer onwards. **οὔτε τὰς μαρτυρίας κτλ.**: the depositions which Conon has drawn up, or should have drawn up. By holding up the proceedings Conon made it impossible to give judgement. **ἀντίγραφα** 'copies' (of the depositions). **τῶν . . . παρόντων ἡμῖν** 'those appearing for me', 'my witnesses'; cf. 59.48. **καθ' ἕν** = ἕκαστον; cf. 2.24, 9.22. The idiom represents a blend of e.g. τῶν παρόντων ἕκαστον and τοὺς παρόντας καθ' ἕνα. **οὑτωσί** 'simply', 'merely'; cf. 39.27. **λίθον**: restored from Harpocration; ousted in MSS by the gloss βωμόν. Arist. *Ath. Pol.* 55.5 speaks of the stone 'at which also the arbitrators swear before giving their judgements and the witnesses swear to their depositions'. Witnesses did not automatically take an oath, but they could choose to swear an oath in support of their testimony. From the present passage and 45.58 it seems that at arbitration either party could compel his opponent's witnesses to take an oath (so, perhaps, at the trial, 52.28). **ἐξ ἑταίρας εἶναι παιδίον αὐτῶι τοῦτο καί:** MSS. There is no reason to alter (to καὶ τοῦτο or τοῦτο δέ). We expect τοῦτον (sc. Κτησίαν), subj. of εἶναι, but οὗτος is often attracted to the gender of the complement; 'that this was his son by a casual mistress and...' Ariston regards this as irrelevant (οὐδὲν πρὸς τὸ πρᾶγμα), but Conon was perhaps anticipating Ariston's argument (§23) that Conon is to blame for the behaviour of his sons. Conon argues that as Ctesias is a bastard he was not admitted to Conon's oikos, so that Conon was not re-sponsible for his education. The claim need not be true. **καὶ πεπονθέναι τὰ καὶ τά:** refers to Ctesias, not Conon (Westermann), which would be obscure without αὐτόν or the like. The original demonstrative force of the article survives in Attic in a number of idiomatic usages; ὁ καὶ ὁ is used to refer vaguely to a number of persons or things instead of listing them (cf. e.g. Lys. 1.23 ἀφικνοῦμαι ὡς τὸν καὶ τόν, 'I called on various people'); trans. 'and that he had been treated in such and such a way'. Conon may be arguing (1) that Ctesias deserves mercy because he has had a difficult life (appeals for pity are standard in Athenian trials), or (2) that Ctesias has 'suffered various things' at the hands of Ariston (i.e. either on the night in question or on previous occasions

Ariston has insulted, assaulted or humiliated Ctesias), (3) Ctesias too
has endured rough treatment from other youths, and this is normal for
young men in Athens, or (4) Ctesias sustained injuries during the fight.
Conon is not simply wasting time. τελευτῶντες 'finally'; the
participles of τελευτάω and ἄρχομαι are often used where we would use
an adverb. αὐτοὶ οὗτοι ἑαυτούς: sc. ἐμίσουν.

27 δ' οὖν: resumptive, 'anyway'. **ποτ'** 'eventually'. **προκαλοῦνται**
'they issued a formal challenge'. Formal challenges (προκλήσεις) figure
prominently in Athenian private litigation. They could take various
forms, a challenge to the opponent to carry out an obligation or observe
its execution by the challenger (cf. 56.13), a challenge to submit or
accept an oath (cf. §40 and 39.2), a challenge to the opponent to submit
his own slaves for interrogation or to agree to the interrogation of the
challenger's slaves (cf. on 37.27, 40f.). Challenges and counter-
challenges are usually no more than manoeuvres intended to give the
litigant a moral advantage in court. Conon offered some slaves of his
(i.e. his attendants on the night in question) for interrogation, to
provide evidence for the trial. The evidence of slaves was only
admissible if extracted under torture. Harrison II 147 observes that there
is no instance in the orators of such a challenge being both accepted
and carried out. The challenge itself was admissible as evidence, and
Conon can use Ariston's refusal to accept it as evidence of the weakness
of Ariston's case. Probably this, rather than a desire for delay, was the
reason for the πρόκλησις. **(ἐπὶ) τῶι μὴ σημανθῆναι τοὺς ἐχίνους** 'to
prevent the sealing of the urns'. At the completion of public arbitration,
if one of the litigants appealed against the arbitrator's decision, all
documentary evidence produced was placed in two urns (one for
prosecution, one for defence); these were sealed, and the arbitrator's
decision recorded; no other evidence could be produced in court (*Ath.
Pol.* 53.2). A.'s point is that by causing delay Conon gains time to
assemble evidence to support his weak case. **ἐθέλειν ἐκδοῦναι περὶ τῶν
πληγῶν παῖδας** 'offering to hand over [lit. 'that they were willing to
hand over'] slaves [for examination] concerning the assault'. **τῶι
δικαίωι τούτωι** 'this argument'. **τῆς διαίτης ἀποφαινομένης:** the word
δίαιτα is used of the arbitrator's decision as well as the process of
arbitration.

28 τὸν πρῶτον πατάξαντα: since A. says πρῶτον, not πρότερον (contrast 47.40, Lys. 4.11) he is probably again accusing Conon of being the ringleader (cf. §33) rather than referring to the formula defining guilt in cases of αἴκεια (ὃς ἂν ἄρξηι χειρῶν ἀδίκων πρότερος 47.40 etc.). **τῶν ἐξ Ἀρείου πάγου:** the modern notion that jurors should as far as possible be ignorant of the issue to be tried was alien to the Greeks. Thus we find soldiers trying cases of desertion and failure to perform military service (see on 39.17). With the present passage cf. Lys. 7.22.

29 εἰ δ' ἄρ' ἠγνόησε ταῦτα: Conon can reply (1) that he did not know the extent of Ariston's injuries, (2) that he did not know that A. was accusing *him* and not Ctesias. A. pre-empts this reply. **οὐ παρεσκευ-άσατ':** the negative in εἰ-clauses is μή, but οὐ is sometimes used, (1) as the negative in statements of fact (a) where εἰ is causal, as after expressions of surprise, where εἰ virtually = ὅτι, (b) where the conditional clause amounts to a quotation of a statement either by the speaker or by someone else (so here, ὡς νῦν φήσει); (2) where the neg. coheres so closely with another word, such as φημί, ἐάω, as to form a single notion (as e.g. Lys. 13.62 οὐ πολλοί = ὀλίγοι). **ἀνεστηκώς** 'having quit my bed', 'when I was up and about'. Cf. 59.58. **ἐν τῆι πρώτηι συνόδωι** 'as soon as we met before the arbitrator' rather than 'at the first meeting with the arbitrator', for §26 suggests that the arbitration only lasted one day. **μαρτυρίαν:** this deposition is included because it was drafted before the completion of the arbitration.

30 περὶ μὲν τοίνυν κτλ.: ταῦτα is object of μέμνησθε, and is explained by τὴν ὥραν, the clause ὧν ἕνεκ' κτλ., and τοὺς χρόνους, all in apposition. **ὧν ἕνεκ' ἐκκρούων:** pleonastic, for delay (ἔκκρουσις) was Conon's motive (ὧν ἕνεκα). The pleonasm gives emphasis (Sandys) – 'his evasive motive in doing this'.

31 The account of Conon's behaviour at arbitration leads naturally to the refutation of his witnesses (§§31–7). The refutation takes two forms, arguments from εἰκός (probability) and character assassination. **οὓς οὐδ' ὑμᾶς ἀγνοήσειν οἴομαι:** implies that these men were notorious; cf. on 39.2. Ariston quotes Conon's deposition verbatim; it is striking (and perhaps significant – see speech intro., *Ariston's action*) that he does not quote his own deposition in answer but paraphrases. **Ἀρχεβιάδης:**

his brother Anaschetus appears as one of the guarantors of the ships for Chalcis, 341/0 (Davies 26, *IG* II² 1623) and Archebiades himself took part in politics (Plut. *Phoc.* 10). **ἀπιέναι** 'were coming from dinner'; cf. on 39.13. **ἀπὸ δείπνου:** see on §7.

32 ὡς ὑμᾶς . . .πιστεύσοντας: the accusative absolute, regular with the participle of impersonal verbs, is sometimes used with personal verbs, usually with ὡς or ὥσπερ. **ἄν:** with ἠθέλησαν; ἄν tends towards the beginning of the sentence. **Νικήρατος:** this may be the Niceratus of Dem. 21. 168, great-grandson of the fifth-century general Nicias. **διαρρήδην μεμαρτυρήκασιν κτλ.:** see speech intro., *Ariston's action.* **ἀγνῶτες ὄντες:** and therefore unlikely to lie for his sake; we cannot assess the veracity of this claim. **κἀπὸ ταὐτομάτου** 'by chance'; cf. 56.14. **πεπονθότα:** the tense suggests that the witnesses arrived on the scene after the event; contrast τυπτόμενον κτλ. above and cf. on §9 ᾤχοντο. **μὴ παθών:** μή because the participle is conditional. **εἰσιέναι:** sc. εἰς τὸ δικαστήριον.

33 τί γὰρ ἄν: sc. τοῦτο ποιοίην. **φαίνεται:** sc. ἀληθῆ ὄντα; 'is true and patently so'. **μὴ παρασχομένωι:** conditional; 'if he had not provided'. **λόγος:** cf. 37.24. **ἑαλωκέναι . . .ὑπῆρχε:** note tense; 'it was open for him to be convicted [once for all]', 'he would have found himself convicted'. This sentence suggests that the arbitrator found for Conon. **συμπόται:** unlike his own witnesses, who are strangers to him. Again A. stresses Conon's addiction to drink. **εἰ δ' ἔσται κτλ.:** a remarkably clumsy sentence, which would be much improved by the deletion of the first πρᾶγμα – 'if such behaviour is to be allowed etc.' **εἰ . . .οὐδέν:** οὐ regularly replaces μή after δεινόν ἐστι, θαυμάζω etc.; cf. on §29.

34–7 Conon's friends claim to be men of rigid austerity, but in reality they are rogues.

34 ἀλλὰ νὴ Δί': this phrase (sometimes simply ἀλλά) is often used to introduce a statement or objection which the speaker intends to demolish. 'Oh, but of course, they are not that sort.' **ἴσασιν . . .πολλοί:** cf. οὐδ' ὑμᾶς ἀγνοήσειν οἴομαι §31 and see on 39.2. **ἐσκυθρωπάκασιν** 'wear a grim expression'; for the verb, and the whole context, cf. 45.68 οὐδ' ἃ πέπλασται οὗτος καὶ βαδίζει παρὰ τοὺς τοίχους ἐσκυθρωπακώς,

σωφροσύνης ἄν τις ἡγήσαιτ' εἰκότως εἶναι σημεῖα, ἀλλὰ μισανθρωπίας.
See also Eur. *Hipp*. 952ff., Juvenal 2.3 (drawn to our attention by
Prof. Kenney). **λακωνίζειν φασί** 'claim to play the Spartan'.
τρίβωνας...ἁπλᾶς: the τρίβων was a short, coarse cloak, worn by
poorer Athenians (e.g. Isae. 5.11), and associated with the Spartans
(Plut. *Nic*. 19, Athen. 12.535e). Plat. *Prot*. 342b speaks of the λακωνί-
ζοντες who βραχείας ἀναβολὰς φοροῦσιν. ἁπλαῖ were thin-soled shoes
(i.e. one thickness of leather). Admiration of Sparta and imitation of
Spartan habits was not uncommon among wealthy Athenians, even
after Leuctra. The clothing described would give scant protection
against the elements, and would be the most obvious way to create an
impression of austerity. Plutarch's description of Archebiades (*Phoc*.
10), πώγωνά τε καθειμένος ὑπερφυῆ μεγέθει καὶ τρίβωνα φορῶν ἀεὶ καὶ
σκυθρωπάζων is largely derived from the present passage. **συλλεγῶσιν:**
i.e. at night.

35 νεανικά 'youthful', hence 'spirited', here ironic; νεανικός/νεανίας
is coupled with λαμπρός as here 18.313, 21.131. **ἑταίρων...καὶ φίλων:**
characterizing gen.; 'isn't that what friends and comrades are for?'
There was a proberb κοινὰ τὰ τῶν φίλων; cf. e.g. Eur. *Andr*. 376f.
ἑταίρων is probably meant to suggest that Conon and friends belong
to a ἑταιρεία; members of political clubs helped each other in litigation;
see G. M. Calhoun, *Athenian clubs in politics and litigation* (Austin 1913)
ch. 3. Since the allegation recurs 21.139, 58.42 (cf. the description of
Boeotus' supporters 39.2, 40.9), we may recognize a commonplace. It
is in the speaker's interest to represent his opponent's witnesses, friends,
συνήγοροι or advisers as part of a conspiracy to pervert justice.
παρέξεται: sc. Ariston; 'what is there in the evidence he will provide
against you that is really (καί) to be feared?' **μηδ':** οὐ plus inf. is the
rule in indirect statement, but μή is often used with verbs denoting
asseveration, belief, confidence; so §31 above μὴ πατάξαι Κόνωνα
'Αρίστωνα. **ἦφθαι:** subject 'Αρίστωνα – 'that he was not even
touched'. **ἐρράφθαι:** this is the first we have heard of stitches, but this
detail may have been included in the doctor's evidence. **τὴν κεφαλήν:**
accusative of the part affected; 'we shall say that you had your head
or some other part of your body fractured'.

Ariston's account of the dishonesty of Conon's friends carries conviction through the vividness of direct statement; in fact no evidence is

offered to show that Conon and his friends belong to a ἑταιρεία nor that any such conversation took place. The conversation is pure fiction; Ariston has quoted Conon's witnesses verbatim, and we know that they testify only that Conon did not strike Ariston; they nowhere suggest that A. beat or stripped Conon.

36 ἰατρούς: see on § 10. **τοῦτ'**: sc. medical evidence. **ὅσα . . .μὴ δι' αὐτῶν**: sc. μαρτυροῦσιν. **ὅση καὶ οἷα** 'the extent and character of their readiness'. **τὸ ὕδωρ**: refers to the water-clock; see Introduction 6.

37 τοίχους . . .διορύττοντες καὶ παίοντες τοὺς ἀπαντ.: summarizes the offences attested in the depositions. We can acquit Conon's friends of the first offence. τοιχωρύχοι (housebreakers) were among the villains classed as κακοῦργοι. If caught in the act they were liable to ἀπαγωγή to the Eleven (see on § 1); if they confessed they were executed, if not they were tried and if convicted executed (Arist. *Ath. Pol.* 52.1). Clearly Conon's friends were never convicted of housebreaking. As to the second charge we do not know (1) whether the depositions cite convictions or simply make allegations (true or false), (2) how many witnesses there were (3) whether the depositions relate to recent acts or offences committed in youth (as in § 14). Probably we have here the kind of serious accusations which Athenian litigants hurl with gay abandon, as e.g. 36.45, 45.79, Andoc. 1.124ff. **γραμματειδίωι**: the diminutive is disparaging (cf. 56.1), 'a scrap of paper'; perjury is a mere trifle for such hardened criminals. **φιλαπεχθημοσύνης** 'viciousness'; coupled with ὠμότης and μισανθρωπία by Isoc. 15.315. **ἀναιδείας** 'unscrupulousness'. **οὐχ οἷοί τε κτλ.**: should not be taken seriously; cf. 21.131.

38–41 It was usual for defendants to bring their children into court to excite the pity of the jury (the practice is satirized by Ar. *Wasps* 568ff., 976ff.). Conon however intends to swear on his children's lives. A. therefore seeks to reduce the effect of this oath on the jury by representing Conon as a man whose oaths are worthless. Demosthenes here expresses horror at Conon's oath, though Dinarchus 1.71 attributes the same oath to Demosthenes, and Demosthenes attributes such an oath to his mother 29.26, 33, 56. At 19.292 Eubulus is represented as

swearing by his children, and Demosthenes criticizes not the form of
the oath but the inconsistency between the solemn oath and Eubulus'
present behaviour. See also Ar. *Frogs* 587, Lys. 12.10, 32.13. The same
oath may be regarded (according to the speaker's needs) as a monstrous
risk to take with one's children's lives (especially as the litigant *must*
regard his opponent's oath as untrue) or as a confirmation, by its very
solemnity, of the truth (this no doubt is Conon's attitude).

38 κατὰ τούτων: κατά plus gen. is regularly used of the person or thing
by which one swears. **δεινὰς καὶ χαλεπάς:** deliberately vague. Cf. on
§9. **ἀκηκοὼς κτλ.:** for sources of information available to a litigant
see Introduction 15f. and A. P. Dorjahn, *TAPA* 66 (1935) 274–95.
ἀνυπόστατα 'irresistible', as explained by what follows. **ἐξαπατῶνται:**
ἐξαπατᾶν is almost the *vox propria* for a verdict favourable to the
speaker's enemies. Athenian juries do not make mistakes; they are
'deceived' by unscrupulous men. **πρὸς τὸν βίον:** Ariston's account of
Conon's life not only undermines the oath but also blackens Conon's
character. No evidence is cited in support of these accusations; this is
the kind of unsubstantiated character assassination which A. deplores
in §15. Such double standards are common in Greek oratory; cf. on
§3, §§38–41 above, 37.45.

39 ἐξ ἀνάγκης: (cf. §17) agrees with Ariston's persona. A. is not the
sort to enquire into such foul matters or to speak of them in public (cf.
§§9, 17) unless forced to, as he is now by Conon's oath. **Βάκχιον:** not
otherwise known. **ὃς παρ' ὑμῖν ἀπέθανε** 'who was executed in your
court' (i.e. 'by your verdict'). Since any panel of jurors represented
the sovereign demos, any judgement by any court and any executive
or legislative decision by the assembly could be attributed to the jury
which the litigant addresses. The names of Conon's companions are
carefully chosen to taint Conon by association. Cf. 39.2. **'Αριστοκράτην:**
perhaps the dissolute mentioned at 38.27. **τὸν τοὺς ὀφθαλμοὺς διεφθαρμένον:** perhaps no more than a detail to enable the jury to recognize
the man. But since traditional belief could regard misfortune as a
punishment of sins either of the individual or his ancestors, and since
we find blindness as a punishment for impiety (as in the legends of
Stesichorus and Tiresias), it is likely that A. connects Aristocrates'
blindness with his (alleged) impiety. Cf. Lys. fr. 53.3. **Τριβαλλούς:**

properly a Thracian tribe, notorious in Athens from the fifth century
for their barbarous tongue and character (Ar. *Birds* 1530, Isoc. *De pace*
50, *Panath.* 227, Alexis fr. 241); also used as a term for idlers and
wastrels, according to Photius and Hesych. s.v. Like the names
mentioned in §13, this title was chosen to indicate the unruly and
unconventional behaviour of the club. London was plagued early in
the eighteenth century by street-gangs of well-to-do young men who
called themselves Mohocks after the North American Indian tribe. τά
θ' Ἑκαταῖα: the MSS have τά θ' Ἑκαταῖα κατεσθίειν (A) / κατακαίειν
(cett.). κατεσθίειν was deleted by Baiter. One cannot feast well on pig's
testicles alone, but a combination of pig's testicles and other delicacies
no doubt makes a filling meal. The interpolation probably arose from
a dittography – Ἑκαταῖα καταια > Ἑκαταῖα κατακαίειν, with the
nonsensical κατακαίειν subsequently 'corrected' to κατεσθίειν (Sandys).
τά Ἑκαταῖα were offerings of food to Hecate made at the meeting of
three roads at the end of the month to avert ill luck. Aristophanes
(*Wealth* 594ff.) speaks (jokingly no doubt) of paupers stealing such
offerings (cf. Luc. *Dial. mort.* 1.1.). But Conon was motivated solely by
bravado and contempt for religion. Such behaviour was a gross affront
to traditional belief (cf. on §17); but it was horrifying as well as
offensive, for it was dangerous to affront a chthonic power in this way.
Cinesias, one of the κακοδαιμονισταί mentioned on §17 above, was
alleged to have fouled the shrines of Hecate, Ar. *Frogs* 366 with schol.
καθαίρουσιν: meetings of the ecclesia and theatrical performances were
preceded by a ritual purification (cf. esp. Ar. *Ach.* 44, *Eccl.* 128, Aeschin.
1.23, Harpocr. s.v. καθάρσιον). A pig was sacrificed and the blood
sprinkled around the periphery of the enclosure. Pigs were regularly
used in ritual purification. According to schol. Aeschin. 1.23 the dead
pigs were thrown into the sea; the sea was by tradition a purifying
element, and objects used in purification were disposed of in this way
from earliest times (Hom. *Il.* 1.314). It is thus difficult to see how the
club could acquire the genitals; but we are not given time to assess the
plausibility of the statement. Since the object used in purification
receives any impurity, it was an act of bravado to feast on it, and a
deliberate affront to common decency to choose the testicles. εἰσιέναι:
sc. εἰς τὴν ἐκκλησίαν / τὸ θέατρον. ῥᾷον ὀμνύναι καὶ ἐπιορκεῖν ἢ
ὁτιοῦν: this charge is lodged with an eye on Conon's oath in court. Cf.
49.65.

40 οὐδὲ πολλοῦ δεῖ 'no, far from it', an idiom common in Demosthenes. With the exception of 20.20 (where οὐδὲ πολλοῦ δεῖ functions itself as a strong negative), a negative statement always precedes, which is repeated in οὐδέ (as here). **μηδέν:** Rennie inserts ἑκών before μηδέν, but the addition seems unnecessary. **ὦν μὴ νομίζετε:** cannot refer to παίδων ('by whom it is not your custom to swear'; ὦν = καθ' ὦν; when antecedent and relative are governed by the same preposition, the prep. is usually omitted with the rel.), for the use of μή, not οὐ, indicates that this is an indefinite rel. clause. Supply μηδέν: 'the man who would not even swear to the truth, and who would not dream of swearing on his children's lives any oath which is contrary to custom'. **νόμιμον:** Rennie follows Blass in inserting κατ' ἐξωλείας αὐτοῦ καὶ γένους καὶ οἰκίας after νόμιμον; but see on §41. **διὰ τοῦ πυρός:** perhaps of an oath taken at an altar while the offerings are burning (καιομένων τῶν ἱερῶν 43.14), διά expressing duration; though the expression is obscure. It is also possible that διὰ τοῦ πυρός is a quotation, i.e. that it is part of the oath formula. Cf. Soph. *Ant.* 264ff. ἦμεν δ' ἕτοιμοι καὶ μύδρους αἴρειν χεροῖν, καὶ πῦρ διέρπειν, καὶ θεοὺς ὀρκωμοτεῖν. There was no trial by ordeal in classical Athens, but such an oath would underline the speaker's conviction. For the shift into direct speech cf. 19.209 βοῶντα ὡς εἰσαγγελεῖ με καὶ γράψεται καὶ ἰοὺ ἰού. However there is much to be said for Sandys's διὰ τοῦ πυρὸς ἰόντος, 'facing any peril' (referring to the 'awful and grim curses' of §38); cf. Ar. *Lys.* 133 and see LSJ s.v. πῦρ II. **ὡς οὐ κατεπιορκησόμενος τὸ πρᾶγμα** 'since I had no intention of letting the case go / be lost by [Conon's] perjury'. For this sense of κατα- cf. e.g. καταπαιδεραστεῖν, καταχορηγεῖν, καταληιτουργεῖν. κατεπιορκεῖν would mean 'lose by perjury'; the middle means 'have something lost by perjury'. **πρόκλησιν:** Ariston's formal challenge (see on §27) consists of an offer to swear an oath to the truth of his allegations against Conon. The oath has no legal significance in itself. But (1) whether the oath is accepted or rejected, A. can use it as evidence of his own veracity, (2) if Conon refuses, A. can use this as evidence of Conon's guilty conscience, thus counteracting the effect of his own refusal of Conon's challenge.

41 τῶν περιεστηκότων 'the bystanders'; the court was surrounded by a railing which separated those involved from the viewing public; cf. on 56.48. **ἦ μήν:** often introduces oaths. **παθὼν κτλ.:** the main idea is in the participles – 'I bring this suit because etc.' **ἐξώλης κτλ.**: A.'s oath differs from Conon's deplorable oath only in that Conon's oath is more specific (restricted to his sons) and more dramatic (since these can appear in court) and that A.'s oath is based on a regular curse formula (as Ant. 5.11 ἐξώλειαν αὐτῶι καὶ γένει καὶ οἰκίαι τῆι σῆι ἐπαρώμενον, Dem. 19.71); only in this narrow sense is A.'s oath more νόμιμον. A. disguises the fact that his own oath is no weaker than Conon's by using a periphrasis for γένος καὶ οἰκία. (This tells against the insertion of the formula in §40 – see ad loc. – for it would damage Ariston's case to juxtapose the two oaths, especially while using the regular form of the oath.) **ἀλλ' οὐκ ἐπιορκῶ**: A. cannot leave the truth of his oath in the balance (εἰ μὲν εὐορκῶ / εἰ δ' ἐπιορκῶ). **διαρραγῆι**: sc. λέγων ὅτι ἐπιορκῶ – 'not if Conon says so till he bursts'. Cf. 18.21. Conon appears to be adopting the same position as Ariston; his (Conon's) oath is true, Ariston's false; since Conon intends to blacken Ariston's character (§14) we may suppose that he will argue (like A.) that his opponent's low character renders his oath worthless.

42 A.'s appeals to emotion now become more direct. The stress on anger in this section (ἄν...ἐμίσει, τὴν ὀργὴν ἔχειν, μισεῖν) shows clearly the difference between Athenian and modern forensic practice; there is no suggestion of rational deliberation on the part of the jury. **μὴ νομίζειν ἴδιον**: it is usual for litigants to aggrandize the issue in this way. This is a private suit, but A. argues that the case concerns the whole community, since it raises questions of principle. **τυχόν**: lit. 'it having chanced' (acc. abs.), i.e. 'perhaps'. **ἐφ' ὅτου**: masc., 'whoever it befalls' (lit. 'in whosoever case it befalls'). **πρὸ...τῶν ἁμαρτημάτων** 'before the offence'. We expect 'during the offence'; two separate forms of the same notion are conflated, 'while committing the offence' and 'before they face the court'. **μήτ' ἔθους**: refers to Conon's oath (§40). **πρὸς τὸ μὴ δοῦναι δίκην** 'in their efforts to evade justice'.

43 δεήσεται...καὶ κλαήσει: for such warnings cf. e.g. 37.48, 53.29 and esp. 45.88 ἐὰν δ' ὀδύρωνται, τὸν πεπονθότα ἐλεεινότερον τῶν δωσόντων δίκην ἡγεῖσθε. Appeals for pity are the defendant's counterpart to the plaintiff's appeal for βοήθεια and his attempts to create resentment against the defendant. **προσυβρισθείς**: Conon's acquittal would be a further outrage (προσ-); cf. §15 and 40.

συμφέρει: such prudential arguments are normal; cf. e.g. 56.48. **ἢ μή:** sc. ἐξεῖναι. **ἐγὼ μὲν οἴομαι μή:** ἐγὼ μὲν συμφέρειν ὑμῖν οἴομαι μὴ ἐξεῖναι τύπτειν καὶ ὑβρίζειν. μέν here is the so-called μέν *solitarium* (Denniston *GP* 380ff.); there is an implied contrast ('whatever others may think'). **ἔσονται:** sc. οἱ τοιοῦτοι. **πολλοί . . . ἐλάττους:** cf. 24.143 ἐὰν μὲν σφόδρ' ὀργίζησθε, ἧττον ἀσελγανοῦσιν, ἂν δὲ μή, πολλοὺς τοὺς ἀσελγεῖς εὑρήσετε, Ant. 2.α.δ.11.

44 A. passes to his own character in public life, which he contrasts with that of Conon's family. 'I might say much, gentlemen of the jury, of the services we have performed, both ourselves and our father while he was alive, serving as trierarchs and as soldiers and obeying orders, and that no such service has been performed by the defendant nor by any of his sons.' It is usual for litigants to quote such services as an obvious way to establish the correct moral character; cf. e.g. Ant. 2.α.β.12, Lys. 7.7, 19.57, Dem. 45.85. The claim that A.'s father or perhaps an older brother or brothers had served as trierarch cannot be checked as we do not know their names. However, as always when A. speaks of his character, the claim is suspiciously brief and allusive, and unsubstantiated by any evidence. The brevity suits A.'s modest persona, but one suspects that there is some truth in the allegation that A. is a wastrel. **τριηραρχοῦντες:** the τριηραρχία was one of the λῃτουργίαι (public services) which acted as a form of wealth tax. In the fifth century the trierarch was provided with a ship and tackle, which he had to maintain in good repair for a year. But already by the end of the fifth century the burden was shared by two men. In 357 the trierarchy was reorganized so that the total burden fell on the 1,200 wealthiest citizens (this is disputed by B. Jordan, *The Athenian navy in the classical period* (Berkeley 1972) 63ff., but his arguments are not conclusive). In 340 Demosthenes was responsible for a further change which assessed individual contributions according to wealth, the 300 richest bearing the greatest share of the burden. **τὸ προστατόμενον ποιοῦντες:** unlike the undisciplined sons of Conon (§§ 3–6). Cf. Lys. 7.7 ἐγὼ γὰρ τὰ ἐμοὶ προστεταγμένα ἅπαντα προθυμότερον πεποίηκα, Dem. 47.48. **οὐδὲν οὔθ' οὗτος οὔτε τῶν τούτου οὐδείς:** sc. χρήσιμος γέγονεν. οὐδέν is acc. of respect. Repeated negatives give emphasis in Greek (which in English can only be represented by an adverb, 'absolutely', 'categorically' etc.); two negatives only cancel out when the simple negative follows a compound negative. **ἀλλ' οὔτε τὸ ὕδωρ ἱκανὸν οὔτε νῦν περὶ τούτων ὁ λόγος ἐστίν:** as the speaker's time was measured by the water-clock, we often find ὕδωρ used as equivalent to χρόνος. Since Greek litigants do not normally avoid irrelevance, we may see here a desire to shed an awkward topic, and suspect that A. could not point to τριηραρχίαι by his family. **ὁμολογουμένως** 'on our own admission'. The same ending is found in Dem. 20, 36, 38, Isae. 7 and 8, and the first sentence (οὐκ οἶδα κτλ.) in Lys. 22.22. The speech has no formal ἐπίλογος.

37 Against Pantaenetus[7]

Date

The only indication of the date of the speech is at §6, where the speaker, Nicobulus, refers to the loan transaction between himself and his partner, Euergus, on the one hand and Pantaenetus on the other as being completed in Elaphebolion (i.e. March–April) in the archonship of Theophilus (who was eponymous archon in 348/7). The loan transaction was completed therefore in March–April 347. The present case probably dates to 346 or 345, since allowance has to be made for the absence from Athens of Nicobulus (who, from §6, sailed for Pontus in spring 347), his clash with the rival creditors on his return, the transference of the processing plant and the slaves to these creditors, and Pantaenetus' final disposal of the property. There is no indication in the content or style of the speech to suggest that it has been wrongly attributed to Demosthenes.

The business transactions

The silver mines at Laurion in southern Attica were owned by the state, which leased areas of them to individual speculators. Pantaenetus had leased a mine for which he owed the state a periodic payment (§22).

The business transactions in the present case involve not the mine, however, but an ἐργαστήριον, or processing plant, and thirty slaves. The transaction between Pantaenetus on the one hand and Euergus

---

[7] The speech is discussed at length by Finley 32ff.; Fine *Horoi* 146ff.; Harrison 274–9.

and Nicobulus on the other was a πρᾶσις ἐπὶ λύσει,[8] i.e., sale on condition that the seller may release the property from the buyer's claim on it. It was not a true sale, but a means of raising a loan on the security of property. The borrower offers as security property which he 'sells' to the creditor; however, provided that the borrower meets his contractual obligations, he has the right to redeem the property by paying back the principal of the debt. Breach of contract (in Pantaenetus' case the failure to meet interest or 'rent' payments) may result in possession of the property by the creditor.

The present case is complicated by the fact that Pantaenetus was involved in more than one such agreement using the processing plant and the slaves. In order to buy from the previous owner, Telemachus,[9] the plant and thirty slaves which accompanied the mine he had leased, Pantaenetus had persuaded Mnesicles and two others to make him the very large loan of 105 minae on the security of the property. When finally sold off (§31, cf. §50) the property fetched 206 minae. Even if allowance is made for sale at a substantial profit, Mnesicles and his co-creditors can hardly have paid the full price of the plant and slaves; the purchase price must have been made up by Pantaenetus. The account of the role of Mnesicles and his co-creditors (§§4f.) is too brief to be very informative, but the nature of the transaction between Pantaenetus and Mnesicles and his partners may be inferred from Pantaenetus' subsequent dealings with Euergus and Nicobulus. When Pantaenetus wished to discharge his debt to Mnesicles and his co-creditors, Euergus and Nicobulus paid 105 minae to them and took over the property and slaves as Pantaenetus' creditors at Pantaenetus' request.[10] A contract was drawn up on the basis of πρᾶσις ἐπὶ λύσει:

---

[8] The actual term πρᾶσις ἐπὶ λύσει does not occur in the sources, but many Attic *horoi* contain a formula involving a form of the participle πεπραμένος with ἐπὶ λύσει. (But for the *horoi* we should be unaware of how common the transaction was.) The expression πρᾶσις ἐπὶ λύσει is a convenient name for the transaction, particularly from the point of view of the debtor.

[9] For Telemachus as owner of the property, see on §5.

[10] We are not told explicitly why Pantaenetus wished to settle with Mnesicles and his co-creditors, though at §49 Nicobulus hints strongly that it was because the period allowed for redemption of the property was running out, which would have entailed for Pantaenetus the loss of the property. Nicobulus also mentions a quarrel between Pantaenetus and Mnesicles (§15). That would be unlikely if Pantaenetus trusted Mnesicles some time after, as Nicobulus indicates at §40. But there is doubt as to whether Nicobulus is lying at §15 or at §40: see ad locc.

Pantaenetus got a lease of the plant and slaves at a rent-interest of 12 % per annum on the loan (§5) and he had the right to redeem the property by repaying the principal within a stipulated time (§5; we are not told how long).

Nicobulus then left Athens on a trading voyage to Pontus. During his absence Euergus, alleging that Pantaenetus had failed to meet his contractual obligations in that he had failed to pay his rent-interest (§7, the only dereliction specifically mentioned though others are claimed), took possession of the plant and slaves, as was his right (see on §14). Euergus also, it seems, appropriated money due to be paid by Pantaenetus to the state for his mining concession, thus causing Pantaenetus to become a state-debtor, the penalty for which was loss of civic rights (see on §22).

When Pantaenetus protested to Euergus he was accompanied by other persons (§7) who claimed that they too had lent Pantaenetus money on the security of the plant and slaves.

Confronted on his return to Athens by this situation, Nicobulus was now faced, he claims, with two alternatives (§10). He could either join with Euergus in running the plant or he could make with Euergus a contract similar to the former one which they both had with Pantaenetus. However, the other alleged creditors of Pantaenetus made a formal offer (§§12f.) either that Nicobulus and Euergus take payment from them of the sum owed them by Pantaenetus and thereby relinquish their claim on the property, or that they (the other creditors) should be paid by Nicobulus and Euergus what was due to them from Pantaenetus, thus making Nicobulus and Euergus sole creditors. At §§13f. Nicobulus declares that he was ready to take the money and be rid of the affair, but that the men who had made the offer then said that they would not pay unless Nicobulus agreed to act as warrantor (πρατήρ; see below) that the property had no debts or claims attached to it. At Pantaenetus' insistence (according to Nicobulus, §14) Nicobulus agreed to this condition and at the same time he received from Pantaenetus a release and discharge from all liabilities with regard to the property. On payment to Euergus and Nicobulus by the other alleged creditors of the sum owed to Euergus and Nicobulus by Pantaenetus the other claimants took over the property on the same basis as Euergus and Nicobulus had originally taken it over (§30). Thus whether the claims of these others were genuine or not, Pantaenetus, it seems, was in the same position as he had been when Euergus and Nicobulus had first advanced their loan to him, and he sold the property outright, probably with one or more of his creditors acting as warrantor (cf. §31), for 206 minae.

The basic procedure involved in the transactions is relatively clear. In each case Pantaenetus is borrowing money on the security of the property. But confusion is caused by the use of the verbs meaning 'buy' and 'sell' and the noun πρατήρ.

(1) ὠνεῖσθαι, ἀποδίδοσθαι: Mnesicles is said to have 'bought' (ὠνεῖσθαι) the property for Pantaenetus from Telemachus (§§5, 9). Then Euergus and Nicobulus 'buy' the property from Mnesicles (§§ 12, 16; cf. §§ 10, 14, 30). But neither Mnesicles and his colleagues nor Euergus and Nicobulus are buying the property outright,[11] but with the condition that Pantaenetus may redeem the property within a stipulated period on repayment of the 105 minae. Moreover Euergus and Nicobulus could not dispose of the property freely as they wished, for Pantaenetus claims (§29) that Nicobulus 'sold' the property παρὰ τὰς συνθήκας, i.e. without Pantaenetus' consent. What was being 'bought' was the property with this encumbrance. In actual fact by this πρᾶσις ἐπὶ λύσει first Mnesicles and his colleagues and then Euergus and Nicobulus were lending money to Pantaenetus. As Nicobulus says, he and Euergus were lending Pantaenetus the money he needed to repay Mnesicles and his colleagues (§4, cf. §§49f., 52ff.). Similarly when Euergus and Nicobulus 'sold' (ἀποδίδοσθαι) the property (§§17, 29, 30) the unnamed 'buyers' were lending Pantaenetus the money to repay Euergus and Nicobulus. Hence the lack of fluctuation in the sum paid by successive 'buyers': always 105 minae. Pantaenetus' debt, with the right to distrain on the property, is transferred in turn from Mnesicles and his colleagues to Euergus and Nicobulus, and then to the unnamed 'buyers'. The basic loan rather than sale nature of the transactions is brought out by the fact that the rent was calculated not on the true value of the security, which was greatly in excess of 105 minae, but on the 105 minae, as interest (§5).[12]

(2) πρατήρ. This noun, meaning literally 'vendor' is used, as are the

---

[11] Even though the 'buyers' could refer to the property as theirs (§§7, 9, 29). See on §7.

[12] Cf. Fine *Horoi* 157. Cf. Libanius in Hypoth. §2 καὶ ἦν τοῦτο τῶι μὲν ἔργωι τόκος, τῶι δ' ὀνόματι μίσθωσις.

verbs meaning 'buy' and 'sell', of conditional sale (πρᾶσις ἐπὶ λύσει).
In § 14 Nicobulus says that Pantaenetus implored Euergus and himself
to become πρατῆρες of the property, and at § 30 he says that Pantaenetus
had implored them to 'sell' because nobody would accept Pantaenetus
as πρατήρ. In §§ 13 and 30 Nicobulus implies that Pantaenetus could
legally have 'sold' the property ἐπὶ λύσει (cf. on § 13), the only obstacle
to such a sale being (if we are to believe Nicobulus) the fact that nobody
trusted Pantaenetus as πρατήρ. The reason for insisting on a reliable
person to act as πρατήρ is that prospective buyers (either ἐπὶ λύσει or
outright) had to depend on the seller to protect their title if a dispute
should arise. Thus there is an emphasis on warranty in the word.[13] The
'buyers' in the present case needed assurance that the property had
no further debts attached to it, so that if they had to seize the property
in the event of Pantaenetus' failure to redeem it by the stipulated date
they would at least know that they would recover their capital. In such
an event the question of title would become very important. Thus the
πρατήρ stands as warrantor that the property does not stand security
for undisclosed debts. Hence Nicobulus can express anger at Mnesicles
(§ 11) for his failure to mention any other claimants on the property,
for Mnesicles had acted as πρατήρ of the property to Euergus and
himself.

The use of these terms without qualification to denote πρᾶσις ἐπὶ
λύσει rather than outright sale was clearly familiar, for we find πρᾶσις
ἐπὶ λύσει described at 33.8 with the words: ὠνὴν ποιοῦμαι τῆς νεὼς
καὶ τῶν παίδων, ἕως ἀποδοίη τάς τε δέκα μνᾶς ἃς δι' ἐμοῦ ἔλαβεν καὶ
τὰς τριάκοντα ὧν κατέστησεν ἐμὲ ἐγγυητὴν τῶι τραπεζίτηι. The
expression ὠνὴν ποιοῦμαι is there used, like ὠνεῖσθαι in the present
speech, of πρᾶσις ἐπὶ λύσει.[14] If the words for buying and selling are
used consistently in the specialised sense relating to πρᾶσις ἐπὶ λύσει
no confusion need arise. But at § 31 Nicobulus also uses ἀποδίδοσθαι

[13] See further Finley 228 n. 33.
[14] In an inscription of 367/6 (*Hesperia* 10 (1941) 14 no. 1, quoted by Finley
295 n. 13) ἀποδομένο alone in l.23 refers to πρᾶσις ἐπὶ λύσει (cf. πριαμένων . . . ἐπὶ
λύσει in ll.33f.). See further Finley 296 n. 16. Finley notes that the omission
of the words ἐπὶ λύσει may be no more than a stone-cutter's error, but points
to Poll. 8.142 (Hyp. fr. 193 Blass): Ὑπερείδης δὲ ἐν τῶι πρὸς Χάρητα ἔφη
ἀποδόμενος ἀντὶ τοῦ ὑποθείς. Pollux noted Hyp.'s use of ἀποδίδοσθαι without
the appended ἐπὶ λύσει and gave an explanation. For further possible cases see
Finley 103.

with its normal connotation of outright sale. He says to Pantaenetus 'for the property which we sold (ἀπεδόμεθα)[15] for 105 minae you later sold (ἀπέδου) for 206 minae'. The word ἀπέδου here means 'sold outright', as we learn from §50: 'property on which you could not borrow (δανείσασθαι) more than 100 minae but which you have sold outright (πέπρακας δὲ καθάπαξ) for 200 minae' (Nicobulus is here using round figures). The terminological confusion at §31 is probably not accidental. Throughout the speech Nicobulus makes no· mention of Pantaenetus' contribution towards the purchase price of the property, and by confusing outright sale and πρᾶσις ἐπὶ λύσει he is able to exaggerate Pantaenetus' profit. He implies that 105 minae was the total price paid for the property when he and Euergus sold it and therefore Pantaenetus' profit was 101 minae. The distortion is intended both to undermine Pantaenetus' charge that Nicobulus 'sold' the property in breach of contract (i.e. if Pantaenetus made a profit of almost 100% Nicobulus can hardly have damaged his interests)[16] and to create an unfavourable impression of Pantaenetus as a man who without risking an obol of his own has made a vast profit from the property, but not content with that is seeking to extract further profit by bringing unjust suits against his creditors (cf. §§49f.).[17]

The case

During Nicobulus' absence on his voyage to Pontus, Euergus, using a slave of Nicobulus, Antigenes, had confiscated a sum of silver due to the state, which Pantaenetus' slave was taking to deposit with the treasury. Through this intervention Euergus had caused Pantaenetus to be registered as a state debtor. In addition Euergus had obstructed the smooth working of the plant and had smelted (and retained) silver which Pantaenetus had mined. For these alleged offences Pantaenetus had successfully prosecuted Euergus and had been awarded damages of two talents.

---

[15] ἀπεδόμεθα and ἐωνήμεθα are variants at this point in the text (see on §31). For the present discussion of the confusion the reading makes no difference because Euergus and Nicobulus had both 'bought' and 'sold' the property.

[16] Cf. Harrison I 277 n. 1.

[17] Cf. 56.3f.

Pantaenetus has now brought the following charges against Nicobulus as Euergus' partner:

1. Nicobulus instructed his slave Antigenes to confiscate silver due to the state from Pantaenetus, so causing Pantaenetus to be registered as a state debtor.
2. Thereafter Nicobulus placed Antigenes in control of the processing plant against the express instructions of Pantaenetus.
3. Nicobulus induced Pantaenetus' slaves καθέζεσθαι εἰς τὸν κεγχρεῶνα to Pantaenetus' detriment (for the meaning of this charge see notes to §§ 26 and 27).
4. Nicobulus smelted silver ore mined by Pantaenetus' slaves and retained the silver from the ore.
5. Nicobulus 'sold' the plant and slaves (i.e. transferred the debt on them) in breach of contract.
6. Pantaenetus also charges Nicobulus with sundry acts of violence and with offences against ἐπίκληροι, acts committed at Pantaenetus' house.

Pantaenetus is suing Nicobulus for two talents' damages (βλάβη, cf. §§ 22, 26), the same amount for which he had successfully sued Euergus. He uses the process of a δίκη μεταλλική. The δίκη μεταλλική came into the 'monthly' class (ἔμμηνος), which meant that the complaints (λήξεις) were accepted by the responsible magistrates, in this case the θεσμοθέται, every month and probably the process was speedier than a straightforward δίκη βλάβης (see on § 2).

Nicobulus has entered a παραγραφή, a countercharge that the prosecution had been brought in a way forbidden by law. The παραγραφή only obviates the need for a defence if successful. When a παραγραφή is brought by the defendant the original action is suspended and the roles of the parties are reversed; the defendant becomes the plaintiff and speaks first, suing his accuser for irregularity in the prosecution, and if the plea fails the original action proceeds.[18] The

---

[18] It has been held either that the παραγραφή issue was merely the first phase of a single debate and that consideration of the substantive issue followed immediately before the same jury (U. E. Paoli, *L'inscindibilità del processo in diritto attico (Studi sul processo attico* (Padova 1933) 77ff.) or that there might even have been no second exchange of speeches if the decision in the παραγραφή went

present speech represents Nicobulus' case for his παραγραφή. But as is usual with παραγραφαί (cf. e.g. Dem. 32–6, 38) Nicobulus does not limit himself to legal argument about the admissibility of the case but also replies to the substantive charges of Pantaenetus. To a certain extent this is only to be expected, for some reference to the events which gave rise to the main action is inevitable if the jury is not to judge the παραγραφή in a vacuum. Moreover the defendant can take the opportunity to use the 'facts' of the case to direct resentment against his accuser. Almost inevitably the plaintiff will then give his version of the 'facts' as well as answering the παραγραφή.[19] There is a further reason for the defendant to raise the main issue while arguing the case for his παραγραφή, a reason indicated by Nicobulus at §21. He must not appear to have recourse to technicalities because his case is weak (cf. Isae. 7.3). Anyone entering a παραγραφή risked creating the impression that he was using his legal expertise to evade justice, and 'excessive' familiarity with the law was regarded with suspicion at Athens as betraying a litigious disposition. But by its very nature the παραγραφή must be based on specific clauses in particular laws. To counter any impression that he is using his legal expertise to evade justice a litigant must convince the jury of the justice of his case. So in the present speech Nicobulus is concerned to defend his own behaviour and to dissociate himself from acts for which Pantaenetus had successfully sued Euergus.

Nicobulus' παραγραφή is based on three grounds:

1. Pantaenetus cannot sue Nicobulus because Pantaenetus had formally relinquished all claims on Nicobulus at the time when the latter agreed to act as πρατήρ of the property.

2. There is no competent magistrate to admit Pantaenetus' case to court. Nicobulus argues that Pantaenetus has combined in a

against the defendant in the main case (A. Biscardi, *Novissimo Digesto Italiano* VII³ (Turin, 1961) s.v. 'Giudizi paragrafici'). These views are based on the fact that speakers did not limit themselves to the issue of the παραγραφή (see below). They have been refuted by H. J. Wolff, *Die attische Paragraphe* (Weimar 1966) 17–86. See Harrison II 108–19. MacDowell (*Law* 215) points to Dem. 36.2, where the speaker says that the motive of himself and Phormion in bringing a παραγραφή was not ἵν' ἐκκρούοντες χρόνους ἐμποιῶμεν.

[19] The only surviving exception is Lys. 23. But that speech exhibits other differences which may be attributed to its early date (cf. MacDowell *Law* 216f.), e.g. the speaker refers to his opponent's ἀντιγραφή (§5) and the normal speaking roles are not reversed.

single suit offences which come under the jurisdiction of different magistrates. (This basis of the παραγραφή was omitted from the formal plea; §34.)

3. Pantaenetus is suing Nicobulus by a δίκη μεταλλική, but the alleged offences do not fall within the μεταλλικὸς νόμος.

Thus there are two general questions to be considered: (1) the validity of Pantaenetus' charges against Nicobulus, and (2) the validity of Nicobulus' παραγραφή.

The case against Euergus

The exact nature of the case against Euergus is not known. Nicobulus says that it was a δίκη μεταλλική (§47) and it is clear that the charges brought against Euergus and against Nicobulus were very similar (cf. §§23, 26, 28, 45ff., 50, 57), though at §§45ff. Nicobulus strongly implies that the accusation concerning ἐπίκληροι (i.e. no. 6 above) was introduced by Pantaenetus in his speech against Euergus and was not contained in the formal charge (see on §47). If Euergus entered a παραγραφή it was obviously unsuccessful. Yet perhaps Euergus had poor grounds for a παραγραφή. Nicobulus' second plea was not available for Euergus because this objection is only introduced by Nicobulus in connection with the charge concerning ἐπίκληροι, which Nicobulus says was not made formally against Euergus, and Nicobulus strongly implies that Euergus did not use this argument (cf. §§45ff.). With regard to Nicobulus' first plea, it is not certain that Euergus had received a release from Pantaenetus; in §§18 and 19 Nicobulus uses plurals, but these plurals could refer to himself alone (cf. ἡμῖν in §9). Only the third plea is left. Perhaps Euergus did not consider this plea strong enough to be the sole grounds for a παραγραφή. It is, however, possible that Euergus did not have this plea available because Pantaenetus brought a straightforward δίκη βλάβης against Euergus and not, as Nicobulus says, a δίκη μεταλλική. If there is truth in this suggestion a possible reason for adopting a different procedure against Nicobulus is that δίκαι μεταλλικαί being ἔμμηνοι (see on §2) were probably generally heard within a month (cf. on §41 with §39). Pantaenetus perhaps felt that this was a safer form of procedure in case Nicobulus went for another of his trading journeys abroad.

It is to be wondered why Pantaenetus did not sue Nicobulus at the time of his action against Euergus, as Nicobulus repeatedly says he should have done. Several possible reasons suggest themselves. Perhaps at that time Pantaenetus was unaware of Nicobulus' part in the actions of Euergus; certainly Nicobulus claims (§15) that Pantaenetus greeted him cordially on his return to Athens.[20] But Nicobulus is charged with actions carried out by his partner Euergus during his absence, and it would suit Nicobulus, in his effort to distance himself from the acts of Euergus, to make this statement, for which he brings no evidence. Perhaps Nicobulus was away from Athens at the time of the first suit. Though Nicobulus often implies (e.g. §9) that he was present in Athens he nowhere explicitly states the fact unless a certain interpretation is accepted which involves an emendation in §18 (see on §18). Or Pantaenetus may simply have been induced to prosecute Nicobulus, who was absent at the time of Euergus' acts, by the success of his action against the easier and more obvious target, Euergus.

The relationship between Nicobulus and Euergus

To several of the charges Nicobulus answers that it is impossible for him to be guilty because he was absent from Athens at the time (§§23, 25, 28, 57), saying that any guilt there was belonged to Euergus (§§26, 28) who has already been convicted on the same charges (§§23, 26). It is very likely that Nicobulus was in fact absent at the time of Euergus' actions against Pantaenetus because he presents evidence of the fact (§§8f.). Though at §26 he grants that Euergus stationed Antigenes, a slave of Nicobulus, at the plant after he had taken possession of it and though he nowhere denies that Antigenes was involved in taking Pantaenetus' silver (see especially §26), he completely fails to take account of the possibility that, as Euergus' partner in the loan and the

---

[20] So Sir John Miles, *Hermathena* 78 (1951) 60. His alternative suggestion, that Pantaenetus moved against Nicobulus because he had been unable to obtain the damages of two talents which had been awarded him in the action against Euergus is even less attractive. Limited as were the means for enforcing judgements in private cases at Athens they appear to have sufficed, for no more elaborate system was deemed necessary (Harrison II 190). If Pantaenetus was having difficulty in extracting two talents from Euergus, he might well hesitate to risk the ἐπωβελία (a hefty 20 minae) simply to extract the same sum from Nicobulus and then face the possibility that Nicobulus too might default.

agreement, he was jointly responsible for Euergus' actions in connection with the property even though he was abroad.

Part of the trouble in assessing the situation is that neither in literature nor in epigraphical texts did the Athenians show concern for precision of language in the matter of multiple creditors.[21] The legal relationship in each instance between debtor and creditors and between one creditor and another may, as Finley suggests, have been clearly fixed among the parties themselves. But as Dem. 56 shows, this relationship was not always shown on the documents.

Though the constituent parts of the loan in Dem. 37 were separate (§4) the loan came under one agreement. We do not however know what was in the agreement, for though Nicobulus refers to clauses in it (§§5–7, 29) he does not submit the text of the agreement in evidence.

Nicobulus indicates that the relationship between himself and Euergus was of a different order from that between the two of them and the other claimants, Nicobulus and Euergus being treated as partners in a single transaction. In §12 the other claimants treat Nicobulus and Euergus as a unit in their challenge, and in §13 it is noticeable that Nicobulus says not only that he agreed to accept the offer of the other claimants but that he persuaded Euergus to do so as well, which perhaps implies that he could not so act alone.

On the other hand for the arguments against the substantive charges he distances himself from Euergus, saying he was abroad and not responsible for the acts of Euergus. He says that after his return from abroad and at least therefore after Euergus had taken over the plant, Pantaenetus greeted him in a friendly way (§15), thus indicating that he and Euergus were quite distinct. Since for the purposes of his answers to the substantive charges it suited Nicobulus to say this, he may be lying.

There is doubt therefore about the exact relationship, but the probability is that as partners in the loan both Nicobulus and Euergus could be held responsible for the acts committed by one of them. At Dem. 35.12 there is a clause in an agreement allowing action against two debtors by the lenders acting either severally or together. Similarly at Dem. 56.45 we read that in the agreement there it was stipulated τὴν πρᾶξιν εἶναι καὶ ἐξ ἑνὸς καὶ ἐξ ἀμφοῖν. Perhaps this was allowed in

---

[21] In Dem. 56.6 though there were two co-creditors only one was named in the agreement. Cf. 42.28f. See Finley 107ff.

Pantaenetus' contract in reverse. But anyway if it was right for Pantaenetus to sue Nicobulus separately and so attempt to be awarded damages twice for the same acts, then it is fair for Nicobulus to represent himself as separate and distinct from Euergus.[22]

Presumably what would be meant by such a clause as that found in 35.12 and 56.45 is that Pantaenetus had the right either to sue both Nicobulus and Euergus together or to sue one for both, not that he had the right to sue each separately. If Euergus and Nicobulus were collectively responsible by virtue of being partners, the legal solidarity should mean both that as a result of the conviction of Euergus Pantaenetus had obtained redress from both partners in the person of one of them, and that having convicted both of them by convicting one of them he was entitled to equal damages from both to a total of the damages awarded at that trial. It may seem odd therefore that Nicobulus does not make a legal issue of this point by including it as a plea for his παραγραφή rather than raising the matter only as an equity issue (§28).[23] The omission may seem especially remarkable because the law on which he depended for his plea concerning ἄφεσις and ἀπαλλαγή and which he has read out at §18, contained the clause preserved at 24.54: ὅσων δίκη πρότερον ἐγένετο ἢ εὔθυνα ἢ διαδικασία περὶ του ἐν δικαστηρίωι, ἢ ἰδίαι ἢ δημοσίαι, ἢ τὸ δημόσιον ἀπέδοτο, μὴ εἰσάγειν περὶ τούτων εἰς τὸ δικαστήριον μηδ' ἐπιψηφίζειν τῶν ἀρχόντων μηδένα, μηδὲ κατηγορεῖν ἐώντων ἃ οὐκ ἐῶσιν οἱ νόμοι; cf. 36.25. But if Nicobulus had argued in this way he must of necessity have identified himself with the actions of Euergus, a very dangerous course if his παραγραφή should fail, because in his answers to the substantive

---

[22] It is possible that Pantaenetus regards Nicobulus as directly responsible for the offences of Euergus. Though it seems clear that Nicobulus was absent from Athens when Euergus took possession of the plant we do not know how long before this Nicobulus had left. It is perfectly possible that the situation was becoming critical *before* Nicobulus left and that he and Euergus *jointly* decided what to do, but that Nicobulus then left and Euergus acted. This would be a possible explanation of Euergus' ability to use Nicobulus' slave Antigenes. Moreover if Nicobulus was not himself physically involved in the offences against ἐπίκληροι (§§33, 45ff.), the charge seems somewhat remote from the charges relating to the plant and slaves and supports the possibility that Pantaenetus is arguing that Nicobulus planned the whole operation even if he did not participate. However, the fact is not altered that Pantaenetus has already obtained ample damages from Euergus.

[23] For his not raising this point as a legal issue see on §18.

charges (§§ 23, 25, 28, 57) he seeks to distance himself from the actions of Euergus by pleading an alibi and claiming he was not responsible for what Euergus had done.[24]

In fairness Pantaenetus should not have expected to receive from Nicobulus damages for offences for which he had already received damages from Euergus. The result of the case is not known; but on this score alone it is to be hoped that Nicobulus was finally victorious – and that he then settled with Euergus for one talent, half the damages awarded against Euergus.

1–3 Introduction

1 δεδωκότων . . . τὴν δίκην: virtually the same words appear *mutatis mutandis* at the opening of 38.1. There are other striking parallels between 37.58–60 and 38.21f. παραγράψασθαι 'to make a plea in bar of action'. See speech intro., *The case*. περὶ ὧν ἄν τις ἀφεὶς καὶ ἀπαλλάξας δικάζηται 'in whatever cases anyone goes to law after releasing and discharging' cf. on §§ 18f. and 38.1 and 5. For a discussion of ἄφεσις and ἀπαλλαγή see Isager–Hansen 228–37. That the terms were originally distinct is suggested by 36.25 καὶ γὰρ ἀφῆκεν καὶ ἀπήλλαξεν, cf. ἀμφοτέρων in 37.1, 38.1, ἀμφότερα in 37.19, 36.25. ἀφιέναι means that a real or potential plaintiff gives up what would otherwise be his right, e.g. to collect what is owed to him or to prosecute someone who has committed an offence against him (cf. 56.26, 28; 37.58f.). ἀπαλλάττειν is used of a man ridding himself of his creditor (33.9, 34.22, 53.11, Isoc. 17.23 (cf. Isoc. 17.19), Isae. 5.28, Plat. *Leg.* 958b) by paying his demands, or of ridding himself of his opponent in a lawsuit by means of bribery (Lys. 29.1) or of getting someone else rid of an opponent (Andoc. 1.122, Isoc. 17.21, 31). Originally τὸ ἀπαλλάττειν seems to have been a protection for a potential defendant; for example, when a debtor ἀπήλλαξεν his creditor, it was acknowledged by the creditor that he no longer had a claim on the debtor.

However, there was confusion in meaning between ἀφιέναι and ἀπαλλάττειν. If a man was ἀφειμένος ('released') ἁπάντων τῶν ἐγκλημάτων he could also be said to be ἀπηλλαγμένος ('rid') τῶν

---

[24] The danger is increased by the fact that though the law at 24.54 does not actually state it, the most natural interpretation is that the law does not allow a second action when *the same person* is the defendant. It is so interpreted at 20.147.

ἐγκλημάτων (Isoc. 17.23, 21 and 26; cf. Dem. 41.4). Nic. plays on this confusion when he claims (§§ 1, 19) that he has from Pant. *both* ἄφεσις *and* ἀπαλλαγή. At the time when Nic. became πρατήρ of the property Pant. ἀφῆκε him (§ 16). By settling the loan transaction Pant. ἀπήλλαξεν Nic. as a creditor, so that Nic. was ἀπαλλαγείς by Pant. But that ἀπαλλαγή protected Pant. from the claims of his creditor Nic., not vice versa. Rather it was by the very fact of being ἀφείς ['released'] πάντων τῶν ἐγκλημάτων that Nic. was ἀπαλλαγείς ['rid'] πάντων τῶν ἐγκλημάτων. Nic. is not in fact protected by two separate acts of Pant. The confusion is again to be seen in Dem. 36. The confusion, caused by the ambiguity of ἀπηλλαγμένος and ἀπαλλαγείς, may have been encouraged by situations in which there was more than one set of creditors and debtors, such as that described in 33.12. **ἀμφοτέρων:** see above. **ὡς ἠκούσατ' ἀρτίως:** after the jury had been selected and ten of their number (one from each tribe) had been chosen by lot, one to be in charge of the clock, four in charge of the voting urns, and five to supervise the receipt of dicastic payment (Arist. *Ath. Pol.* 66.2f.), the presiding magistrate then εἰσκαλεῖ τὸν ἀγῶνα (Arist. *Ath. Pol.* 67.1) or καλεῖ τὴν δίκην/γραφήν (cf. §42, 58.43), i.e. announced the business and summoned the parties, whereupon the clerk of the court (γραμματεύς) read out the charge or claim (Aeschin. 1.2., cf. Ar. *Wasps* 894). **παρεγραψάμην . . . μὴ εἰσαγώγιμον εἶναι τὴν δίκην** 'I demurred to the admissibility of the suit'. The regular construction with παραγράφεσθαι is pleonastic μή with the acc. and inf. as with verbs of 'denying' etc. Nic. is pleading that because Pant. gave him a release and discharge the case should not be brought to court by the responsible magistrate, who is said to εἰσάγειν δίκην. The magistrates, in this case the thesmothetae, must have had to decide whether the case should be brought to court, there being no public arbitration in a δίκη ἔμμηνος (see on §2), and in this case their decision must have been that the suit lay. By this παραγραφή Nic. is challenging their decision. **ἀφεῖσθαι:** perf. pass., with a play on ἀφείς: 'thinking that I should not have been released from this right', i.e. in addition to being released by Pant. from all charges. **καὶ ἀπηλλαγμένον:** Paley followed by Gernet rejects these words as interpolated, but cf. 38.9. ἀπηλλαγμένον is unexceptionable. It could be passive, 'had been got rid of' as a legal opponent (cf. Lys. 29.1), or middle, 'had come to terms, had become reconciled' (cf. Ar. *Clouds* 1194, Plat. *Leg.* 768c, 915c). There is ambiguity again at Xen.

Mem. 2.9.6, where a third meaning is possible for ἀπαλλάττεσθαι, 'to give up one's prosecution' (cf. Dem. 21.151, 198). More worrying is the reflexive ἐμαυτόν rather than ἐμέ. Gernet may be right with his suggested καὶ ἐμαυτὸν ἀπηλλαγμένον: 'when I prove that this man has granted a release and that I have been discharged' or 'that I am rid of him'. For the confusion of ἀφιέναι and ἀπαλλάττειν, see above. ἐπὶ ταύτης τῆς σκήψεως 'relying on this plea', i.e. that the action is illegal. εἰσελθὼν . . . ἐπιδεῖξαι: since the construction depends on οἰόμενος δεῖν Nic. should have said εἰσελθόντα, or if the construction were to depend on οἰόμενος alone he should have said ἐπιδείξειν. It is a fairly simple anacoluthon, an error whose commission is all the more understandable in such a long and complicated sentence.

2 ἐν οἷς τὸ συμβόλαιον . . . ἐγένετο 'in which the agreement...existed', i.e., was in force. Not 'at which the agreement...came into being' if, as is likely, it is the agreement *par excellence*, the agreement concerning the loan and lease (§5), to which reference is made. The wrongs which Pant. alleges he has suffered were committed after that agreement was made. Several times (e.g. §§9, 18, 57) Nic. says that Pant. should have sued him at the time when he sued Euerg. It is less likely that he is referring to an agreement whereby he became πρατήρ of the property and Pant. granted him an ἄφεσις (§16). **ἐμμήνων** 'monthly', i.e. the suits came into that class for which complaints (λήξεις, see on 54.1) were accepted at monthly intervals. The traditional explanation of δίκαι ἔμμηνοι as cases which had to be decided within a month of being initiated (e.g. Lipsius 901; Bonner–Smith II 91, 116; Harrison II 16, 24, 154) has been shown to be misleading by Cohen 23–36. The main evidence, apart from the present passage, is Dem. 33.23 with 26 and 7.12. Thus in the present passage Nic. is saying that Pant. would have brought his case when the agreement was in force since (μέν) complaints for these cases were accepted every month and (δέ) both Pant. and himself were in Athens. That interpretation gives more point to Nic.'s statement than the traditional one.

Yet the smooth working of the system of δίκαι ἔμμηνοι would demand that cases accepted in one month be at least normally completed before the next cycle of cases began. The process of the present case, Nic. says, had been initiated 'last month' (see on §41 with §39). Speed could be achieved by there being no public arbitration, though private arbitration remained a possibility (33.14ff., 34.18). Cohen suggests that there may have been no ἀνάκρισις (see Introduction and on 54.1).

For a list of δίκαι ἔμμηνοι at the time of Arist. *Ath. Pol.* (in addition to δίκαι μεταλλικαί and δίκαι ἐμπορικαί) see *Ath. Pol.* 52.2 (on the δίκη αἰκείας, see on §33).

παρ' αὐτὰ τἀδικήματα 'precisely at the moment of the wrongs'. Cf. 18.13, 21.26, 32.7 (παρ' αὐτὰ τἀδικήματα Paley). For the sentiment cf. 36.53, Thuc. 3.38. **τὴν πρὸς Εὔεργον δίκην:** see speech intro., *The case* and *The case against Euergus.* **συκοφαντεῖ:** see on 39.2. **ὑπόλοιπόν ἐστι** 'the only course left to me is'. Cf. §18.

3 δεησόμαι κτλ.: Cf. 38.2. **μέτρια καὶ δίκαι':** so S and in 38.2 FQ; δίκαια καὶ μέτρια vulg. and in 38.2 SA. **εὐνοϊκῶς:** see on 54.2. **πολλῶν γὰρ δικῶν κτλ.:** cf. Isae. 8.5 (and Dem. 27.7). **λαχών:** see on 54.1.

4–17 Narration.

4 ἐπ' ἐργαστηρίωι . . . καὶ τριάκοντ' ἀνδραπόδοις: Three *horoi* (*IG* II² 2747–9 = Finley, nos. 88–90) recording cases of πρᾶσις ἐπὶ λύσει couple ἐργαστήρια and ἀνδράποδα. Plant and slaves were often regarded as one unit for such purposes as sale and security (cf. S. Lauffer, *Die Bergwerkssklaven von Laureion* 1 (Wiesbaden 1956) 97ff.).

The ἐργαστήριον would consist of equipment for grinding the ore (see on §26) and a washing table for separating the heavier metal-bearing particles prior to smelting. A photograph of washing tables may be found in J. F. Healy, *Mining and metallurgy in the Greek and Roman world* (London 1978) 161 pl. 41.

ἐν τοῖς ἔργοις ἐν Μαρωνείαι: cf. 21.167, Xen. *Vect.* 4.5: Maroneia was a district in the silver-mining area of Laurion in southern Attica; see on §25. **Μνησικλεῖ μὲν Κολλυτεῖ . . . Φιλέαι δ' Ἐλευσινίωι καὶ Πλείστορι:** Collytus was a deme of the tribe Aigeis and Eleusis was a deme of the tribe Hippothontis. The fact that Pleistor is not given a demotic perhaps means that he was not an Athenian. **τάλαντον:** one talent equals 60 minae. Pant.'s debt to Mnesicles and his co-creditors was 105 minae, the same as his subsequent debt to Euerg. and Nic.

5 πρατὴρ . . . ὁ Μνησικλῆς ἡμῖν γίγνεται: for πρατήρ see speech intro., *The business transactions.* At §29 Nic. says that Mnes. became πρατήρ at Pant.'s request. If the time limit for redemption was close (cf. §49) it would be most important for Pant. to raise money to repay Mnes. Yet Mnes. could have proved an obstacle and could have caused the property to become his if Euerg. and Nic. insisted on his being πρατήρ and he refused. But Mnes. seems to have been more than willing to help the 'sale' through (cf. § 11, προὐξένησε). That in itself does not preclude the possibility of a quarrel between Pant. and Mnes. (cf. speech intro. n. 10). **καὶ γὰρ ἐώνητ' ἐκεῖνος . . . κεκτημένου**: Fine (*Horoi* 147) argues that since the plant and slaves were subsequently sold for 206 minae (§31, cf. §50) it is inexplicable why Telemachus as the original owner had been willing to sell it to Mnes., in the interest of Pant., for only 105 minae, and he concludes that Pant. was the original owner and that he borrowed 105 minae from Telemachus by πρᾶσις ἐπὶ λύσει, using the plant and slaves as security. However, the description of Mnes. at §9 as ὅσπερ ἐξ ἀρχῆς αὐτὸς ἐώνητο (cf. §49) can only mean that Mnes. was the first in the series of creditors and that Telemachus was the original owner. The discrepancy between the loan of 105 minae and the outright sale of the property for 206 minae is explicable if the original purchase price was 105 minae plus an unknown sum, the unknown sum being the amount contributed by Pant., and the 105 minae being borrowed by Pant. from Mnes. and his partners by a πρᾶσις ἐπὶ λύσει. For ἐώνητο see speech intro., *The business transactions*. **μισθοῦται δ' οὗτος . . . τοῦ μηνὸς ἑκάστου**: the *horoi* show that in πρᾶσις ἐπὶ λύσει it was usual for the debtor to retain possession of the property. In this case it was vital for Pant. to keep possession in order to carry out his ore-processing activities. Here Pant. leases the property for 105 drachmae a month. Since the loan was 105 minae and one mina equals 100 drachmae, the interest rate on the loan was 1 % a month or 12 % per annum. We have meagre information on the rates of interest in πρᾶσις ἐπὶ λύσει. See Finley 86. The fact that the rent was calculated not on the value of the security but on the amount of the loan shows that the Athenians thought of πρᾶσις ἐπὶ λύσει not as a sale but a loan (cf. speech intro., *The business transactions*). **λύσις . . . ἔν τινι ῥητῶι χρόνωι**: λύσις generally signifies release from an obligation or condition, e.g. a debt or captivity. Here it refers to Pant.'s right to release the property (by repaying the loan) from the claim which Euerg. and Nic. have on it as security for the loan. We are not informed on the time limit stipulated in the agreement for Pant. to exercise this right. Nor is there direct evidence available in Athenian sources concerning the usual duration of a period of right of redemption. For a possible case of a redemption period of one year see Finley 36 on *horoi* nos. 71 and 152.

6 ἐλαφηβολιῶνος . . . ἐπὶ Θεοφίλου ἄρχοντος: March–April 347. For the significance of these words for dating the speech see speech intro., *Date*. **εἰς τὸν Πόντον:** for trading purposes, it appears from § 10. Nic. probably speculated in grain, for Pontus was one of the main grain-producing areas and Athens relied heavily on imported grain (cf. intro. to 56). **τὰ . . . πραχθέντα τούτοις πρὸς αὐτούς:** for the construction cf. § 9 and Thuc. 4.121.2. **οὔτ᾽ ἀεὶ ταῦθ᾽ οὗτος:** in fact the two claims of Pant. which are actually specified (as opposed to ἀλλ᾽ ὅτι ἂν βούληται) are not mutually exclusive. **ἐκπεσεῖν:** ἐκπίπτειν is commonly used for the pass. of ἐκβάλλειν; cf. § 59. **παρὰ τὰς συνθήκας:** from the frankness at § 14 with which Nic. emphasizes that he and Euerg. were in possession of the plant and slaves it is quite definite that Euerg. was acting within his rights in taking possession when Pant. defaulted in his interest payments. Part of Euerg.'s fault may have lain in using force (cf. βίαι) instead of using the δίκη ἐξούλης (cf. on 39.15) or in taking over possessions of Pant. which were not part of the security (cf. §§ 22ff.). **αὐτὸν αἴτιον αὐτῶι πρὸς τὸ δημόσιον γενέσθαι τῆς ἐγγραφῆς:** i.e. by seizing Pant.'s payment due to the state. Cf. § 22. In his ἔγκλημα against Nic. Pant. says αἴτιος ἐμοὶ γενόμενος ἐγγραφῆναι τὸ διπλοῦν τῶι δημοσίωι. Here in § 6 τῆς ἐγγραφῆς takes the place of ἐγγραφῆναι and πρὸς τὸ δημόσιον takes the place of τῶι δημοσίωι.

7 ἐκεῖνος: sc. φησίν. The reference is to Euergus. **ἁπλῶς:** in contrast with Pant.'s shifting allegations. **ἀπολαμβάνων:** the nuance of ἀπο- is receiving what is one's due. Cf. §§ 12, 38. **τῶν ἄλλων τῶν ἐν ταῖς συνθήκαις ποιοῦντος οὐδέν:** the other transgressions are nowhere specified. **παρ᾽ ἑκόντος τούτου:** Euerg. denied that violence was used (cf. § 6, βίαι). **τὰ ἑαυτοῦ:** using as evidence this passage, § 9 (ἡμέτερον) and § 29 (τὰ ἡμέτερ᾽), and the fact that there was a regular μίσθωσις (§ 5), Fine (*Horoi* 148f.) argues that in πρᾶσις ἐπὶ λύσει ownership was transferred to the creditor. However, Pant. was not an ordinary lessee but had a redemption right to the property (§ 5; cf. Harrison 1 277 n. 1). Nic. and Euerg. did not own the property in the sense that they could sell it outright. They could only sell it in the sense that they could pass the encumbered property to other creditors of Pant. (§§ 16, 29f.); but that, it seems from §29, could by the terms of the agreement only be done with Pant.'s permission. (On Pant.'s right to sell, see on §13.) While it suits Nic. to say that the property was 'theirs', it is so only in the sense that they had bought it ἐπὶ λύσει (see below). τοὺς ἀμφισβητήσοντας 'men to lay a claim' to the property. According to §12 they had loaned money to Pant. on the security of the plant and slaves, but according to Nic. he knew nothing of these claimants. The fact that Nic. never counters their claim with the assertion that it was legally impossible makes it plain that property sold ἐπὶ λύσει could stand as security for another debt (cf. on §12). In an inscription in *Hesperia* 10 (1941) 14 no. 1 ll. 1–39 from the *poletai* records of 367/6 (discussed by Finley 36 and 111ff. and *Studi in onore Vincenzo Arangio-Ruiz* (Naples 1953) III 473ff.; Fine *Horoi* 150ff.; and Harrison I 270f.) there is recorded the sale of a confiscated house which had stood security for four loans. At least one πρᾶσις ἐπὶ λύσει transaction existed alongside other encumbrances on the property, and in fact there were probably two separate loans contracted by πρᾶσις ἐπὶ λύσει. If we have here a case of two transactions by πρᾶσις ἐπὶ λύσει then ownership certainly did not pass to the creditor (see above). While it is possible for these claimants to have a legal claim, it is unknown whether their claim was based on πρᾶσις ἐπὶ λύσει or on another form of security.

8 ἔχει δίκην ἧς ἐτιμήσατ' αὐτός 'he has satisfaction the amount of which he himself estimated', i.e. two talents in damages from Euerg. (§46). The laws about damage prescribed payment of double the amount if the damage was committed intentionally but of the simple amount if it was committed unintentionally (Dem. 21.35, 21.43, 23.50). τιμᾶσθαι with the genitive is used of the litigant's estimating the penalty in an ἀγών τιμητός (see Introduction), τιμᾶν and the genitive is used of the court estimating or awarding the penalty. αὐτός brings out the fact that as Pant. himself fixed the damages he cannot fairly say that they were insufficient (see below). **καὶ οὐ δήπου κτλ.**: in saying that it is not right for Pant. to receive damages for the same wrongs from both Euerg. and himself Nic. has a good point, but not necessarily because Euerg. was the perpetrator and he was abroad, for he thus fails to take into account the fact that as Euerg.'s partner he could be considered jointly responsible for Euerg.'s actions. (Cf. § 18 and speech intro., *The relationship*.) τοῦ μηδ' ἐπιδημοῦντος: the attributive participle negatived with μή can be generic. But here and at §§ 28 and 57 it is circumstantial and involves a condition 'if I was not even at home'; cf. 18.247 (referring to himself in his relations with Philip) ὁ μὴ λαβὼν καὶ διαφθαρεὶς νενίκηκε τὸν ὠνούμενον. Cf. § 25. See Goodwin *MT* 330, 335f.

9 πρατὴρ ἦν . . . ἐώνητο: see on § 5. For πρατήρ and ἐώνητο see speech intro., *The business transactions*. ἡμέτερον ὄν: see on § 7. τοῖς . . . πρὸς Εὔεργον τούτωι πραχθεῖσιν: see on § 6. ἔλαχέν τε δίκην: see on § 3. καὶ οὐδὲν πώποθ' ἡμῖν ἐνεκάλει 'and never in all this time [imperf.] made any charge against me'. There is a strong implication that Nic. was in Athens at the time when Pant. raised suit against Euerg. but subject to the reading in § 18 he never explicitly says so. Cf. on § 13.

10 σχέδον τι πάντ' ἀπολωλεκὼς ὅσ' ἔχων ἐξέπλευσα: there is no way of knowing whether or not this is true. If true, it may be a reason for Nic.'s promptness in seizing the opportunity to recoup the money he had lent Pant. (§ 13). But Nic. may just be rousing sympathy for himself among the jurors. ἀκούσας καὶ καταλαβών 'after hearing and finding'. καταλαμβάνειν means 'to find on arrival' (LSJ s.v. καταλαμβάνω II.2). ἀφεστηκότα 'had given up'. Cf. 21.181 ὧν εἷλεν ἀποστάς 'giving up all claim to what he had won at law'. Nic. here accepts Euerg.'s version (§ 7); Pant. would say ἐκπεπτωκότα (§ 6). ἔχοντα καὶ κρατοῦνθ' 'had and had power', a formula found in three *horoi* on secured property (Finley, nos. 1, 2 and 10). They marked exceptional circumstances whereby the creditors would occupy the premises till the debt was liquidated. The expression does not indicate ownership (Finley 12 and 204 n. 11; but cf. Harrison 1 270 n. 2). ἐωνήμεθα: see speech intro., *The business transactions*. θαυμαστῶς ὡς ἐλυπήθην: a not uncommon attraction from θαυμαστόν ἐστιν ὡς... Cf. Plat. *Phd.* 66a ὑπερφυῶς, ἔφη ὁ Σιμμίας, ὡς ἀληθῆ λέγεις. More remarkable is Plat. *Rep.* 350d μετὰ ἱδρῶτος θαυμαστοῦ ὅσου. περιεστηκὸς εἰς ἄτοπον 'had come to a pretty pass'. ἢ γὰρ κοινωνεῖν . . . συμβόλαιον ποιεῖσθαι: by the first stated alternative, both Nic. and Euerg. work the plant and take the profits; by the second, Euerg. works the plant and presumably by the new agreement pays interest to Nic. But it is only the plant and slaves

which they can take over, Pant.'s right of redemption remaining. The ore belongs to Pant., and, so far as we are told, they have no mining rights by which they can mine ore; nor are we told that the ore of other people was available for them to process. It is true that Euerg. seems to have processed Pant.'s ore, but that was later held to be illegal (§28). Nic. does not spell out this problem because he is being charged with the illegality involved. It is hardly surprising that he was unhappy with a situation (§§ 10f.) in which both his stated alternatives involved illegal action. In fact it must have been open for them to take what in the short term would have been the costly course of keeping possession of the plant and slaves, who would need to be maintained, until either Pant. redeemed the property or Pant.'s time limit for redemption was reached, in which case the property would be theirs to sell.

Nic. gives these alternatives as the only ones open to him. Unless they were prevented by the agreement from breaking the partnership, there seems no obvious reason why theoretically Nic. should not have as additional alternatives the two courses of action which he says (§12) were proposed by the other claimants, i.e. that he should buy Euerg. out or that Euerg. should settle with him by paying him what he was owed. But it would probably have required Pant.'s permission to 'sell' the encumbered property (cf. §29) and Pant. may not have agreed to such a move unless the terms of the necessary new agreement were altered in his favour. Or again these alternatives would not exist in practice if there was unwillingness or financial inability to buy out or unwillingness to be bought out (cf. Nic.'s statement that he had lost almost everything on his trading journey). Nic. seems to be giving only the practical alternatives which faced him, involving as they did illegal acts which were committed.

προῃρούμην: not 'I preferred neither of these alternatives to the other', but 'I deliberately chose neither of these alternatives', i.e. he would have been happier with another course of action. Possible is 'I undertook neither of these alternatives' or 'I proposed to do neither of these alternatives', meaning he was at an impasse.

11 ἀηδῶς . . . ἔχων . . . τούτοις: cf. 20.142. τὸν Μνησικλέα τὸν πρατ-ῆρα . . . γεγενημένον: cf. on §5. λέγων . . . προὔξένησέ μοι 'telling him what sort of fellow he had introduced to me'. προξενεῖν means to represent the interests of a foreign state in one's own state. From these

duties of a πρόξενος, προξενεῖν meant to manage anything for someone else and to introduce or recommend one person to another for business purposes (cf. 53.13; Plat. *La.* 180c; *Alc.* 1.109a). At Delphi the πρόξενοι acted on behalf of all the visitors and their duties included introducing them when they wished to consult the oracle, which they could not do without a sponsor (Eur. *Hel.* 146; cf. Eur. *Ion* 335, 551; *Andr.* 1103; *Med.* 724). **τῶν μὲν ἀμφισβητούντων κατεγέλα:** in his capacity as πρατήρ of the property Mnes. was the proper person for Nic. to ask concerning the question of other debts on the security of the property. (See speech intro., *The business transactions.*) The fact that he asked Mnes. indicates that the other alleged creditors said that their claims predated the 'sale' of the property to Nic. and Euerg. **καὶ παραινέσειν τούτωι . . .καὶ οἴεσθαι πείσειν:** perhaps this is a general reference to Pant.'s future behaviour made with nothing specific in mind concerning his breaches of contract (§7). If Pant. had to pay the state double what he owed (§§6, 22) it is unlikely that he was in a financial position to pay Nic. and Euerg. the interest he owed them. But perhaps the reference is to the other, unspecified, breaches of contract.

12 οἱ . . .φάσκοντες 'the men who alleged'. **ἃ ἡμεῖς ἐπριάμεθα παρὰ Μνησικλέους:** for ἐπριάμεθα see speech intro., *The business transactions*, 108. Nic. *implies* that their claim was impossible, but that is not so (see on §7) and he never actually says that it was legally impossible for other creditors to have a claim on the property. **ὑγιές** lit. 'healthy'; so 'sound', 'wholesome'. **τοῦ Μνησικλέους βεβαιοῦντος ἡμῖν** 'Mnesicles making confirmation in our favour', i.e. as πρατήρ (see speech intro., *The business transactions*). Mnes. confirmed that when he 'sold' it the property did not stand as security for these other debts.

Were these claimants authentic? Nic. declares that he has the support of Mnes. in maintaining that they were not, but since we do not know the specific contents of the μαρτυρίαι at §14 we have no real guide to help decide whether to believe him or not. He represents them as being brought in against Euerg. and himself by Pant. (§§7, 14) and to deny their claim helps him to rouse prejudice against Pant. Certainly their actions helped Pant. out of a bad situation, for after the transaction between them and Nic. and Euerg. Pant. was in a position to recover his property and sell it for 206 minae (§31) instead of having to face the prospect of losing it entirely when his period of redemption was up.

If the claimants were genuine, their subsequent actions are explicable. We do not know if Pant. had defaulted on his contractual obligations to them also, but even if he had they may well have thought it best to avoid the unpleasant situation in which Nic. says he found himself by Euerg.'s taking possession (see on § 10). Yet the convenience for Pant. of their existence is suspicious. Fine (*Horoi* 149) considered that these creditors were probably fictitious and agents of Pant., comparing §§ 39 and 48. If they wanted to help Pant., why did they not lend him the money necessary to redeem the property without professing a claim? In the first place by professing a claim they could attempt to get money out of Nic. and Euerg. (see below). Moreover in the property's present state of being conditionally forfeit to Nic. and Euerg. it may well have been impossible for Pant. to use it as security (even if the prospective lenders would take it thus) without the permission of Nic. and Euerg. (At § 30 Nic. says that Pant. had the right to sell ἐπὶ λύσει, but that is in a situation where Nic. and Euerg. are obviously giving their permission.) As claimants rather than prospective lenders they could put pressure on Nic. and Euerg. (see on § 13). They may not have realized how Nic. felt about the situation (§§ 10f.) and there is no evidence that Euerg. felt the same way (see on § 35). They might have thought that if there were no other claimants, Nic. and Euerg. would be willing to hold out till the property became fully theirs; as claimants they were reducing the size of the profits in that event.

The ignorance of Nic. (and Mnes.?) of the claimants' existence is not helpful in deciding whether or not the claims are valid. If Nic.'s ignorance is genuine, it renders the claims suspicious; but if he is denying the validity of the claims to rouse prejudice against Pant. (see above) he obviously has to profess ignorance of the claimants' existence.

προκαλοῦνται πρόκλησιν ἡμᾶς: double accusative: 'make us a challenge'. For challenges see on 54.27. In addition to the challenge demanding or offering a slave for torture (see on § 27) there were also challenges either to fulfil an obligation (see 56.40; cf. 48.34, Isoc. 17.15, Lys. fr. 16 Th.) or to accept fulfilment of an obligation (cf. 50.31ff.). In case of litigation such challenges could be admitted as evidence. See further on § 13. **ὡς οὐ δεξομένους** 'thinking that / on the grounds that we would not accept it'. **ἐνεκάλουν** 'demanded as their due'. Cf. Lys. 3.26. **αἰτιώμενοι πολλῶι πλείονος . . . χρημάτων** 'alleging that he had property worth much more than the money we had lent'. Cf. LSJ s.v.

αἰτιάομαι 11.2. The property was worth almost double the loan; Nic. and Euerg. had lent 105 minae and the property was ultimately sold for 206 minae.

The claimants made their allegation in support of their argument that they had a right to compensation for their loans on the property. But this argument could only have any force if two conditions were satisfied.

(1) If the property was worth more than the money which *all* the creditors had lent. This sense is gained by taking the subject of ἐδεδώκεμεν to be all the creditors; but since Nic. denies the validity of the claims that interpretation is hardly possible. But perhaps the property was in fact worth more than all the claims for loans made on it.

(2) If Pant. failed to redeem the property. Since at §31 Nic. can say that Pant. had the right to sell ἐπὶ λύσει, Pant. still had the right of redemption. If Nic. and Euerg. settled the claims of the other creditors and Pant. then redeemed the property, not only would they have gained nothing but they would have the trouble of recovering from Pant. the money they had paid to the claimants. If on the other hand Pant. failed to redeem the property, the excess (ὑπεροχή) of the value of the property over the debts would not then have to be shared with the other creditors.

The motive of the claimants in making the challenge to Nic. and Euerg. to take their money and get out is to set Pant. up with his business again, as can be seen from what actually follows (cf. on §12). Their motive in asking Nic. and Euerg. to buy them out depends on whether their claim was genuine or not. If it was not genuine, they would make money out of Nic. and Euerg. If it was genuine, they would get what they were owed with no dispute, and they would not have to share the (perhaps short-term) difficulties which faced Nic. with the property currently under Euerg.'s control (§§ 10f.).

13 παραχρῆμα, οὐδὲ βουλευσάμενος 'immediately, not even deliberating'. Not 'immediately and not (καὶ οὐ) deliberating'. **κομίσασθαι συνεχώρησα:** it is little wonder that Nic. agreed. He has already referred to the difficulties of his present position (§§ 10f.). Now if he insisted on denying the rights of the claimants, he risked a troublesome lawsuit, all the more troublesome if the claimants said that their claim had priority. On the other hand if he allowed the justice of their claim any long-term profit to be made out of the (as yet unknown) ὑπεροχή would be diminished both by the amount of the other creditors' loan and their share of the ὑπεροχή. **τὸν Εὔεργον ἔπεισα:** This may imply that one of the partners in the loan could not make the move without the other, a fact which would perhaps have some bearing on the question of Nic.'s joint responsibility for the action of his partner (see speech intro., *The relationship*). What in fact they were agreeing to do was to 'sell' the property in the same way as it had been 'sold' to them by Mnes. (§§ 16, 29f.; see speech intro., *The business transactions*), so that Pant.'s debt to them passed to the claimants. Pant. for his part doubtless would give his permission (see on § 7) because he knew what he would get out of the transaction. Nic. says Pant. was eager for the 'sale' (§§ 14, 16, 30). **ἀπολαμβάνειν:** see on § 7. **οἱ . . . ἐκεῖν' ἐπαγγειλάμενοι** 'the men who had made that offer unasked / of their own free will'. See LSJ s.v. ἐπαγγέλλω 4. **εἰ μὴ πρατῆρες γιγνοίμεθ' ἡμεῖς:** for πρατῆρες see speech intro., *The business transactions*. Cf. § 30: οὐδεὶς γὰρ ἤθελεν δέχεσθαι τοῦτον πρατῆρα. In saying that no one would accept Pant. as πρατήρ because he was untrustworthy, Nic. indicates that Pant. had the right to sell ἐπὶ λύσει. Since two πράσεις ἐπὶ λύσει on the same property were probably legally possible (see on § 7), in general a debtor probably had the right to sell again ἐπὶ λύσει. But this right may well have been restricted, at least by contract, in being subject to the permission of existing creditors. It is most unlikely that when the property was conditionally forfeit, as in the present case, the defaulting debtor had an unrestricted right to sell either ἐπὶ λύσει or outright. But in the present situation Nic. and Euerg. would have given Pant. permission to 'sell' the property (cf. on § 13).

We can believe Nic. when he says the other creditors did not trust Pant. If their claim was genuine and Nic. genuinely did not know of it (cf. on § 12) then Pant. had already duped Nic. If their claim was not genuine, they would not want to be the victims of the same duplicity themselves. Though having Mnes. as πρατήρ had not helped Nic., it might still appear to the claimants to lessen the danger to have someone other than Pant. as πρατήρ. **οἵ' ἐσυκοφαντούμεθ':** cf. § 8. These words imply that the case against Euerg. was at least under way at the time of the transaction with the claimants. Strictly it should mean that Nic. was involved in the litigation, but that cannot be pressed. The imperf.

perhaps implies that the case was not completed. This is another indication that Nic. was in Athens when Pant. brought the case against Euerg. Cf. on §9. (See speech intro., *The case against Euergus*.)

14 τὰ . . . χρήματ' οὐ προΐενθ' 'were not letting their money go'. Cf. §36. **ἡμεῖς δ' εἰκότως . . . κρατεῖν:** see on §6. For ἐωνήμεθα see speech intro., *The business transactions*. For κρατεῖν see on § 10. **ἱκέτευεν, ἐδεῖτο, ἠντεβόλει:** commonly put together in the speeches. Nic. emphasizes Pant.'s attitude (cf. ἀξιοῦντος . . . τί οὐ ποιήσαντος;) because it is part of Pant.'s accusation that Nic. sold the property contrary to the agreement (§29). **πρατῆρας:** see speech intro., *The business transactions*. **καὶ τοῦθ' ὑπέμεινα:** This is pretence to indicate how accommodating he was. In fact he was very glad to comply. (Cf. on § 13.)

15 ὁρῶν δ' αὐτὸν κτλ.: there follows an unsubstantiated attack on Pant.'s general nature and behaviour. **τὸ μέν** 'on the one hand' followed by πάλιν δ'. Below τὸ μέν is followed by ἐπειδὴ δέ. **ἐξ ἀρχῆς . . . πρὸς ἡμᾶς:** perhaps a quarrel between Pant. and Mnes. had been the reason for Pant.'s desire to change his creditor (cf. on §5). On the other hand Nic. indicates that some time later Pant. was willing to trust Mnes. (§40), but the latter statement may be false (cf. on §40). **τούτωι:** he points to Euerg. **προσκεκρουκότα:** cf. 39.18, 54.3. **τὸ μέν:** see above. **κατέπλευσα** 'I had sailed in', i.e. back to Athens from Pontus; cf. §§6, 10. **ἄσμενον φάσκονθ' ἑορακέναι με** 'alleging/pretending that he was glad to see me'. Since Euerg. had taken possession of the property during Nic.'s absence (§ 10) this would be an indication that Pant. did not associate Nic. with the wrongs he had suffered at Euerg.'s hands. Thus, Nic. implies, he should not do so now in the charges. See speech intro., *The case against Euergus* and *The relationship*. This friendly attitude suits Nic.'s answers to the charges (cf. §§23, 25, 28, 57) and we have only his word for it. He is very vague about when Pant.'s attitude changed (ἐπειδὴ δ' ἔδει τὰ δίκαια ποιεῖν). **πάλιν** 'in turn'. **καὶ ἅπασι μέχρι κτλ.:** a vague and unsubstantiated assertion.

16 ἀπαλλαττόμενος 'becoming reconciled' or 'withdrawing from the fray'. See on § 1. The word is used deliberately because of its undertones of ἄφεσις and ἀπαλλαγή which he goes on immediately to mention. **πρατήρ:** see speech intro., *The business transactions*. **πάντων ἀφεθεὶς τῶν**

ἐγκλημάτων καὶ ἀπαλλαγείς: see on §§ 1 and 19. οὖτος . . . ἀφῆκεν ἁπάντων ἐμέ: this is the first basis for the παραγραφή, dealt with in §§ 18f. καθάπερ αὐτὸς ἐπριάμην παρὰ Μνησικλέους: so §§ 29f. Cf. § 5. μά: though not in itself either affirmative or negative, μά followed by the accusative of the thing appealed to is used chiefly in negation. Cf. § 53. οὐδ' ἂν . . . λαχεῖν . . . τουτονί: ἂν (repeated) goes in sense with λαχεῖν. For δίκην λαχεῖν see on §3. The position at the end of the sentence emphasizes τουτονί. εἴ τι γένοιτο 'come what may'.

17 τὴν δίκην . . . παρεγραψάμην μὴ εἰσαγώγιμον εἶναι: see on § 1. συκοφαντούμενος: for once the accusation of bringing a malicious charge may have some foundation. See speech intro., The relationship. ἀφιέμην . . . καὶ ἀπηλλαττόμην: See § 16 and on § 1. τῶν ἐωνημένων . . . ἀπεδόμην: see speech intro., The business transactions. κελεύοντος . . . ἐκέλευσεν: see on § 14.

18–20 Argument for the παραγραφή on the grounds that Pant. has granted Nic. ἄφεσις and ἀπαλλαγή.

18 μάρτυρες: in § 17. In view of the deposition of witnesses who were present at the time there can be little doubt that Nic. was in fact granted the ἄφεσις, for which see on § 1. Cf. on § 19. λαγχάνων . . . τὴν δίκην: see on §3. ἐμαρτύρει . . . ὑπόλοιπον εἶναι: if indeed Nic. was present in Athens. See below and speech intro., The case. οὖτος: deleted by Blass because of the hiatus after ἐμαρτύρει. While Dem. became increasingly careful about hiatus, in general it is unjustifiable to emend because of hiatus what would otherwise be unexceptionable. μηδὲν ἔγκλημ' ὑπόλοιπον εἶναι 'that he had no complaint outstanding against me'. τῶν αὐτῶν ἀδικημάτων παρόντων, ἀμφοῖν δ' ὁμοίως ἐγκαλῶν: only S has δ', other MSS ἀμφοῖν ὁμοίως. 'if the same wrongs existed and he was making the same charge against both' (Euerg. and Nic.). The reading of Blass, which is adopted by Gernet, is τῶν αὐτῶν ἀδικημάτων, παρόντοιν ἀμφοῖν ὁμοίως ἐγκαλῶν. This would bring out an important point, only implied elsewhere (see on §9), namely that Nic. was present in Athens when Pant. brought his case against Euerg. The genitive τῶν αὐτῶν ἀδικημάτων could depend on ἐγκαλῶν (causal, cf. on 54.1 and on §33 below) or on ἐδικάζετο (cf. e.g. § 19, Lys. 10.12, Dem. 22.27). But there is little to be said for the change and there is some

awkwardness in the casual way the important idea in παρόντοιν is dragged in. **οὐκ ἐῶσιν οἱ νόμοι περὶ τῶν οὕτω πραχθέντων πάλιν λαγχάνειν:** for λαγχάνειν see on 54.1. The law on which Nic. is here depending had as its first clause (cf. 36.25) the prohibition on cases where there had been ἄφεσις or ἀπαλλαγή (§19, cf. on §1. In the law itself the two terms were probably linked by ἤ not καί because the point of 36.25 depends on the conjunction ἤ). Among other things this law contained a clause which made it illegal for a case to be brought on matters about which a court decision had already been made (§§19f.). The relevant part of the law has been preserved at 24.54, quoted in speech intro., *The relationship*.

Yet while with περὶ τῶν οὕτω πραχθέντων Nic. is vague, his reference is to a situation in which an ἄφεσις has been granted. In §17 witnesses to his ἄφεσις have deposed and in §18 he has argued that Pant. also 'testifies' by his behaviour that the ἄφεσις took place. In §§19f. it is ἄφεσις alone which concerns him.

Thus πάλιν λαγχάνειν does not mean 'prosecute again', 'bring a second prosecution'. He is not appealing to the clause in the law which forbids a magistrate to allow a case to be brought concerning which a court judgement had already been given. The phrase πάλιν λαγχάνειν means here 'prosecute subsequently' (cf. 38.1 δεδωκότων...τῶν νόμων παραγράψασθαι περὶ ὧν ἄν τις ἀφεὶς καὶ ἀπαλλάξας πάλιν δικάζηται; cf. 38.4). On Nic.'s failure to make the plea that the case had already been decided see speech intro., *The relationship*.

19 τοῦ νόμου . . . μηκέτι τὰς δίκας εἶναι: a paraphrase of the first clause of the law. See on §§1 and 18. **ἀμφότερ':** see on §1. **ἠκούσατε τῶν μαρτυριῶν:** in §17. See on §18. Nic. states that he was πάντων ἀφεθεὶς τῶν ἐγκλημάτων καὶ ἀπαλλαγείς (§16). In judging the validity of this basis for the παραγραφή we are greatly hampered by Nic.'s failure to specify exactly the sphere of the claims from which Pant. had released him. The release cannot have been a blanket release (despite πάντων); it cannot relate to any wrong whatever which he may have committed or may in the future commit. Since the release was granted at the time he became πρατήρ and at the time of the settlement of Pant.'s debt, the release probably related to claims concerning the agreement and perhaps his acting as πρατήρ (yet he does not bring his ἄφεσις as a defence in §29). If it is true that Antigenes also received a release (§51) the release must have covered the taking over of the plant and slaves. Nic. was probably therefore protected against charges arising out of the terms of the agreement, and so should not have been subjected to the charges in §§ 25, 26, and 29, which involved simply taking over the plant by the terms of the agreement. But it is improbable that he was protected by the release from the charges involving theft (§§ 22, 28) or from those concerning violence and wrongs to ἐπίκληροι (§§ 33ff.). The extent of the release was probably not made crystal clear, because the magistrates had allowed the charges to go forward despite the law addressed to them (24.54, quoted in speech intro., *The relationship*; cf. on § 18). ἁπάντων μὲν τοίνυν κτλ.: for the thought cf. 36.25. ἃ μὲν γὰρ τὸ δημόσιον πέπρακεν: an example of τὰ ἐν τοῖς νόμοις ἀπειρημένα. In the law (24.54, quoted in speech intro., *The relationship*) it is forbidden to allow a suit concerning what τὸ δημόσιον ἀπέδοτο, i.e. confiscated property. Thus the buyer of such property could protect himself by a παραγραφή against legal actions in connection with the property (cf. Harrison I 218f.). οὐ προσήκοντα 'what did not belong to it'.

20 καὶ περὶ ὧν ἔγνω τὸ δικαστήριον: a second example of τὰ ἐν τοῖς νόμοις ἀπειρημένα. Cf. 24.54 (quoted in speech intro., *The relationship*) ὅσων... δίκη περί του ἐν δικαστηρίωι. ἃ δ' αὐτὸς ἐπείσθη: contrasted with ἃ μὲν... πέπρακεν καὶ περὶ ὧν ἔγνω... From §§ 16 and 12 there is a strong if unintended impression that any 'persuasion' of Pant. took the form of blackmail on the part of Nic., that he pretended he was willing to become πρατήρ only on condition that he received a release. τοῖς ὑφ' ἑαυτοῦ: i.e. τοῖς ὑφ' ἑαυτοῦ δικαίοις ὡρισμένοις οὐκ ἐμμένει.

21–32 The charges of Pantaenetus.

21 οὐκοῦν... ἐπέδειξα: in §§ 16f. ὅτ' ἐγιγνόμην τῶν ἀνδραπόδων πρατήρ: for πρατήρ see speech intro., *The business transactions*. Cf. § 16 πρατὴρ τῶν κτημάτων. It has been calculated from Xen. *Poroi* 4.3 that the average cost of a slave working in the mines was 150 drachmas, so that thirty slaves, the workforce of Pant.'s plant, would cost about 45 minae, which was the amount of Nic.'s personal loan. From the words τῶν ἀνδραπόδων πρατήρ it has been assumed therefore that Nic.'s loan was on the slaves and Euerg.'s loan of 60 minae was on the plant. But the real value of the plant and slaves was 206 minae (§ 31). At 27.9 Dem.

uses μαχαιροποιούς and κλινοποιούς in apposition to ἐργαστήρια. In the present passage he says 'slaves' where he means 'plant and slaves' viewed as a unit (cf. on §4 and Finley 259 n. 110). ἵνα δ᾽, ὦ ἄνδρες κτλ.: Nic. now embarks on his replies to the charges of the substantive case. On his reasons for doing so see speech intro., *The case*. ἁλισκόμενον 'because I have the worst of it'. Cf. Plat. *Theaet.* 179b.

22 ΕΓΚΛΗΜΑ: the word in its technical sense was confined to a claim in a private suit (Lipsius 817). ἔβλαψέ με Νικόβουλος κτλ.: the first clause of the ἔγκλημα, further clauses being given at §§25, 26, 28, 29. As with the ἔγκλημα given at 45.46 there is no reason to suspect that the clauses are not genuine. (Cf. E. Ardaillon, *Les Mines du Laurion dans l'antiquité* (Paris 1897) 180f.) They contain details which could not have been gleaned from the speech itself (§22 ἀφελέσθαι... ἐνενήκοντα μνῶν, §25 ἐπὶ Θρασύμωι, §26 καθέζεσθαι εἰς τὸν κεγχρεῶνα, §28 καὶ κατεργάσαμενος κτλ.). Some of these details are too obscure (ἐπὶ Θρασύμωι, κεγχρεῶνα) to be the work of a forʳer. The document perhaps owes its survival to the fact that it is necessary for an understanding of this part of the speech. ἔβλαψέ με Νικόβουλος ἐπιβουλεύσας ἐμοί: these words (cf. §26 ἐπὶ βλάβηι τῆι ἐμῆι) mark the nature of the case as a δίκη βλάβης. (See speech intro., *The case*.) Cf. Dinarchus' charge against Proxenus in Dinarchus fr. 42 1.85 Sauppe (= No. 14 Burtt [Loeb *Minor Attic orators* II]) *ap.* Dion Hal. *Din.* 3 ἔβλαψέ με Πρόξενος (then a statement of how) ἐπιβουλεύσας τούτοις. So here ἐπιβουλεύσας (of §23) marks the fact that Pant. was claiming that Nic. had intentionally caused him damage. The word seems to have been regularly used to make this allegation. It is an important word because anyone convicted of committing damage intentionally had by law to pay double the amount of damage whereas if the damage was unintentional only the simple amount had to be paid (Dem. 21.43) Cf. on §8. ἐπριάμην: for the use of this verb and πωλεῖν of leasing the mines see Arist. *Ath. Pol.* 47.2 ἐνενήκοντα μνῶν: according to Arist. *Ath. Pol.* 47.2 mines were leased from the state for three years or (probably – the text is uncertain) ten years. Lessees paid by instalments (καταβολαί) at regular intervals, probably each prytany. On this basis Pant.'s instalments would be 300 drachmas per prytany if his lease was for 10 years. For the whole question of tenure and payment see R. J. Hopper, *BSA* 48 (1953) 224–39. ἐγγραφῆναι τὸ διπλοῦν τῶι δημοσίωι: a man defaulting on payment due to the state was liable for double what was owed and he suffered ἀτιμία till he paid , i.e. he was excluded from the agora and from all procedural protection of his rights as a citizen, he was banned from addressing the ecclesia and the boule and from going to holy places and participating in public rites (cf. Harrison II 169–76).

23 μεμαρτύρηται . . .διαφοραί: i.e. between Pant. and Euerg. Cf. §§8f. **οὐ μὴν ἀλλά:** used to introduce a supplementary argument which takes such marked precedence over the previous argument (μεμαρτύρηται μὲν δὴ κτλ.) that it is represented as contrasted with it rather than reinforcing it. See Denniston *GP* 29f. **ὑπογράψας** 'having sketchily written', i.e. having made the vague charge. See LSJ s.v. ὑπογράφω II.2; cf. also LSJ s.v. II.3 and Bond's note on Eur. *HF* 1118. **ἐπιβουλεῦσαι:** see on §22. **πῶς γὰρ ἐγὼ προσέταξα . . .ᾔδειν:** in the literal sense of his words Nic. can of course be believed. But both here and at §26 he completely fails to take into account that as Euerg.'s partner in the loan he was jointly responsible for Euerg.'s actions in connection with the loan. See speech intro., *The relationship.*

24 πόση μωρία: exclamation, 'What folly . . . !' **λέγονθ' . . .γεγραφέναι:** sc. αὐτόν. Omission of the article in this type of expression is comparatively rare and the subject is usually expressed. Cf. Ar. *Clouds* 819 with Dover's note. **ἐπεβούλευον:** see on §22. **ἀτιμῶσαι:** see on §22. **ἃ οὐδὲ πολίτης . . .ποιῆσαι:** Nic. means that only the state could impose ἀτιμία (cf. 18.82 of a jury) not another citizen, much less a mere slave. This is not of course an answer to the charge at all inasmuch as Nic. is confusing the indirect with the direct agency. **λόγος:** cf. 54.33.

25 καὶ ἐπειδὴ ὦφλον κτλ.: see on §22. **ἐπὶ Θρασύμωι:** here and at Aeschin. 1.101 MSS give ἐπὶ Θρασύλλωι; Harpocration says that the area was named after a monument to Thrasyllus. But records of mining leases refer to a mining area called Θράσυμος. Hopper (*BSA* 48 (1953) 217) rightly insists that this form should be read in Dem. and Aeschin. The corruption, evidently an old one, is due to uncial confusion of M and ΛΛ. Since Thrasymos was separate from, though presumably close to, Maroneia (M. Crosby, *Hesperia* 19 (1950) 213 reconstructs no. 5 line 33 to speak of 'the road from Thrasymus to Maroneia'), the phrase ἐν τοῖς ἔργοις ἐν Μαρωνείαι in §4 is used loosely. **τῶν ἐμῶν**: Euerg. was perfectly within his rights to take over the plant and slaves (see on §6) but not in using violence nor in interfering with Pant.'s unencumbered property. Nic. however chooses not to make the distinction in his reply, but simply to deny his own personal responsibility. **τὸν μὴ παρόντα . . .τῶι μὴ παρόντι**: the μή here is both generic and conditional. See on §8. For Nic.'s plea that he was not present see on §23. Though Nic. cannot have taken an active part, he could conceivably have approved and helped plan with Euerg. the seizure of the plant. **ὅ γ' ὤν** 'inasmuch as I was', 'since I was'. γε in a participial clause denotes that the main clause is only valid in so far as the participial clause is valid, whether or not the participial clause is in fact known to be valid. Thus, depending on the context ὅ γ' ὤν could mean 'inasmuch as I was' or 'in so far as I was'. See Denniston *GP* 143f. **πῶς γάρ** ; 'How could I?'

26 πλημμελῶν: a metaphor from music, 'make a false note', and so 'offend', 'err', a euphemism in view of the fact that Euerg. was convicted for his actions and ordered to pay two talents by way of damages. Nic. is admitting that Euerg. acted unlawfully, but not in taking over the property itself (see on §§6, 14). **ὧν**: i.e. ταῦτα ὧν 'in respect of these things for which he has paid the penalty'. **οἴκοθεν λαβὼν παρ' ἐμοῦ**: it is very noticeable here that Nic. does not make a straightforward denial of Euerg.'s authority to use his slave. It must be considered very probable that Euerg. used Antigenes on the basis of his partnership with Nic. See speech intro., *The relationship*. **ὡς αὑτόν**: Euerg. stationed the slave 'to [i.e. at] himself' (i.e. the property). **τί γάρ , εἰ κατέστησεν Εὔεργος, ἐγώ σ' ἀδικῶ** ;: an outright denial that he was jointly responsible for the acts of his partner. On the validity of the argument see speech intro., *The relationship*. **κἄπειτα πείσας κτλ.**: see on §22. **πείσας**: a natural word rather than κελεύσας for Pant. to use in the ἔγκλημα if he wished to hide the fact that Euerg. had a right to be in the plant and to order his slaves. Having legitimately taken possession (not ownership) of the slaves (see on §6) presumably Nic. and Euerg. could give them whatever orders they pleased provided that they did not interfere with Pant.'s unencumbered property (cf. on §25). **καθέζεσθαι**: see on §27. **εἰς τὸν κεγχρεῶνα**: the meaning of κεγχρεών, a word not found elsewhere, is uncertain. κέγχρος, properly 'millet' was

used of the spawn of fish (Hdt. 2.93) and small beads (Athen. 12.525c);
cf. Eur. *Ph.* 1386, where ἀσπίδος κεγχρώματα is taken to mean the
eyelet holes in the rim of a shield the size of a millet-grains. Probably the
κεγχρεών was that part of the plant where the ore was ground in
mortars to the size of κέγχροι (cf. Diod. 3.13.1, where ore from the
Nubian gold-mines was first ground to the size of vetch) before being
ground to a fine powder for separating on a washing table. (See
R. J. Hopper, *BSA* 48 (1953) 204, *BSA* 63 (1968) 298, J. F. Healy,
Mining and metallurgy in the Greek and Roman world 141ff.) ἐπὶ βλάβηι
τῆι ἐμῆι: see on §22.

27 ἐκ τοῦ προκαλεῖσθαι...μὴ 'θέλειν: it is not known at what stage
the challenge was issued, but it was not part of Nic.'s counter-challenge
to Pant. (§43), for that was later read out (see on §43).

The evidence of slaves was only admitted when it was given under
torture (cf. §40). To be valid the evidence of slaves had to be given with
the consent of both parties. A litigant therefore issued a challenge,
normally before witnesses (Lys. 7.34, Dem. 45.61, 54.27, 59.123), to his
opponent to hand over a slave for torture or to accept a slave of his
own for torture (cf. §42). A litigant could capitalize, as here, on his
opponent's refusal to accept and the challenge itself could be used as
evidence and is so used in this chapter (cf. 49.58, Ant. 1.11, 5.38, 6.27,
Lys. 4.12; cf. on 54.27). In addition to the distrust with which the
evidence of slaves was generally viewed (see on §41), in this instance
Pant. may well have had good reason to fear the outcome of his
accepting Nic.'s challenge. Even if his charge was true with regard to
Euerg., he might well doubt that slaves under torture (on terms
proposed by Nic.) would give an answer suitable to him to the question,
'Did Nicobulus persuade you...?' since Nic. himself was not present.
ἔπειθον 'For what reason did I try to persuade them?' With the imperf.
Nic. moves the act which he denies to the realm of the unfulfilled. He
uses ἔπειθον not ἐκέλευον, taking up the words of the ἔγκλημα (cf. on
§26). **ἵνα...αὐτοὺς κτήσωμαι**: Pant. might argue that Nic. and Euerg.
hoped to gain ownership of the slaves by reason of Pant.'s inability to
redeem them in the stated time by repaying the principal of the loan;
and if that time was fairly near he might argue that they told the slaves
to go and sit in the κεγχρεών so that they should not work his ore and
that he should be placed in even deeper financial difficulties than he

already was and thus should not be able to redeem the slaves. There is no need to believe that this was truly Nic.'s (Euerg.'s) motive: Pant. could have made the claim without revealing that Euerg. was legitimately in possession of the slaves and the plant. In fact such a motive is unlikely to be correct, for he also claims that Nic. and Euerg. worked his ore. (See on §28.) **νὴ Δι'**: used to introduce contentions supposed to come from antagonists (LSJ s.v. νή II.2). Cf. §50. **ἀλλ' αἱρέσεώς μοι . . . κομίσασθαι:** this does not in itself answer Pant.'s claim because by Nic.'s own account this choice only became open to him when the other creditors, whose claim was initially denied by Mnes., gave him the choice, and it may be that their claim made it worth while for him to take his share of the loan rather than to wait for a share that would be smaller than expected of the proceeds of a sale of the security in the event of Pant.'s failure to redeem it.

Nic. meets the charge in this clause with a denial. He denies that he persuaded the slaves, thus simply varying his answer that he was abroad at the time, but he does not specifically deny that they were persuaded. This makes it likely that at some point the slaves were ordered to stop work. That he does not argue that it was legitimate for Euerg. to order them to stop work is in keeping with his simply denying his own personal responsibility in §§25f. and not making a distinction between what was legitimate action on Euerg.'s part and what was not. If Pant.'s alleged motive is wrong the truth may be that for a short period, perhaps at the actual time that Pant. was ejected (by force? §6), the slaves were ordered to the κεγχρεών and that subsequently they were ordered to work the silver ore (cf. on §28).

καὶ ταῦτα μεμαρτύρηται: in §13.

28 ταύτην . . . οὐχὶ δεξάμενος τὴν πρόκλησιν: see on §27. **καὶ κατεργασάμενος κτλ.:** see on §22. **τὴν ἀργυρῖτιν** 'the silver ore'. **τῶι μὴ παρόντι:** see on §8. Nic. returns to his old defence, again refusing to countenance the possibility of his joint responsibility with Euerg. See speech intro., *The relationship.* **καὶ περὶ ὧν Εὐέργου κατεδικάσω:** a reminder, again without pressing the point, that Euerg. has already paid the damages claimed. Cf. on §18. Nic. does not deny that Euerg. acted as charged.

29 καὶ ἀποδόμενος κτλ.: see on §22. **ἀποδόμενος:** see speech intro., *The business transactions.* **τὰς συνθήκας:** see §5. **ἐμισθώσαμεν . . . καὶ ἄλλ'**

οὐδέν: presumably Nic. could not have presented the text of the agreement as evidence for his claim even if he had wanted to because it would have been destroyed at the end of the financial transaction. But despite what Nic. says here the agreement did contain, in addition to terms of the lease proper, conditions of the loan (§5: καὶ λύσις... ἔν τινι ῥητῶι χρόνωι). In view of this accusation it is highly probable that the agreement contained a clause forbidding Euerg. and Nic. to dispose of the encumbered property, i.e. sell the debt, without Pant.'s consent. τῶν τόκων: see §5. τὰ ἡμέτερ': see on §7. πρατήρ: see speech intro., *The business transactions*. τούτου παρόντος καὶ κελεύοντος: see on §5.

30 ἀπεδόμεθα . . . ἐπρίαμεθα: see speech intro., *The business transactions*. **ἐφ' οἷσπερ αὐτοὶ ἐπριάμεθα:** by the terms of the transaction with the new creditors, Pant. was in the same position as he was when Nic. and Euerg. became his creditors. **οὐ μόνον κελεύοντος . . . ἀλλὰ καὶ ἱκετεύοντος** 'not only urging' (as in the case of Mnes.) 'but also begging', cf. §§14, 16. Nic. does seem to be right in his answer that so far from Pant. preventing him from 'selling' the property he asked him to become πρατήρ because in Pant.'s circumstances these 'buyers' were a godsend to him if not actually his agents (see on §12). This charge of Pant.'s seems especially malicious. **οὐδεὶς γὰρ ἤθελεν δέχεσθαι τοῦτον πρατῆρα:** see on §13. **τί οὖν . . . ἐνέγραψας:** see on §29. Nic. now addresses Pant. directly for dramatic effect, a device he continues to use in §31. **ἐωνήμεθ' . . . ἀπεδόμεθα:** see speech intro., *The business transactions*.

31 μαρτυρεῖς κτλ.: Nic. is arguing that the fact that Pant. ultimately did so well out of Nic.'s 'selling' the property shows that so far from opposing Nic.'s action he encouraged it. Put in that form it is a *non sequitur*. Nic. attempts to mislead the jury by confusing πρᾶσις ἐπὶ λύσει and outright sale, portraying Pant. as a profiteer. See speech intro., *The business transactions*. **ἃ γὰρ ἡμεῖς . . . ἀπέδου σύ** 'For what we sold for 105 minae you later sold for three talents 2,600 drachmas' (i.e. 206 minae). Cf. §50. Nic. is deliberately confusing πρᾶσις ἐπὶ λύσει (ἀπεδόμεθα) with the sale outright (ἀπέδου).

ἀπεδόμεθα, the reading of SA, is to be preferred to the variant ἐωνήμεθα because it is in the context of the circumstances of Nic.'s 'sale' (§30) that the point is made. It was probably failure to understand the situation and Nic.'s deliberate confusion which gave rise to the reading ἐωνήμεθα. But if ἐωνήμεθα is the true reading it would refer to buying ἐπὶ λύσει (from Mnes.) and makes no difference to Nic.'s confusion.

Pant. had a right to sell outright, and since the sale ἐπὶ λύσει to the new creditors had been on the same terms as the 'sale' to Nic. and Euerg. (§30) Pant. had this right when he first had them as ċreditors. It was presumably impossible for him to sell the property outright at the time when it was conditionally forfeit to Euerg. and Nic. and to pay them from the proceeds what he owed, not only because of the difficulty in finding a buyer for currently forfeit property but also by reason of a clause in the agreement. Euerg. and Nic. presumably did not allow the possibility of the disappearance of the profit from the ὑπεροχή.

καίτοι τίς ἂν καθάπαξ πρατῆρά . . . μίαν ;: usually rendered along the following lines: 'And yet who having you as warrantor in the outright sale would have given you one drachma?' Cf. §50 πέπρακας δὲ καθάπαξ, 19.118 καθάπαξ πέπρακεν ἑαυτόν. Harrison (i 278 n. i) rejects the sense 'warrantor of a sale outright': 'καθάπαξ is emphatic by position; but Nikoboulos is not saying "who having you as warrantor *for a sale outright...?*"; rather "who having *you* as a warrantor...?"' It would ruin his argument to imply that Pantainetos might have been satisfactory as warrantor in a sale ἐπὶ λύσει'. Harrison prefers to follow Dareste and Gernet in taking καθάπαξ πρατῆρα to mean 'you only, without other warrantors'. But (1) it is difficult to see a position in which καθάπαξ would be less emphatic; (2) it is doubtful if καθάπαξ can bear this meaning; and (3) in view of the parallels for the usage of καθάπαξ with πεπρακέναι meaning 'to sell outright', that seems the most natural area of meaning here.

However, Harrison's point is valid in that Nic.'s argument would be ruined by the implication that Pant. might have been satisfactory as a warrantor in a sale ἐπὶ λύσει. The text may be preserved if καθάπαξ can be taken with τίς, 'who at all (καθάπαξ) having you as warrantor...?' (i.e. nobody at all). But this interpretation is open to the third objection above and no parallel can be advanced to support it.

The difficulties would be removed by the deletion of καθάπαξ. Nic. would then be asking his question with reference to both relevant sales. It is possible that καθάπαξ began life as a gloss explaining what is in this speech an unusual meaning of ἀπέδου.

32 ἐπείσθη: i.e. the price was acceptable to him. **πρατῆρα**: see speech intro., *The business transactions*. **καθ' ὃ συνέβαλον ἀργύριον** 'in respect of the sum which I had lent him'. The new creditors had lent the same sum as Nic. and Euerg. (§30). Nic. therefore acted as warrantor for the property to that value. **δυοῖν ταλάντοιν**: the sum for which Pant. had successfully sued Euerg. (§46). **προσδικάζεται**: the nuance of προσ- is 'in addition' to these benefits he has received.

33–4 Argument for the παραγραφή on the grounds that there is no εἰσαγωγεύς for Pantaenetus' suit.

33 Though Nic. has said that he proposes to show Pant. is lying καθ' ἕκαστον ὧν ἐγκαλεῖ (§21) he makes no attempt to answer the charge in the remaining part of the ἔγκλημα. Instead he tries to show Pant.'s failure to bring the charge before the proper magistracy. Not enough is known concerning the circumstances of the alleged offences (the only information is given at §45) to make any judgement of Nic.'s guilt. If these offences were in truth committed by Euerg. (and from §47 it appears that he was only charged with them in the course of Pant.'s speech) and if they were committed in an attempt to uphold the rights held by himself and Nic. by virtue of the loan agreement, then perhaps the question of Nic.'s guilt depends yet again on whether or not he should be considered jointly responsible for the actions of his loan partner. (See speech intro., *The relationship*.) **αἴκειαν καὶ ὕβριν**: see on 54.1. **βιαίων**: the δίκη βιαίων was an action for forcible theft of property (and covered rape). The genitive after ἐγκαλεῖ (understood) is causal (see on 54.1 and cf. on §18), but it appears strange among the accusatives αἴκειαν, ὕβριν and ἀδικήματα (cf. τὰ τῶν βιαίων (τὰ περὶ τῶν βιαίων A) below). The speaker seems unwilling to use the form βίαια. It seems that, unlike the situation with αἰκείας and ὕβρεως, δίκη βιαίων was felt to be a unit to such an extent that the genitive came most readily to the speaker's mind. **ἐπικλήρους**: if a man died leaving no legitimate male issue but only female issue, a woman in such a situation was called ἐπίκληρος. It was the duty of the nearest male relative of the dead man to marry her, even if a divorce was thereby made necessary on either or both sides. It was thus hoped that she might produce a son who would inherit the property left by the dead man and continue the oikos. See MacDowell *Law* 95–8 (with references) and D. M. Schaps, *Economic rights of women in ancient Greece* (Edinburgh 1979) 25–47. A public prosecution for wronging an ἐπίκληρος could be brought by *eisangelia* (see on §§ 45f.). ἡ μὲν αἴκεια . . .πρὸς τοὺς τετταράκοντα: on the Forty see Harrison II 18–21. They were responsible for all cases which would normally go to arbitration, i.e. all private suits except δίκαι ἔμμηνοι (see on §2), homicide suits, and probably suits dealing with the family and family property.

Here the δίκη αἰκείας (see speech intro. to Dem. 54 and on 54.1) is said to come before the Forty (cf. schol. Plat. *Rep.* 464e). Yet Aristotle (*Ath. Pol.* 52.2) lists it as one of the δίκαι ἔμμηνοι which came before the εἰσαγωγεῖς. The status of the δίκη αἰκείας must have been changed between the date of this speech and Arist. *Ath. Pol.* (i.e. *c.* 325/4). The εἰσαγωγεῖς in the sense of the five special officers with this title had probably not been instituted at the date of this speech (see below on περὶ ὧν οὐκ εἰσὶν εἰσαγωγεῖς). For a possible reason for the change of status of the δίκη αἰκείας see Cohen 17 n. 41.

αἱ δὲ τῆς ὕβρεως πρὸς τοὺς θεσμοθέτας: this is confirmed by Isoc. 20.2 and it appears in the law given at Dem. 21.47 and Aeschin. 1.16, though it is omitted from Aristotle's list of γραφαί which came before the thesmothetae (*Ath. Pol.* 59.3). ὅσα δ' εἰς ἐπικλήρους, πρὸς τὸν ἄρχοντα: see on §46. ἀντιλαγχάνειν: here used of entering a παραγραφή. Contrast the use at 39.38. The process implied is that of making a counter-move to an opponent's λῆξις (see on §3). περὶ ὧν οὐκ εἰσὶν εἰσαγωγεῖς 'in regard to which there are no introducing magistrates' (see Wolff 97 (see p. 111 n. 18), Harrison II 121f.). Here and at §34 εἰσαγωγεύς is used in a general sense with reference to the magistrate who δίκην εἰσάγει (see on §1). Aristotle (*Ath. Pol.* 52.2) gives a list of δίκαι ἔμμηνοι (see on §2) which by *c.* 325/4 were dealt with by the college of five εἰσαγωγεῖς. Dem.'s general use of the term here was used by Gernet (*Droit et société dans la Grèce ancienne* (Paris 1955) 173ff.) to argue that the college of εἰσαγωγεῖς had not been instituted at the date of this speech.

The law Nic. is using seems to have rendered a suit inadmissible if the plaintiff could not bring it by a δίκη allotted to a specific magistrate as its introducer. This is not however what Nic. is arguing. He is saying that Pant. has put together in one complaint (which he maintains in §§ 35–8 should not be covered by a δίκη μεταλλική) charges which should have been brought by several δίκαι (and a γραφή) each allotted to different magistrates. In other words, he is arguing not that there is no relevant magistrate but that the wrong magistracy has been used. But he attempts to give the impression that there is a general law relating to that situation *different from* the particular law defining the conditions under which a δίκη μεταλλική may be brought. If there was such a law he fails to produce it.

Harrison (II 122 n. 3) says that Nic. appears to be arguing that though each of Pant.'s complaints was maintainable in itself, there was no εἰσαγωγεύς for them when lumped together. That is less likely in view of his words οὐκ ὄντων εἰσαγωγέων τῶν θεσμοθετῶν ὑπὲρ ὧν λαγχάνει. If that is his meaning he has not expressed it clearly.

34 καὶ οὐκ ὄντων . . . Πανταίνετος 'and though the thesmothetae are not the introducing magistrates in matters about which Pant. is bringing suit'. This is not what the law covered unless these words are given the far-fetched meaning that the thesmothetae are not εἰσαγωγεῖς of the matters about which Pant. is bringing suit when he lumps them together. But whichever interpretation is adopted the question depends on whether the matters should be introduced by the thesmothetae in a δίκη μεταλλική, something he has yet to consider (§§ 35–8). **ἐξαλή-λιπται:** perf. pass. of ἐξαλείφω, which means 'plaster' or 'wash over'. With the meaning here 'erase' (from the written complaint) and the metaphorical use of ἐξαλεῖψαι below cf. 39.39 and see note *ad loc.* **τὸ δ' ὅπως, ὑμεῖς σκοπεῖτε** 'As for the question how [sc. ἐξαλήλιπται], *you* consider.' Cf. 3.10 τὸ δ' ὅπως, τοῦτο λέγε. Nic. implies underhand work, perhaps collusion. (For the vagueness of the charge, cf. 57.33.) But presumably this basis of the παραγραφή has been struck out simply because the law in question did not apply and because he is attempting to show that the situation is covered by two laws whereas in reality it is covered only by the μεταλλικὸς νόμος (§§ 35–8). See on § 33. If Harrison's interpretation of Nic.'s argument is correct (see on § 33) it may have been struck out because the matter would be decided by the jury's judgement on his arguments concerning the μεταλλικὸς νόμος.

35–8 Argument for the παραγραφή on the grounds that the alleged offences do not fall within the definition of the μεταλλικὸς νόμος.

At 35.47–9 from the other point of view the speaker opposing Lacritus' παραγραφή enumerates the various courts that he could not go to if his suit were rejected by the emporic court. Cf. 34.43.

Having drifted into the grounds for the παραγραφή by way of answer to one of Pant.'s charges (§§33f.), Nic. continues his arguments in support of the παραγραφή.

35 εἰσαγώγιμον: see on § 1. The inference is that the mining law *defined* cases which could be brought by a δίκη μεταλλική. Cf. below. **χάριτος** 'thanks' from Pant. for allowing him to recover his property. **ἐάν τις ἐξίλλῃ τινὰ τῆς ἐργασίας:** this clause in the law makes the δίκη ἐξούλης (see on 39.15) available to those who had leased from the state , so putting the lessee on the same footing as someone who had bought from the state (cf. Harrison I 234 n. 1). **ἐγὼ δ' οὐχ ὅπως αὐτὸς ἐξίλλω** 'not only did I not eject him myself'. For οὐχ ὅπως cf. 56.43. For ἐξίλλω cf. on 39.15. Even if Nic. were here to allow that he was jointly responsible for the acts of Euerg. (see speech intro., *The relationship*) what he says is true since Euerg.'s taking over the plant was legitimate (see on §6). But though he did not use the word ἐξίλλειν Pant. accused Nic. of ejecting him from the processing plant (§25). That clause would seem to give Pant. his excuse for bringing a δίκη μεταλλική even though he is suing for damages in the terms of a δίκη βλάβης. (Cf. on §§22, 36.) **ἄλλος ἀπεστέρει:** i.e. Euergus. While it suits Nic. to put all the blame on Euerg., these words perhaps imply that Euerg. was not so unhappy with the situation after they had taken over the property as Nic. says he himself was (§§ 10f.). **ἐγκρατῆ:** Cf. on § 10. **πρατὴρ . . . ἐγενόμην:** § 16. For πρατήρ see speech. intro., *The business transactions*.

36 κἂν ἄλλο τι ἀδικῇ τις περὶ τὰ μέταλλα: Nic. gives specific instances, but what he says here may imply that the law contained a final compendium clause with these words which Nic. chooses to ignore. If so, although Euerg.'s actions did not concern the mine directly, Pant. might argue that by preventing him from using the plant Euerg. and Nic. were rendering his mining activities impossible, since if he was not producing marketable silver he could not buy supplies or replace the necessities of working. **ἂν τύφῃ τις** 'if anyone causes smoke', in a malicious or dangerous way. Cf. Ar. *Wasps* 1079. Filling workings with smoke was not necessarily malicious or dangerous, since fire was used for breaking down the rock (R. J. Hopper, *Trade and industry in classical Greece* (London 1979) 185). This reading of Bekker (τυφῆι A) is preferable to ὑφάψηι (FQ) which would mean 'sets on fire from underneath' (by setting fire to the pit-props?). That would be too specific in reference for the context. Presumably τύφηι > ὑφῆι (S, which is meaningless) > ὑφάψηι. ἂν ὅπλ' ἐπιφέρηι 'if he makes an armed attack'. The smoking and armed-attack clauses would allow a δίκη μεταλλική to be brought even though actual ejection was not achieved. The law provides a remedy for injuries which prevented the smooth working of the mine. ἂν ἐπικατατέμνηι τῶν μέτρων ἐντός 'if he makes additional cuts within the boundaries'. Cf. Hyp. *Eux.* 35 φήναντος γὰρ Λυσάνδρου τὸ 'Επικράτους μέταλλον...⟨ὡς⟩ ἐντὸς τῶν μέτρων τετρημένον. κατατέμνειν is used of cutting mines (Xen. *Por.* 4.27); ἐπι-signifies 'in addition'.

The precise nature of the offence is uncertain. We expect this clause in the law, like the two which precede, to be concerned with an offence against another lessee, not an offence against the state. The boundary of a mine would be reached underground by measuring from a vertical shaft, and the distance (μέτρον) to which a mine operator could go marked the boundary of the mine. To extend the mine beyond such μέτρα was to cut into the boundaries and so to pass within them (cf. R. J. Hopper, *BSA* 48 (1953) 220f.). To do so would mean extracting ore for which one was not entitled by one's lease. This breach of the law, an offence against the state, is shown by Hyp. *Eux.* 35 to have laid a man open to φάσις, being a special case of misappropriating state property (cf. Harrison II 218–21). It was presumably by this procedure that Lycurgus succeeded in having Diphilus executed for τοὺς μεσο-κρινεῖς ὑφελεῖν and for having unlawfully enriched himself by mining operations ([Plut.] *Mor.* 843a = *Vit. Lyc.* 44). Hopper (op. cit. 222) argues that the μεσοκρινεῖς were dividing pillars, possibly sections of rock wall pierced by passages. But since the present clause of the μεταλλικὸς νόμος should involve a wrong committed against an individual, not a wrong against the state, it refers to cutting into another's area and extracting ore which another lessee was legally entitled to extract. Either τῶν μέτρων ἐντός has become a stylized expression taken from the law concerning the offence against the state or we must understand it to mean cutting within (another's) μέτρα, the victim being unexpressed as in the clauses which immediately precede. πρὸς ὑμᾶς 'against you', the members of the jury. προεῖντο . . .προϊεμένους: cf. on §14.

37 πρίηται: cf. on §22. προεισφοράν 'advance war tax'. The εἰσφορά was a war tax which took the form of a capital levy and it was raised by decree of the people as occasion demanded. For the payment of the

tax those eligible were divided into 100 symmories. The ἡγεμόνες of the
symmories together with the δεύτεροι and τρίτοι advanced the tax to
the state (προεισφέρειν), later recovering it from the other members of
their symmories. Cf. A. H. M. Jones, *Athenian democracy* (Oxford 1957)
23–38, esp. 26–8.

38 ἂν ὅλως ἄλλο τι 'if, in short, he has any other ground for action'.
So ὅλως below. **συντρήσασιν** 'bore'. Properly συντετραίνειν means to
unite by running one passage or channel into another. Here it refers
to running one gallery into another. **ἀπειληφότι:** see on § 7. **γλίσχρως**
lit. 'stickily', i.e. 'with difficulty'. **πρός:** adverbial, 'in addition'; cf.
§49, 39.23. **οὐδ' ἐγγύς** 'I should say not!' Cf. 18.12.

39–44 The challenge and counter-challenge concerning the evidence
of the slave.

39 εἰσαγώγιμος: see on § 1. **οὐδὲν . . . λέγειν** 'though he was able to say
not one single thing that was right'. **περὶ ὧν ἀφῆκε δικαζόμενος:** cf.
§§ 18–20. **τοῦ ἐξελθόντος μηνός** 'last month'. Cf. Hyp. *Eux.* 35. See on
§ 2. **εἰσιέναι τὴν δίκην** 'to enter the court' (LSJ s.v. δίκη IV.2). **τῶν
δικαστηρίων ἐπικεκληρωμένων** 'when the lawcourts had already been
allotted' to the jurors. Cf. 47.17. See Arist. *Ath. Pol.* 59.5. **ἐργαστήριον**
'gang'. Cf. on 39.2. **τῶν συνεστώτων** 'conspirators'. Cf. §48.

40 πρόκλησιν: see on §27. Nic. says that the challenge was made at
the very last moment before the hearing (cf. §42). In a case which
involved arbitration a πρόκλησις was only allowed up to the sealing
of the evidence by the arbitrator (54.27), but since the present case was
a δίκη ἔμμηνος (see on §2) there was no arbitration. The implication
of 48.3 is that with the consent of both parties a suit could be withdrawn
from the jury at the last moment (cf. Isoc. 18.39, Isae. 5.31, Dem.
34.18); and in Isae. 5.17 a compromise was reached even after the votes
had been cast but not counted. At 52.14 a plaintiff withdraws a case
from a public arbitrator. **μακράν:** the implication is that the length of
the challenge was designed to confuse Nic. The terms of the challenge,
which was written (§42: τὴν πρόκλησιν ἀνοίξας), contained the
questions which were to be put to the slave (cf. Ant. 1.10), the manner
in which the torture was to be carried out (cf. 45.61), and the person

who was to conduct it (see below and §42). The text of a πρόκλησις is given at 59.124. **βασανίζεσθαι:** see on §27. **κἂν μὲν ἦι ταῦτ' ἀληθῆ κτλ.:** acc. to Nic., Pant.'s challenge included a compromise whereby the issue was to be settled in favour of the one whom the slave's evidence favoured. **τὴν δίκην ἀτίμητον ὀφλεῖν αὐτῶι:** in an ἀγὼν τιμητός (see Introduction) such as a δίκη βλάβης, the plaintiff stated in his charge what the amount of his claim was (§§32, 41), and in the case of conviction, the defendant submitted an alternative penalty (cf. on 56.18, 43). According to Nic., by accepting the challenge he was accepting Pant.'s assessment of damages, thus in effect making the case ἀτίμητος, though, of course, now it would not come before a court. **τὸν βασανιστὴν Μνησικλέα:** cf. Isoc. 17.15, Ant. 1.10. See below. **ἐπιγνώμον' εἶναι τῆς τιμῆς τῆς τοῦ παιδός:** the proposal was that Mnes. was to assess how much Pant. was to pay Nic. for bodily damage suffered by the slave as a result of the torture. Cf. 59.124, Ar. *Frogs* 624 (for a list of tortures see Ar. *Frogs* 618ff. with Stanford's note). It may be doubted whether Pant. would really be willing to have Mnes. in this position if he had quarrelled with him (cf. on §15). In fact these terms may really reflect those of Nic.'s counter-challenge rather than Pant.'s challenge (cf. on §41). **ἐγγυητάς:** sureties that Nic. would abide by the terms of the challenge. The acceptance of the terms constituted a contract. The present passage and that at Isoc. 17.15ff. provide the only definite cases where it is claimed that a challenge was at first accepted. (At 47.5 the challenge itself is in question.) Nowhere do we have an example of the terms of the challenge actually being carried out (see on §41).

41 ποῦ γάρ ἐστι δίκαιον κτλ.: though he himself issued a challenge (§27) Nic. justifiably suggests that the evidence given by a slave under torture is suspect. In fact on the subject of the reliability of slaves' evidence orators say what suits them (cf. on 54.3, 38). Antiphon (5.31) says explicitly that a slave was likely to say what would please his questioners in order to end his torture (cf. Ant. 1.40) and Lysias (7.35) points to the likelihood of slaves ridding themselves of their torture by incriminating their masters 'to whom they are naturally κακονούστατοι' (cf. Lys. 7.16). Lycurgus however (*Leocr.* 29) states that his opponent's slaves would have been much readier to deny the truth than to invent lies against their master, presumably because they feared

punishment. Dem. 30.37, repeating Isae. 8.12 almost verbatim, says
that the evidence of slaves is more reliable than that of free men because
whereas the latter have been thought not to have told the truth, no slave
who has been tortured has ever been convicted of telling lies (cf. Ant.
1.8, 6.25, Isoc. 17.54, Dem. 47.8). Aristotle (*Rhet.* 1373b 31ff.) gives the
rhetorical possibilities of either line of argument. The fact that we have
no single instance of the terms of a challenge being carried out is strong
evidence that in reality the evidence given by slaves under torture was
not generally considered trustworthy. At least some of the many people
challenged must have recognized either that such evidence was
intrinsically untrustworthy (cf. Harrison II 147f.) or that the terms of
the challenge (cf. §42) made it untrustworthy. **ἢ μηδὲν . . . ζημιοῦσθαι:**
since the case would not go before a jury, Pant. would not now risk
being fined the ἐπωβελία (for which see on 56.4). The alternatives
presented by Nic. (either I have to pay or he gets off scot-free) are not
true alternatives. Any unfairness lay in the fact that Nic. had something
to lose and nothing to gain. **προσκαλεῖται μέν με τὴν δίκην πάλιν:** the
first stage of a suit. The plaintiff summoned (προσκαλεῖσθαι) the
defendant, before witnesses, to appear before the relevant magistrate
on a stated day, declaring the charge. Cf. on §3. **ἐπειδὴ θᾶττον:**
τάχιστα is more usual. Cf. Plat. *Prot.* 325c ἐπειδὰν θᾶττον. **ἀνείλετο
τὰς παρακαταβολάς:** παρακαταβολή is not used in its narrower sense
of a deposit which was paid in claims against the state for property
wrongfully confiscated and sold and in certain inheritance claims
(Harpocr. s.v. παρακαταβολὴ καὶ παρακαταβάλλειν; see Harrison II
179–83). As at Isoc. 20.2 the word here has the wider meaning of 'court
deposit'. Apart from παρακαταβολή in the narrower sense, there were
two kinds, the παράστασις which was paid by the plaintiff in many
kinds of public suit, and the πρυτανεῖα, to which reference is made here
(cf. with reference to a δίκη βλάβης Isoc. 18.12). It was a deposit made
by both the plaintiff and the defendant to the state and forfeited if the
case was lost, the losing party reimbursing his opponent. The amount
was related to the matter in dispute, being 30 drachmas if the sum at
issue was, as in this case, over 1,000 drachmas. See Harrison II 92–4.
The implication of the present passage is that the plaintiff (and
presumably the defendant) was entitled to recover the πρυτανεῖα if the
matter at issue was settled out of court at least by a πρόκλησις.
οὕτως . . . δικαίοις: this depends on Nic.'s version, whereby he quickly

accepted Pant.'s challenge. But Nic. brings no testimony (not even his
ἐγγυητής) in support either of his account of the timing of Pant.'s
challenge or of the unauthorized changes: he merely has his own
counter-challenge read (§43). Possibly Nic. was unwilling to accept the
challenge, probably because he felt that the evidence of the slave would
be damning to himself (and it may be that Pant. in fact named himself,
not Mnes., as βασανιστής), possibly because, like others, he refused to
have his case decided by a slave's evidence. However, rather than give
Pant. the advantage conferred by the refusal of a challenge (cf. on §27,
Dem. 54.27 and 40) he issued a counter-challenge, which may have
named Mnes. as βασανιστής. In fact the terms attributed to Pant.'s
challenge may reflect rather the terms of Nic.'s counter-challenge.
Pant.'s hasty resumption of the prosecution (again unsupported by
evidence) is not surprising. If, as is likely, Nic. did not accept or reject
Pant.'s challenge immediately, Pant., quite properly in view of his
challenge, recovered his deposits because he was not going on with the
case as arranged, but as his challenge was made in the near certain
knowledge that Nic. would refuse (cf. above) and as there was still no
settlement he equally properly initiated another suit, keeping his eye on
the date for the acceptance of λήξεις for δίκαι μεταλλικαί (see on
§2).

42 τὸ μέλλειν καλεῖσθαι τὴν δίκην: see on §1; cf. §39. **προκαλοῦμαί
σε ταυτί κτλ.:** the short sentences bring out the haste with which Nic.
claims the challenge was put to him and the pressure under which it
was accepted. **τὸν δακτύλιον** 'the ring' for sealing the challenge.
ἐγγυητής: cf. on §40. **ἐποιησάμην:** middle, 'I had no copy made nor
anything else of that sort.' Nic. is giving a reason why he could not
compel Pant. to abide by what he gives as the original terms of Pant.'s
challenge. **ἑτέραν...πρόκλησιν:** the claim that the terms of a sealed
document had been changed is highly suspect, and Nic. brings no
evidence on the point. Cf. on §41. **αὐτὸς βασανίζειν:** obviously it was
in Pant.'s interest and against Nic.'s that Pant. rather than a third party
such as Mnes. should be βασανιστής, since Pant. could continue the
torture till he had extorted the evidence which was in his own favour.
τὸν ἄνθρωπον 'the fellow' (i.e. the slave), with a sense of pity as at
21.91. **εἷλκεν:** imperf., denoting the length and incomplete nature of
Pant.'s action: 'he attempted to drag him away'. Cf. 21.221 μηδέν'

ἕλξειν μηδ' ὑβριεῖν μηδὲ τυπτήσειν. For the nuance of dragging with wanton violence see LSJ s.v. ἕλκω II.3.

43 τὸ καταπεπλάσθαι τὸν βίον 'that one's way of life should be feigned'. καταπεπλάσθαι is the emendation of Emperius of καταπεπλῆχθαι, which renders no satisfactory meaning even with Wolf's addition, τὸ ⟨μὴ⟩ καταπεπλῆχθαι, 'the not being shy' (cf. LSJ s.v. καταπλήξ 2). For καταπεπλάσθαι cf. Lys. 19.60 (πλάσασθαι). Rennie compares Dem. 45.68 (πεπλασμένοις), with which LSJ (s.v. πλάσσω IV Med.) compare Thuc. 6.58. A doubt must hang over καταπεπλάσθαι because the parallels are with πλάττειν not with καταπλάττειν, which means 'to plaster', 'to poultice', and is not otherwise attested in the metaphorical sense till the first century A.D., though Menander (*Misoumenos* 364 (Sandbach)) uses καταπλαστός meaning 'affected'. **καταφρονούμενος . . . ζῆν** 'because I was despised by reason of my simple and natural life', as contrasted with τὸ καταπεπλάσθαι τὸν βίον. Nic. is putting on an air of injured innocence. **ταῦτ' ἀνεχόμενος** 'by putting up with this behaviour'. **δ' οὖν** 'however that may be'. Nic. returns to his main topic after giving his generalizing reflection on his situation. See Denniston *GP* 463f. **ἠναγκαζόμην:** with the imperf. Nic. indicates that he did not come quickly and easily to his decision to issue a counter-challenge. **παρ' ἃ ἡγούμην δίκαι' εἶναι:** cf. §41. **ἀντιπροκαλεῖσθαι:** attested only here in classical Greek. ἀντιπρόκλησις is attested only in Hesychius. **παρεδίδουν** 'I offered to hand over', i.e. on my own terms. It is imperf. because the action was not completed. **λέγε τὴν πρόκλησιν:** since Pant. is said to have refused both the terms of what was read and the terms of his own challenge (§44), what was read was Nic.'s counter-challenge, which proves absolutely nothing.

44 φυγών μὲν . . . φυγὼν δ': in agreement with the subject of ἐρεῖ, not with ἔγωγε. **θεάσασθε:** Nic. presents the slave Antigenes to the jury. We may assume that he was physically incapable of committing outrages – if he was alone. **οὐδ' αὐτὸς ἐγκαλεῖ:** Pant. does not make this clear in the ἔγκλημα (§§22, 25, 26, 28), and underlying Nic.'s alibi answer is the assumption that Pant. did imply this in his ἔγκλημα. Nic.'s statement here underlines his failure to take account of the possibility that he could be held responsible for his partner's actions. See speech intro., *The relationship*.

45–7 Consideration of the case against Euergus.

45 ἐξαπατήσας: cf. on 54.38. **τὰς αὐτὰς οὔσας ἀπολογίας:** Nic. cannot mean that his defence is the same as Euerg.'s was, because Euerg. lost his case. He means that his defence with regard to the alleged happenings at Pant.'s house would have applied equally well in Euerg.'s case but Euerg. did not make it; if he had, Pant. would not have secured a conviction. By linking his answer to these charges with Euerg.'s case, Nic. attempts not only to prove that the action against Euerg., which involved the same charges as his own case (§23), was malicious (ὅσπερ...σεσυκοφαντῆσθαι), but also to offset the fact that he was pleading in the shadow of Euerg.'s conviction by at least giving the impression that he is using arguments which if used by Euerg. would have prevented his conviction. **εἰς ἀγρὸν ὡς αὑτόν** 'to his house in the country'. **ἐπὶ τὰς ἐπικλήρους εἰσελθεῖν καὶ τὴν μητέρα τὴν αὑτοῦ:** see on §33. It is not stated how the ἐπίκληροι came to be in Pant.'s house.

For the seclusion of Athenian women so far as practical considerations of supervision and wealth allowed cf. on 39.9 and see Dover 95–8, 209–13. From 47.38 it can be seen that a decent man would avoid invading the privacy even of an enemy's womenfolk. Pant. is exploiting this ethic, first against Euerg. and now against Nic. The occurrence of the same charge at Lys. 3.6 and at Dem. 21.79 suggests that such accusations may have been commonplace. It is interesting that Dem. here despises the sort of charge he himself makes at 21.79. Cf. above on §41.

πρὸς τὸ δικαστήριον: the reason for the emphatic position at the end of the sentence is that Nic. asserts that Pant. did not raise the matter until he came to court. See on §47.

46 πρὸς μὲν τὸν ἄρχοντα κτλ.: in addition to his duty to act as the presiding magistrate in cases of wrongs against ἐπίκληροι (cf. §33), orphans and others, the archon, by a law quoted at 43.75, had the right and duty to act himself in 'looking after' (ἐπιμελείσθω) orphans, ἐπίκληροι, families that were becoming extinct, and women who remained in the house of a dead husband claiming to be pregnant by him (cf. Arist. *Ath. Pol.* 56.6f.). If anyone committed ὕβρις (see on 54.1) or any illegal act against these classes of people, the archon could fine the offender up to the level of his competence (κατὰ τὸ τέλος: for this

expression and the imposition of fines by magistrates see Harrison II
4–7), or if the offence seemed too serious for that remedy he could bring
the offender before a court (by εἰσαγγελία, see below on οὐδ'
εἰσήγγειλεν) with a proposal for what he considered the proper penalty
(cf. 35.48, Isae. 7.30, Aeschin. 1.158). Looking after orphans and
ἐπίκληροι would mostly involve ensuring that orphans were duly
assigned to guardians and ἐπίκληροι to husbands. Nic.'s use of ἐπιμελεῖσθαι shows that he has this law in mind. By specifically mention-
ing Pant.'s not having had the matter examined (ἐξήτασται) before the
archon he implies that, if Pant. had gone to the archon, the archon
could have added the weight of his office to the prosecution. Pant.'s
failure to do this, he suggests, is suspicious. **παρ' ὧι τῶι μὲν . . . βοήθεια:**
the man bringing the charge before the archon suffered no penalty
whether or not the archon took up the prosecution himself (cf. below
on οὐδ' εἰσήγγειλεν). The penalties after conviction in a case brought
by εἰσαγγελία were severe (Isae. 1.39, 3.47, 3.62, 11.13, 11.35). The
expression ὅτι χρὴ παθεῖν αὐτὸν ἢ ἀποτεῖσαι is used in a law, quoted
at 24.105, of the court deciding corporal or pecuniary punishment for
someone who had committed the grave offence of violating a ban on
attendance at holy places. **οὐδέπω . . . ἐξήτασται:** see above. In
addition Nic. is claiming that the charge was not considered *at all* before
the case came to court (see on §47). **οὐδ' εἰσήγγειλεν:** the normal
procedure for wrongs against ἐπίκληροι or against orphans was
εἰσαγγελία (for ἐπίκληροι: Isae. 3.46, Dem. *ap.* Poll. 8.53; for orphans:
Isae. 11.6, 15), which followed the rules for γραφαί (and so has to be
distinguished from the εἰσαγγελία procedure used in relation to
treason and atheism: Harrison II 50–9, MacDowell *Law* 58, 64, 183–6).
Though Aristotle (*Ath. Pol.* 56.6) lists ὀρφανῶν κακώσεως, ἐπικλήρου
κακώσεως and οἴκου ὀρφανικοῦ κακώσεως in a list of δίκαι and γραφαί
which were the responsibility of the archon, the εἰσαγγελία procedure
would be adopted because the prosecutor was liable neither to a court
fee, which would be forfeit if he lost the case, nor to a penalty if he failed
to gain a certain proportion of the votes (Isae. 3.47). Cf. Harrison I
117–19. **ἐν δὲ τῶι δικαστηρίωι κτλ.:** contrasted with πρὸς μὲν τὸν
ἄρχοντα . . . οὐδέπω . . . ἐξήτασται, οὐδ' εἰσήγγειλεν . . . because Nic.
asserts that the matter was not raised and investigated before it was
brought up in court. **δυοῖν ταλάντοιν:** Pant. was suing Nic. for the
same amount (§32).

47 ἐν δὲ μεταλλικῆι δίκηι: for some doubt as to whether Euerg.'s case was a δίκη μεταλλική see speech intro., *The case against Euergus*. περὶ ὧν οὐδ᾽ . . .κατηγορηθήσεσθαι: the λῆξις (see on 54.1) would have included the formal charge. Nic. must mean that in Euerg.'s case the charge about the ἐπίκληροι did not appear formally in the λῆξις but was brought up by Pant. informally in the course of his speech in court. ἡ δ᾽ ὀργή: the indignation felt by the members of the jury at Euerg.'s alleged wrongs against the women (see on §45).

48–51 Having 'shown' that Pant. deceived an earlier jury, Nic. considers Pant.'s general character and behaviour, and includes some invective against his witnesses.

48 ἐξηπατηκότα . . .ἐξαπατᾶν: cf. on 54.38. τοῖς πράγμασιν . . .τοῖς λόγοις: 'the facts' and 'the assertions/arguments' are contrasted. τοῖς συνεστῶσιν: cf. §39. τῶι μεγάλωι τούτωι 'that big man'. Nic. points to him. τῶι πιθανωτάτωι πάντων ἀνθρώπων καὶ πονηροτάτωι: the alliteration conveys the contempt with which Nic. spits out the words. Cf. 34.6 πρᾶγμα ποιεῖ πάντων δεινότατον. καὶ τῶι. . .κλαήσειν καὶ ὀδυρεῖσθαι 'and in his readiness to weep and wail with no reserve or shame'. μηδὲν ὑποστελλόμενον 'without restraint'. This phrase, a metaphor from reefing sails, is common: cf. 4.51, 19.156, 19.237, 19.338, 21.70.

49 ὅς γ᾽ 'inasmuch as you...seek'. (The verb does not come till the end of the sentence.) Cf. on §24. ὀφείλων: to Mnesicles and his co-creditors (§4), who are also referred to by τοῖς συμβαλοῦσιν ἐξ ἀρχῆς (cf. §9). χωρὶς ὧν . . .ἠδίκεις 'apart from the wrongs you committed in respect of the agreement itself' (see §7). πρός: see on §38. ἀτιμῶσαι: cf. §24. It is not clear how loss of civic rights was a prospect. It would be a possibility if it was a τίμημα of the plaintiff in an εἰσαγγελία for κακώσεως ἐπικλήρου (cf. on §46). ἐξισταμένους τῶν ὄντων 'giving up possession of their property', i.e. becoming bankrupt. Cf. 33.25, 36.50, 45.64. σοὶ δ᾽ ὁ συμβεβληκώς 'but in your case the one who has lent to you', i.e. Euerg. (δανείσας τάλαντον, cf. §4). δύ᾽ ὤφληκεν: §46.

50 τετταράκοντα μνᾶς δανείσας: §4. δυοῖν ταλάντοιν: §32. πέπρακας δὲ καθάπαξ 'you have sold outright'. See on §31. The sum given in

§31 is 3 talents 2,600 drachmas. Here Nic. is using round figures.
τέτταρ' . . . τάλαντα: i.e., 2 talents awarded against Euerg. and 2
talents claimed against Nic. νὴ Δία: see on §27. τίς δ' ἂν . . . τῶν
αὑτοῦ: Pant.'s reference would be to the charges in §§ 22 and 25, and
if violence was used in ejecting Pant. from his property (cf. § 6 βίαι),
Antigenes is unlikely to have acted alone. δίκην λαχών: see on § 3.
ὑπεύθυνον 'responsible, answerable'. Here the word is used generally.
Properly it is used of an officer of the state who is liable to account for
his administration (εὔθυναι). The statement of Nic. is justified: why was
it fair that he, represented by the slave, should have to pay damages
for the same actions as those for which Euerg. has paid damages?

51 ἀφῆκε τῶν τοιούτων αἰτιῶν ἁπασῶν: if this statement is literally
true in the sense that Antigenes was included in Nic.'s ἄφεσις (and it
may have been testified at § 17), any ἄφεσις given to Antigenes could
only relate to the taking over of the property; it could not relate to all
the terms of the agreement (cf. on § 19). It is possible that Nic. got
a blanket ἄφεσις for Antigenes because Pant. never believed that
Antigenes was acting without orders. But even so it remains question-
able if it would have included the theft of the silver and violence. But
probably Nic. is using ἀφῆκε figuratively, arguing that (cf. γάρ) Pant.
failed to institute a suit against Antigenes but has done so against
Nic.; thus he shows that he has released Antigenes. τὴν πρόκλησιν:
§ 40ff. λαχόντ' . . . τὴν δίκην . . . εἴληχεν . . . λαχών: see on § 3. ταῦτα
δ' οὐκ ἐῶσιν οἱ νόμοι: there was a general law that a master was liable
for the payment of compensation for the acts committed by his slaves
(Hyp. *Athen.* 22; cf. Dem. 53.20). There is a case of a slave being sued
in his own right at Dem. 55.31f., which indicates that the rule was that
when the slave was acting on his master's orders the master should be
sued direct; but when the slave had acted on his own initiative, the
slave should be sued direct but the master was liable for any penalty
incurred (cf. Harrison I 173ff.). So here Nic. is saying that since he did
not order Antigenes to act as he did, Pant. should institute the case not
against Nic. but against Antigenes direct: he should not institute the
case against Nic. and then accuse Antigenes as if he were acting on his
own initiative (ὥσπερ κυρίου).
    At 53.20 it is said that the master καὶ δίκας ἐλάμβανε καὶ ἐδίδου
whenever a slave κακόν τι ἐργάσαιτο. The words are too vague to make

it clear whether the master as κύριος actually appeared in court or whether the words mean simply that he was liable for any penalty incurred (cf. διώκειν here).

Of course Pant. does not consider Antigenes to have acted on his own initiative. He is suing Nic. as being jointly responsible with Euerg., who gave the order to the slave.

52–6 Nic. deals with his own character and physical attributes to counteract prejudice against money-lenders in general and those with his physical attributes.

52 μισοῦσι . . . 'Αθηναῖοι τοὺς δανείζοντας: advantage could be gained by presenting one's opponent as a professional money-lender (cf. 45.69f.). The fact that Athenian credit was overwhelmingly for consumption (for instance, to meet personal crises, to maintain existing business) rather than of a productive nature (see Paul Millett in Peter Garnsey, Keith Hopkins and C. R. Whittaker (eds.), *Trade in the ancient Economy* (London 1983) 43, 188 n. 15) encouraged the attitude that, while to lend to those in difficulties was good, it was despicable to make a financial gain out of other people's misfortunes by taking interest. Cf. Theophr. *Char.* 6.3. **φησίν:** since the case involves a παραγραφή Nic. speaks first. While Pant. could well ridicule Nic.'s voice and manner in a comparison of his own career and that of Nic. (cf. Dover 240 n. 15), it is highly unlikely that in anticipating this particular argument Nic. had any definite source of information. More probably he is attempting to counter prejudice which he knew to exist against him, at the same time scoring off Pant. by suggesting that he was so mean and ridiculous as to seek a verdict on totally irrelevant grounds. **ταχέως βαδίζει, καὶ μέγα φθέγγεται, καὶ βακτηρίαν φορεῖ:** for fast walking and a loud voice being annoying to other people, cf. 45.77 τῆς μὲν ὄψεως τῆι φύσει καὶ τῶι ταχέως βαδίζειν καὶ λαλεῖν μέγα, οὐ τῶν εὐτυχῶς πεφυκότων ἐμαυτὸν κρίνω· ἐφ' οἷς γὰρ οὐδὲν ὠφελούμενος λυπῶ τινας, ἔλαττον ἔχω πολλαχοῦ (cf. §55 below). Aristotle (*EN* 1125a 13ff.) says that the traits of the μεγαλόψυχος are κίνησις βραδεῖα . . . καὶ φωνὴ βαρεῖα καὶ λέξις στάσιμος· οὐ γὰρ σπευστικὸς ὁ περὶ ὀλίγα σπουδάζων, οὐδὲ σύντονος ὁ μηθὲν μέγα οἰόμενος· ἡ δ' ὀξυφωνία καὶ ἡ ταχυτὴς διὰ τούτων.

Perhaps walking fast was regarded in the same light as τὸ βαδίζειν ἀρρύθμως which Alexis (fr. 263) said was a mark of οἱ ἀνελεύθεροι (= 'rude', 'unpolished', cf. Ar. fr. 685). In Theophr. *Char.* 4 speaking in a loud voice is a mark of the ἄγροικος (cf. Cratinus fr. 374 ἀγροβόας ἀνήρ). Old men carried sticks (cf. e.g. Aesch. *Ag.* 75, 80, Eur. *HF* 254, Ar. *Ach.* 682) and so did cripples (cf. Lys. 24.12), but otherwise carrying a stick was a mark of those who ἐλακωνομάνουν (Ar. *Birds* 1283, cf. *Eccl.* 74, Plut. *Nic.* 19.4) and of a fop (Ephippus fr. 14). Theophrastus describes the ἄρεσκος (*Char.* 5, in a passage which some editors transpose to *Char.* 21 the μικροφιλότιμος) as δεινὸς... κτήσασθαι...βακτηρίας τῶν σκολίων ἐκ Λακεδαίμονος.

All in all Pant. would seem to be describing Nic. as boorish and pretentious.

53 τέχνην...πεποιημένοι 'having made a trade of' (derogatory). Cf. Ar. *Knights* 68, Luc. *Merc. cond.* 30, *Peregr.* 18, *Salt.* 9. **μήτε συγγνώμης μήτ' ἄλλου μηδενός εἰσιν ἀλλ' ἢ τοῦ πλείονος** 'have no thought of pity or anything else except profit'. μή is generic. For τοῦ πλείονος 'the excess' cf. P. Cair. Zen. 661 (3rd cent. B.C.). In view of the unusual construction συγγνώμης...εἰσιν doubts have been expressed about the soundness of the text. But the manuscript reading is supported by Priscian (*Inst.* 18.285), who lived in the early sixth century A.D., some four hundred years before the date of our earliest manuscripts of Dem. He wrote: *Attici* συγγνώμης οὐκ ἔστιν οὗτος, *id est 'nemini dat veniam'*; and he then quotes μιμεῖσθαι...πλείονος (with τινός for μηδενός). **μὰ Δία:** cf. on § 16.

54 πλέων: used of trading overseas. (Cf. Ar. *Peace* 341, Plat. *Gorg.* 467a.) **εὐπορήσας...μιχρῶν** 'having made small gains'. The gen. with εὐπορεῖν usually marks that for which the subject is well off. But cf. Xen. *Hell.* 1.1.10, Arist. *Metaph.* 996a 16, where, as here, εὐπορεῖν seems to approximate to τυγχάνειν. **μὴ λαθεῖν διαρρυὲν αὐτὸν τἀργύριον:** sc. βουλόμενος, lit. '[wishing] his money not to escape his notice having flowed through', i.e. 'not wanting his money to slip through his fingers without his being aware of it'. **εἰς ἐκείνους τιθείη** 'class him with them', i.e. with οἱ τέχνην πεποιημένοι (§53). **εἰ μὴ τοῦτο λέγεις κτλ.:** splendid irony; a withering *reductio ad absurdum* of Pant.'s argument. **τίς...ἄνθρωπος** 'what sort of person'. Cf. 39.25.

55 ὁ ταχὺ βαδίζων: see on §52. **ὁ ἀτρέμας:** sc. βαδίζων, 'the man who walks in a leisurely way'. **τῆς διαλέκτου:** see on §52. **οὐ τῶν εὐ πεφυκότων...ἑαυτοῖς:** cf. 45.77 (quoted in note on §52). **λυσιτελούντων:** so MSS. Rennie accepts Naber's λυσιτελούντως (sc. πεφυκότων) because of εὐτυχῶς πεφυκότων at 45.77. But the MS text is unexceptionable. **μηδέν:** this is used and not οὐδέν because it is in a subordinate clause within a Conditional. It could also be generic, but against that is 45.77: ἐφ' οἷς γὰρ οὐδὲν ὠφελούμενος λυπῶ τινας, ἔλαττον ἔχω πολλαχοῦ.

56 τῶι δεῖνι 'to so-and-so'. Dat. of δεῖνα, which is always used with the article but is sometimes not declined (as at Ar. *Th.* 622). Cf. 13.5 ὁ δεῖνα τοῦ δεῖνος τὸν δεῖν' εἰσήγγειλεν. **διὰ ταῦτα:** i.e. my physical attributes. **προσοφλεῖν:** sc. χρή. προσ- signifies 'in addition'. δίκην ὀφλεῖν = 'lose one's case'. **οὐδὲ εἷς:** emphatic for οὐδείς. **τἄλλα... ταῦθ':** i.e. the physical attributes. **καὶ φύσει...οὐκ εὔπορόν ἐστιν:** For the sentiment cf. Ar. *Wasps* 1457f. **ἐπιπλῆξαι:** either sc. αὐτὸν ἐπὶ τούτοις, 'reprove/punish him for these attributes', or sc. αὐτῶι ταῦτα, 'cast these attributes in his teeth'.

57–60 Summary and conclusion.

57 ἀλλὰ τί τούτων ἐμοὶ πρὸς σέ 'But which of these attributes has any bearing on my dispute with you?' Cf. 54.17. **λαγχάνειν:** see on §3. **πρατῆρ'...ὑποστῆναι** 'to undertake this position of warrantor'. See LSJ s.v. ὑφίστημι Β.ΙΙ.b. For πρατήρ see speech intro., *The business transactions.* **ὁ μὴ παρὼν μηδ' ἐπιδημῶν:** see on §8.

58 εἰ τοίνυν ὡς οἷον κτλ.: the start of a striking parallel with 38.21f. See on §1. Now, at the end of his speech, Nic. emphasizes the binding nature of an ἄφεσις. **ἐρεῖν:** Pant. spoke after Nic. since the case involved a παραγραφή (cf. on §52). **ἐκεῖνό γ'...ὅτι:** cf. 56.1. **ἀκούσιοι φόνοι:** apart from lawful killings (e.g. the death of a patient under the doctor, or of a boxer or wrestler in an athletic contest, or killing in self-defence, cf. MacDowell *Law* 113f.) there was an important distinction between intentional (ἑκούσιος) and unintentional (ἀκούσιος) homicide. Whereas Scots Law and English Law distinguish between an act planned in advance (i.e. premeditated murder) and an act committed in a moment of passion or anger (cf. Arist. *EN* 1111b 18f.), for the Athenians this distinction had no legal significance. Athenian law treated ἐκ προνοίας as a synonym for ἑκούσιος. So Arist. *MM* 1188b 29–38 ὅταν γάρ τις πατάξηι τινὰ ἢ ἀποκτείνηι ἥ τι τῶν τοιούτων ποιήσηι μηδὲν προδιανοηθείς, ἄκοντά φαμεν ποιῆσαι, ὡς τοῦ ἑκουσίου ὄντος ἐν τῶι διανοηθῆναι...ἐνταῦθα ἄρα τὸ ἑκούσιον πίπτει εἰς τὸ μετὰ διανοίας. If a man deliberately harmed another and killed him without meaning to, he was regarded as guilty of ἑκούσιος φόνος (cf. 54.25, 28). If on the spur of the moment one man killed another intentionally, he was guilty of ἑκούσιος φόνος. Similarly Athenian law treated ἀκούσιος φόνος and φόνος μὴ ἐκ προνοίας as synonyms (cf. 23.50). So W. T. Loomis, *JHS* 92 (1972) 86–95, against R. S. Stroud, *Drakon's law on homicide* (Berkeley 1968) 41. The practical effect of treating ἀκούσιος and μὴ ἐκ προνοίας as synonyms is to narrow ἀκούσιοι φόνοι to accidental killings, where there was no intention to harm, let alone kill.

Part of the law of homicide dealing with unpremeditated (μὴ ἐκ προνοίας) homicide, i.e. ἀκούσιος φόνος, is given in *IG* I² 115. (A better text than that previously available has been published by Stroud, op. cit.)

59 ὥστ' ἐὰν . . .οὐκέτ' ἐκβαλεῖν κύριος τὸν αὐτόν ἐστιν: the penalty for ἀκούσιος φόνος was exile within a specified period after conviction and by a fixed route. A convicted man had to remain in exile until pardon (αἴδεσις) was extended to him by the relatives of the dead man. If the victim's father, brother or sons survive it may be given by them but only if they are unanimous. If none of them survives it may be granted by more distant relatives of the victims as far as first cousin once removed, again only if they are unanimous. If no relative survives within that degree, pardon may be granted by ten members of the phratry chosen by the ephetae according to their rank (ἀριστίνδην) (*IG* I² 115.11–19; Dem. 23.72). (In theory, the phratry comprised distant relatives (cf. on 39.3), but not necessarily in practice, because when a non-citizen was granted citizenship he was often allowed to choose his phratry: cf. e.g. *IG* I² 110.15–17.) The present passage shows that when this pardon was granted it could not be revoked. **μὴ καθαρόν:** if a man was guilty of φόνος, either ἑκούσιος or ἀκούσιος, he was believed to be polluted, so that he was regarded as likely to suffer some disaster at the hands of the gods and as liable to spread this pollution to others who consorted with him and to the whole state unless steps were taken by the victim's relatives to bring him to justice (cf. the beginning of Soph. *OT*). On pollution related to homicide see R. Parker, *Miasma* (Oxford 1983) 104–43.

The man guilty of ἀκούσιος φόνος not only had to stay clear of Athens, he also had to keep away from those festivals and ceremonies which were open to all Greeks (cf. MacDowell *AHL* 121). If he returned after being pardoned by the victim's family, the law specified sacrifice, cleansing and certain other actions (Dem. 23.72). If we may trust dramatists on precise legal details the sacrifice might include a pig (Aesch. *Eum.* 283) or new-born lambs (Eur. *IT* 1223f.). The evidence for the procedure is discussed by L. Moulinier, *Le Pur et l'impur dans la pensée des Grecs* (Paris 1952) 87–91. Cf. Parker, op. cit. 370–4.

οὐδὲ γ', ἂν ὁ παθών . . . τοῦτο τὸ ῥῆμα: it was the duty of the relatives of a murder victim, whether the φόνος was ἑκούσιος or ἀκούσιος, to take the appropriate actions against the killer in order to deter others from murder, to extract vengeance for the dead man and to free the community of pollution. To fail in this duty was not only a disgrace (cf. 58.28f.) but might lead to a conviction for impiety (cf. 22.2 with MacDowell *AHL* 8–11). According to the present passage, however, the relatives were relieved of this duty if the victim released the killer with his dying breath. This is the only circumstance in which such duty was removed: it underlines the vengeance aspect of the duty. **ἐκπίπτειν καὶ φεύγειν . . . καὶ τεθνάναι:** for ἐκπίπτειν as the pass. of ἐκβάλλειν see on §6. The inclusion of καὶ τεθνάναι shows that release by the victim applied to ἑκούσιος φόνος as well as to ἀκούσιος φόνος. The penalty for ἑκούσιος φόνος was death, but after the first of his two speeches at his trial a defendant so charged could go into voluntary exile without waiting for the verdict (see MacDowell *AHL* 110–17). Thus while ἐκπίπτειν and φεύγειν could apply to both types of φόνος, τεθνάναι can only apply to ἑκούσιος φόνος. Pardon it seems could not be granted by the victim's family to someone in exile guilty of ἑκούσιος φόνος. (Cf. MacDowell *AHL* 124f.) If it had been possible for relatives to pardon in cases of ἑκούσιος φόνος, Nic. would surely not have distinguished ἀκούσιος φόνος.

60 ἐφ' ἡμῶν 'in our day'.

39 Against Boeotus

Personalities

This and the speech which follows in the corpus (Dem. 40) were delivered during the prolonged dispute between two sons of Mantias. Mantias served as ταμίας εἰς τὰ νεώρια in (probably) 377/6 and was trierarch in (perhaps) 365/4. He may be the Mantias who was strategus in 359 (Diod. 16.2.4–3.5).[25] The disputes περὶ τοῦ ὀνόματος (39) and περὶ προικὸς μητρώιας (40) result from his relations with two women, both from prominent Athenian families. Mantitheus, the plaintiff, is Mantias' son by the daughter of Polyaratus, a rich man and public figure;[26] she had previously been married to Cleomedon, the son of the fifth-century politician Cleon. The defendant, Boeotus, is Mantias' son by Plangon, daughter of Pamphilus, who was strategus in 389/8, but was subsequently convicted of embezzlement and his property sold (Ar. *Wealth* 174f., Plat. Com. fr. 14).

Date

The arbitration of the suit περὶ τοῦ ὀνόματος had been completed by the time the Athenian forces under Phocion returned from Euboea probably in 348 (39.16; see ad loc.). The present speech then will have been delivered late in 348. The speech περὶ προικός was delivered while Cammys was tyrant of Mytilene (40.37); Cammys' rule ended in 347. Speech 40 will have been delivered before the end of 347. Dion. Hal. *Din.* 13 says that speech 40 was delivered 'two or three years' after speech 39, but the context there shows that Dion. means 'a short time', as opposed to a long interval; he is not being precise.

Mantias' sons

According to Mantitheus the facts are as follows. Mantitheus is the legitimate son of Mantias by the daughter of Polyaratus. Both during his marriage and after his wife's death Mantias kept a mistress, Plangon, by whom he had two sons, Boeotus and his younger brother Pamphilus, both born after Mantitheus. At least, Plangon claimed that

---

[25] For Mantias' career see Davies 367.   [26] For Polyaratus see Davies 461.

they were Mantias' sons. However, Mantias steadfastly refused to believe that the children were his. When Boeotus came of age, he brought a suit against Mantias to compel him to recognize Boeotus as his legitimate son. Mantias was unwilling to go to court, fearing that his political enemies might use the trial as a means to attack him. Accordingly he made a private arrangement with Plangon before the case came to arbitration. Mantias was to challenge Plangon to affirm on oath that Boeotus was his son. Plangon (for a payment of 30 minae) was to refuse the oath. But when the case came before the arbitrator Plangon broke her promise and swore that Boeotus and Pamphilus were Mantias' sons. Mantias' opposition collapsed, and he acknowledged them as his legitimate sons by enrolling them in the phratry, under the names Boeotus and Pamphilus. Since Boeotus (if not Pamphilus too) was already of age, the next step was enrolment in the deme.[27] But Mantias died before this could be accomplished. Boeotus proceeded to enrol himself in the deme by the name Mantitheus. This, the name of the paternal grandfather, had been borne by the speaker since birth, with Mantias' full approval. Partly because of the real inconvenience caused by their possession of the same name, as described in 39.7–19, 40.34f., partly out of indignation that the name given him by his father should be used by another against his father's wishes, Mantitheus has brought the present suit to compel Boeotus to resume his former name.

Mantitheus is certainly telling the truth about his own mother.[28] She came from a wealthy family, and did not have to accept the inferior position of mistress. Mantitheus has witnesses to the various acts which

[27] A lost speech of Isaeus (fr. 6) was entitled πρὸς Βοιωτὸν ἐκ δημοτῶν ἔφεσις. Davies (365) takes it as 'an appeal by Mantitheos against the acceptance by the deme of his half-brother under the name Mantitheos after Mantias' death'. It is unlikely that Mantitheus could appeal, for *Ath. Pol.* 42.1 indicates only two matters of dispute during enrolment in the deme, age and status; and appeal was granted only to the rejected candidate. The title of the lost speech suggests that the speaker was the appellant and Boeotus the accuser (cf. Dem. 57 πρὸς Εὐβουλίδην). The Boeotus named was a member of the deme Κειριάδαι, of the Hippothontid tribe, to which Plangon's family belonged (39.23, 28). It is probable that he is either our Boeotus or his eponymous uncle (39.32). The speech could represent an appeal following expulsion from the deme as a result of the general scrutiny of all members in all demes authorized by the Demophilus decree of 346/5, or an appeal after the annual scrutiny of new deme members.

[28] Boeotus appears to reverse Mantitheus' claim. It was Plangon who was the wife and Mantitheus' mother who was the mistress; 40.20.

established and reaffirmed the formal marriage of Mantias and Polyaratus' daughter; the giving of the dowry (40.6), his admission to Mantias' oikos in infancy (see on §20), his enrolment in the phratry as a child (39.20) and in the deme as an adult (39.5). We cannot doubt Mantitheus' legitimacy. But there is a strong *prima facie* case against Boeotus' legitimacy. Plangon's father was ruined. Mantitheus claims (40.22) that Pamphilus' estate did not cover the debt to the treasury, so that Pamphilus is still listed as a debtor. Plangon's marriage prospects were poor, and she might well, with her brother's approval, consent to be Mantias' mistress for the relative security thus gained.[29] Boeotus could in theory be Mantias' illegitimate son by his mistress.

However, this is unlikely. Not only does Mantitheus never explicitly deny that Plangon was married to Mantias: neither did Mantias. For from 40.10 it appears that Mantias' only reason for rejecting Boeotus was that he did not believe that Boeotus was his son, not that he had never been married to Plangon. Still more significant is Mantias' eventual acknowledgement of Boeotus' legitimacy. Mantitheus says that Mantias was afraid to face Boeotus in court because of his political enemies. But if Plangon was never anything more than Mantias' mistress, Mantias' case was strong. Boeotus was not asking Mantias to admit paternity; he was asking Mantias to acknowledge his legitimacy by enrolling him in the phratry, for at this enrolment the father swore that the offspring was his *by a formally married wife of citizen birth*. If Mantias was never married to Plangon, Boeotus was asking him to lie on oath to his phratry, and to rob his legitimate son Mantitheus of part of his inheritance. As well as witnesses to prove that he was never married to Plangon, Mantias would have a strong argument from probability ('why should a public figure marry into a ruined house?') and a strong moral position ('how could he be expected to lie to his phratry?'). Political enemies or not, Mantias' position was not weak, and the interests of his legitimate son demanded that he resist Boeotus vigorously. However, his position would be weakened if he had been married to Plangon, and if Plangon could prove it. His position would be almost untenable if, as Boeotus claims (39.22, 40.28), Mantias had formally acknowledged him as a child, and if Plangon could prove it. On this assumption Mantias' attempt to bribe Plangon becomes readily

[29] That such arrangements, made with the approval of the woman's family, were not unknown, is suggested by Isae. 3.39.

intelligible. It is likely that Mantias had been married to Plangon, and that Boeotus was born during this marriage, whether or not he was Mantias' son.

When was Mantias married to Plangon? Mantitheus (39.27ff.), seeking to refute Boeotus' claim that the name Mantitheus belongs to him as the eldest of Mantias' sons, insists that Boeotus is younger than himself. But there is reason to doubt this. Boeotus sued Mantias when grown to manhood (40.9 αὐξηθείς), i.e. eighteen years of age or more. Mantitheus married at the age of eighteen (40.12). It is clear from 40.12 that the dispute between Boeotus and Mantias was already in progress when Mantitheus married. We may reasonably infer that Boeotus is the elder.[30] This is strongly supported by 39.27ff., where Mantitheus tries to refute Boeotus' claim to seniority. Mantitheus' argument there is evasive and unconvincing; he hurries through his argument with evident discomfort, and we may infer that Boeotus is indeed the elder. Plangon was Mantias' first wife, Mantitheus' mother his second. Thanks to Rudhardt,[31] we can establish within narrow limits the ages of the half-brothers and the dates of Mantias' marriages. In 347 Mantitheus has a daughter of marriageable age (40.4, 56), i.e. about fourteen to sixteen.[32] Mantitheus married at eighteen. If the daughter was born c. 363–361 the marriage can be dated c. 364–362[33] and

[30] J. Rudhardt, *MH* 19 (1962) 39–64, 42f.

[31] The figures given in the text are adapted from Rudhardt. J. Kirchner, *Prosopographia attica* (Berlin 1901–3), II 49, 53 gives c. 380 for Mantitheus' birth and c. 362 for his marriage. We cannot hope for precision, given the nature of the subject. Thus we suppose that Mantias' daughter was married at fourteen to sixteen, but we cannot exclude a slightly higher age. We suppose that Boeotus and Mantitheus were born within five years of each other, because Mantitheus claims it is impossible to tell which is older (39.29). But since they had different mothers, and ageing varies according to genetic factors and way of life, the age gap could be greater. Marriages cannot be dated accurately from subsequent births, since the time required for procreation varies, as those who have tried will appreciate.

[32] W. K. Lacey, *The family in classical Greece* (London 1968) 104, 162.

[33] This is not the date at which Plangon tricked Mantias before the arbitrator. Mantias was dead by 357 (40.18). Yet the enrolment in the deme had not taken place. One cannot envisage Boeotus tolerating a delay of five years. Probably the dispute continued for some time after Mantitheus' marriage. It looks as though Mantias, perhaps already in ill health (the opposite is implied at 40.13 but Mantias' insistence on haste at 40.12 suggests that he believed himself near death) was seeking to delay Boeotus' attempt to have his legitimacy recognized,

Mantitheus' birth to *c*. 382–380. Mantias' second marriage can therefore be dated to 381 at the latest. If we suppose Boeotus to be two to five years older than Mantitheus he will have been born *c*. 387 at the earliest and 382 at the latest. As an ambitious politician Mantias will not have married into Pamphilus' family after his ruin; we can therefore date Mantias' marriage with Plangon to *c*. 388 at the latest.

Clearly Mantias divorced Plangon, probably because he suspected her (or claimed to suspect her) of infidelity.[34] Hence his refusal to accept that Boeotus was his son. This refusal dates to the time of the divorce, for Boeotus lived with Plangon (40.9, 50); normally on divorce the children would remain in the father's house.

What then of the third son Pamphilus? Pamphilus never emerges as a personality in either speech. He appears to have remained aloof; at least, Mantitheus ignores him. It has been supposed[35] that Pamphilus was younger than Mantitheus, the result of a resumption of Mantias' relationship with Plangon after the death of Mantitheus' mother. Mantitheus certainly claims that Plangon was Mantias' mistress after his mother's death (40.9). But there is little to be said for such a supposition. The only apparent point in its favour is that Mantitheus nowhere seeks to refute a claim of seniority from Pamphilus; the debate concerns only himself and Boeotus. But it is hardly surprising that Pamphilus made no claim to be the oldest brother; he had no reason to quarrel with his full brother Boeotus; the debate about seniority involved no financial or other advantages, merely the possession of a name which Pamphilus had never claimed. Even if Pamphilus were, or claimed to be, older than himself, Mantitheus had nothing to gain

in order to leave only one legitimate son to inherit his estate, probably for financial as well as emotional reasons. It is far from certain (see on 39.9) that after the division of the estate any of Mantias' sons belonged in the liturgical class. Mantias did, as no doubt would Mantitheus if he were sole heir. As sole heir Mantitheus could follow his father into a public career.

[34] It is possible that the charge of infidelity was an excuse to dispose of Plangon. The dowry had not been paid to Mantias by the time Pamphilus was ruined (40.20ff.). B. claimed (ibid.) that Mantias received the residue of Pamphilus' estate from the boule as Plangon's dowry. But he offers no evidence (40.21), and he failed to satisfy an arbitrator. Probably the dowry was never paid; and to an ambitious politician the connection with a ruined house was embarrassing. But this is conjecture. Certainly Mantias' only official ground for rejecting Plangon's sons was doubt about paternity.

[35] Rudhardt 48ff.; cf. Davies 367.

and everything to lose by taking issue with Pamphilus, for (a) his claim to be older than Boeotus would be weakened if he also had to prove himself older than Boeotus' younger brother, (b) to raise the subject would be to complicate the issue, while Greek litigants are at pains to over-simplify. The arguments against the view that Pamphilus is the son of a later liaison between Mantias and Plangon are strong. (1) There is no evidence to support Mantitheus' claim that Plangon was Mantias' mistress after the death of Mantitheus' mother. (2) It is difficult to see why Plangon's brothers, impoverished but presumably not without pride, should allow their sister to become the mistress of a man who had divorced her. (3) Mantias and Plangon did not part amicably; Boeotus describes her as 'badly treated' (39.24). (4) It is difficult to see why Mantias persisted in his refusal to enrol Boeotus in the phratry. (5) Pamphilus was accepted by Mantias as a result of Plangon's oath. But if Plangon was only Mantias' mistress at this time Pamphilus had no right to be enrolled as a legitimate son in the phratry and Mantias no reason to enrol him. Problems 2 and 5 may be avoided if we suppose that Mantias remarried Plangon. But there are still obstacles. (a) Why was Boeotus still not enrolled in the phratry? (b) If Pamphilus was accepted by Mantias as legitimate, why was he not enrolled in the phratry in infancy, as was the custom? (c) Boeotus' claim that he never lived in his father's house (40.50; cf. Mantitheus' statement that Mantias did not co-habit with Plangon after the death of Mantitheus' mother, 40.9) makes no sense if Mantias remarried Plangon. We might suppose that Pamphilus was Plangon's son by a lover after her divorce. But from 40.10 it would seem that Mantias' challenge to Plangon included both Boeotus and Pamphilus. Mantias would not include Pamphilus in the challenge if it were out of the question that he was Mantias' son. We conclude that Pamphilus was at least conceived before the divorce.

This raises a problem. We must suppose an interval of at least one year between the births of Boeotus and Pamphilus. It was customary for children to be admitted to the phratry in infancy. If Mantias lived with his wife long enough to sire another child, why did he not enrol the first child? Conversely, if Mantias doubted that Boeotus was his son, why did he continue to live with his wife? The difficulty disappears on the following hypothesis.

Mantias believed at the time of Boeotus' birth that Boeotus was his son. The normal time to enrol children was at the Apaturia in the Pyanepsion (September–October) following the birth. According to the time of year when Boeotus was born, there could be an interval of up to twelve months (if he were born in Pyanepsion but after the Apaturia) between Boeotus' birth and his enrolment. Mantias intended to enrol Boeotus. But during the interval Plangon became pregnant, and Mantias suspected that the child was not his. This caused him to have doubts about the existing child. Boeotus was not admitted to the phratry; Plangon, pregnant, was sent home. This was all Mantias needed to do to repudiate his sons. The recognition of legitimate offspring was not a single act but a series of acts performed between birth and the age of majority.[36] Mantias refused to complete the process.

Mantitheus' action

Mantitheus seeks to prevent his half-brother from using the name of the paternal grandfather. The action may have been a δίκη βλάβης.[37] Certainly Mantitheus appears to seek financial compensation from Boeotus. The most natural interpretation of Mantitheus' claim at 40.35 (ἠνάγκασέ με λαχεῖν αὐτῶι δίκην περὶ τοῦ ὀνόματος, οὐχ ἵνα χρήματα παρ' αὐτοῦ λάβω, ὦ ἄ. δ., ἀλλ' ἵν', ἐὰν ὑμῖν δοκῶ δεινὰ πάσχειν καὶ βλάπτεσθαι μεγάλα, οὗτος κάληται Βοιωτός, ὥσπερ ὁ πατὴρ αὐτῶι ἔθετο) is that although Mantitheus claimed compensation, his primary aim was to compel Boeotus to abandon the name Mantitheus. The phrases δεινὰ πάσχειν καὶ βλάπτεσθαι μεγάλα in 40.35 and ἀλλὰ ταῦτα μὲν ἡ πόλις βλάπτεται· ἐγὼ δ' ἰδίαι τί (sc. βλάπτομαι) 39.13, and the prominence given in speech 39 to the argument that Mantitheus' interests suffer as a result of Boeotus' conduct, suggest a δίκη βλάβης. But there are problems. The MSS give the title πρὸς Βοιωτόν; with a δίκη βλάβης we expect κατὰ Βοιωτοῦ. The MSS may be mistaken. But more serious is the fact that a δίκη βλάβης usually envisages actual financial loss by the plaintiff, while Mantitheus alleges only inconvenience. Mantitheus may be interpreting (and asking the jury to interpret) the notion of damage loosely. The cases of damage envisaged by the laws, inappropriate as they were, may be the nearest parallel for his own situation.

---

[36] Rudhardt 56ff.　　　　[37] Lipsius 652, Bonner–Smith II 108.

To win his case Mantitheus needs to establish two points: (1) that the two half-brothers cannot use the same name, (2) that he himself has the better claim to the name. The first point is demonstrated effectively. On the second point Mantitheus fails to satisfy. Both Boeotus and Mantitheus are legitimate sons of Mantias. Mantitheus proves (39.20) that he was given the name Mantitheus in infancy, and that he was enrolled as a child in the phratry and as a man in the deme under this name; he also proves (which Boeotus does not deny) that Boeotus was enrolled by Mantias in the phratry under the name Boeotus, and that it was Boeotus, not Mantias, who enrolled Boeotus in the deme by the name Mantitheus. Mantitheus' claim rests ultimately on the clearly expressed wishes of Mantias. But Boeotus claims (39.22) that Mantias gave *him* the name Mantitheus as a child, and he bases his claim to the paternal grandfather's name on the grounds of seniority. Since Mantitheus has no adequate reply to the former claim we may accept that at the naming ceremony the infant son of Plangon was given the name Mantitheus, not Boeotus. That Mantias should then proceed to name the son of his second marriage (the speaker) Mantitheus is hardly surprising, for, having repudiated the sons of his first marriage, he regarded our Mantitheus as his first-born. If Mantitheus could refute either, preferably both, of Boeotus' claims he might have a strong case. As it is it would appear that both brothers have an equal right to the name.

We are in an unusually fortunate position with this speech in that we know the jury's verdict. At 40.17f. Mantitheus says that in Mantitheus' claim for his mother's dowry from Mantias' estate the arbitrator found against Boeotus by default. Boeotus rejected the decision on the grounds that the arbitrator found against Boeotus, while his own name was Mantitheus. Accordingly Mantitheus filed the same action against Boeotus under the name Mantitheus. Mantitheus' acquiescence can only mean that the jury in the suit περὶ τοῦ ὀνόματος found for Boeotus, thus establishing his right to the name Mantitheus. There is also external evidence. An inscription of the late 340s (*IG* II² 1622.435f.) records the payment of a debt of Mantias' by his heirs Πάμφιλος Θορίκιος...Μαντίθεος Θορίκιος...Μαντίθεος Θορίκιος. If Mantitheus had won his case Boeotus could not have used the name. The jury reached the only reasonable verdict on the evidence presented.

1–5 Prooemium (§ 1) and διήγησις (§§ 2–5) are not neatly separated as in Dem. 54 but blended.

1 οὐδεμιᾶι φιλοπραγμοσύνηι: the Athenians disapproved of litigiousness (cf. on 54.17), and we often find speakers claiming inexperience in litigation (as e.g. Lys. 12.3, Dem. 34.1). The speaker must be a simple man, telling the plain truth in unadorned language, and untainted by professionalism; consequently we find litigants denying any skill in public speaking (Plat. *Ap.* 17c–d, Dem. 40.4, 55.2) or where this is impossible allaying the suspicion which such skill arouses (Dem. 21.189; cf. 32.31). The prominent position of the phrase shows the speaker's awareness that the present suit is unusual, and that the jury will suspect that he is coming to court over a trivial issue. It is therefore important for him to show that real inconvenience is caused by their possession of the same name. **δίκην . . .ἔλαχον:** see on 54.1. **ἄτοπον** 'strange', 'bizarre'. **εἰ:** causal, 'because'. **κριθῆναι:** impersonal, 'it was necessary that the issue be decided in your court'.

2 μὲν οὖν: οὖν is connective; μέν looks forward to νῦν δέ. **περίεργος** = φιλοπράγμων; 'it would be right to think me a busybody for caring what he chooses to call himself'. **κατασκευάσας ἐργαστήριον συκοφαντῶν** 'having drummed up a gang of crooks'. Cf. 32.10 ἐργαστήρια μοχθηρῶν ἀνθρώπων, 37.39 περιστήσας...τὸ ἐργαστήριον τῶν συνεστώτων, 40.9 παρασκευασάμενος ἐργαστήριον συκοφαντῶν. The phrase is only half-metaphorical, for ἐργαστήριον denotes business premises, and these men are (alleged to be) professional prosecutors. The origin of the noun συκοφάντης and the verb συκοφαντέω is obscure. When we first meet them (in Ar. *Ach.*), they describe a professional informer. In some public actions there were rewards for prosecutors, and it was only to be expected that unscrupulous men would bring such actions for gain. But there were other ways in which an unscrupulous man could profit from litigation, by blackmail using the threat of litigation (Lys. 7.39, 25.3), or by hiring one's services to one of the parties to a lawsuit, to prosecute (and so embarrass or silence) his opponent (Dem. 21.103). More generally, a man might use his legal expertise to escape conviction when guilty, or bring private suits for gain. However, the notion of gain is not always present; the words may describe a man who brings an unjust prosecution (Dem. 57.34). In the orators noun and verb imply any or all of these activities. Claims that the speaker's opponent is a sycophant are commonplace. It is not clear whether ἐργαστήριον συκοφαντῶν refers to a permanent club or to a temporary alliance of hirelings. ὃν ἴσως γιγνώσκετε πάντες: implies notoriety, not fame; cf. 54.31, 34. Athenian litigants often appeal to the personal knowledge of the jurors (as below §§ 16 and 25), but we cannot always assume that such claims are true. Sometimes this type of expression is used simply to mask a complete lack of evidence. In a large jury, each juror might well suppose that he alone was ignorant of the facts, as in the tale of the emperor's clothes. Cf. Arist. *Rhet.* 1408a 34 πάσχουσι δέ τι οἱ ἀκροαταὶ καὶ ᾧ κατακόρως χρῶνται οἱ λογογράφοι, 'τίς δ' οὐκ οἶδεν;' 'ἅπαντες ἴσασιν·' ὁμολογεῖ γὰρ ὁ ἀκούων αἰσχυνόμενος, ὅπως μετέχῃ οὗπερ καὶ οἱ ἄλλοι πάντες and Dem. 40. 53f. περὶ ὧν ἂν μὴ ἔχῃ μάρτυρας παρασχέσθαι, ταῦτα φήσει ὑμᾶς εἰδέναι, ὦ ἄ. δ., ὃ πάντες ποιοῦσιν οἱ μηδὲν ὑγιὲς λέγοντες κτλ. Cf. e.g. 57.8, 33, 60 and see on 54.31. **Μενεκλέα:** described in 40.32 as the ἀρχιτέκτων of Boeotus' plots against Mantitheus. **τὸν τὴν Νῖνον ἑλόντ':** probably not descriptive but pejorative ('who had the poor girl Ninus convicted' – Paley). Menecles is associated with a *cause célèbre*, and Boeotus is tainted by association with Menecles. Cf. 32.11 and see on 54.39. From Dem. 19.281 and schol. it appears that Ninus was executed for impiety, involving witchcraft and the introduction of a new mystery religion. The priestess mentioned by Josephus, *Adv. Ap.* 2.267 as having been executed ὅτι ξένους ἐμύει θεούς could be Ninus, but equally she could be Theoris, prosecuted for impiety by Demosthenes (Plut. *Dem.* 14, Harpocr. s.v. Θεωρίς, Dem. 25.79f.). **ἐδικάζεθ' κτλ.:** since the result of Boeotus' success was Mantias' enrolment of Boeotus in the phratry (§4), at which ceremony Mantias had to swear that he was enrolling a son born to him by an Athenian woman to whom he was formally married (cf. 57.54, Isae. 8.19), it is clear that Mantitheus distorts Boeotus' case; Boeotus claims not simply that he is Mantias' son but that he is Mantias' *legitimate* son. The nature of Boeotus' suit is not clear. Bonner–Smith II 108 see a δίκη βλάβης. The suggestion is plausible but unprovable (Harrison I 79 is sceptical). **Παμφίλου:** see speech intro. **τῆς πατρίδος ἀποστερεῖσθαι:** probably not mere rhetoric on B.'s part. Legitimacy was not a prerequisite for citizenship in Athens (the issue is controversial; for the view that bastards had citizen rights see Harrison I 63ff., D. M. MacDowell, *CQ* n.s. 26 (1976) 88ff.; the

opposite view is maintained by S. C. Humphries, *JHS* 94 (1974) 88ff.,
P. J. Rhodes, *CQ* n.s. 28 (1978) 89ff. and notes on *Ath. Pol.* 42.1), but
Athenian birth on both sides was. When Mantias denied paternity he
made it impossible for Boeotus to prove that he satisfied the conditions
for citizenship. Hence the fact that B., though fully grown (40.9), had
not yet been enrolled in the deme (39.5, 40.34), and the repeated
association of Boeotus' claim to be Mantias' son with his claim to
citizenship (39.2, 39.31, 39.34, 40.10, 40.42, 40.48).

3 To avoid having to face Boeotus in court, Mantias made a private
arrangement with Plangon; the arrangement is described in slightly
greater detail in 40.10f. Mantias was to issue a formal challenge to
Plangon, bidding her affirm on oath that he was the father of her sons;
Plangon (for 30 minae) was to refuse the oath, and her brothers were
to adopt her sons, thus confirming the latter in their citizen rights.
Plangon, however, despite her promise accepted the challenge and
swore that Boeotus and his brother were Mantias' sons. The arbitrator
found for Plangon. For προκλήσεις in general see on 54.27. In 54.40
we had a πρόκλησις in which the challenger offers to swear an oath;
here the challenger offers to tender an oath to his opponent. Plangon's
oath was decisive not because as mother she should know the father
of her children (for at Isae. 12.9 we are told that the plaintiff's mother
swore to his paternity, but the oath decided nothing) but because it
was sworn as a result of Mantias' challenge. Either Mantias' πρόκλησις
laid down that Plangon's oath was to be binding on him or Mantias
felt that his position was almost hopeless when Plangon accepted the
πρόκλησις (προκλήσεις in Attic litigation were almost always refused),
especially as he would not dare to reveal his deal with Plangon. The
affair became notorious; see Arist. *Rhet.* 1398b περὶ τῶν τέκνων αἱ
γυναῖκες πανταχοῦ διορίζουσι τἀληθές [but see above]. τοῦτο μὲν γὰρ
Ἀθήνησι Μαντίαι τῶι ῥήτορι ἀμφισβητοῦντι πρὸς τὸν υἱὸν ἡ μήτηρ
ἀπέφηνεν. **πᾶσα γὰρ εἰρήσεται ἡ ἀλήθει':** Boeotus will naturally have
harped on Mantias' unwillingness to face him in court as evidence of
his own legitimacy. Mantitheus contrives to give a pleasing impression
of his own candour by admitting to facts which he might be expected
to suppress; cf. 45.4. Bond ad Eur. *HF* 222 observes: 'the parenthesis
removing a scruple is a rhetorical device which gives greater emphasis'.
μή τις . . . ἀπαντήσειεν αὐτῶι: the Athenians saw nothing wrong in

principle in the use of the lawcourts as an arena for settling personal and political feuds; it was a commonplace from the archaic period onwards that a man had a duty to hurt his enemies and a right to use any means at his disposal – Solon 13.5, Plat. *Meno* 71e, Theognis 363f., Eur. *Ion* 1046f. Thus at Dem. 53 init., 59 init., Aeschin. 1.1f. we find the speaker openly avowing private reasons for bringing public indictments. However, such motivation is only tolerable when it is accompanied by concern for the welfare of the state (in public cases) and when the charge is justified; cf. Lycurg. *Leocr.* 6 and see also Dem. 57.8, where the speaker asks us to disapprove of an unjust accusation brought solely for the purpose of revenge. The reasons alleged by Mantitheus are therefore such as would appear plausible to an Athenian jury. But the issues at stake were so important that it is unlikely that even this deterrent would keep Mantias from court, and one suspects that Plangon could prove (1) that she had been married to Mantias, (2) that Mantias had acknowledged Boeotus as an infant (see speech introduction and notes on §§ 20 and 22). **αὐτῆς** 'voluntarily', 'of her own accord', 'unbidden'. **ἦ μήν:** cf. on 54.41. **ἐὰν ὅρκον . . . δίδωι:** ὅρκον διδόναι is the usual expression to denote 'administer an oath'. **μὴ ὀμεῖσθαι:** cf. on 54.35. **μεσεγγυησαμένης ἀργύριον** 'having had a sum of money deposited with a third party'. The sum was 30 minae (40.10). **ἐπὶ τούτοις** 'on these terms'.

4 τὸν ἀδελφόν: the implication of this passage and 40.10 that Pamphilus did not sue Mantias is confirmed by Arist. (loc. cit.), τοῦτο μὲν γὰρ ᾿Αθήνησι Μαντίαι τῶι ῥήτορι ἀμφισβητοῦντι πρὸς τὸν υἱὸν ἡ μήτηρ ἀπέφηνεν. The present passage suggests that Mantias' challenge concerned Boeotus alone, but that Plangon included Pamphilus in her oath; at 40.10 it is stated that the challenge referred to both. The latter passage is supported by the fact that Mantias seems to have raised no objection to the enrolment of Pamphilus into the phratry, as he would surely have done had Pamphilus been excluded from the terms of the challenge. **εἰσάγειν εἰς τοὺς φράτερας:** in theory all members of a phratry, as descendants of a common ancestor, were distant relatives. But this was not necessarily so in practice, since new citizens could enrol in the phratry of their choice, e.g. *IG* II² 558.20f. Although the phratries, as subdivisions of the old four tribes, had lost all political significance through the reforms of Cleisthenes, they continued to function for social and religious purposes. Membership was hereditary, and was confined to legitimate male issue. Admission took place at the Apaturia, the feast of the phratries, held in Pyanepsion (September–October). The festival lasted three days, the third of which (called κουρεῶτις) was the occasion for the presentation of children to the phratry. It was usual to introduce a child in infancy, at the first Apaturia after the birth (Et. M. 118, 55, Isae. 8.19). The father offered a victim for sacrifice; this offering was called μεῖον, 'the lesser' (Harpocr. s.v. μεῖον, *IG* II² 1237 = *SIG* 921). The boy was again presented to the phratry at puberty, and another offering was made, called κουρεῖον (for the importance of this occasion see *IG* II² 1237.26ff., 115ff.); at this stage the boy became a full member of the phratry. In the case of Boeotus and Pamphilus the process will have been accelerated. **ἐποιήσατο:** ποιεῖσθαι can mean not only 'adopt', but also 'acknowledge as one's child', as 40.26. **Βοιωτόν** 'as Boeotus', 'by the name Boeotus'.

5 συμβάσης . . . τελευτῆς: in 357 (40.18). **τὰς εἰς τοὺς δημότας ἐγγραφάς:** at the age of eighteen an Athenian male assumed full citizen rights and responsibilities. Each year the demesmen conducted a scrutiny (δοκιμασία) of sons of demesmen of the appropriate age to ascertain (1) if they were old enough, (2) if they were genuinely of Athenian birth on both sides. If they were accepted their names were entered in the deme register (ληξιαρχικὸν γραμματεῖον), Arist. *Ath. Pol.* 42.1. **Μαντίθεον ἐνέγραψεν ἑαυτόν:** since a youth undergoing *dokimasia* was presented to the deme by his father, it is unlikely that Boeotus would have succeeded in having himself enrolled as Mantitheus if Mantias had still been alive. With Mantias dead the situation was changed. The enrolment in the phratry had no legal significance in itself; hence the name used for the phratry enrolment was not binding on Boeotus. Boeotus argued at the time of the present trial (§§ 22ff.) that Mantias gave him the name Mantitheus at birth. Armed with this argument, and the fact that Mantias finally acknowledged paternity, Boeotus had himself enrolled as Mantitheus. **ὅσα βλάπτει:** suggests a δίκη βλάβης (see speech intro., *Mantitheus' action*). ὅσα is internal object, ἐμέ and ὑμᾶς direct objects. **ὑμᾶς:** it is usual for litigants in private suits to argue that public issues are at stake; cf. on 54.42.

6 returns to the thoughts of the opening chapter. For this device (ring-form, ring-composition) see on 54.13. **σκαιός** 'crass'. **ἀλόγιστος**

'irrational', 'unreasonable'. τῶν μὲν πατρῴων . . . συγκεχωρηκέναι τὸ τρίτον νείμασθαι μέρος: Mantitheus in fact had no choice (as he acknowledges 40.13) once Mantias acknowledged Boeotus and Pamphilus as his legitimate sons. In the absence of a principle of primogeniture, all legitimate sons shared equally in the estate (Isae. 6.25). It was possible to show a slight preference in wills (see Harrison I 152), but the shares must still be roughly equal. ἐγίγνετο 'which *were becoming* mine', i.e. 'were coming to me', 'would have been mine'. Cf. Lys. 7.12, 13, Andoc. 1.117, Isae. 3.42. στέργειν 'to rest content'. ζυγομαχεῖν: a metaphor from oxen under the same yoke, used fittingly here of a family quarrel. ἀτιμίαν ἔφερε καὶ ἀνανδρίαν 'would bring great disgrace and [the stigma of, charge of, reputation for] cowardice'; this kind of compendious expression is common, especially with κτάομαι and ὀφλισκάνω.

According to Mantitheus' claim that Plangon was not Mantias' wife nor Boeotus his son, clearly Mantitheus cannot give up his name under any circumstances; if anyone yields, it must be Boeotus.

7–38 πίστεις. Mantitheus seeks to prove (a) that it damages his interests (and those of the state) for the two to bear the same name (§§ 7–19), (b) that he has a right to the name and Boeotus has not (§§ 20–38). §§ 7–19 are subdivided into (1) inconvenience caused in public life (§§ 7–12) and (2) inconvenience caused in private life (§§ 13–19).

7 τίν' . . . τρόπον: adverbial; 'by what style/formula', lit. 'in what way'. ἐπιτάξει: see on 56.16. οἴσουσι 'will propose' for public service (λῃτουργίαι); see on 54.44. οὐκοῦν 'so', 'eh bien'. **Μαντίθεον Μαντίου Θορίκιον:** an Athenian's full name comprised his personal name, patronymic and demotic. Since Boeotus and Mantitheus shared the same patronymic and demotic (for deme membership was transmitted in the male line), if both were called Μαντίθεος they would be indistinguishable. **χορηγόν:** it was the duty of the choregus to pay for the training and attire of a chorus competing at a state festival. A man could be choregus for the tragic and comic performances at the City Dionysia or Lenaea, for the dithyrambic competitions at the City Dionysia, Thargelia, Panathenaea, Prometheia, and Hephaesteia (for the last two festivals see [Xen.] *Ath. Pol.* 3.4, *IG* II² 1138 and J. M. Moore, *JHS* 91 (1971) 140f.), for the pyrrhic dance at the Panathenaea, or for the Athenian representatives at the musical competitions on Delos (Arist. *Ath. Pol.* 56.3). From *Ath. Pol.* 56.3 it appears that where the competition was between tribes (as in the dithyramb) the choregi were selected by the tribes and the names submitted to the magistrate in charge of the festival, but where there was no competition between tribes, as in the tragic contests at the Dionysia and the contests on Delos, the choregus was appointed by the relevant magistrate. (An exception appears in the comic contests at the Dionysia, where by the time of the composition of *Ath. Pol.* in the 320s the five choregi were selected by the tribes.) Mantitheus here envisages the former procedure. **γυμνασίαρχον:** the function is narrower than the name suggests. Torch-races took place at the Great Panathenaea, Prometheia, Hephaesteia and the festival of Pan. Competition was between tribes; hence the tribes chose the gymnasiarch, whose function was to meet the expenses of his tribal team. **ἑστιάτορ᾽:** the ἑστιάτωρ had the job of feasting his tribe on festal occasions, especially the Dionysia and Panathenaea (schol. Dem. 20.21). **σέ:** i.e. Boeotus.

8 καὶ δή 'suppose', a common idiom, e.g. Eur. *Med.* 386 καὶ δὴ τεθνᾶσι. **καλεῖ** 'summons' (to accept the burden or offer an objection). **ὁ ἄρχων ἢ πρὸς ὅντιν᾽ ἂν ἦι ἡ δίκη** 'the archon or whoever has jurisdiction'. In the case of the choregia for the men's and boys' choruses at the Dionysia and Thargelia the archon dealt with objections from the tribal nominees, since he had control over the festivals for which they were appointed. The Basileus would likewise hear objections from those nominated for the γυμνασιαρχία, since he had control over all torch-races (*Ath. Pol.* 57.1). Mantitheus assumes that he and Boeotus will each claim that the other is meant. Blass deleted ἡ δίκη to avoid hiatus, but the phrase is found in a law at 43.71, and the hiatus may be justified as a quotation of a legalistic formula, perhaps from the law governing ληιτουργίαι. **ταῖς ἐκ τῶν νόμων . . . ζημίαις:** for refusing to perform the ληιτουργία (οὐ ληιτουργοῦμεν) without appearing before the archon to give cause when summoned (οὐχ ὑπακούομεν). **συμμορίαν:** for the payment of εἰσφοραί (extraordinary war-taxes levied on property) the 1,200 wealthiest citizens were divided after 378/7 into boards (συμμορίαι). The method of collection underwent various changes in the fourth century; at the time of the present speech the 300 richest of those liable paid the levy in advance and recovered the sums due from the members of their συμμορίαι. Cf. on 37.37. **τριήραρχον:** cf. on

54.44. Trierarchs were appointed by the strategi, who also handled litigation arising from disputes (Dem. 35.48, 42.5). By the 320s one strategus alone administered the trierarchy (*Ath. Pol.* 61.1). τῶι: τίνι. κατειλεγμένος: the strategi were responsible for drawing up the list of those liable for military service (κατάλογος).

9 ἀρχή 'official', lit. 'office', a common use. **καθιστῆι:** these are liturgies appointed by state officials, unlike those of § 7, where the official simply accepts the tribe's nominee. **οἶον** 'for instance', 'say'. **ἄρχων:** the archon appointed the choregi for the tragic competitions at the City Dionysia and for the competition at Delos. **βασιλεύς:** as the administrator of the Lenaean festival (*Ath. Pol.* 57.1), the Basileus will have appointed the choregi for the competitions in tragedy and comedy at the Lenaea. **ἀθλοθέται:** every fourth year the Panathenaea were celebrated with great pomp and splendour. To the ritual of the annual ceremony were added contests in music and athletics. This festival was called the Great Panathenaea to distinguish if from the annual festival. The competitions, which were Panhellenic (unlike the choral contests at the annual Panathenaea), were organized by ten ἀθλοθέται, selected by lot, who held office for four years. **προσπαρα-γράψουσι** 'they will further add', lit. 'write in addition (πρός) alongside (παρά)'. To his personal name a man would add (παρα-γράφειν) his father's name and his deme; Mantitheus envisages a further addition (πρός), the mother's name. **νὴ Δία:** introducing a possible reply; cf. on 54.34. **τὸν ἐκ Πλαγγόνος:** we might expect the nominative (προσπαραγράψουσι νὴ Δία 'ὁ ἐκ Πλαγγόνος'), but in Greek brief quotations are usually drawn into the syntax of the sentence. Cf. e.g. Plat. *Crat.* 398d τὸ τοῦ ἔρωτος ὄνομα ὅθεν γεγόνασιν οἱ ἥρωες, Ar. *Wasps* 97f. **Πλαγγόνος:** probably a pet name (ὑπο-κόρισμα), for the word properly denotes a wax puppet or doll (Call. *h. Dem.* 92). For such pet names cf. 59.121 Φανὼ τὴν Στρυβήλην καλουμένην, Isae. 3.30ff. (a female called Clitarete at birth but known as Phile). Though Plangon's name is mentioned once in the present speech, eight times in the speech περὶ προικός, we are never told the name of Mantitheus' mother. D. Schaps, *CQ* n.s. 27 (1977) 323ff., shows that Greek litigants regularly suppress the names of women relatives, even where these women are important to the case (thus in Dem. 57 the speaker names his mother only once, §68, and only where for formal

reasons it becomes unavoidable, despite her obvious relevance to the
question of his disputed citizen status) but are less reticent about women
of low character, and women related to the opponent (according to
Mantitheus Plangon would fall under both categories). Athenian
women were as far as possible segregated, ideally unknown to males
outside the family (see esp. Thuc. 2.45.2); to use a woman's name in
a male gathering was perhaps to suggest that she was known to more
men than was proper, and to expose her to malicious gossip. (It should
however be noted that this applies only to the middle and upper classes,
for poorer men could not afford the luxury of closeting their womenfolk
and losing a pair of working hands; cf. Dover 95ff.) See also on 37.45.
κατὰ ποῖον νόμον: there was no law to forbid such an addition, but
there was no precedent for it and no reason for the Athenians to make
an exception to the general form of nomenclature. In fact, in *IG* II²
1622.435f. both brothers are alike denoted Μαντίθεος Θορίκιος. ποῖος
often, as here, indicates contempt, dismissal, incredulity. **ὧν:** connective
relative (more common in Latin than in Greek), where we would use
a demonstrative.

Davies (368) concludes from the hypothetical tone of this section that
none of Mantias' sons had been called upon to support a liturgy; he
notes that 'none of them is subsequently attested in the liturgical class'.
See further on §25.

10 §§ 7–9 have dealt with burdens which both will seek to avoid. §§ 10–12
deal with honours or advantages which both will claim. Mantitheus is
dealing here with posts which were filled by lot from among candidates
who presented themselves. Unlike the preceding hypotheses, in the cases
envisaged here both Mantitheus and Boeotus would know which was
meant unless both had presented themselves for the same office; but
of course the public would not know, and it would still be possible for
the brother who had not presented himself to claim the office. **κριτής:**
not a juror (δικαστής) but a judge in a competition, such as the
dramatic contests at the City Dionysia and Lenaea. It was typical of
Athenian democracy that such judges were ordinary men selected by
lot. **κέκληκεν:** sc. the official in charge of the competition. **κληροῖ**
'assigns by lot' (the person selected λαγχάνει ἀρχήν). **βουλῆς κτλ.:**
these are defining genitives. The construction is more English than
Greek; the accusative (in apposition to ἀρχήν) would be more normal.

σημεῖον 'device', 'mark'. ὥσπερ ⟨ἂν⟩ ἄλλωι τίνι 'as on anything else'. ἂν is not in the MSS; it was inserted here by Blass. Cf. §27. τῶι χαλκίωι: a bronze ticket, bearing the full name of the candidate, used as a lot; the πινάκιον of §12. ὁποτέρου ἐστίν: sc. τὸ σημεῖον or τὸ χαλκίον. To anyone outside their immediate acquaintance, such private signs would be meaningless.

11 καθιεῖ: (καθίζω) 'will cause to sit'. The sentence means only that one of the brothers will take legal action, but the phraseology, by suggesting that the court is specially convened for their dispute, makes their inconvenience that of the city. τοῦ . . . κοινοῦ καὶ ἴσου 'the right granted equally to all'. πλυνοῦμεν 'will insult, abuse [sling mud, throw dirt]', a colloquialism found in Aristophanes, e.g. *Ach.* 381 κἀκυκλοβόρει κἄπλυνεν; cf. Dem. 58.40. Since the verb literally means 'wash' the metaphorical use is at first surprising; but the word is used of garments etc. (λούω and νίζω of people) and suggests the manhandling involved in laundering clothes. ὁ τῶι λόγωι κρατήσας: the two half-brothers have to argue their right to office, whereas for others the lot is final. ἄρξει 'will hold office', 'will serve'. καὶ πότερ' ἂν κτλ.: the sweet voice of reason.

12 Here M. suggests not a source of dispute but a way in which the brothers might manipulate the confusion to their own advantage. If both stood for an office which only one desired, on the prior agreement that the other would not claim the office if the lot of 'Mantitheus son of Mantias of Thoricus' were selected, this would double the chances of the real candidate. This passage is our only source for the law forbidding the use of two lots by one man. The severity of the penalty is not surprising, for such an offence struck at the roots of democracy. τὸ . . . κληροῦσθαι: subject; 'what else is the election of one man with two lots', i.e. 'what else is this but...', 'this is nothing but...' πάνυ γε 'yes indeed', 'of course'. This is Boeotus' supposed reply. τὸ γοῦν κατ' ἐμέ 'at least, as far as I'm concerned'. Such villainy may not, of course, be beyond the rascally Boeotus. ἐξὸν μή: sc. ἔχειν: accusative absolute, 'when we need not'.

13ff. The private inconveniences. There is considerable skill and economy in the way character assassination is achieved without digression. Boeotus' villainy emerges naturally from Mantitheus' account of possible problems.

13 ἡ πόλις βλάπτεται: only the last possibility could really be described as 'damaging' the city. In all the other cases one or other of them would, if only after legal action, perform the liturgy or hold office. In order to strengthen his case (cf. on §5) Mantitheus contrives to identify damage to his own public life with damage done to the city. A more accurate (but less effective) antithesis would be ἀλλὰ ταῦτα δημοσίαι μὲν βλάπτομαι, ἰδίαι δὲ τί; **ἠλίκα:** sc. βλάπτομαι. **τι . . . λέγειν** 'to make sense', 'talk sense', 'be right'; οὐδὲν λέγειν is 'to talk nonsense', 'be quite wrong'. **χρώμενον** 'that he was familiar with / kept company with'. The present infinitive/participle in indirect statement may represent either a present or an imperfect in direct statement. Usually (as here ἕως μὲν ἔζη) the context makes clear that the infinitive/participle represents an imperfect indicative. For the verb cf. e.g. 53.4 μᾶλλον ἀλλήλοις ἤδη ἐχρώμεθα διὰ τὸ γείτονές τε εἶναι καὶ ἡλικιῶται. **ἔζη:** sc. Μενεκλῆς. **τὰ τοιαῦτ':** the behaviour implied in §2 and described in what follows. **ἴσως ἔστιν:** δεινότης need not be a virtue; it can denote 'cleverness', in contrast to 'wisdom', here the purely technical expertise of the sycophant. δεινότης is not a quality claimed by litigants at Athens (cf. on 54.17); hence the alacrity with which Mantitheus accepts Boeotus' (alleged) claim.

14 ἂν οὖν κτλ.: the hypothetical form of the argument indicates that Boeotus has undertaken no prosecution which might cause him to be regarded as a sycophant; he is tainted by association with Menecles. **γραφαί:** public indictments; see on 54.18. **φάσεις** 'denunciations' (< φαίνω). This procedure was available for a wide variety of offences (Harrison II 218f.). The prosecutor lodged with the appropriate magistrate (according to the offence) a written denunciation that someone had broken a law. The prosecutor received half of any goods seized and sold or any fine imposed. **ἐνδείξεις, ἀπαγωγαί:** ἀπαγωγή is summary arrest; see on 54.1. In ἔνδειξις the prosecutor, instead of arresting the guilty party (as in ἀπαγωγή), submitted his accusation to a magistrate, who then had to make the arrest. It was confined to cases where a man held an office, performed a function, or entered a place from which he was barred owing to ἀτιμία or pollution. See

Harrison II 229ff. The same list occurs at Andoc. 1.88 as the most significant public actions. ἐπίστασθ' ὑμεῖς κοσμίους ποιεῖν: clearly the way the jurors (and the demos, Ar. *Knights* 1121ff.) liked to imagine themselves. ἐγγεγραμμένος: listed as a debtor to the state. νὴ Δί': cf. §9.

15 τυχόν 'perhaps'; acc. abs. μὴ ἐκτεισθῆι: debts to the treasury were not cancelled by death. The partial ἀτιμία (see on 37.24) of the state debtor was inherited by his legitimate issue, and continued (as in the case of the original debtor) until the debt was repaid. τῶν ἐμῶν: genitive of comparison = μᾶλλον ἢ οἱ ἐμοὶ παῖδες. δίκην ἐξούλης: (< ἐξίλλειν) 'a suit for ejectment'. Such an action could be brought by a person whose attempts to take possession were resisted by the occupant. This measure was available in a limited number of cases, viz. (1) where a court had established his claim to the property, (2) where a mortgaged property was seized for non-payment of the mortgage, (3) when the entrant was the legal heir, (4) when the entrant was the tenant or purchaser of state property (see Harrison I 217ff.). If the jury found for the plaintiff, the defendant had to pay to the state a fine equal to the sum awarded to the plaintiff. Mantitheus claims at 40.34 that the possibility envisaged here had actually taken place. κυρίαν ... ποιησάμενος: sc. τὴν δίκην. ἐγγράψαι: optative, sc. τῶι δημοσίωι. For the active cf. 53.14. εἰσφοράς 'property-taxes'; cf. on §8.

16 περὶ τοὔνομα 'connected with the name Mantitheus'. ὅλως 'whatsoever', 'in general.' δίκην ἀστρατείας 'an indictment for failure to serve in the army' ('draft-dodging'). δίκη here is used in the broadest sense, for this action was a γραφή. The penalty was ἀτιμία. εἰς Ταμύνας: in 349 the tyrant of Eretria, Plutarchus, asked for aid from Athens. Early in 348 the Athenians sent a force under Phocion. Phocion was deserted by Plutarchus, but succeeded in defeating Callias, the tyrant of Chalcis, at Tamynae, though in a disadvantageous position (Dem. 5.5, Aeschin. 3.86–8, Plut. *Phoc.* 12). Demosthenes opposed the expedition (5.5). (The date of the expedition, and therefore of the present speech, is not certain. The absence of any reference to the campaign in the three Olynthiac orations suggests that the conflict in Eretria began in or after autumn 349; 59.4 suggests that the operations in Euboea took place at the same time as Athenian aid to Olynthus

in 348.) **τοὺς Χοᾶς** ' the feast of jugs', the second day of the Anthesteria, held on the 11th, 12th and 13th days of Anthesterion (January–February). The day was named after the vessel known as a χοῦς, miniature versions of which were given to children on that day. **τοῖς Διονυσίοις:** the City Dionysia in Elaphebolion (February–March). The suggestion seems to be that Boeotus evaded service by lingering in Athens and then performed in a chorus (dithyrambic or dramatic) at the Dionysia to escape prosecution, since choral duty earned exemption from military service. But choregi were appointed soon after the archon took office in Hecatombaion (*Ath. Pol.* 56.3), and we may suppose that they began at once to choose choristers; certainly they would not wait until immediately before the contest. Boeotus was left behind because he was already in training. He had trained as a chorister in boyhood, § 23. **οἱ ἐπιδημοῦντες:** imperfect, ' those who were in town'.

17 ἀπελθόντων δ' ἐξ Εὐβοίας: in the summer. **λιποταξίου προσεκλήθη:** the γραφὴ λιποταξίου strictly referred to desertion rather than evasion of service (ἀστρατεία), but the distinction was not observed (cf. Lycurg. *Leocr.* 147 and see McDowell *Law* 160). The jury in both cases consisted of fellow-soldiers (Lys. 14.5). Anyone who missed a campaign, even with good reason, was exposed to such charges, as was Demosthenes himself, who served as choregus in the festival in which Boeotus was chorister, 21.103; cf. also 59.26f. The attitude of the speaker to such accusations varies according to his rhetorical needs; the charge against Demosthenes is grossly unfair, that against Boeotus (we are to believe) entirely just. Cf. on 54.3. **κατὰ τοὐνόματος τοῦ ἐμαυτοῦ πατρόθεν** ' against my own name and my father's'; cf. *IG* II² 1237.115ff. ἀπογράφεσθαι τῶι πρώτωι ἔτει ἢ ὧι ἂν τὸ κουρεῖον ἄγηι τὸ ὄνομα πατρόθεν καὶ τοῦ δήμου καὶ τῆς μητρὸς πατρόθεν καὶ τοῦ δήμου πρὸς τὸν φρατρίαρχον, Arist. *Ath. Pol.* 63.4. **δέχεσθαι:** complaints could be received by the secretary of the appropriate magistrate, 58.32, but εἴσηγον ἄν indicates that Mantitheus was to preside at the trial, for δίκην εἰσάγειν is the term used of the admission of a case into court by the presiding magistrate. In Lys. 15.1 the court is presided over by the strategus; from the present passage it appears that a taxiarch could preside, perhaps when there was a large number of cases. **εἰ μισθὸς ἐπορίσθη:** at 5.5 Dem. describes the Euboean war as πόλεμος ἄδοξος καὶ δαπανηρός. The difficulty of financing military operations was

chronic in fourth-century Athens. The drain on the exchequer caused
by the Euboean campaign and the Olynthiac war was such that there
was a temporary lack of funds to pay the jurors; hence lawsuits were
suspended. For another such suspension see Dem. 45.3f. **τὴν λῆξιν** 'the
complaint', 'the charge'. **δῆλον ὅτι:** not the main clause (δῆλόν ἐστιν
ὅτι); δῆλον ὅτι is usually felt, as here, as an adverbial phrase, 'clearly',
'evidently'. **σεσημασμένων...τῶν ἐχίνων:** the arbitration of the
present suit was completed before the charge was brought against
Boeotus, or before the army returned, or before it set out; whichever
is meant, it was impossible to introduce evidence relating to the matter.
See on 54.27.

18 ξενίας προσκληθείη 'if he were charged with illegal usurpation of
citizen rights'. The punishment on conviction in a γραφὴ ξενίας was
enslavement (schol. Dem. 24.131). The charge of ξενία was freely hurled
in Athens; but the circumstances of his recognition by Mantias left
Boeotus especially exposed to such an accusation. **οὐκ ἐποιεῖθ'** 'was
refusing to acknowledge him'. **οὕτως γεγονώς** 'with his origin as it is',
i.e. uncertain. **πάλιν** 'on second thoughts', not 'again'. Cf. §§22, 24.
ʼκεῖνος: Mantias. **ψευδομαρτυρίων** 'false testimony'. Anyone proposing to bring a δίκη ψευδομαρτυρίων against a witness appearing for
the opponent had to signify his intention before the votes were cast in
the original trial (*Ath. Pol.* 68.4). The penalty was pecuniary, but three
convictions brought ἀτιμία. **ἐφ' οἷς ἐρανίζει:** i.e. ἐπ' ἐκείνοις ἃ ἐρανίζει,
'for his contributions to his cronies'. ἔρανος is (1) a meal to which each
brings his own share, (2) an interest-free loan collected from a number
of friends by or on behalf of a person in need (thus we find a man raising
an ἔρανος to pay off a loan contracted to ransom him from pirates at
Dem. 53.10ff., and a prostitute raising an ἔρανος from loyal clients to
buy her freedom at Dem. 59.31), and repaid in instalments (φοραί or
εἰσφοραί), (3) a mutual-aid society. The third use postdates Demosthenes. From the second use we get the metaphor here. The metaphor
is commonly used of aid contributed to a common cause, as Thuc. 2.43,
Lycurg. *Leocr.* 143. Here the members of the ἐργαστήριον συκοφαντῶν
to which Boeotus belongs band together to contribute false testimony
whenever one of them is engaged in a lawsuit. **ἐρήμην** 'undefended',
'by default', i.e. by failing to appear. Mantitheus could have made his
point by saying εἰ ψευδομαρτυρίων ἅλοι but he further blackens

Boeotus' character by suggesting that his guilt would be so obvious (and conviction so inevitable) that Boeotus would not take the trouble to defend himself. **δόξης καὶ . . . ἔργων:** hendiadys, 'the infamy of his conduct'.

19 There is considerable skill in the postponement of this piece of evidence until the end of the discussion. After this string of hypotheses the jury may feel that Mantitheus' fears were far-fetched. It is at this point that doubt is crushed with concrete examples. **γραφὰς . . . πέφευγεν** 'has had public indictments brought against him'. **τῆς ἀρχῆς:** the office of taxiarch; 40.34, χειροτονησάντων ὑμῶν ἐμὲ ταξίαρχον, ἧκεν αὐτὸς ἐπὶ τὸ δικαστήριον δοκιμασθησόμενος. **ἐχειροτονήσατε:** military officials were elected by show of hands, not lot, since proven skill and experience were needed. The second person because the jury represents the whole demos. **πολλὰ καὶ δυσχερῆ:** in 40.34 we hear that Boeotus was convicted in a δίκη ἐξούλης but claimed that it was his half-brother who was convicted. This may be one of the 'many inconveniences' referred to here.

20 οὐ δήπου κτλ.: there is a double antithesis, τὸ μέρος τῶν χρημάτων ἔχειν / ἀφαιρεθῆναι τοὔνομα, ἀναγκασθείς / βουλόμενος κτλ. **τὴν ἐγγραφὴν ἐποιήσατο** = ἐνέγραψεν. Any verb may be replaced by its cognate noun plus ποιεῖσθαι. The mannerism elevates. **τὴν δεκάτην:** this, the naming ceremony for the new-born child, is probably to be identified with the ἀμφιδρόμια, the ceremony at which an Athenian father formally admitted his child to the οἶκος (see however L. Deubner, *RhM* 95 (1952) 374ff.). The ceremony took place on the fifth, seventh or tenth day after birth.

21 ἐπὶ τοὐνόματος τούτου 'in possession of this name'. **πάντα τὸν χρόνον:** in this context 'all my life'; cf. e.g. Soph. *Ant.* 461. **πρὸς τοῖς δημόταις** 'before, in the presence of, the demesmen', at the *dokimasia*. **τολμᾶν κτλ.:** Boeotus shows a want of filial devotion; cf. on §31.

22 In 40.28f., Isae. 3.30 the celebration of the δεκάτη is evidence of legitimacy. A bastard, excluded from the ἀγχιστεία ἱερῶν καὶ ὁσίων (Harrison 1 66; see on §35), could not be a full member of the οἶκος. Boeotus is arguing that Mantias acknowledged him as his legitimate son in infancy, and gave him the name Mantitheus, but subsequently denied paternity. **καὶ μάρτυράς τινας παρείχετο**: like Mantitheus (§20) Boeotus provides witnesses to his δεκάτη. In the absence of a central register of births the provision of witnesses to the ceremony was a necessary procedure; in this as in other respects (such as marriage; the only proof that marriage had taken place was the testimony of witnesses to the ceremonies connected with it, as e.g. Dem. 57.41) Athens in the fourth century remained an oral culture. Here and in 40.28f. Mantitheus seeks to discredit Boeotus' witnesses. In 40.29 he stresses the small number of the witnesses (two, Timocrates and Promachus, 40.28) to the event; though witnesses would no doubt be scarce several decades after the birth. Here and at 40.28 he asserts that the witnesses were never close associates of Mantias. Since no evidence is adduced, we cannot test the assertion, but even if it is true it does not follow that the witnesses are lying. Plangon may have provided witnesses from among the friends of her own family, to protect her son's interests. At 40.59 Mantitheus claims that Timocrates is no older than Boeotus. Again, no evidence is offered. But even if M. is telling the truth it does not follow that T. is lying. One of the few exceptions to the bar against hearsay evidence was that the words of a dead man could be quoted; T. could be attesting that an older relative, now dead, witnessed the ceremony.

Since the issue of the δεκάτη is important, the surprising brevity of Mantitheus' attack on the witnesses (here and in Dem. 40) together with absence of evidence indicates that Boeotus is telling the truth.

μὴ νομίζων: dates Mantias' disbelief to the time of Boeotus' birth. Certainly Mantias later denied paternity, but he may have had no doubts at the time of Boeotus' birth. μή, not οὐ, because the participle is conditional – 'if he did not believe'. **ἔξαρνος**: probably not formal renunciation (ἀποκήρυξις) but a simple refusal to enrol Boeotus in the phratry; see on §39.

23 πρὸς ὀργὴν ἦλθεν: Boeotus claims that Mantias' subsequent rejection of him was the result of a quarrel with Plangon (cf. 40.29). If (as argued in the speech intro.) Boeotus' account is true, the quarrel may have concerned the paternity of Plangon's sons. Mantias may have come to doubt that they were his. **ἑαυτοῖς**: ἀλλήλοις, as often. **καταλλάττεσθαι**: the same argument is used at 40.29. Like all arguments from εἰκός, it has some plausibility, but it fails to take account of the

bitterness, injustice and pusillanimity which can arise in personal
relationships, and it collapses once the possibility is accepted that the
dispute was actually about the paternity of the children. **πρός:**
adverbial; 'in addition'. Cf. 37.38, 49. **φάσκειν συγγενὴς εἶναι:**
insidious. Mantitheus does not say simply συγγενὴς εἶναι; the implication is that Boeotus and Plangon are lying. **εἰς Ἱπποθωντίδ' ἐφοίτα
φυλήν:** Thoricus (Mantias' deme) belonged to the Acamantid tribe,
but Plangon sent her son to learn dancing in a school of the Hippothontid
tribe, presumably the tribe of her family. Mantitheus' argument seems
nugatory at first sight. What difference does it make where Boeotus
went to school? Schools were run by private individuals, not by the state
or the tribe. But Mantitheus is not referring to ordinary schooling.
Dancing did not form part of basic Athenian education, and it is
anyway clear that Mantitheus refers to an establishment devoted to
choral dancing (χορεύειν refers to choral dance, not solo dance), not
an ordinary school. χορεύσων here probably refers to training for the
dithyrambic contests, in which competition was between tribes (see on
§7). Thus the argument, though weak (see on ἐξῆν below), is not as
fatuous as it appears. Boeotus as a boy trained for such contests and
the tribe he was to represent was Hippothontis, not Acamantis. **ἐφοίτα:**
the usual word for going to school.

24 ἄν: with πέμψαι. **ὁμοίως:** sc. ὡς εἰς τὴν Ἱπποθωντίδα. **ἐξῆν:** if
Mantias refused to acknowledge Boeotus officially by enrolling him in
his phratry, it is unlikely that Boeotus could represent Mantias' tribe
at a festival. Boeotus eventually took legal action to compel Mantias
to acknowledge him; such action could perhaps have been taken earlier
on his behalf (this is not certain; if as M. claims at 40.22 Plangon's
brothers had not yet paid their father's debt to the treasury, as ἄτιμοι
they could not address a court as plaintiff, defendant or witness, and
could not therefore sue Mantias for Boeotus). But the real inconveniences of Mantias' refusal to recognize Boeotus would not be felt
while Boeotus was a child, and Plangon's family might hesitate to sue
Mantias simply to vindicate B.'s right to dance for Acamantis. **ὁμοίως
ἐξῆν** is a gross exaggeration. M. returns to the argument in §28. **καὶ
ἐφαίνετ' ἂν κτλ.** 'and the tribe [which you represented] would be seen
[or would have been seen] to be consistent with the [alleged] giving
of the name' (not of course 'would have seemed' = ἐφαίνετ' ἂν
εἶναι).

25 παρά 'through', 'by reason of'; see LSJ s.v. c iii 7. **εὐήθειαν:** not 'foolishness' but 'guilelessness'. The open, honest Mantias (as M. represents him) was no match for the unscrupulous Plangon (as M. would have us see her). **δίκας κτλ.:** these suits are discussed in slightly greater detail in 40.16f. During the division of Mantias' estate Mantitheus demanded that the sum of one talent, representing his mother's dowry, be set aside for himself. Boeotus put in a counter-claim for the same sum, representing (he claimed) Plangon's dowry (40.14; at 40.20 B. is represented as demanding over 100 minae). This is what is meant by αἷς πρότερόν μ' ἐσυκοφάντει. At the arbitration over Boeotus' claim judgement was given against B., whereupon he filed other financial suits against Mantitheus – δίκας δύ' ἢ τρεῖς εἴληχεν here. These appear to have concerned money allegedly left by Mantias with M., of which B. is claiming a share. **πρὸς αἷς:** i.e. πρὸς ἐκείναις ἃς ἐσυκοφάντει. **ἐσυκοφάντει:** for συκοφάντης, συκοφαντεῖν, see on § 1. **πάντας . . . ὑμᾶς εἰδέναι:** see on § 2. **τίς ἦν χρηματιστής** 'what sort of a businessman' (cf. 37.54); i.e. a bad one, so that the money claimed by Boeotus does not exist. *IG* ii² 1622.435f. records the payment of a (relatively small) debt of Mantias by his heirs. Davies attributes the (possible) disappearance of Mantias' sons from the liturgical class (above §9) to Mantias' poor head for business. This is to go far beyond the evidence. Since the lower limit for the liturgical class was approximately 3 talents (Davies xxiii–xxiv) and since all legitimate children shared equally in an estate, Mantias' estate could have been worth over 8 talents but his sons would still fall outside the liturgical class. Mantias was far from destitute when he died, for a house worth at least one talent could be set aside (pending the result of the cross-suits for the dowries) before the division of Mantias' estate (40.14f.).

26 ἐάσω ταῦτα: as a decent son, M. refuses to dwell on his father's defects; but is he really moved by filial piety, or an awareness of weak argument? **εἰ δίκαι' ὀμώμοκεν:** i.e. when she swore that Boeotus and Pamphilus were Mantias' sons. This sentence is explained by what follows. If Mantias kept two houses, as (according to M.) Plangon's oath implies, he cannot have left much money when he died (at 40.51 M. claims that Plangon lived lavishly at Mantias' expense). Mantitheus is distorting Boeotus' argument. Boeotus maintains that Plangon was Mantias' wife, not his mistress (40.20, cf. 39.22). Mantitheus' argument is presented in such an evasive manner (no details, no witnesses) that we may reasonably conclude that he sets little store by it. **ταῖς δίκαις ταύταις:** instrumental with ἐπιδεικνύει ('proves him by these suits of his') or modal with συκοφάντην, sc. ὄντα ('an unscrupulous litigant in these suits'). **γάμωι γεγαμηκώς . . . ἑτέραν εἶχε γυναῖκα:** formal marriage versus a vague informal liaison. **πῶς ἄν:** i.e. he could not have done.

27 δίκαιον μὲν οὐδὲν ἕξει λέγειν: common in anticipation of the following speaker's arguments; cf. 36.18, 37.52, 40.20, 35.49, Lys. 14.16, 28.12, 30.7. **ἐπηρέαζεν:** according to Boeotus (cf. §32), the name Boeotus was given as a calculated insult. The insult could perhaps reside in a hint at the proverbial stupidity of the Boeotians (Pind. *O.* 6.90, Hor. *Epist.* 2.1.244); however, from what follows (ἀξιοῖ δὲ κτλ.) it seems more likely that the insult consists in the withholding of the paternal grandfather's name, which B. regards as his right. **πειθόμενος ὑπ' ἐμοῦ:** since Boeotus claims that the name Boeotus was given at the instigation of Mantitheus he cannot be referring to his infancy, for even if Mantitheus was alive then (i.e. if as he claims he is the elder, which is unlikely – see below) he can only have been a child. B. must be referring to the time of his enrolment in the phratry (i.e. after his suit with Mantias), when Mantitheus would be old enough to make the alleged suggestion. See further on §32. **ὡς δὴ πρεσβύτερος ὤν:** δή is ironic, as often, citing a statement with unconcealed disbelief. The paternal grandfather's name is a πρεσβεῖον (§29), the privilege of the eldest son; cf. 43.74. **βραχέα:** arguments and accounts are often introduced with a promise of brevity; see on 54.2. **οἶδα . . . ὁρῶν:** imperfect, 'I know I saw him'; see on §13. **οὑτωσί** 'casually'; see LSJ s.v. IV. **οὐ μὴν ἰσχυρίζομαι τούτωι:** all Mantitheus can offer as evidence is appearance, and he promptly drops the argument; to insist on the point would be silly (εὔηθες). But why should the insistence be silly, if the fact were true?

28 ἠξίους χορεύειν: Mantitheus reverts to a (marginally) stronger argument. **θείης** 'assume'; LSJ s.v. B II. **εἰ γὰρ Μαντίθεον:** sc. ὄνομ' ἂν θείης σαυτὸν ἔχειν δικαίως.

29 τὸν . . . τοῦ δικαίου λόγον 'the computation of justice' (cf. 6.8 τοῦ δικαίου λόγον ποιούμενοι) ; 'it is difficult to be precise about years, but you can all calculate justice'. A splendid red herring.

Mantitheus' reply to Boeotus' claim of seniority is odd.

(1) In §28, instead of urging forcefully his own seniority, M. simply cites appearance, and then undermines the limited value of this evidence by saying that it would be foolish to insist on the point. The evidence *is* weak, but we expect a man who is confident of his cause to use to the full whatever evidence he has.

(2) In §29 M. is content to stress the difficulty of proving who is older. He would have us believe that there is no objective means of proving seniority where the age gap is not obvious from appearance. But it would have been easy to adduce witnesses to prove his seniority. Years at Athens were dated by the eponymous archon. The Panhellenic festivals were another obvious means of dating. Though there were no birth certificates, Mantitheus could bring witnesses to link his birth, or the celebration of his δεκάτη, or even his enrolment in the deme (the group enrolled in each year were assigned the name of an eponymous hero, Arist. *Ath. Pol.* 53.4, 7) to the archon lists or some other datable event such as the Olympic games to prove that he is older. Since M. offers no such evidence we must conclude that he has none to offer.

(3) M. is happy to escape the argument from seniority, and take refuge in other arguments, Boeotus' choir training in the Hippothontid tribe (§28), the date of the admission to the phratry (§29).

(4) Equally surprising is the brevity of the argument. When Mantias enrolled Boeotus in the phratry he swore that B. was legitimate. Whether or not the oath was true (i.e. whether B. was the son of Mantias' first marriage or, as Mantitheus claims, a bastard), the effect was the same. It gave B. all the rights of a legitimate son. Before the law both B. and M. are legitimate sons of Mantias. Boeotus' claim to the name is based in part on seniority. The issue is therefore of some importance. But Mantitheus hurries through his argument with evident discomfort.

We must conclude that Boeotus is the elder. Mantitheus, aware that Boeotus' case is unassailable, is content to obfuscate the issue; his aim is merely to raise a degree of doubt in the mind of the jury. As we have seen (speech intro., *Mantitheus' action*), there is external evidence that Boeotus won the case. The case turns in part on the issue of seniority, and if Boeotus can produce evidence of seniority where Mantitheus can only offer vague assertions, the jury will be impressed by the evidence.

ἔστι δὲ οὗτός τις: M. shifts ground to the main argument for his own claim to the name, stressing the strength of his case to bolster up the weakness of his claim to seniority. ἐποιήσατο: see on §4.

30 Ἀκαμαντίδος φυλῆς: partitive; 'how comes it that you have become a member of the Acamantid tribe?' **τῶν δήμων:** partitive; 'of the demes, a member of that called Thoricus' (Paley); cf. Plat. *Euthyphro* 2b9, Arist. *Ath. Pol.* 21.4. **ὅτι...Μαντίας:** Boeotus' reply, supplied by Mantitheus. This imaginary cross-examination, in which Boeotus complacently condemns himself in reply to the dispassionate questions of Mantitheus, prepares effectively for the sudden release of emotion in §31, where M. pounces. A litigant could be compelled to answer his opponent's questions (Dem. 46.10; see e.g. Lys. 12.24–6, Plat. *Ap.* 24d–27e); Arist. *Rhet.* 1419a gives instruction on how to conduct a cross-examination. M. could have put these questions to B. personally; but a real cross-examination might not have gone so smoothly (Arist. loc. cit. also tells how to circumvent the opponent's questions).

31 The argument used in §§30f. is logically weak, esp. Mantitheus' demand in the name of Mantias that Boeotus keep the name under which he was enrolled in the phratry. A father may demand obedience from his sons, but a son cannot make such a demand on behalf of his dead father. But the strength of the appeal lies not in logic but in emotion. The Greeks felt strongly the need for respect to parents. Honour towards parents is one of the 'Three Commandments' of the Greeks (see Thompson–Headlam on Aesch. *Eum.* 269–72). In Athens, the right of parents to support in old age by their children and to proper burial, and the protection of parents from physical and other abuse, were guaranteed by the γραφὴ κακώσεως γονέων, the penalty on conviction being total ἀτιμία (see e.g. Xen. *Mem.* 2.2.13, Aeschin. 1.28). One of the questions asked at the δοκιμασία of the archons was γονέας εἰ εὖ ποιεῖ (Arist. *Ath. Pol.* 55.3; cf. e.g. Dem. 57.70, Dinarchus, *Aristog.* 17). It is from this common morality reinforced by law that Mantitheus' demand derives its considerable emotional appeal. This fine display of righteous indignation is skilfully used to cloak the speaker's embarrassment on the subject of seniority. **παραγράφειν** 'call yourself by another patronymic', 'style yourself the son of someone else'; cf. on §8.

32 νὴ Δί': introducing a statement or objection which the speaker intends to demolish, as often. M.'s point is that since B. regarded his

mother's family with respect the name of his maternal uncle can hardly
have been given as an insult; one of Plangon's brothers was called
Boeotus (40.23). But for B. the insult probably resided in the refusal
of the name Mantitheus (see on §27). **ἐπειδὴ κτλ.:** M. argues that
Boeotus was enrolled in the phratry as Boeotus because he himself had
already been enrolled as Mantitheus; therefore Mantias could not enrol
B. as Mantitheus. M. does not say, as we expect, that B. was enrolled
as Boeotus because that was the name he had always held. From §§21
and 28 it seems that B. claims that he has always been called
Mantitheus, and M. tacitly accepts this here. It seems probable that
B. has been calling himself Mantitheus since he was a child. He only
acquired the name Boeotus when he was admitted to the phratry as
an adult. When B. enrolled himself in the deme register as Mantitheus,
he was simply resuming the name he had always used. For B. the name
Mantitheus was his own; it was moreover (as the name of Mantias'
father and privilege of Mantias' eldest son) inextricably connected with
his claim to legitimacy, and to the esteem which Mantias had always
denied him. **ἠναγκάζετο:** M. never tires of reminding B. (and the jury)
that Mantias only acknowledged B. against his will. **ἐπεὶ σὺ δεῖξον**
'otherwise you must prove', lit. 'for/since [if it is not as I say] prove'.
Cf. Soph. *El.* 352, Ar. *Wasps* 72.

33 τὸν προσήκοντ' 'a true son' (Paley), lit. 'one who is related [to
them]'. **οὐκ ὢν δ':** sc. οἷον δεῖ τὸν προσ. κτλ. For the participle
resuming a finite verb in the first part of the sentence see Denniston,
Greek prose style 95f. In English cf. Fitzgerald's *Omar*⁵ 71 'The moving
finger writes; and having writ moves on.' **ἀπωλώλεις:** for such claims
cf. on 54.22. **οἱ περὶ τῶν γονέων . . . νόμοι:** see on §31 for the laws
protecting parents. These are completely irrelevant to the present case,
but again it is the emotional effect (πάθος) of the appeal to deep-seated
feeling which matters, not the cogency of the argument. **εἰσβιαζομένων:**
used instead of βιαζομένων as suggesting wrongful intrusion as well as
compulsion. Cf. Ar. *Birds* 32. **ἄκοντας:** qualifies the unexpressed object
of εἰσβιαζομένων (τοὺς πατέρας supplied from τοῦ πατρός above).

34–6 Mantitheus now changes his tone, from vituperation to the calm
voice of reason and patience. He is no longer a man attempting simply
to protect his own rights but one as much concerned for his opponent
as for himself.

34 πόλις: see on §2. **οὔκουν ἔγωγε** 'certainly not I', 'not I at least'.
βλασφημῆις: climactic. **εἰς ἀλλότρι' ἐμπεσών κτλ.** 'it will be thought
that you have forced your way into property which does not belong
to you and that your use of it shows that it is not properly yours'. We
have translated ἀλλότρια as 'another's property' (cf. 21.150 of Midias'
abuse of his citizen rights: τῶν οὐ προσηκόντων ἀγαθῶν κύριος
γεγονώς...οὐδέν' οἶμαι τρόπον φέρειν οὐδὲ χρῆσθαι τούτοις δύναται,
ἀλλὰ τὸ τῆς φύσεως βάρβαρον καὶ θεοῖς ἐχθρὸν ἕλκει καὶ βιάζεται, καὶ
φανερὸν ποιεῖ τοῖς παροῦσιν ὥσπερ ἀλλοτρίοις...αὐτὸν χρώμενον).
But it could mean 'a family which is not your own'; Boeotus' treatment
of Mantias' family proves that he does not really belong to it (cf. Lycurg.
Leocr. 48, Dem. 40.47). Both ideas may be intended. **οὕτω:** sc.
ἐπιβουλεύων, δικαζόμενος, φθονῶν, βλασφημῶν.

35 τὰ μάλισθ': with the whole sentence rather than with ὄντα alone;
'even if you *were* his son and my father *did* refuse to recognize you'.
ἀδικῶ: is 'be in the wrong', 'be guilty' as well as 'do wrong', hence
the present, where ἠδίκηκα could equally well have stood (so τίκτω is
'be the parent of' as well as 'bear', νικάω 'be the victor' as well as
'win'). **οὐκ ἐποιεῖτο ... ἐποιήσατο:** the imperfect expresses Mantias'
continued refusal to recognize Boeotus, the aorist the fact of his eventual
recognition. **προσήκονθ' ἡγούμην:** sc. σε. **τῶν πατρώιων ἔχεις τὸ
μέρος:** M. offers this as evidence of his own acceptance of B. as his
brother. But once Mantias accepted B. as his legitimate son M. had no
legal right to refuse him his share of the estate. Cf. on §6. **ἱερῶν, ὁσίων
μετέχεις:** in the context of Mantias' estate, this refers to the ἀγχιστεία
ἱερῶν καὶ ὁσίων, the right of succession (Isae. 6.47, 9.13, Dem. 43.51).
The oikos was a religious as well as an economic and social unit, and
membership involved not only a claim on property (ὅσια) but also a
share in the family cult (ἱερά). The religious observances of the family
included burial rites and the annual offerings to the dead, and the
worship of the family gods (see Lacey, *The family in classical Greece* 147ff.).
ἀπάγει: probably here a synonym of ἐξάγειν, the *vox propria* for the
refusal by the possessor of a property to allow a claimant to take
possession (e.g. Isae. 3.62; see Harrison I 219); the claimant would then
bring a δίκη ἐξούλης. In the context of an inheritance the word is
appropriate; see on §15. **κλάηι καὶ ὀδύρηται:** for such displays see on

54.42. **κατηγορῆι ἐμοῦ**: this may refer to Boeotus' complaint (40.50) that M. was given all the advantages (financial and emotional) of Mantias' recognition while B. was spurned, to the continuing financial suits (see on §25), or to Boeotus' attempt to have M. tried for τραῦμα ἐκ προνοίας (40.32f.). There were doubtless other accusations. **μὴ περὶ τούτων ὄντος τοῦ λόγου νυνί**: character assassination is irrelevant when it is directed against oneself; cf. e.g. Lys. 9.1 and see on 37.45. μή because the participle is conditional – 'if [as is the case] the present argument does not concern these'; οὐ plus causal participle ('since etc.') would have served as well. **κληθέντι**: the aorist is ingressive; 'having assumed the name', 'under the name Boeotus'.

36 μηδαμῶς: sc. φιλονίκει; 'you must not'. **ἐθελέχθρως** 'malicious', 'unrelenting'. **οὐδὲ γὰρ ἐγὼ πρὸς σέ**: sc. ἐθελέχθρως ἔχω. οὐδὲ γάρ = καὶ γὰρ οὔ. **τὸν ἀκούσαντ'**: i.e. anyone who hears the name Mantitheus mentioned. **πότερος**: ἐστιν οὗτος or the like. **ὃν ἠναγκάσθη ποιήσασθαι**: M. contrives, while feigning concern for B., to rub in yet again the unfortunate circumstances of Mantias' recognition of B.; cf. on §32. **ἐρεῖ**: i.e. the person who mentioned the name Mantitheus.

37 εὐορκήσετε: at the beginning of the year the jurors swore an oath. At Dem. 24.149–51 occurs what purports to be the text of this oath. The document can hardly be genuine, for it omits clauses known to be part of the oath and includes others which can only have occurred in the oath for a limited period or which make little sense. But some clauses certainly are genuine, the pledge to judge according to the laws, not to accept bribes, to listen impartially to both parties and to vote on the issue under dispute (see in general Bonner–Smith II 152ff. and Harrison II 48). Litigants often remind the jurors of their oath, e.g. Lys. 10.32, Isae. 2.47, Aeschin. 3.6, Dem. 20.118, 36.61 (εὐορκήσετε), 45.88. The reference may be to a specific clause, as below §40, Aeschin. 3.6, or as here the speaker may remind the jury of the general tenor of their oath, which is to be just. **κατέγνω . . . ἂν ἔχειν** 'gave judgement against himself that it would be right for him to have the name Boeotus'; for the construction cf. e.g. Thuc. 3.45.1. **ἠντεδίκει . . . ὡς ὢν Βοιωτός** 'he contested the suit as Boeotus'. M. claims that by defending the suit lodged against him under the name Boeotus he accepted that this was his name. The argument is nugatory. B. may have been as keen as M. to have the issue decided. **ὑπώμνυθ'** 'sought an adjournment'. If either party were unable to appear, before an arbitrator as here or before a court, he might apply for an adjournment by deposing on oath his inability to attend. **ἐρήμην ἐάσας καταδιαιτῆσαι:** sc. τὸν διαιτήτην. καταδιαιτάω (prefix as in καταγιγνώσκω) is 'decide [as arbitrator] against' someone, ἀποδιαιτάω (prefix as in ἀποψηφίζομαι) 'decide [as arbitrator] for' someone.

38 ἀντιλαγχάνει μοι τὴν μὴ οὖσαν 'he moved a non-suit'. When decision at arbitration had been given by default, it was open for the litigant who had failed to appear to apply within ten days to have the case reopened, ἀντιλαγχάνειν τὴν μὴ οὖσαν (sc. δίκην; at Dem. 21.86 the phrase τὴν δίαιταν ἀντιλαχεῖν is used). This involved swearing that the absence was unavoidable (Poll. 8.60). The details of the process are unknown. Cf. on 37.33. **Βοιωτὸν αὐτὸν προσαγορεύσας:** this may be a tactical blunder by Boeotus; but was it possible for him to have the decision quashed on the grounds that the wrong name was used when the action itself concerned the name? Certainly once Boeotus' right to the name Mantitheus was confirmed in court he was quick to take the advice here given by M. At 40.17f. M. says: 'The action in which I was suing him at that time was decided against him by default, when though he was in town he did not appear before the arbitrator. The defendant not only failed to appear then and present his case, gentlemen of the jury, but also denied that I had secured a judgement against *him*; for he said his name was not Boeotus but Mantitheus...' Predictably, although M. here regards this as the right course for B. to take (§38) if he really believed in his right to the name Mantitheus, at 40.17 he comments: καὶ οὕτως ὀνόματι ἀμφισβητῶν ἔργωι τὴν προῖκά με τῆς μητρὸς ἀποστερεῖ. **ἀντίληξιν:** Boeotus' written application to have the arbitrator's decision set aside.

Blass, followed by Sandys, wished to bracket §§37f. as a later addition by Demosthenes, since these sections appear to interrupt the natural transition from §36 (the names given by Mantias) to §39 (the validity of Mantias' action). This then compels us to bracket καὶ κατὰ τὴν τούτου προσομολογίαν in §41. But in fact there is a natural progression from the last sentence of §36 through §§37f. to 39. Mantitheus establishes first that Mantias gave the names, then that Boeotus accepted his right to do so, and finally that the law likewise accepts this right.

39 νόμος: this is our only evidence for this law. Since the law defined the father's rights it is not surprising that Mantitheus does not cite it, for it does not give him any legal right to prevent B. from using the name Mantitheus. If M. is citing the law accurately it seems that if Mantias had lived B. would have been unable to enrol himself as Mantitheus in the deme register in the face of Mantias' opposition. But now that Mantias is dead the situation is not so simple. B. argues (probably truthfully) that Mantias named him Mantitheus at birth. The jury is thus offered a choice between two expressions of Mantias' will in this matter, the name Mantitheus given in infancy and the name Boeotus given at the enrolment in the phratry. **ἀλλὰ κἂν πάλιν ἐξαλεῖψαι βούλωνται:** ἀλλὰ καὶ πάλιν ἐξαλεῖψαι ἂν βούλωνται. **ἐξαλεῖψαι** 'erase'. Possibly metaphorical here, indicating merely the father's right to remove his son's name. This right appears to be connected with that of *apokeryxis*. It is not clear whether the reference is to the personal name or the patronymic, or both. However, the verb may be literal. ἐξαλείφω is used at Ar. *Knights* 877 of disfranchisement for prostitution (removal from the ληξιαρχικὸν γραμματεῖον), at Xen. *Hell.* 2.3.51 of Critias' removal of Theramenes from the list of 3,000 (cf. Arist. *Ath. Pol.* 36.2), at Arist. *Ath. Pol.* 49.2 of the removal of names from the list of cavalry. Here it may refer to removal from the phratry register, which would perhaps follow expulsion from the oikos. **ἀποκηρῦξαι:** this is the only reference in the orators to the process of ἀποκήρυξις, which is otherwise known only from later lexicographers. The word indicates a public proclamation whereby a father expels his son from the oikos. This is as much as we are told (e.g. Dion. Hal. *Ant. Rom.* 2.26 τιμωρίας τε κατὰ τῶν παίδων ἔταξαν ἐὰν ἀπειθῶσι τοῖς πατράσιν..., ἐξελάσαι τῆς οἰκίας ἐπιτρέψαντες αὐτοὺς καὶ χρήματα μὴ καταλιπεῖν, Suda s.v. ἐκποίητον γενέσθαι, ὁ μὲν ἀποκήρυκτος ἐπὶ κολάσει ἐκβάλλεται). The lexicographers indicate that *apokeryxis* was a punishment for (serious) misconduct by a son. There is no reason to suppose (and no hint in the present passage) that *apokeryxis* was used to disown a son when a father had come to doubt paternity, as supposed

by Gernet II 10, followed by Harrison I 77 and MacDowell *Law* 91;
so rightly Rudhardt, *MH* 19 (1962) 51, who observes that since the
recognition of a son was not a single act but a series of acts, from birth
to manhood (admission to oikos, phratry and deme), a father could
disown a son whose legitimacy he now doubted by refusing to complete
the process. Certainly there is no suggestion in this passage that Mantias
had used *apokeryxis* against Boeotus, as Gernet suggests.

40 ὧν γ᾽ ἂν μὴ ὦσι νόμοι γνώμηι τῆι δικαιοτάτηι δικάσειν: this clause,
added to the jurors' oath to judge according to the laws and decrees
of the Athenian people (κατὰ τοὺς νόμους καὶ τὰ ψηφίσματα τοῦ δήμου
τῶν Ἀθηναίων), is omitted from the jurors' oath quoted at Dem.
24.149, but is found (beside the present passage) at Dem. 20.118, 23.96,
57.63 and attested by Pollux 8.122. M. argues that in the present case
both clauses could apply equally well, for the strict letter of the law and
justice coincide. Although the jurors were not actually asked, as this
clause suggests, to decide cases in which the accused was not charged
with transgression of a specific law or laws, there were many acts not
explicitly covered by laws. Athenian laws not infrequently named
offences without defining them or listing cases (see E. Ruschenbusch,
Historia 6 (1957) 266, 271). There was no concept of precedent to enable
the scope of the laws to be defined by tradition. Consequently it fell
to the jurors to decide whether a given act counted as an offence under
the law cited by the plaintiff as well as deciding questions of fact. In
such cases (of which the present suit may be one – see speech intro.,
Mantitheus' action) the jurors would decide γνώμηι τῆι δικαιοτάτηι. Cf.
MacDowell *Law* 60.

41 ὃ δίκαιον τῆι γνώμηι . . . ὑπειλήφατε: deliberately recalls γνώμηι
τῆι δικαιοτάτηι. The jurors' 'opinion of justice' or 'most just opinion'
in the present case must coincide with that which they would apply in
their own case. **εὐσεβές:** i.e. in accordance with your oath. **ὥστε κτλ.:**
this sentence is all we are given by way of an ἐπίλογος. **τὴν τούτου
προσομολογίαν:** as described in §§ 37f. **οὐδ᾽ εἰωθότα γίγνεσθαι** 'quite
unprecedented'; substituted for οὐδὲ δίκαια both for variety and to
present a more striking close.

56 Against Dionysodorus

Trade and finance

The speaker Darius[38] and his partner Pamphilus have lent to the traders Dionysodorus and Parmeniscus 3,000 drachmas as a maritime loan with the ship of Dionysodorus and Parmeniscus as security for it. In this case Darius is attempting to recover the money which he alleges Dionysodorus and Parmeniscus owe to him and his partner as a consequence of the loan.

The essentials of Athenian maritime trade are that a merchant buys a cargo at Athens, sails to another port and sells the cargo at a profit there, takes on a fresh cargo, returns to Athens and sells that cargo there at a profit.

Before setting out he may take out a maritime loan.[39] By the general terms of a maritime loan a merchant (ἔμπορος) or ship-owner (ναύκληρος) borrowed money for the duration of the voyage (cf. on §3), using as security either the cargo, in whole or in part, or (if the borrower was the ship-owner) the ship itself. The loan and interest were repaid only on condition that the ship or cargo arrived safely at its destination. If as a result of shipwreck or piracy the ship or the cargo was lost, the debt was cancelled and the lender lost his money.

The maritime loan can thus be seen as a kind of insurance policy[40] by which the risk of loss was shifted from the borrower to the lender, and this view may be true if a loan was taken by a relatively wealthy trader. But traders were usually not men of great resources,[41] and at 34.51 the speaker, Chrysippus, can say that neither ship nor ship-owner nor supercargo can put to sea if the part contributed by those who lend

[38] The name is known from the Hypothesis but not from the speech itself. The information may have come from a document which was cited in full in a branch of the manuscript tradition which we do not now possess. The document could not however have been the συγγραφή, for Darius says that he was not named in it (§6); but perhaps he was named in the πρόκλησις (§17).

[39] On maritime loans see G. E. M. de Ste Croix, in H. Edey and B. S. Yamey (eds.), *Essays in honour of W. T. Baxter* (London 1974) 41–59. Cf. also Paul Millett, in Peter Garnsey, Keith Hopkins and C. R. Whittaker (eds.), *Trade in the ancient economy* (London 1983) 36–52.

[40] So Finley, 87; *The ancient economy* (London and Berkeley 1973) 141; see de Ste Croix, op. cit. 42f.

[41] J. Hasebroek, *Trade and politics in ancient Greece* (London 1933) 7–10, 36f.

money is taken away. Even when allowance is made for the fact that this statement is made by a lender who is trying to persuade the jury that it is in their own interests that the case be decided in his favour and against the borrower,[42] it would weaken Chrysippus' case to make a claim that was obviously false. The insurance factor should not be exaggerated. It seems that most maritime traders borrowed not from choice but in order to stay in business, in order to pay for their cargoes.[43] Naturally the merchant would expect to make sufficient profit on his cargo to pay back the loan with interest and still have profit to spare.

A loan could be made for one leg of the voyage only (ἑτερόπλουν) or, as in the present case, for the outward and return voyage (ἀμφοτερόπλουν). Presumably because of the dangers involved in sea travel, maritime loans commanded a higher rate of interest than other loans. Thus at 34.23 we hear of an ἀμφοτερόπλουν loan from Athens to Bosporus made at the rate of 30% while the interest on real security was $16\frac{2}{3}$%.[44] Since a journey to Bosporus and back took between two and three months,[45] the interest, if calculated on an annual basis, would be between 120% and 180%. At 50.17 there is a ἑτερόπλουν loan from Sestos to Athens at $12\frac{1}{2}$%. Moreover the rate of interest could vary depending on the anticipated danger involved in the voyage. At 35.10, in a preserved contract, the ἀμφοτερόπλουν loan is made at the rate of $22\frac{1}{2}$%; but if the voyage from Pontus to Hieron is made after the rising of Arcturus (about the middle of September) the interest rate is to rise to 30%.

Various conditions could be agreed upon, such as a lower limit on the value of the cargo (34.6f.; 35.18), or restrictions on where the ship should go and return to (56.5). Sometimes alternative routes could be allowed (35.10). There could also be a penal clause, effective in the case of contravention of the loan agreement (cf. 34.26, 33). Usually there was a written contract setting out in detail the terms and conditions of the loan. A good idea of the possible complexity of a maritime loan agreement is given by the contract preserved at 35.10–13.

According to Darius, the conditions of his loan were that it was ἀμφοτερόπλουν; that the ship should sail from Athens to Egypt and then return to Athens; that interest was payable (but the rate is not

[42] De Ste Croix, op. cit. 43.   [43] Millett, op. cit. 42–7.
[44] Millett (op. cit. 186 n. 2) notes that the commonest rate of interest on landside loans in classical Athens was one per cent per month.
[45] Cf. Isager–Hansen 60.

stated); that the ship was the security; that the debt was cancelled if
the ship was lost; that failure to comply with the terms of the contract
doubled the liability (the penal clause); and that either or both of the
borrowing partners could be sued.

The case

Darius and Pamphilus were probably metics. Δαρεῖος is certainly a
foreign name, and Πάμφιλος is the name of a metic mentioned elsewhere
(21.163: τὸν μέτοικον…τὸν Αἰγύπτιον, Πάμφιλον).

To judge from the way in which Darius argues, it seems that
Dionysodorus and Parmeniscus were neither Athenian citizens nor
metics resident at Athens. The point involves the restrictions applied
to transporting corn to any port other than Athens. At 35.50f. (dated
before 338) the speaker says that the law is severe if any Athenian
transports corn to any port other than Athens or lends money for that
purpose. The law cited refers only to the lending of money, but it shows
that the illegality included Athenians καὶ τῶν μετοίκων τῶν ᾿Αθήνησι
μετοικούντων. At *Leocr.* 27 (dated 330) Lycurgus refers to the illegality
involved if an Athenian transported corn to anywhere other than
Athens, and the speaker of 34.37 (dated 327/6), with particular
reference to Lampis who was probably a slave, says that the laws have
prescribed the severest penalties εἴ τις οἰκῶν ᾿Αθήνησιν ἄλλοσέ ποι
σιτηγήσειεν ἢ εἰς τὸ ᾿Αττικὸν ἐμπόριον. He brings the law to bear on
Lampis who is described as οἰκῶν μὲν ᾿Αθήνησιν, οὔσης δ᾽ αὐτῶι
γυναικὸς ἐνθάδε καὶ παίδων. Thus it was illegal for an Athenian or a
metic resident in Athens to transport corn anywhere other than to
Athens or to lend money for such a voyage. Now on several occasions
Darius alleges that Dionysodorus and Parmeniscus did in fact transport
corn from Egypt to Rhodes and that they sold it there (§§3, 9f., 11, 13,
20, 21, 23, 25, 34, 47) and that they lent money on voyages to Rhodes
and Egypt (§17). Yet at no point does Darius specifically claim that
they were acting illegally in so doing except in so far as they were in
breach of contract. At §47 he certainly describes his opponents as τῶν
καὶ ἡμᾶς καὶ ὑμᾶς ἠδικηκότων, but nowhere does he invoke the law
concerning the transportation of corn: they had 'wronged' Athens by
acting to her disadvantage, but Darius does not invoke the corn law
and he would certainly have accused them of illegality if he could. Since
shortly before the date of this speech (323 or 322, see below, *Date and*

authenticity) there had been a serious shortage of corn (see below, *The corn crisis*), the law is unlikely to have been relaxed since 327/6. The conclusion is that in all probability Dionysodorus and Parmeniscus were neither Athenians nor metics living at Athens.

The case for the recovery of the money claimed to be owed to Darius and Pamphilus is brought against Dionysodorus alone. That is in accordance with the terms of the contract which stated τὴν...πρᾶξιν εἶναι καὶ ἐξ ἑνὸς καὶ ἐξ ἀμφοῖν (§45). Since the ship had not returned to Athens, Parmeniscus, who sailed with it, was presumably still on board.

A situation in which only one partner prosecuted would not in itself be surprising, for active solidarity is exemplified in a clause of the contract cited in 35 at §12. It would, however, be remarkable if Darius alone sued in the present case because at §6, though he says he had a share in the loan, he also adds that only Pamphilus' name appeared in the contract. It is true that the Athenians did not show concern for precision of language in situations where more than one creditor was concerned (cf. intro. to 37, p. 115) but the present case is a δίκη ἐμπορική (see Appendix) and the written contract was vital in the δίκη ἐμπορική. Since Darius has no written contract, it is difficult to see how he could sue without at least Pamphilus' affirmation that Darius was a lender with himself. But though Pamphilus was present in court (Πάμφιλος οὑτοσί, §6) his testimony is not called in the speech. Darius in fact spends no time whatever in establishing his right to prosecute. It is highly likely therefore that Dem. 56 is a speech in support of Pamphilus, who has already spoken. This likelihood is strengthened by the abruptness and obscurity of the opening sentence of the speech,[46] abruptness and obscurity which are particularly evident when it is borne in mind that, since this speech is for the prosecution, this sentence would be the first the jurors would learn of the case if Darius spoke first. But the fact that Darius' speech is complete with a long narrative section means that Pamphilus said little other than by way of introducing Darius.[47]

---

[46] κοινωνός εἰμι τοῦ δανείσματος τούτου. Whose partner? What loan? Why τούτου?

[47] Cf. Dem. 36, where Phormio can only have spoken a few words before leaving his case to a *synegoros*. Phormio's reason is τὴν...ἀπειρίαν τοῦ λέγειν and ἀδυνάτως ἔχει (36.1). Perhaps his Greek was weak. If Pamphilus' Greek was bad he may quickly have passed the case on to his partner.

The case is one for damages (δίκη βλάβης).[48] Darius claims that, though Dionysodorus and Parmeniscus had borrowed 3,000 drachmas for a voyage to Egypt and back on the security of the ship and on the condition that it should return to Athens, the ship was taken to Rhodes and the cargo was sold there contrary to the agreement. He alleges that though the seaworthiness of the ship is proved by the fact that it has been plying between Rhodes and Egypt, the ship (the security) has not been produced in Athens and the money owed to him and Pamphilus has not been paid. Since the terms of the contract have been violated he invokes the penal clause, whereby his opponents' liability is doubled. Dionysodorus, on the other hand, said that the ship had been damaged. He offered to repay the capital of the loan and the interest as far as Rhodes, pointing out that other creditors had agreed to this arrangement. Darius says that he and Pamphilus had insisted that the interest should be paid for the whole voyage, and he claims that the ship had put into Rhodes because his opponents could get a higher price for their cargo there than at Athens.

A notable feature of the speech is that Darius produces no testimony whatever to substantiate what he alleges to be true.[49] Especially remarkable is his failure to produce evidence in support of his claim that the ship is still intact and is plying between Egypt and Rhodes. Again, his allegations concerning the reasons for the sale of the cargo at Rhodes are entirely unsubstantiated.

One strong point which he appears to have is that if the ship was lost Dionysodorus and Parmeniscus were not liable to pay anything to Pamphilus and himself; but if they offered payment of the sum owed as far as Rhodes, they were admitting that the ship was not lost; and if the ship was not lost, his opponents should have fulfilled their contractual obligation by bringing it to Athens and paying the debt in full. Darius rests his case on the terms of the contract, which seems only to have allowed for the ship to be either σεσωισμένη or διεφθαρμένη. What Dionysodorus is claiming is that the ship ἐρράγη, which does not necessarily mean that it was lost, but could mean that it was holed (see on §§ 12, 23). Probably the ship had put into Rhodes for repairs, and since it could not sail on to Athens the cargo had to be sold there. If the ship was neither σεσωισμένη nor διεφθαρμένη the offer of payment

---

[48] On the use of κατά (not πρός) Dionysodorus see Harrison II 79.

[49] In this respect the speech is comparable with Lys. 9.

of what was due as far as Rhodes seems to have been a compromise. In the present case Dionysodorus would probably seek some kind of 'equity' ruling.

Contracts

In §2 Darius says that he is dependent on laws which declare that all agreements voluntarily entered into shall be valid. By 338, the latest date for Dem. 35, which preserves a contract at §§ 10–13, maritime loans had become the subject matter of agreements of such length and complexity that committing them to writing was the only adequate protection against conflict, even against misunderstanding. Moreover one of the conditions for the δίκη ἐμπορική was that there should be an agreement in writing (see Appendix). At §26 Darius' statement οὐδ' ἐστὶν ἡμῖν οὐδὲν κυριώτερον τῆς συγγραφῆς may reflect a clause in the contract (see on §26). Certainly in his speech he relies very heavily on the contract.[50]

It seems strange therefore that he introduces no witnesses to prove the validity of the agreement. The agreement in this case was in writing, but generally what was important about agreements was not that they were in writing, but that there were witnesses to their having been made.[51] At the end of the written contract cited at 35.10–13 the names of three witnesses are given, and more appear at §14, where the witnesses depose. When a written agreement was drawn up it was entrusted to a third party (cf. 48.46–8) who, if not already one of the witnesses, would be available for proof in addition to the other witnesses (cf. 35.14, 48.11). In the present case the contract may have been entrusted to the banker (cf. §15). Certainly the banker would have been regarded as a respectable and trustworthy witness. So respectable were bankers that according to Isoc. 17.2 it was unusual to bring witnesses

[50] Of 113 instances of the noun συγγραφή and the verb συγγράφομαι (in the sense 'enter into a contract') which appear in the Demosthenic corpus, no fewer than 105 cases occur in speeches concerned with maritime loans. The present speech has a very high proportion of the 105 occurrences, no fewer than 48 cases compared with five in Dem. 32, 32 in Dem. 35 and 20 in Dem. 34. The exceptionally high frequency of the words in the present speech (and in addition there are two uses of the rare verb παρασυγγράφεω: see on §28) is indicative of the strong reliance Darius places on his bond.

[51] Cf. 34.30. Aristotle ascribes no special evidentiary weight to writing at *Rhet.* I. 1376a 33ff.

to agreements with them; they 'have many friends, handle a lot of money, and have a reputation for trustworthiness because of their profession'.

Thus the absence of witnesses did not invalidate an agreement. In Lys. P. Oxy. no. 1606 fr. 6(b) (Grenfell and Hunt) the speaker had loaned his friend Theomnestus thirty minae without witnesses and a case has been brought against Theomnestus. The absence of witnesses simply made the agreement more difficult to prove.

It may be thought that Darius' failure to produce witnesses to testify to the contract may be explained at least in part by the fact that in δίκαι ἐμπορικαί the writing of agreements had an importance not found in other types of case. However, witnesses are provided at 35.14, which is a speech in response to a παραγραφή, but from §§45–9 it is apparent that the case is presented as a δίκη ἐμπορική. The importance of the written contract in δίκαι ἐμπορικαί would perhaps be likely if anything to increase the need felt for witnesses to depose to the genuineness of the document rather than to reduce that need.

Date and authenticity

An indication of the date of the speech is given in § 7, where Darius says of Dionysodorus and Parmeniscus: ἦσαν γάρ...ὑπηρέται καὶ συνεργοί...Κλεομένους τοῦ ἐν τῆι Αἰγύπτωι ἄρξαντος. (For Cleomenes and his position of power in Egypt see on § 7.) The most natural meaning of the aorist participle is that at the time of the speech Cleomenes was no longer in power. Usually the aorist participle stands in a temporal relationship to the main verb, but an attributive aorist participle can refer to time absolutely past.[52] Thus at 59.110 (τὴν θυγατέρα...ἐξέδωκε Θεογένει τῶι βασιλεύσαντι, καὶ αὕτη ἔθυσε τὰ ἱερὰ τὰ ἄρρητα ὑπὲρ τῆς πόλεως...) the aorist participle is not past with reference to ἐξέδωκε: see 59.79, 84. Again at 21. 178 (ἕτερος ἀδικεῖν ποτ' ἔδοξεν ὑμῖν...καὶ κατεχειροτονήσατ' αὐτοῦ παρεδρεύοντος ἄρχοντι τῶι υἱεῖ...ἦν δ' οὗτος ὁ τοῦ βελτίστου πατὴρ Χαρικλείδου, τοῦ ἄρξαντος), while παρεδρεύοντος and ἄρχοντι refer in an important way to the time of κατεχειροτονήσατε, ἄρξαντος cannot refer to time earlier than ἦν; it refers to time past from the point of view of the speech. Cf. also 9.22. In all these cases the power is finished at the time of

[52] Cf. Goodwin *MT* 52f.

speaking.[53] At 56.7 ἄρξαντος cannot refer to a time before that of ἦσαν. The natural conclusion is that Cleomenes' power in Egypt was over at the time the speech was written.

After Alexander died on 10 June 323[54] Ptolemy received the satrapy of Egypt and Cleomenes became ὕπαρχος to him, his second in command (Arr. *Succ.* 1.5). According to Pausanias (1.6.3) after crossing into Egypt Ptolemy executed Cleomenes in the belief that Cleomenes was disloyal to him in the interest of Perdiccas. The chronology is uncertain.[55] Ptolemy opposed the supremacy of Perdiccas from the period immediately after Alexander's death till the death of Perdiccas in May or June 320.[56] The downfall of Cleomenes cannot be earlier than autumn 323 and is unlikely to be later than summer 320.[57] Thus the speech cannot be earlier than the later part of 323.

At §50 Darius refers to the jury with the words τῶι πλήθει τῶι ὑμετέρωι, which may provide some indication that he was addressing a democratic jury. It is doubtful if this would have been said after the suppression of democracy by the Macedonians at the end of 322.[58] Thus the probable *terminus ante quem* for the speech is 20th Boedromion 322,

---

[53] In his introduction to the speech Sandys wrote that the aorist need only imply that Cleomenes was in power at the time of the action described without showing whether he was in office or not when the speech was delivered. But usage elsewhere is against that view, and Sandys agreed that if Cleomenes were still in office the most natural tense would have been the present.

Any notion that the aorist participle at 56.7, 59.110 and 21.178 is ingressive is to be dismissed, because it is difficult to see why it would be used in preference to the imperfective (at 21.178 alongside the imperfective) when the two amount to the same and the ingressive aorist adds an unnecessary complication.

[54] See A. E. Samuel, *Ptolemaic chronology* (Munich 1962) 46f.

[55] For a discussion of events from 323 to 320, see R. M. Errington, *J.H.S.* 90 (1970) 49–77.

[56] Errington, op. cit. 75.

[57] The wording of Paus. 6.1.3 seems to indicate that the execution of Cleomenes was one of Ptolemy's first actions: αὐτὸς δὲ ἐς Αἴγυπτον διαβὰς Κλεομένην τε ἀπέκτεινεν...καὶ Μακεδόνων τοὺς ταχθέντας τὸν ᾿Αλεξάνδρου νεκρὸν ἐς Αἰγὰς κομίζειν ἀνέπεισεν αὐτῶι παραδοῦναι. But it was not till spring or early summer 321 that the cortège was ready to leave Babylon. See Errington, op. cit. 64f.

[58] But the words at §50 do not provide conclusive evidence for the end of 322 as the *terminus ante quem*. It is possible that the traditional language was maintained in the courts after that date, as it was in inscriptions. Cf. *IG* ii/iii.1 380.7 and 381.10 which belong to 320/19: ἔδοξεν τῶι δήμωι.

the date on which a Macedonian garrison occupied Munychia (Plut. *Phoc.* 28).

Since δίκαι ἐμπορικαί were in all likelihood heard between Boedromion and Munichion, i.e. about September to April (see Appendix), the most probable date for the speech is between Boedromion and Munichion 323/2, though the first part of Boedromion 322 cannot be totally discounted.

At § 5 Darius says that the loan was made πέρυσιν τοῦ μεταγειτνιῶνος μηνός (i.e. about August), and at §§ 4, 16, 34 and 45 he says that his opponents have had the use of the loan for over a year. If the speech belongs to the period between Boedromion and Munichion 323/2 the loan was made in Metageitnion 324, while if the speech belongs to the earlier part of Boedromion 322 the loan was made in Metageitnion 323.

Since Demosthenes did not commit suicide till 16th Pyanepsion 322 (Plut. *Dem.* 30), i.e. about the end of October or the beginning of November, by this dating it was physically possible for him to have composed the speech after his return from exile in 323. In the circumstances of the Lamian War it may be doubted that he took on the writing of a speech for such an apparently trivial case.[59] To judge by stylistic criteria it is most improbable that he wrote it. The sentence structure can be padded and laboured; see especially §§ 10 and 16, which consist of single long and awkward sentences quite unlike Demosthenes. The speech is unattractively repetitious: §§ 3f., part of the proem, anticipate in detail much of the narrative section, thereby causing unnecessary repetition; and the recapitulation of the case at §§ 45ff. does not bear the stamp of Demosthenes. Moreover these doubts are increased by a consideration of quantifiable stylistic criteria. In Speech 27 of 363 B.C., Demosthenes' first forensic speech, avoidable hiatus is found on average 12 times in 100 lines and there is an average of 17 avoidable runs of three short syllables per 100 lines. In Speech 21, composed around 348 B.C., avoidable hiatus averages only 2 cases in 100 lines and avoidable tribrachs average 11 in 100 lines. In Speech 18, the great public speech of 330 B.C., the average for avoidable hiatus remains at 2 per 100 lines and the number of avoidable tribrachs drops to 3 per 100 lines. Compared with these speeches which are known to

[59] Yet the associations of the people involved are not known. There is a Pamphilus whom Dinarchus (*In Dem.* 43) accuses Demosthenes of making a citizen in return for money. The connection is obviously very tenuous.

be genuine, Speech 56 shows a marked lack of sensitivity towards avoidable hiatus with an average of 21 per 100 lines, and towards avoidable runs of three short syllables with an average of between 13 and 14 per 100 lines. While the speech was probably not therefore written by Demosthenes (cf. on §50), there is no reason to doubt that it is a genuine courtroom speech.

The corn crisis[60]

At §§7–9 Darius tries to make forensic capital out of associating Dionysodorus and Parmeniscus with the activities of Cleomenes (see on §7), whereby he ran a conspiracy to fix the price of corn in the Aegean area and which were associated in the minds of the Athenians with the high price of corn.

That the corn supply was a matter of the greatest importance to Athens is testified by the law making it illegal for an Athenian or a metic living at Athens to transport corn to any market other than Athens or to lend money for such a voyage (see above, *The case*). Athens depended heavily on imported corn for her supply. In 330 Demosthenes can say at 18.87 that the Athenians consumed more imported corn than anyone else, and from 20.31 it appears that Pontus was the most important source of supply. Egypt and Sicily were other important sources.

A series of honorary decrees for the Cypriot Heracleides of Salamis erected in 325/4 (*IG* II/III.1 360) marks honours granted to him by Athens because in 330/29 he had sold 3,000 medimni of wheat at only five drachmas the medimnus though he was the first merchant to reach harbour, and because in 328/7 he had presented the city with 3,000 drachmas for the purchase of corn.[61] (Cf. *IG* II/III.1 1628, 346–9, 363–8 (of 326/5).) With the shortage of corn to be detected in these decrees is to be associated an inscription (Tod 196) of the early 320s,[62] found at Cyrene, which gives a list of the persons and communities (including Athens) to whom Cyrene supplied corn ὅκα ἁ σιτοδεία ἐγένετο ἐν τᾶι

---

[60] The corn crisis is discussed in Isager–Hansen 200–8.
[61] Cf. the three crises mentioned at 34.38 (327/6), the first of which was in 335.
[62] Cf. Isager–Hansen 204f.

Ἑλλάδι. The range of places covers all areas of Greece and includes Epirus and perhaps Illyria.[63]

That a blight was the cause[64] is suggested by the fact that in the Cyrene inscription small places are mentioned, such as Larissa and Tanagra, places which might be considered small enough not normally to need imported corn. But if a blight was a cause, other factors, such as inflation, inefficient distribution and profiteering[65] made a bad situation worse. The lessening of the value of money brought about by the large amount which came into the Mediterranean area from Asia as a consequence of Alexander's conquests must have caused difficulty with price arrangements. Bad distribution and profiteering existed, as the activities of Cleomenes show. At §7 Darius can say that by the activities which he describes Cleomenes did much harm to Greece by his price-fixing.

If the speech belongs to 323 or 322 (see above, *Date and authenticity*) Darius is ascribing (without any evidence) to his opponents collusion with Cleomenes in 324 or 323. There seems to have been some shortage then which was only relieved by the arrival of ships from Sicily (§§9f.). We have only Darius' word for it that Dionysodorus and Parmeniscus were in fact part of Cleomenes' large profiteering conspiracy, and the charge may well be totally false. However, if he can make the charge stick, he is drawing on a large reserve of hatred.

1–4 Introduction.

1 κοινωνός εἰμι τοῦ δανείσματος τούτου: Dar. says that he is a sharer in the loan because his name did not appear on the contract (§6). For Dar.'s position see speech intro., *The case*. ἡμῖν τοῖς τὴν . . . προῃρη-μένοις: lit. 'us who have chosen for preference the working at sea', i.e. 'us whose business lies in maritime commerce'. Cf. §§48, 50. ἐργασία can be used either of manual work (manufacture: Plat. *Gorg.* 449d, *Theaet.* 146d; working at a material: Plat. *Chrm.* 173e, Thuc. 4.105; agriculture: Isoc. 7.30) or of trade, business (banking: Dem. 36.6; maritime commerce: §4, Dem. 33.4). ἐκεῖνο μέν 'this at least'. The

---

[63] See Tod p. 275.
[64] Cf. Tarn in *CAH* vi 448.
[65] Cf. W. L. Westermann, *American Historical Review* 35 (1930) 18; H. Michell, *The economics of ancient Greece*² (Cambridge 1957) 275.

primary function of μέν is to emphasize an idea, to concentrate attention on it, and this original sense is found in classical Greek. By isolating one idea μέν can prepare the way for a contrasting idea, and in the latter function μέν commonly introduces the first part of an antithesis; but sometimes the contrasting idea is not expressed (μέν solitarium). The distinction between the emphatic use, as here, and the contrasting use can be fine. See Denniston *GP* 359ff., esp. 364ff., 380ff.

φανερὸν καὶ ὁμολογούμενον 'for all to see and acknowledged [by all to exist]'. In the context ὁμολογούμενον cannot mean 'agreed upon by the two parties' nor can it have anything to do with witnesses to the contract. Dar. means that whereas the lenders give hard cash they are given in return only a flimsy contract (see below) which may be disputed. Mercantile money-lending was more insecure than other forms of usury inasmuch as if a ship or cargo which served as security was lost at sea the loss was the lender's; he had to accept the vagaries of the elements and to deal with ship-owners and merchants who might have considerable opportunity to cheat him. However the very high interest rates in maritime loans (cf. speech intro., *Trade and finance*) were intended to cover such losses and the profit was great. **ἐν γραμματειδίωι . . . καὶ βυβλιδίωι μικρῶι πάνυ**: a single document (the contract) is meant. The diminutives γραμματείδιον, βυβλίδιον are contemptuous (cf. 54.37). **δυοῖν χαλκοῖν**: genitive denoting price. A χαλκοῦς was worth one-eighth of an obol, one-forty-eighth of a drachma. In the Eleusinian accounts of 329/8 and 327/6 (*IG* II–III² 1672f.) unskilled workers get 1½ drachmas a day, skilled workers 2 or 2½ drachmas. (For the value of money in the fifth and fourth centuries see A. H. M. Jones, *Athenian democracy* (Oxford 1957) 135.) The sum of two χαλκοῖν was therefore very small. **ἡμεῖς δ' οὐ φαμὲν δώσειν** '*We* don't [merely] *say* that we shall give.' In a different context the words could mean 'We say that we shall not give.'

2 καὶ τί λαβόντες τὸ βέβαιον, προϊέμεθα; 'and what is the security we get when we lend on risk?' **τὸ βέβαιον**: lit. 'the secure thing' in the midst of this uncertainty. For the construction, cf. § 15. **προϊέμεθα**: used of lending on risk at §50. Cf. 36.6, Plat. *Demod.* 384c. It is found in the active of lending at Ar. *Clouds* 1214. **ὅσα ἄν τις ἑκὼν . . .κύρια εἶναι**: cf. 37.27; 47.77; Hyp. *Athen.* 3. On this law and for the question of what constituted a valid agreement see speech intro., *Contracts*. **καὶ**

δυοῖν θάτερον . . . αἰσχυνόμενος: θάτερον could conceivably be the complement of ἦι but δυοῖν θάτερον is usually adverbial; cf. 9.11, 18.139, 19.106, 176, 51.16. So perhaps at §27 below. At 27.45 δυοῖν θάτερον is the object of διαπράττεσθαι.

3–4 Darius gives a highly rhetorical preliminary outline of his case.

3 ἐν τῆι πέρυσιν ὥραι: ὥρα is a period of time within a longer natural period (cf. Plat. *Phdr.* 229a τήνδε τὴν ὥραν τοῦ ἔτους τε καὶ τῆς ἡμέρας). At 54.26 and 57.12 it refers to the time of day (cf. 21.84). Commonly it means the time of year (e.g. 50.23; cf. Thuc. 6.70). It is doubtful whether in classical Greek it can mean the year generally. 'In the season of last year' probably refers to the sailing season. Since the loan was made in Metageitnion (§5) the ship should have returned by the end of the sailing season, and while it is not known how long Dion. and Parm. had by the terms of the contract to pay what they owed after the return of the ship, it was probably only a matter of days, to judge from 35.11. See speech intro., *Date and authenticity.* **τοὺς νόμους:** Dar. speaks vaguely. In view of παρὰ τὴν συγγραφήν he is probably referring to the laws mentioned in §2, to the effect that a voluntary agreement is binding, and in §10, to the effect that ναύκληροι and those on board should sail to the port agreed. He does not say specifically that Dion. and Parm. transgressed the law forbidding anyone resident at Athens to transport corn anywhere other than Athens, and if that law had applied in the present case Dar. would have stated the fact somewhere in the speech (see speech intro., *The case*). However, if any members of the jury saw that reference so much the better for Dar. **οὐδέπω καὶ νῦν:** lit. 'not even yet even now', i.e. 'not to this very day'. When a negative is strengthened as in 'even now' the strengthening usually carries on the negative, οὐδέ not καί. But οὐδέπω καὶ νῦν is a fixed expression which appears again at §§40 and 45. **οὔτε τὸ ἐνέχυρον καθίστησιν εἰς τὸ ἐμφανές** 'nor has he produced the security'. The security (cf. ἐχυρός, 'strong', 'secure') is the ship. The words are a reference to the δίκη εἰς ἐμφανῶν κατάστασιν (cf. Harrison I 207ff. and §38).

4 δεύτερον ἔτος τουτί 'for over a year now'. See speech intro., *Date and authenticity.* **καρπούμενος τὰ ἡμέτερα** 'making a profit from our money', as explained in §17. **τὴν ἐργασίαν:** see on §1. **ὑποκειμένην:**

τίθημι or, more frequently, ὑποτίθημι, is the usual verb used for setting as security for a loan, 'mortgaging'. **δῆλον ὡς ζημιώσων κτλ.:** in this highly rhetorical passage, Dar. says that in addition to the violations of the contract Dion. intends to cause Pamph. and himself more distress by the court case. He intends to give the impression that Dion. is spitefully ruthless; but it was, after all, Dar. who brought the case, not Dion. **τῆι ἐπωβελίαι:** a fine of one-sixth of the sum in litigation, an obol for each drachma (hence the name).

There is much uncertainty both as to the types of private case in which a litigant was liable to the ἐπωβελία and as to the circumstances in which it was exacted; see in general Harrison II 183ff. In the present passage we have the only evidence for the ἐπωβελία being exacted from a plaintiff in a δίκη ἐμπορική. (The context of 35.46 indicates that the reference there is to the imposition of the ἐπωβελία in παραγραφαί.) It is not surprising that an attempt was made to discourage frivolous prosecution in courts specifically established for the benefit of those engaged in commerce (see Appendix).

Both the defendant and the plaintiff were liable to the ἐπωβελία in the case of a παραγραφή (Isoc. 18.3; cf. 18.12) and very probably in the case of an ἀντιγραφή (Dem. 47.64, but cf. Poll. 8.58 and Harrison II 184). But apart from the uncertain evidence of Pollux concerning φάσις (8.48; cf. Harrison II 184, 220f. with Cohen 88ff.) there is no reason to believe that the *defendant* was liable to ἐπωβελία in any other type of case.

It is not certain whether simple failure to win the case would cause Dar. to be fined the ἐπωβελία. At 27.67 Dem. says that he will incur it ἄν...ἀποφύγηι μ' οὗτος. Again Isoc. at 18.3 says that in the case of a παραγραφή it is incurred by ὁπότερος...ἄν ἡττηθῆι. Simple failure to win is given as the condition for it for one prosecuting χρηματικήν τινα δίκην by the schol. on Plat. *Leg.* 921d and for prosecutors in general by Harpocration (see below). However from Isoc. 18.12 in a case of διαμαρτυρία a litigant had to obtain less than one-fifth of the votes cast before he became liable to it and Pollux (8.48) mentions one-fifth of the votes in the case of φάσις. It is probable that at 27.67 Dem. is using exaggerated language (he goes on to say that he will suffer ἀτιμία but he would not in fact become a state debtor since at 28.18 he says he would pay the ἐπωβελία to his opponent). It is likely that the ἐπωβελία was only payable when a litigant received less than one-fifth of the votes, because the purpose of imposing the fine must have been to discourage prosecutions which had no hope of succeeding.

It is fairly likely that the ἐπωβελία was paid to the defendant, if one may generalize from 28.18 and (in a case of an ἀντιγραφή) 47.64. Cf. Harpocration s.v. ἐπωβελία: ἐπιτίμιον...ὅπερ ἐδίδοσαν οἱ διώκοντες τοῖς φεύγουσιν, εἰ μὴ ἕλοιεν.

εἰς τὸ οἴκημα: οἴκημα is a euphemism for δεσμωτήριον, 'prison' (cf. Plut. *Sol.* 15, Hesych. s.v. οἴκημα) and is so used at 32.29 and Lys. fr. 75.4.

By law defendants in δίκαι ἐμπορικαί who failed to win their case could be imprisoned till they paid the penalty adjudged against them (33.1) and at 21.176 we hear of a successful plaintiff, Euandrus of Thespiae, who arrested his defeated opponent, Menippus of Caria, after the latter had left Athens but had returned at the time of the celebration of the Mysteries. (This arrest was in violation of the law concerning the Mysteries, but in other circumstances, apparently, it would have been lawful.) At 35.46f. (the defence in a παραγραφή case) the speaker, setting out the consequences for him if the παραγραφή is successful, gives imprisonment if he incurs τὰ ἐπιτίμια and does not pay. While the ἐπωβελία applies to the παραγραφή case (see above) the matter of imprisonment for failure to pay arises probably because this case involves a παραγραφή in a δίκη ἐμπορική. Just as Dem. 56 provides the only evidence for the ἐπωβελία being exacted in a δίκη ἐμπορική (see above) so this is the only evidence unconnected with a παραγραφή to give definite indication that failure to pay the ἐπωβελία rendered the plaintiff in a δίκη ἐμπορική liable to imprisonment.

The reason for imprisonment may have been that litigants in such cases might often be not normally resident at Athens and might prove difficult to find for the exacting of payment (cf. 21.176). Another consideration may have been the importance to Athens of her corn imports: in the interest of trade foreign merchants and lenders would have to feel confident that they would have every possible opportunity to obtain reparation for failure to honour a contract and that every attempt was made to ensure that no frivolous suit would be brought against them in the matter of a contract.

5–18 Narrative of the background to the case.

5 πέρυσιν τοῦ μεταγειτνιῶνος μηνός 'in the month of Metageitnion last year'. Metageitnion, the second month of the Attic year, corresponds to the latter part of August and the first part of September. See speech intro., *Date and authenticity*. **ἐξ Αἰγύπτου εἰς 'Ρόδον ἢ εἰς 'Αθήνας:** alternative choices are found in the contract for a maritime loan at 35.10: 'Αθήνηθεν εἰς Μένδην ἢ Σκιώνην, καὶ ἐντεῦθεν εἰς Βόσπορον, ἐὰν δὲ βούλωνται, τῆς ἐπ' ἀριστερὰ μέχρι Βορυσθένους, καὶ πάλιν 'Αθήναζε.

6 ἀποκριναμένων δ' ἡμῶν . . .ἀλλ' ἢ εἰς 'Αθήνας: Dar. makes it clear to the jury that he and Pamph. had declined the proposal that the voyage might be to Rhodes, (1) in order not to seem to have connived at corn being carried to a port other than Athens or to have lent money for that purpose (cf. §11); (2) in order to make it appear plain that from the outset Dion. and Parm. had the possibility of this voyage in mind; and (3) in order to forestall the possibility of Dion.'s pleading that the thought of such a voyage was in the lenders' minds or that Parm. could not have known that it was not. **προσομολογοῦσι** 'agreed [in addition to the other things agreed]', i.e. in addition to the other terms of the proposal which were *ab initio* agreed upon by both parties. **ἐπὶ ταύταις ταῖς ὁμολογίαις** 'on these terms.'. Cf. §11. **ἀμφοτερόπλουν** 'for a return voyage'. A technical term in maritime loans; see speech intro., *Trade and finance*. **συγγραφὴν ἐγράψαντο** 'they had the contract written', 'they allowed the contract to be written' (middle). **ἔξωθεν:** lit. 'from outside'. See on §1. **ἀναγνώσεται:** i.e. the secretary of the court will read the συγγραφή. Cf. §17.

7 καὶ ὁ...Παρμενίσκος ἐπέπλει ἐπὶ τῆς νεώς: presumably as ναύκληρος Parm. was still with the ship and it was for this reason that Dar. was suing Dion. alone. Dion. could be sued alone by the terms of the contract: see §45 τὴν δὲ πρᾶξιν εἶναι καὶ ἐξ ἑνὸς καὶ ἐξ ἀμφοῖν. **ὑπηρέται καὶ συνεργοὶ πάντες οὗτοι:** Dar. brings no evidence to substantiate his claim that Dion. and Parm. were part of a conspiracy.

Either πάντες includes friends, witnesses and perhaps *synegoroi* whom Dion. had with him in court or the word is used illogically but effectively to give the impression of a large conspiracy. There is no need to emend to πάντων, the tentative suggestion of Rennie, who compares 32.16. The emendation produces two genitives, πάντων and Κλεομένους, which stand awkwardly in different relationship to ὑπηρέται καὶ συνεργοί.

Κλεομένους . . . ἄρξαντος: the aorist participle indicates that C.'s power was now at an end. For the importance of the words for dating the speech, see speech intro., *Date and authenticity*.

Cleomenes was a Greek from Naucratis on the Canopic branch of the Nile. The position given him by Alexander when the latter had conquered Egypt in 332/1 was one of civil control of the Sinai peninsula and financial control of all Egypt (Arr. *An.* 3.5.2–5, Curt. 4.8.5). At some date Alexander probably made him satrap of Egypt ([Arist.] *Oec.* 1352a 16, Paus. 1.6.3, cf. Arr. *Succ.* 1.5, Dexippus (= *FGrH* 100) fr. 8), though it has been doubted whether Alexander ever formally appointed a Greek financier from Naucratis as satrap of Egypt (see W. W. Tarn, *Alexander the Great* II (Cambridge 1948) 303 n. 1). Alexander certainly seems to have shown trust in him (cf. Arr. *An.* 7.23.6–8), perhaps because he raised revenue so well. After Alexander died in 323 and Ptolemy became satrap of Egypt, C. became Πτολεμαίωι ὕπαρχος (Arr. *Succ.* 1.5). Ptolemy put him to death because of suspicion of disloyalty in acting for Perdiccas (Paus. 1.6.3).

Whether or not he was ever appointed satrap he was undoubtedly important (cf. Arr. *An.* 7.23.6–8) and he acted as satrap. When Ptolemy came to Egypt he got 8,000 talents there (Diod. 18.14.1), the result, no doubt, of the work of the unpopular C. Among the financial exploits recorded at [Arist.] *Oec.* 1352a 16ff., at the time of the corn shortage in the Greek world (see speech intro., *The corn crisis*) when Egypt was not so badly hit, we read that he forbade the export of corn from Egypt; and when the civil governors (νομάρχαι) protested on the grounds that if there was no export of corn they would be unable to pay their taxes, he allowed export but clapped on a heavy export charge, thus getting the duty on the export, cutting down export, and depriving the nomarchs of their excuse. On another occasion he bought up the whole supply of Egyptian corn for ten drachmas a measure and sold it at 32 drachmas for the same measure.

The present passage at Dem. 56.7ff. gives an insight into his manipulation of the corn market in the Aegean area. His name must have been synonymous with dear bread, and by linking Dion. and Parm. with C.'s information service, Dar. is drawing on a deep store of hatred.

παλιγκαπηλεύων: the schol. on Ar. *Wealth* 1156 distinguishes the κάπηλος (a local trader who bought from the producers, one who bought and sold in his own country; cf. Plat. *Rep.* 371d, *Sph.* 223d), the ἔμπορος (a merchant who bought for sale in another country, i.e. a trader who carries wares from state to state; cf. Plat. *Sph.* 223d), and the παλιγκάπηλος (ὁ ἀπὸ τοῦ ἐμπόρου ἀγοράζων καὶ πωλῶν). Cf. the corn-sellers of Lys. 22 who bought corn from the importers and resold it (at an exorbitant price). We should not insist on the Ar. schol.'s exact meaning. The word is used simply contemptuously of Hermes at Ar. *Wealth* 1156 and it is used contemptuously and metaphorically at 25.46 κάπηλος ἐστι πονηρίας καὶ παλιγκάπηλος καὶ μεταβολεύς. The pejorative use perhaps derives from the fact that the παλιγκάπηλος does not produce or transport but merely distributes. συνιστὰς τὰς τιμάς 'settling the prices', 'fixing the prices'. καὶ αὐτὸς καὶ οὗτοι μετ' αὐτοῦ: an anacoluthon which emphatically brings the jury's attention back to the gang of which Dion. and Parm. are alleged to be members.

8 ἐπέπλεον 'used to sail in charge of'. ταῖς ἐμπορίαις: lit. 'the carryings of cargo' (cf. Lys. 32.25), i.e. 'the shipments'. οὐχ ἥκιστα 'most of all', a common litotes. συνετιμήθη τὰ περὶ τὸν σῖτον: τιμᾶν and τιμᾶσθαι can mean 'to value', 'to estimate'. Cf. 27.8 (speaking of his guardians) συνετιμήσανθ' ὑπὲρ ἐμοῦ ταύτην τὴν εἰσφορὰν εἰς τὴν συμμορίαν, 'they jointly set for themselves [if the middle has force] by assessment this tax for the symmory on my behalf'; and 28.11. So here by a slight extension, lit. 'the corn situation was jointly set by assessment', i.e. 'the price of corn was fixed'. There is no need to emend with Wolf and Paley to ἐπετιμήθη (for which see 34.35, 50.6), though συν could have come into the text from συνιστάς or from συνεργιῶν. ἐκ τῶν τοιούτων ἐπιστολῶν καὶ συνεργιῶν: for a slightly different type of conspiracy involving the corn supply at Athens, cf. Lys. 22, esp. 13ff.

9 It is alleged (1) that Dion. and Parm. allowed Athens as the sole port of return because of the high price of corn there and (2) that Dion. sent a message to Rhodes to inform Parm. of the subsequent lower price. No evidence whatever is produced to support these allegations. ἐπιεικῶς ἔντιμον 'fairly dear'. ὑπέμειναν . . . γράψασθαι 'they did not object to having it written'. ὁ Σικελικὸς κατάπλους 'the arrival of the ships from Sicily'. Pontus, Egypt and Sicily were the most important Athenian

sources for corn. The case of Dem. 32 concerns a cargo of corn from
Syracuse. Cf. Isager–Hansen 19–27, esp. 25f. The reference appears to
be to a convoy, travelling together (perhaps with an escort of triremes)
for protection against pirates. **ἀνῆκτο εἰς Αἴγυπτον** 'had put to sea for
Egypt'. **ἐνθένδε:** lit. 'hence' because of the ἀπο- in ἀποστέλλει.
ἀκριβῶς εἰδώς . . . εἰς 'Ρόδον: for traders breaking their journey at
Rhodes on their way to Athens, see Lycurg. *Leocr.* 18 (cf. Diod. 20.81).
It is not known if Parm. stopped at Rhodes on the way to Egypt. If
he did, the messenger, if he existed, may have been too late to catch
him there on the outward journey. Sailors had an easy voyage from
Athens to Egypt because they ran before the prevailing wind. On the
return journey they presumably used the north wind along the coast
of Syria and sailed to Cyprus, then along the south coast of Asia Minor
past Phaselis to Rhodes; then, rounding the southern tip of Asia Minor
at Cnidus, they sailed west past Naxos and Paros to Athens. (See
Isager–Hansen 61.)

10 πέρας δ' οὖν, λαβὼν γὰρ κτλ. 'Anyway, in the end, having
received . . .' The γάρ is explanatory after πέρας δ' οὖν. For the
construction, cf. Aeschin. 2.46 τέλος δὲ πάντων· ἔγραψε γὰρ ἡμᾶς
στεφανῶσαι. . . (Hyp. *Athen.* 4 τέλος δ' οὖν, ἵνα μὴ μακρολογῶ,
μεταμεμψαμένη γάρ με. . . In the Paris papyrus, from which we have
the text, γαρ is written by the scribe above μεταμεμψαμένη.) **λαβὼν γὰρ
ὁ Παρμενίσκος κτλ.:** the construction is irregular: λαβών . . . ὁ
Π . . . . καὶ πυθόμενος . . . ἐξαιρεῖται . . . καὶ ἀποδίδοται, καταφρονήσαντες
μὲν . . . καταφρονήσαντες δέ . . . The subject is ὁ Παρμενίσκος and the
verbs ἐξαιρεῖται and ἀποδίδοται are singular; but then the two
participles, καταφρονήσαντες μέν and καταφρονήσαντες δέ are plural,
referring to both Dion. and Parm., though ὁ Παρμενίσκος alone is the
subject of the main verbs. The speaker makes the change from singular
to plural as though in his own mind he considers the acts of Parm. to
be the work of both Parm. and Dion. **τὰς ἐνθάδε καθεστηκυίας:** the
otiose τοῦ σίτου after ἐνθάδε is best deleted with Richards (cf. § 25). The
meaning is probably 'on learning the prices prevailing/current here',
which seems the natural sense, especially in view of πρὸς τὰς καθεστηκυίας
τιμάς at § 8 and τὰ ἐνθένδε καθεστηκότα at § 9. The possibility of the
meaning suggested by Paley, 'on learning that the prices here had
settled', i.e. 'that the prices here were about average', seems doubtful

from the classical usages listed in LSJ (B.b.4). ἐξαιρεῖται τὸν σῖτον κτλ.:
it is very noticeable in this passage that Dar. makes no mention of any
violation of the law forbidding Athenian citizens and metics living at
Athens to transport corn to any port except Athens (see speech intro.,
The case). Since he would have made much of it if it had applied, we
may infer that Dion. and Parm. were foreigners. καταφρονήσαντες: see
on § 12. τῶν ἐπιτιμίων: the penalty prescribed in the contract for
non-compliance, i.e. payment of double the money due (§§ 20, 27, 45).
Cf. 34.26, 33. οἱ κελεύουσι . . . ἐνόχους: laws otherwise unknown. τοὺς
ἐπιβάτας: ἐπιβάτης (lit. 'one who goes upon') has a variety of
technical meanings in different contexts, e.g. a marine on a warship
(Thuc. 3.95.2), a fighting man on a chariot (Plat. *Criti.* 119b). Here
it means a merchant on board ship, 'supercargo' (cf. 34.51). Thus at
§ 24 reference is made to the ἐπιβάται despatching their own goods.

11 Dar. states how dismayed and annoyed he and Pamph. were at the
unloading of the corn at Rhodes and he specifically mentions his fear
that he and Pamph. would be suspected of having connived at it (cf.
on § 6). τούτωι τῶι ἀρχιτέκτονι: Dar. refers to Dion. because he stayed
at home while Parm. sailed with the ship (§ 7). ἀρχιτέκτονι 'contriver'
or 'director' of the entire plot. ἀρχιτέκτων meant a master-builder,
chief artificer, director of works. At Athens it was the name of the post
of the manager of the theatre and of the Dionysia. The metaphor is a
natural one. Cf. 40.32. ἀγανακτοῦντες 'expressing our indignation'.
ἐπὶ ταύταις ταῖς ὁμολογίαις: cf. § 6. τοῖς βουλομένοις . . . εἰς τὴν
'Ρόδον: see on § 13. οὐδὲν μᾶλλον: Dar. and Pamph. complained that
Dion. and Parm. brought them under suspicion of complicity. The
point of οὐδὲν μᾶλλον is that the lenders did not even have the ship
back in Athens by way of compensation for that situation. Dar.
probably exaggerates the danger; contrast 35.50 (dealing with similar
circumstances): εἰς τοὺς ἐσχάτους ἂν κινδύνους ἀφικόμην . . . εἰ μή μοι
ἡ συγγραφὴ ἐβοήθει . . . καὶ ἐμαρτύρει ὅτι εἰς τὸν Πόντον ἔδωκα τὰ
χρήματα καὶ πάλιν 'Αθήναζε.

12 ἀλλὰ . . . γε 'at least' in the sense of a *pis aller*. ἀλλά alone can have
the same nuance but is less emphatic. See Denniston *GP* 12f.
τὸ . . . δάνειον 'the capital'. ὑβριστικῶς: Dar. consistently represents
Dion. as an arrogant man who makes and breaks rules to suit himself.

Cf. καταφρονήσαντες (§ 10) νομοθετῶν (§ 12), εὐήθεις ἔφη (§ 18) and see
on §§ 16 and 41. **τὸ πρὸς μέρος τοῦ πλοῦ τοῦ πεπλευσμένου** 'the sum
proportionate to the voyage actually completed'.

For Dion.'s offer to pay the loan and the interest due as far as Rhodes,
see § 13, where it was made in front of witnesses. The strong likelihood
is that Dion. did in fact make the offer as a compromise because the
ship had been damaged and had therefore been forced to put into
Rhodes (cf. §§ 21, 23, 38, 40). Partial loss, under specific circumstances,
of the hypothecated cargo was covered by the contract in Dem. 35 at
§ 11. But if the ship of Dion. and Parm. had been damaged but not lost,
the contingency was not covered by the contract, for here Dar. can say
that in making the offer Dion. was not complying with the terms of the
contract and Dion. could simply have quoted such a clause in his
defence. Dion.'s compromise offer, if it was such, was perhaps accepted
by other creditors (cf. § 22). See on § 16. **νομοθετῶν:** see above on
ὑβριστικῶς.

13 λογιζόμενοι ὅτι . . . ὁμολογοῦμεν: if the ship had been damaged but
not lost (see on § 12) this fear on Dar.'s part may just conceivably be
genuine and may explain the *raison d'être* of the case and the argument
which Dar. adopts in the speech. It could be that, unlike the other
creditors, Dar. felt that if he and Pamph. had accepted the offer they
could be placed in an awkward situation. The contract would be
removed from the man with whom it had been deposited (see on § 14)
and thus there would be no written proof that that he and Pamph. had
not *originally* contravened the law by lending money for the transporting
of corn to a port other than Athens (cf. 35.50, quoted in note on § 11;
see speech intro., *The case*). If Dar. has witnesses to the fact that he and
Pamph. had insisted in the contract on Athens as the port of return he
does not produce them in this case (cf. speech intro., *Contracts*). Anyway
neither the contract nor witnesses to it could testify that they had
accepted the money on the basis of a clause covering damage to the
ship of such a nature that it could sail again after repairs. There would
however be witnesses to their accepting money for a voyage which had
in fact ended at Rhodes (see above), and Dar. may not have had much
faith in the possibility of obtaining the merchants on board Parm.'s ship
as witnesses of the fact that the ship had been damaged and so forced

to be laid up at Rhodes. If the ship was in fact now sailing, as Dar.
alleges (§23), the danger may have seemed great to him. If he truly
felt that he and Pamph. dared not accept the loan and the interest only
as far as Rhodes, and if Dion. refused to pay what was due if the ship
came safe to Athens (cf. § 12), then in order to get anything Dar. would
have to sue for *all* that was owed; and to sue for all he had to claim
that the ship was σεσωισμένη and to insist, Shylock-like, on his bond.
Yet although his bringing the case and the form of his argument may
possibly be explained thus in terms of self-defence, he was not compelled
to demand the double damages stipulated in the contract for violation
(see on §20; cf. on §18). That demand smacks of greed rather than
self-defence. **ἔτι μᾶλλον ἐπέτεινεν** 'exerted himself even more', 'was
yet more pressing'. A metaphor from tightening a bowstring or tuning
a lyre (cf. Arist. *EN* 1138b 23). Cf. §24. **μάρτυρας πολλοὺς παραλαβών:**
it was usual to have witnesses when money was repaid. Cf. 34.30 and
see speech intro., *Contracts*. **οὐδὲν μᾶλλον κτλ.:** Dar. means that Dion.
brought witnesses not because he intended to pay but rather because
he expected Dar. and Pamph. not to accept the money. They were
brought, he claims, to witness the offer and refusal. **λαβεῖν:** the reading
of A and the word used of the other creditors at §26. The other MSS
read ἀπολαβεῖν, which can have the nuance 'take a part' (cf. Thuc.
6.87.3). Cf. §§ 16, 33, 41. ἀπολαβεῖν does not have this nuance at §46.
Cf. also § 12 and on 37.7. **τὰς ὑπούσας αἰτίας:** sc. τῶι λαβεῖν. Cf. § 11.
ἐδήλωσε δὲ αὐτὸ τὸ ἔργον 'The result itself made this clear.' The result
and events leading up to it are related in §§ 14–16. For the expression,
cf. 57.25 τὸ ἔργον ἐδήλωσεν.

14 τῶν ὑμετέρων πολιτῶν: the fact that they are citizens is perhaps
brought out to give the advice greater respectability in the eyes of the
jury, Dar. and Pamph. being themselves probably metics (see speech
intro., *The case*). Moreover it gave the jury the impression that Dar.
and Pamph. had solid citizens on their side. If the claim is true, it is
odd that these citizens do not appear as witnesses. **ἀπὸ ταὐτομάτου** 'by
chance', 'by coincidence', i.e. without being asked or called upon. The
phrase belongs grammatically with παραγενόμενοι (e.g. LSJ, Gernet),
not with συνεβούλευον (Paley); cf. 54.32. Perhaps Dar. in fact had
people with him to witness his accepting Dion.'s money as *part payment*
of what was owed. **τὸ . . . διδόμενον** 'what was being offered' (imper-

fective). **ἐλαττοῦσθαί τι:** it is difficult to see what disadvantage there was in accepting Dion.'s offer as part payment and then having a legal decision made over the sum in dispute. If Dar. and Pamph. did not take up Dion.'s offer as part payment they would have to go to law over the whole sum. The notion of Dar. making a concession lessens the impression of respect for strict legality which he gives elsewhere. For his part Dion. could not afford to agree to the proposal of Dar. and Pamph., which included only the partial cancellation of the contract (see §15), because Dar. could then argue in court that Dion.'s willingness to leave the contract in existence was an admission of the weakness of his case. Only by withholding the sum which he offered could he hope to force Dar. to compromise. **μὴ δοκεῖν φιλόδικοι εἶναι:** see on 54.17, 24, 39.1. **ὁμόσε πορευομένους:** the expression ὁμόσε ἰέναι is fairly common in military contexts meaning 'to close with' the enemy. For metaphorical usages cf. Plat. *Euthyd.* 294d ὁμόσε ᾔτην τοῖς ἐρωτήμασιν, Plat. *Rep.* 610c, Arist. *Metaph.* 1089a 3. A hostile nuance could give the general meaning 'seeing us proceeding against him he told us to cancel the agreement'. The sense 'seeing us ready to stand on our rights and not give up altogether the interest from Rhodes to Athens' (Paley) does not suit the context in which Dar. is emphasizing his 'concession'. Perhaps therefore the meaning is that of moving towards agreement (LSJ s.v. ὁμόσε 1.3), i.e. 'seeing us coming to meet him, willing to meet him half-way'. But since such a nuance is without parallel, the expression may describe a metaphorical battle of wills (as distinct from a real legal dispute) i.e. 'seeing us closing with him' in the sense of 'calling his bluff'. **ἀναιρεῖσθε** 'cancel', 'rescind'. Cf. 33.12, 34.1. A contract was deposited with a third party (48.46–8). See speech intro., *Contracts.* When cancellation of the agreement was made, the document was removed from the person with whom it had been deposited and it was destroyed, usually before witnesses. There is no mention in the orators of written receipts.

15 ἀναιρώμεθα: the subjunctive is commonly used in repeating what has just been said. **οὐδέν γε μᾶλλον ἢ ὁτιοῦν:** lit. 'in no respect more than anything whatever', i.e. 'That's the last thing we'll do!' **τοῦ τραπεζίτου:** the contract may have been deposited with the banker. For the trustworthiness of bankers, see speech intro., *Contracts.* **τί γὰρ ἔχοντες . . . ἀντιδικήσομεν** 'What can we claim, on what will our case rest when we plead it…?' **τὸ ἰσχυρόν:** lit. 'the strong point'. For the construction cf. §2. If the contract was annulled, any action by Dar. and Pamph. to recover more money could have been stopped by a παραγραφή (cf. 33.12). **διαιτητήν** 'arbitrator'. Cf. §16. For arbitrators see on 54.26–9. Not all cases came to court. The state-appointed arbitrators, i.e. public arbitrators, heard many private cases, but among those not heard by them were cases dealt with by the thesmothetae, which included δίκαι ἐμπορικαί. The reference here therefore must be to private arbitration. Private arbitrators were agreed upon by the litigants themselves, and whereas appeal was possible against the judgement of a public arbitrator, the decision of an arbitrator or of joint arbitrators mutually agreed upon by two disputants was binding.

16 ταῦτα δὲ ἡμῶν . . .κριθῆναι 'when we said this, gentlemen of the jury, and asked Dionysodorus here not to alter nor to annul the contract admitted even by them themselves to be binding, but to pay us back as much of the money as he himself was agreeing to do, but as for the sum in dispute, when we were ready to have the matter decided…' ὄντων is co-ordinate with λεγόντων…καὶ ἀξιούντων, ὄντων being introduced by δέ by way of an anacoluthon, and κριθῆναι is dependent on ἑτοίμων. With the manuscript reading, ὡς ἑτοίμων ὄντων, κριθῆναι must depend on ἀξιούντων and is a third infinitive in the series (i) μὴ κινεῖν μηδὲ…ποιεῖν and (ii) ἀποδοῦναι. But ὡς ἑτοίμων ὄντων cannot refer to ἡμῶν. The meaning cannot be 'when we asked him…with regard to the money in dispute to have the matter decided by arbitration on the understanding that we were ready to have it so decided' because ἡμῶν would be expected to be expressed in the phrase. Nor is it satisfactory to take ὡς ἑτοίμων ὄντων as referring to τῶν ἀντιλεγομένων. Used of money ἕτοιμος means 'ready money', 'money in hand'. To say that they asked that the settlement of the sum in dispute should be left to one or more arbitrators on the understanding that the money was in hand makes little sense, and in any case the notion of ready money is alien to the context. While Weil's emendation of ἑτοίμων to ἐν τῶι μέσωι (cf. 4.5) solves that difficulty, it results in the tautologous 'about the contested money as being the subject of dispute between us'. It is simplest to delete ὡς with Bekker and Richards. **κινεῖν:** just possibly 'to move' in the sense of 'to annul' (cf. on §14). But since κινεῖν can be used of changing laws (Plat. *Leg.* 797b, Arist.

Pol. 1268b 28) it probably means 'to alter'. **κἂν πλείοσι:** three arbitrators figure in Dem. 33, one agreed by both disputants and one selected by each. Cf. also 59.45. **τῶν ἐκ τοῦ ἐμπορίου:** as being men who have experience in business. **οὐκ ἔφη . . .οὐδενί:** if Dar.ʼ actually made the suggestion of arbitration, it is understandable that Dion. should not wish to avail himself of it if there had been a partial shipwreck. He may well have felt that one arbitrator or, say, three might not be so easily persuaded of the justice of his compromise when faced with the strict legalistic approach of Dar. pleading the contract. Dion. may well have preferred to take his chance, if necessary, with a more suggestible jury. Cf. Dar.ʼs version of his reasoning in § 18. **ἀπολαμβάνοντες:** cf. on § 13. **ἐπέταττεν** 'ordered', 'commanded', giving the impression that Dion. was acting in a high-handed manner. The word is used of ἡ πόλις at 39.7. See on §§ 12, 41. **δεύτερον ἔτος:** cf. on § 4.

17 Dar. alleges that Dion. is using his and Pamph.ʼs money to make loans for voyages to Rhodes and Egypt. The allegation may, of course, be totally false, because he brings no evidence, such as the testimony of men who had borrowed money from Dion. But by the allegation Dar. depicts Dion. as an unscrupulous rogue, who is not acting in the interests of Athens. He does not say, however, that in lending for voyages to Rhodes and Egypt Dion. is acting contrary to the Athenian corn laws. Thus this is another indication that Dion. and Parm. were not Athenian citizens nor metics resident at Athens (see speech intro., *The case*). **ναυτικοὺς τόκους:** for the high rate of interest that was received on maritime loans, see speech intro., *Trade and finance*. **ὅτι δ' ἀληθῆ . . .προὐκαλεσάμεθ' αὐτόν** 'To prove that I am telling the truth, he [the secretary of the court] will read to you the challenge which we made to him concerning these matters.' The πρόκλησις was a challenge to bring the ship to Athens (§ 40) and to submit to the decision of an arbitrator (§ 18). It was posted in a public place (§ 18). This πρόκλησις, of course, in itself *proved* nothing at all; certainly it did not prove what Dar. has just said concerning maritime loans.

18 εὐήθεις ἔφη . . .καταθεῖναι τὰ χρήματα: there may actually be an element of truth in the reasons Dar. gives Dion. for his refusal to go to arbitration: see on § 16. However, if Dion. actually said what Dar. attributes to him, he did not show much sense; but there is no evidence to indicate that he actually did say it. **εὐήθεις ἔφη**: Dion.'s alleged reply shows the arrogance which Dar. consistently ascribes to him; see on § 12. **εἶτ' ἐὰν μὲν . . . παρακρούσασθαι**: in addition to putting words into Dion.'s mouth, Dar. tries to build up prejudice against him by alleging that he considers the jurymen to be fools who are not to be taken seriously (cf. § 43). **τηνικαῦτα καταθεῖναι τὰ χρήματα**: Dion. would have to base his case, it seems, on an equity ruling to the effect that as his ship was prevented from journeying further than Rhodes it was only right that he should have to pay only the loan and the interest as far as there. It is probable that he hoped, even if the case went against him, that he would avoid paying the penalty stipulated in the contract of double the sum owed (cf. on § 20). From § 43 it seems that the present case is an ἀγὼν τιμητός (see Introduction 2) and that Dion. 'estimated' the loan and interest without doubling. It is also clear that the penalty prescribed in the contract was in no way binding on the jury. (L. Gernet, *Droit et société dans la Grèce ancienne* (Paris 1955) 78f., considered that any suit concerning a contractual obligation was an ἀγὼν τιμητός.)

19–36 Refutation of Dionysodorus' case.

19–20 Introduction.

19 οἴομαι δ' ὑμᾶς κτλ.: Dar. attempts to create prejudice against Dion. by the assumption that he has no case. **πάλαι**: the position makes it emphatic. **εἴ τις ἄνθρωπος**: not simply 'if a man' (εἴ τις); there is a nuance that Dion. is not behaving like a rational human being.

20 διπλάσια τὰ χρήματα: the penalty for failing to bring the ship to Athens or otherwise violating the contract. Such a penalty clause does not appear in the contract cited at 35.10–13, but cf. 34.26, 33. See §§ 27, 38, 45 and cf. on § 18.

21–2 Dar. gives three alleged points of Dion.'s defence in order that he may refute them. The question arises whether what Dar. says truly represents Dion.'s case, but the answer can never be known. See Introduction 15f.

21 φησὶ γάρ: emphatic. Cf. § 1.

22 φησὶ γὰρ ἑτέρους κτλ.: Dion.'s point is that Dar. is isolated in his refusal to accept the claim that the ship was damaged, the implication being that Dar. is motivated by greed. **ἑτέρους τινὰς δανειστάς**: the implication is that before the ship set out from Athens Dion. borrowed from others at Athens as well as from Dar. and Pamph. (cf. on §25). However, at §29 Dar. represents the lenders as being in Egypt. **σωθείσης τῆς νεώς**: σώιζειν and σώιζεσθαι are frequently used (usually with an adverb or prepositional phrase expressing goal of motion) to mean 'bring safely' (σώιζειν) or 'arrive safely' (σώιζεσθαι). Cf. on §32.

23–5 Answer to the first alleged argument, viz. sailing from Egypt the ship was damaged and so put into Rhodes where the cargo was unloaded. As proof Dion. says that boats were hired at Rhodes and that some of the cargo was brought to Athens (cf. §21).

23 Dar. deals with the alleged statement and the alleged proof separately. Against the statement that the ship was damaged Dar. makes two points.

(1) If the ship had been damaged (ῥαγῆναι, see below) it would not have arrived safely at Rhodes, yet it obviously reached Rhodes safely. It is significant that when Dar. is putting forward the alleged argument of Dion. he uses the word ῥαγῆναι (§§21, 23, 40, 43), not διαφθαρῆναι. ῥαγῆναι means not necessarily 'be wrecked' (cf. LSJ s.v. B.3) but 'be holed', 'spring a leak'. Since Dion. argues that he was forced to put in at Rhodes (§§20, 40), he cannot be claiming that the ship actually sank. He must mean by ἐρράγη that it was incapacitated. For Dion. ῥήγνυσθαι = θαλαττοῦσθαι. But in the present passage for Dar. ῥήγνυσθαι = διαφθείρεσθαι. Hence he is able to claim that if the ship ἐρράγη ('was wrecked' according to Dar.'s interpretation of the word) it could not have reached Rhodes. Dar. is deliberately over-simplifying the issue (because the contract only allowed for the ship to be σεσωισμένη or διεφθαρμένη); he acknowledges only two types of ship, floating or sunken (cf. on §32). It is perfectly possible that having been holed the ship required lengthy repairs at Rhodes.

(2) If the ship had been damaged it would not now be seaworthy, whereas it sailed from Rhodes to Egypt and is now sailing everywhere except to Athens. Perhaps necessary repairs had now been carried out. Perhaps having made the compromise offer (see on §12) Dion. and

Parm. decided to get on with their business. It is, however, to be expected at the least that some evidence would have been adduced concerning the ship's sailing πανταχόσε πλὴν οὐκ εἰς Ἀθήνας, even if these last words are ironic; yet no such evidence appears in the speech. ὅταν μὲν . . . ὅταν δέ κτλ.: although the specific use of the article in τὸν σῖτον ἐξελέσθαι shows that Dar. is referring to the voyage which forms the subject of the dispute, the indefinite construction is used to imply a plurality of voyages at the time of the present suit. ῥαγῆναι φάσκειν . . . πλόϊμον οὖσαν φαίνεσθαι: with φάσκειν Dar. casts doubt on what Dion. is saying, and with φαίνεσθαι and the participle the nuance is that what he himself is saying is patent fact, whereas in truth it is mere allegation. τηνικαῦτα δέ: δέ is apodotic, as not uncommonly in the fourth century in a complex antithesis: see Denniston *GP* 183ff.

24–5 Dar. deals with what he alleges Dion. will say to prove his alleged statement, viz. that he hired other boats and transhipped the cargo to Athens. Dar. replies (1) that Dion. and Parm. did not own the entire cargo and that merchants travelling on board had to hire boats to convey their goods to Athens; (2) that from their own goods Dion. and Parm. transhipped to Athens only those whose price had risen.

24 οἱ ἐπιβάται: see on § 10. It may be wondered how Dar. knew the reason he gives, for none of the ἐπιβάται is produced to testify and it is noticeable that Dar. uses οἶμαι in parenthesis. Cf. on § 25. ἐκλεγόμενοι τίνων αἱ τιμαὶ ἐπετέταντο: lit. 'picking out of what things the prices had been tightened'. For ἐπετέταντο see on § 13. Perhaps the nuance of the Indirect Question construction is that of making a careful and purposeful selection. However τίνων may possibly represent an Indefinite Relative (i.e. τίνων = ὅτων, 'all goods whose price...'). The substitution of τίς for ὅστις in Indefinite Relative clauses is rare before the Hellenistic era (for examples see Pfeiffer on Call. fr. 75.60), but there is a solitary fifth-century example at Eur. fr. 773.2 N². There is no need to emend (εἴ τινων Dobree and G. H. Schaefer, τιν' ὧν Madvig). Cf. on § 25.

25 τί . . . τὸν σῖτον . . . κατελίπετε: Dion. and Parm. may have been legally obliged to honour a commitment to take passengers' goods to their destination. With regard to their own goods which were sent to Athens, there are two possibilities.

(1) The cost of hiring boats to ship their customers' goods to Athens would have eaten a sizable hole in their profits, and they would have been presented with the prospect of further loss if yet another boat (or other boats) had to be hired to transport the grain. If that was the case, the sensible course would be to sell the grain in Rhodes and to send to Athens, perhaps in one of the boats already hired, any high-priced but compact commodity from the cargo owned by themselves. Thus perhaps Dar.'s τίνων...ἐπετέταντο is factually correct but his interpretation of motives false.

(2) As Gernet (III 133 n. 4) suggests, the goods which were sent on may have been hypothecated to other creditors (cf. §§ 26–30). The incapacity of the ship may not have freed Dion. and Parm. from their contractual obligation to present their security in Athens in the case of hypothecated goods. Dar. gives the jury to understand that the other creditors lent money on the ship, but if the goods in question were hypothecated, to say so would weaken his case.

By either of these possibilities the unexpected costs involved in hiring boats must have reduced the expected profit of Dion. and Parm. substantially, and the obvious course was to cut their losses and sell the grain at Rhodes.

ἀνειχέναι: used as the opposite of ἐπιτείνω (cf. on § 13) with regard to a bow or stringed instrument (see LSJ s.v. ἀνίημι II.7). Again Dion.'s alleged motive is supported by no evidence.

26–30 Answer to the second alleged argument, viz. that the other creditors have agreed to accept the interest due for the voyage as far as Rhodes and all Dion. is doing is to ask Dar. and Pamph. to do the same (cf. § 22).

26 ὑμῖν: Dar. is addressing Dion. and Parm. Below σοι refers to Dion. alone. **οὔθ' ὁ δοὺς οὔθ' ὁ πείσας:** the variant reading in F and Q. 'For if anyone has remitted to you anything that belonged to him, no wrong is suffered either by the man who has made the gift [i.e. who has made the remission] or by the man who has persuaded him to do so [i.e. Dion.].' There is no other example of διδόναι as 'make a concession', but δούς well brings out the idea that the concession was something to which Dion. was not entitled (cf. Lys. 10.24, where undeserved success in a lawsuit is a δωρεά; and διδόναι can mean 'grant', 'concede' in argument – see LSJ s.v. III.2). The common manuscript reading is ὁ πεισθεὶς ἢ ὁ πείσας, 'no wrong is suffered by the man who has been persuaded or the man who has been active in persuading'. But ἤ is wrong: after οὐδέν we expect 'nor' or 'neither...nor'. The word ἤ can be neatly explained by postulating that ἢ ὁ πείσας was first given as a variant for ὁ πεισθείς. Bekker read οὐδὲν ἀδικεῖται ὁ πεισθείς, a reading which leaves ὁ δούς in F and Q unexplained. Reiske emended to οὔθ' ὁ δοὺς οὔθ' ὁ πεισθείς. (ὁ δούς is the man who has paid the interest, i.e. Dion., and ὁ πεισθείς is the creditor who has been persuaded to accept the money and to make the remission.) The reading οὔθ' ὁ δοὺς οὔθ' ὁ πείσας is to be preferred to this. The slip of a scribe's eye from the first οὔθ' to the second may have resulted in the nonsensical οὔθ' ὁ πείσας, which may have been emended for the sake of sense to ὁ πεισθείς. If the reading ὁ πείσας was known from some source, the words ἢ ὁ πείσας may have been added, at first as a variant, and thus have given the common manuscript reading. **οὐδὲν κυριώτερον:** at 35.13, 39 a contract stipulates κυριώτερον δὲ περὶ τούτων ἄλλο μηδὲν εἶναι τῆς συγγραφῆς. Cf. *IG* XII 7.67, 27 and 76. So presumably did Dar.'s contract. Cf. speech intro., *Contracts*.

27 Dar.'s first argument against Dion's second alleged point of defence is that the waiving of interest by others is none of his concern, for what matters to him is the συγγραφή. The συγγραφή has been freely entered into by the defendants, he argues, and so its provisions in the case of default should be put into effect. That Dion. entered freely into the contract is the meaning of αὐτὸς σὺ σαυτῶι ὥρισας. **δεῖξον οὖν... ἡμῖν κυρία:** by a fairly common idiom τὴν συγγραφήν, ὡς οὐκ ἔστιν ἡμῖν κυρία = ὡς οὐκ ἔστιν ἡμῖν κυρία ἡ συγγραφή. **ὡς οὐ δίκαιος εἶ κτλ.:** lit. 'that you are not just to do everything in accordance with this', i.e. 'that it is not right that you should do everything in accordance with it'.

28 ὁτωιδήποτε τρόπωι 'by whatever [dishonest] means'. Dar. is implying some form of collusion. Cf. 35.6, 40.8. **παρασυγγεγράφηκας** 'cheated by violation of contract'. An uncommon word. Apart from its use here and its intransitive use at §34 ('violate a contract') it is not found in classical Attic. (Cf. speech intro., *Contracts*.) **οὐκ οἴομαί γε:** Dar. has asked the question οὐδὲν ἀδικεῖς ἡμᾶς; 'are you doing us no wrong?', which he answers with, 'No, I do not consider [sc. that you are doing us no wrong].' ἐπεὶ ὅτι γε κτλ. 'For the fact that even the alleged waiving of the interest, if indeed it has actually taken place, as these men say, has been to the advantage of the lenders is clear to all of you.' With ἄρα Dar. casts doubt on the entire claim. In this sentence Dar. turns to his second argument against Dion's alleged defence point, namely that it was to the advantage of the other creditors to waive interest.

29 οἱ γὰρ ἐκ τῆς Αἰγύπτου δανείσαντες κτλ. 'For those [in Egypt] who lent money to them for a single voyage from Egypt to Athens, when they [i.e. these lenders] arrived at Rhodes and they [i.e. Dion. and Parm.] took the ship there, it did not, I think, make any difference to them [i.e. the lenders] to relinquish their claim to the interest, recover the capital at Rhodes, and put the money to work again on the route to Egypt. This was much more to their advantage than to sail back here [i.e. to see the ship sail back to Athens and collect the loan and the whole of the interest here]. The voyage there is minute [see on §30] and it was possible for them to operate twice or three times with the same money; but if they had been here in the city they would have had to let the bad weather go past and wait for the sailing season.' The construction is irregular. οἱ δανείσαντες, the intended subject, is left hanging when an impersonal main verb is used, οὐδὲν... διέφερεν. οὗτοι (subject of κατεκόμισαν only) refers to Dion. and Parm. (cf. §20).

The position of ἐκ τῆς Αἰγύπτου indicates that Dar. represents the creditors cited by Dion. in his defence (cf. on §22) as based in Egypt, not in Athens as Dion. appears to say. Dar. raises the spectre of Egyptian money-lenders for two reasons.

(1) Since men who had lent money in Athens would expect the ship to sail to Athens so that they would receive payment in full, a compromise with such creditors would be evidence of the truth of Dion.'s claim that the ship was holed (cf. on §23). To counter this argument by saying that a compromise suited the creditors, Dar. has to suppose creditors for whom a journey from Rhodes to Athens involved no more profit than a return to Egypt.

(2) For collusion to be possible the creditors had to be on the ship when it made its stop at Rhodes. A creditor who had lent money on a round trip (ἀμφοτερόπλουν) did not normally travel with the ship; a creditor who had lent money on a single trip (ἑτερόπλουν) travelled

on board, sent an agent on board, or arranged for payment to an agent at the destination. Hence for Dion.'s version of Athenians who had lent on a round trip Dar. substitutes Egyptians who had lent on a single trip. As Gernet observes, if the lenders were really based in Egypt, we should expect Dar. to insist on the point.

ἑτερόπλουν: for rates of interest on a loan ἀμφοτερόπλουν and on a loan ἑτερόπλουν and the method of calculation, see speech intro., *Trade and finance*.

30 ἀκαριαῖος 'tiny', 'minute', 'brief'. To say that a journey from Rhodes to Egypt (approximately 700 km) is shorter than one from Rhodes to Athens (approximately 450 km) is a gross misstatement. But Dar.'s audience had no time to check the statement and had no reference work available; many, if not most, will have been neither to Rhodes nor to Egypt, and there was no opportunity for discussion to enable a knowledgeable juror to refute such a falsehood. ἀκαριαῖος is used of measurements which are literally minute, and if it is the true reading Dar. is consciously indulging in 'a grotesque exaggeration' (Sandys).

ἀκαριαῖος is the reading of A, while SFQD have ἀκέραιος. Either reading could have arisen from the other, but the rarer ἀκαριαῖος is more likely to have been changed to ἀκέραιος than vice versa. Moreover ἀκέραιος properly means 'pure', 'unmixed', then 'whole', 'unharmed'; but here it would have to have the unattested active sense 'involving no risk', 'not dangerous'. If this is the true reading, Dar. is still lying. The journey from Rhodes to Egypt was not entirely safe; for although winds in the Mediterranean are generally less fierce than those in the same latitude in the Atlantic, Dion. can claim even in autumn to have run into difficulties, and it is clear from Thuc. 3.69.1 that sudden and violent storms could assault ships in the waters in which the ship was sailing. Rennie accepts Sandys' ἀεὶ ὡραῖος ('always in good weather'). Like the manuscript readings, this too would be a lie.

δὶς ἢ τρίς: If ἀκαριαῖος is the true reading, Dar. presumably means that the distance between Egypt and Rhodes is so small that two or three trips can be made (in reality up to about 2,100 km, or 4,200 km if three round trips are made) before winter, whereas if they came to Athens there would be time for no further sailing (cf. παραχειμάζειν ἔδει καὶ περιμένειν τὴν ὡραίαν). τὴν ὡραίαν: sc. ὥραν. The expression can mean harvest time or the campaigning season, during which troops kept the field.

31–3 Answer to the third alleged argument, viz. that Dion. has to pay Dar. and Pamph. only if the ship is σεσωισμένη (cf. on §§22, 23).

31 μὴ οὖν ἀποδέχεσθε τούτου κτλ.: ἀποδέχεσθαι is fairly common in the sense 'admit into the mind' and so 'receive favourably'. Thus, e.g. Plat. *Rep.* 531e ἀποδέξασθαι λόγον, Plat. *Prot.* 329b ἀποδέξασθαι τὴν ἀπόκρισιν. It can be used, as here, with the genitive of the person and a participle added, e.g. Plat. *Phd.* 92a, e ἀποδέχεσθαί τινος λέγοντος, 'receive a statement from someone to the effect that...'. Here 'Don't just accept it from him when he cheats you and...' (By an extension the construction can be used without the participle expressed, e.g. Plat. *Phd.* 96e οὐκ ἀποδέχομαι ἐμαυτοῦ ὡς τὸ ἓν δύο γέγονεν.)

32 ἡδέως δ' ἂν κτλ.: at first sight this argument of Dar. appears to be a strong one. If the ship is διεφθαρμένη, he argues, there should be no dispute about the payment of interest, whereas if it is σεσωισμένη payment should be made as agreed in the contract. However, the argument does not appear to be so strong if the ship has been so badly damaged that it needs lengthy repairs (cf. on §23). As in §23 Dar. is once more over-simplifying. (1) He again posits only two states for the ship – either it sails or it does not. (2) He exploits the different nuances of σώιζεσθαι, which can mean (usually with an expression of the goal) 'reach in safety', but also (without such an expression) 'be saved or preserved' and hence in the perfect 'be safe', 'be intact'. The contract actually stipulated that the full interest was payable *if the ship reached Piraeus safely* (§§22, 36). But Dar. here ignores the significance of the prepositional phrase; the money is payable if the ship survives. Thus he can substitute the words εἰ δ' ἐστὶν ἡ ναῦς σῶς at §32 and ὅτι μὲν σέσωισται καὶ ἔστιν σῶς at §37. **οὔτε γὰρ τοὺς τόκους κτλ.:** if the ship had sunk the obligation of the debtor would have been cancelled.

33 To show that the ship is σεσωισμένη, Dar. puts forward as his best proof the fact that it is now sailing. By repeating the allegation made at §23 (again with no supporting evidence offered) Dar. apparently hopes the jury will regard the statement as an established fact, which it is not. **ἀπολαβεῖν:** cf. on §13.

34 ἄφεσιν 'remission'. Cf. §§26, 28. **παρασυγγεγραφηκότες:** see on §28. **παρὰ τὴν σιτηγίαν** 'because of [i.e. by] the carrying of corn'. See LSJ s.v. παρά III.7. **καρπούμενοι:** see §17. No evidence is offered. **δεύτερον ἔτος τουτί:** see speech intro., *Date and authenticity*.

35 τὸ μὲν γὰρ δάνειον κτλ.: by over-simplifying Dion.'s case Dar. succeeds in convicting him of inconsistency. **καίτοι ἡ συγγραφὴ . . . ἡ αὐτή:** probably true. Cf. speech intro., *The case*.

36–8 ΣΥΓΓΡΑΦΗ: The MSS give three fragments, supposedly from the contract. Doubt is aroused about their authenticity by the fact that the two quotations in §36 are not even whole clauses (contrast 37.22ff.). The second quotation is especially odd, since we should expect a reference to *the obligation to pay* the money back if the ship returned safe. It is possible that we have here simply cue words, which Dar. did not speak (see Introduction 5, written into the speech by the author. But all the quotations could without effort have been cobbled together by a later writer from the text of the speech. See on §38.

37–44 Having dealt with the alleged case of Dion., Dar. turns to positive proofs of his own argument. He repeats several points he has made before (cf. Gernet, *Dem.* III ad loc.).

37 σέσωισται καὶ ἔστιν σῶς: for emphasis Dar. gives the situation both as the present result of previous action and as the present circumstances. Cf. on §32. **παρ' αὐτῶν τούτων ὁμολογεῖται:** Dar. means that they admit the fact only by implication, as is shown by the parenthesis. Cf. §§12 and 39.

38 δι' αὐτὸ τοῦτο: Dar. suggests that Dion. is using as his defence the act which constituted his offence. **τὰ ὑποκείμενα:** cf. on §4. The contract too (if genuine) uses the plural. This was presumably a legal expression, perhaps stylised from a time when goods only were hypothecated (cf. F. Pringsheim, *Der Kauf mit fremdem Geld* (Leipzig 1916) 14f.). The word is used in the plural in the contract at 35.12, but the reference there is to cargo. ἐμφανῆ καὶ ἀνέπαφα 'plain to see and free from legitimate claim by a third party'. Cf. 35.11, 24. The clause requiring the debtor to present his security in Athens at the end of the voyage was no doubt regular in maritime loans; the security remained in the power of the lender until the debt was paid in order to protect the lender against default by the borrower. Cf. §§ 39, 40. διπλάσια τὰ χρήματα: on the penalty clause, which Dar. clearly wishes to be applied (cf. § 44), see on §§ 18 and 20. ἐὰν δὲ κτλ.: Dar. has listed three stipulations in the contract: failure to pay what is owed, failure to present the security, and violation of the agreement in any other way. The citation from the agreement lists only the latter two. If the citation is genuine we should probably posit a lacuna (Blass); if it is forged (see on § 36) the forger has relied on § 39, where the first stipulation is omitted. This is reached only at § 41. ἀποδιδότωσαν: the form normally used is ἀποδιδόντων. The ending in -τωσαν became common in the Hellenistic period (in Attic inscriptions from c. 300 B.C.). Yet the form here does not *prove* that the citation is a forgery (see on § 36; cf. above) for ἔστωσαν is found at Thuc. 8.18 and Eur. *Ion* 1131 and ἴτωσαν at Eur. *IT* 1480.

39 ὁμολογῶν σῶν εἶναι αὐτός: Dion.'s admitting this was by implication at § 37; now Dar. makes it a plain statement of fact.

40 καὶ γὰρ τοῦτο 'Yes, this too.' Cf. 4.12, 18.123, 19.314, 21.167. θεάσασθε τὴν ὑπερβολήν 'Just see how far he goes.' τὸ μετὰ τοῦτο: cf. § 43. The expression is analogous to τὸ νῦν, τὸ πάλαι etc. ἐπεσκευάσθη καὶ πλόϊμος ἐγένετο: cf. on § 12. οὐδέπω καὶ νῦν: see on § 3. ἐμφανῆ καὶ ἀνέπαφον: see on § 38. προκαλεσαμένων: presumably the demand that Dion. surrender his pledge formed part of the challenge cited at § 17.

41 διπλάσια τὰ χρήματα: see on §§ 18 and 20; cf. § 38. προστάττεις 'command'. Cf. πρόσταγμα. See on §§ 12 and 16. According to Dar. (§ 13) Dion. had said he was ἕτοιμος to pay the loan and the interest due as far as Rhodes; then (§ 16) Dion. ἐπέταττεν Dar. and Pamph. to accept his offer; now the language is made more offensive by heightening προστάττεις with a comparison between Dion.'s πρόσταγμα and the contract. Sandys compares Isoc. 4.176, where the

Peace of Antalcidas is said to be no equitable agreement (συνθῆκαι) and is denounced as dictated (προστάγματα) by the King of Persia. ἀπολαβεῖν: cf. on § 13. κυριώτερον: chosen deliberately to contrast the clause in the contract οὐδὲν κυριώτερον τῆς συγγραφῆς. See on § 26. ἐφ᾽ ὧι...ἀποθάνοις: if this statement refers to the fact that the ship did not reach Athens safely rather than to Dion.'s daring to say that it did not, the language is not so extravagant as it may appear. At 34.50 reference is made to the case of a respected citizen who after impeachment had been condemned to death for failing to deliver securities to his creditors. The circumstances of that case are not known.

42 διὰ τίνα γὰρ μᾶλλον κτλ. 'For who rather is to blame, men of the jury, for the fact that the ship has not come safely to the Piraeus?' The MSS have ἄλλον, which must be wrong when there is a choice given (πότερον...ἤ). Gernet follows Blass in deleting. The question then arises as to how ἄλλον got into the text. Rennie's emendation to μᾶλλον is neat, though we expect 'Who is to blame?' rather than 'Who is more to blame?' ἐπὶ ταύταις ταῖς ὁμολογίαις: cf. on § 6.

43 ἐρράγη: see on § 23. τὸ μετὰ τοῦτ᾽: cf. on § 40. ἐπειδὴ ἐπεσκεύ-ασαν...ἐμίσθωσαν αὐτήν: there is no proof of Dar.'s repeated statement. He seems to work on the principle of the Bellman in Lewis Carroll's *Hunting of the Snark*: 'What I tell you three times is true.' ὡς ὑμᾶς...τὸ ἀκούσιον σύμπτωμα: no proof has been adduced to show that the ship was sailing, but even if it had now been repaired and was now sailing, it is possible that Dion. and Parm. felt that having made a justifiable offer which was refused they were going to get on with their business and use the ship on voyages which presented themselves: if these had not yet included Athens that was unfortunate. It is also possible that in view of the present trouble about the ship they were not going to strive too hard to bring it to Athens till the troublesome matter had been settled. σύμπτωμα 'occurrence', 'mishap'. προσεξημαρτήκασιν: προσ- signifies 'in addition'. καὶ ὥσπερ...εἰσεληλύθασιν 'and they have come here contesting the suit in a spirit of mockery'. Dar. is attempting to prejudice the jury against Dion. in a way similar to § 18. He is suggesting that his opponents do not take the dignity of the court seriously. Cf. §44. ὡς ἐπ' αὐτοῖς . . . καὶ τοὺς τόκους: see on §18.

44 ἐπὶ δυοῖν ἀγκύραιν ὁρμεῖν 'to ride at two anchors'. The equivalent English expression is 'to have two strings to one's bow'. Warships usually carried two anchors, merchantmen two or more. The ship rode at anchor with the stern facing the shore, to which it was attached by a cable, while an anchor was let down from the prow. Two anchors were used if the sea was rough. Hence 'two anchors' became proverbial for security (cf. Pind. *O.* 6.101). But the number is itself significant, since the two anchors are the alternatives which Dion. (according to Dar.) believes are open to them: if they are successful they will keep what belongs to others, and if they lose they will have to pay only what they owe for a voyage to Athens, i.e. they will not pay double as prescribed in the penalty clause (see on §§18 and 20). ἐὰν δὲ μὴ . . . ὑμᾶς: cf. §§18 and 43. ἐξαπατῆσαι: see on 54.38. αὐτὰ τὰ ὀφειλόμενα 'simply (αὐτά) what is owed', and not double as is prescribed in the penalty clause. See on §18. Cf. §§38 and 43. καὶ ταῦτα οὐχ ἧττον ἡμῶν συνηδικημένους: the idea that Athens has suffered by the actions of Dion. and Parm. is exploited in §§47–50.

45–50 Summary and conclusion.

45 δεύτερον ἔτος 'for over a year'. See speech intro., *Date and authenticity*. οὐδέπω καὶ νῦν: see on §3. τὴν δὲ πρᾶξιν εἶναι καὶ ἐξ ἑνὸς καὶ ἐξ ἀμφοῖν 'the money may be recovered from [either] one or from both'. Thus by the terms of the contract, Dion. alone may be sued for the recovery of the money; it was not necessary also to sue Parm. (who was presumably still with the ship: cf. §7). It was written into the contract at 35.12 that the lenders could act either singly or jointly in the case of default on the part of the borrowers. Cf. speech intro., *The case*.

46 ἀπολαβεῖν: see on §13.

47 Dar. takes up the last word of §44 by appealing to the jury's self-interest. Corn imports were of great importance to Athens, and Dar.

plays on the jury's anxieties about the corn supply, which only recently had been a matter of concern at Athens (see speech intro., *The corn crisis*). Yet it is again noticeable that Dar. does not accuse his opponents of breaking the law in transporting grain to Rhodes: another indication that Dion. and Parm. were foreigners (see speech intro., *The case*).

48–50 On the same theme of self-interest, Dar. urges the jury not to create a precedent for those who wish to break contracts. He plays on the notion that the business of the market will be decreased if Dion. is acquitted.

48 παρεστᾶσι: courts met in the open. Thus anyone could watch if he wanted to. See on 54.41. **τῶν κατὰ θάλατταν ἐργάζεσθαι προαιρουμένων:** cf. on § 1. The end of the speech returns effectively to the beginning (see on 54.13). Dar. began by speaking of the insecurity of his profession, whose only protection lay in the lawcourts and the law; here he begs the jurors not to increase this insecurity. **προήσονται:** see on § 2. **οἱ ἐπὶ τοῦ δανείζειν ὄντες:** lit. 'those who are on lending', i.e. those who make money-lending their business.

50 προέσθαι: see on § 2. **τῶι πλήθει τῶι ὑμετέρωι:** see speech intro., *Date and authenticity*. A final appeal to the jury's self-interest. **ἐγὼ μὲν οὖν...συνειπεῖν:** cf. end of 34 ἐγὼ μὲν οὖν ὅσαπερ οἷός τ᾽ ἦν εἴρηκα· καλῶ δὲ καὶ ἄλλον τινὰ τῶν φίλων, ἐὰν κελεύητε. For the role of the συνήγορος see Introduction 7f. **δεῦρο Δημόσθενες:** cf. end of Andoc. 1 δεῦρο, Ἄνυτε, Κέφαλε, ἔτι δὲ καὶ οἱ φυλέται οἱ ᾑρημένοι μοι συνδικεῖν, Θράσυλλος καὶ οἱ ἄλλοι. If the reference here is to Demosthenes the famous orator and if these words are genuine, then it must be considered highly likely that Demosthenes had at least a say in the preparation of Dar.'s speech (see speech intro., *Date and authenticity*). But Demosthenes was not an uncommon name; the reference may be to another Demosthenes; and it is possible the speech may have been wrongly included in the Demosthenic corpus because of these last words. On the other hand it is possible that the last words have been added to enhance the value of a speech not by Demosthenes. Cf. 58.70 βοήθησον ἡμῖν ὁ δεῖνα, εἴ τι ἔχεις, καὶ σύνειπε. ἀνάβηθι. There it seems as if a formulaic ending has been added. Blass, who believed that Dem. 56 was spurious, emended Δημόσθενες to ὁ δεῖνα.

Appendix: Mercantile cases[66]

Dem. 56 is a speech for the prosecution in a δίκη ἐμπορική (mercantile case). The rise of the 'monthly' δίκαι ἐμπορικαί between 355 (the earliest date for Xen. *Por.* 3.3) and 342 (Dem. 7.12) was an important development in Athenian law,[67] for it placed merchants of all states on an equal footing at Athens. The state depended on merchants for its corn supplies and the merchants' activities were a source of revenue. Speed and efficiency in the settling of disputes in which they were involved were to the advantage not only of the merchants but also of the state.

The scope of the δίκαι ἐμπορικαί is set out at 32.1: οἱ νόμοι κελεύουσιν, ὦ ἄνδρες δικασταί, τὰς δίκας εἶναι τοῖς ναυκλήροις καὶ τοῖς ἐμπόροις τῶν Ἀθήναζε καὶ τῶν Ἀθήνηθεν συμβολαίων καὶ περὶ ὧν ἂν ὦσι συγγραφαί. (Cf. also 33.1, 34.42.) Three conditions had to be fulfilled. First, one of the litigants had to be an ἔμπορος or a ναύκληρος.[68] Since in Dem. 34, 35 and 56 it is the defendant who is an ἔμπορος or ναύκληρος, the wording of 32.1 (and 33.1) cannot be taken literally as showing what the law was, at least in practice. Secondly, the case had to arise out of a trading voyage to or from Athens. Thirdly there had to be a written contract.[69]

---

[66] The subject is dealt with by Cohen, *passim.*

[67] Cohen 158ff. sees three stages in the historical development: in the first half of the fourth century they were not 'monthly' and were presided over by the *nautodikai* (cf. Lys. 17.5); in the middle of the century they became 'monthly' and were placed under the *eisagogeis* (cf. Poll. 8.101); finally at the time of the corn crisis of 330–326 (see speech intro., *The corn crisis*) they were transferred to the thesmothetae (cf. Dem. 33.1, Arist. *Ath. Pol.* 59.5). Cf. MacDowell *Law* 231ff. For the view that the development of the δίκαι ἐμπορικαί should be related to the collapse of the empire following the Social War rather than to any developments of a purely commercial nature, see Claude Mossé, in Peter Garnsey, Keith Hopkins and C. R. Whittaker (eds.), *Trade in the ancient economy* (London 1983) 53–63.

[68] An ἔμπορος, who bought goods in one city and sold in another, would normally sail on a ship which was transporting his goods. A ναύκληρος was in command of a merchant ship, either owning it himself or being an employee of the owner. He was a merchant who carried his wares aboard his own ship; an ἔμπορος was not necessarily a ship-owner.

[69] The precise scope of δίκαι ἐμπορικαί has been the subject of debate, an account of which is given in J. Vélissaropoulos, *Les Nauclères grecs. Recherches sur les institutions maritimes en Grèce et dans l'Orient hellénisé* (Geneva 1980) 236ff. For

The δίκαι ἐμπορικαί were ἔμμηνοι, 'monthly', i.e. complaints were accepted every month. The process would usually be swift, for the smooth working of the system would demand that the cases accepted in one month should be completed before the next cycle of cases began (see on 37.2).

The period for the monthly initiation of δίκαι ἐμπορικαί is given at 33.23: αἱ δὲ λήξεις τοῖς ἐμπόροις τῶν δικῶν ἔμμηνοί εἰσιν ἀπὸ τοῦ βοηδρομιῶνος μέχρι τοῦ μουνιχιῶνος, ἵνα παραχρῆμα τῶν δικαίων τυχόντες ἀνάγωνται. The words at 33.26, ὅτι δ' ἐπεδήμει πέρυσιν, ὅτε αἱ δίκαι ἦσαν, λαβέ μοι τὴν μαρτυρίαν, show that the meaning of §23 is that δίκαι ἐμπορικαί were heard only in the part of the year mentioned, not that they were heard throughout the year but were not ἔμμηνοι outside the stated period.[70]

According to the unanimous testimony of the MSS,[71] the period for δίκαι ἐμπορικαί was from Boedromion to Munichion, i.e. approximately September to April, a time outside the normal sailing season. A possible reason for this arrangement may be seen to be to allow merchants to trade unhindered during the sailing period by confining litigation to the period in which they were inactive and free to sue. However, Paoli[72] saw a contradiction between the courts' functioning in the winter and the purpose given at 33.23 for the δίκαι ἐμπορικαί, viz. ἵνα παραχρῆμα τῶν δικαίων τυχόντες ἀνάγωνται. Paoli proposed therefore that the names of the months be transposed,[73] thus placing the hearing of δίκαι ἐμπορικαί during the sailing season. Foreign merchants would no doubt find it easier to be in Athens during these months. In fact, however, 33.23 can be readily reconciled with the

the interpretation of 33.1 adopted here, by which a case could only be brought as a δίκη ἐμπορική if *both* the second and third conditions applied, see Isager–Hansen 151f. For the interpretation by which the speaker is saying that ναύκληροι and ἔμποροι can bring δίκαι ἐμπορικαί *either* about agreements (written or verbal) concerning trading to or from Athens *or* about other matters provided there is an agreement in writing, see L. Gernet, *Droit et société dans la Grèce ancienne* (Paris 1955) 186f.

[70] Cf. Cohen 29f.

[71] μουνυχιῶνος codd.

[72] U. E. Paoli, *SZ* 49 (1929) 473–7, reprinted in *Studi sul processo attico* (Padova 1933) 177–86.

[73] Paoli's transposition of the months has been accepted by Gernet, I 141 n. 2 and Harrison II 86. Against the transposition are Cohen 42–59 and MacDowell *Law* 232.

reading of the manuscript tradition. παραχρῆμα may be taken with τυχόντες as referring to the speedy process of δίκαι ἔμμηνοι; or παραχρῆμα may be taken with ἀνάγωνται, the clause meaning 'in order that having attained their rights they may put to sea immediately' when the sailing season begins. At first sight, however, 33.25 may seem to provide an argument in favour of Paoli's transposition. There the speaker puts forward as an argument of Apaturius for his failure to prosecute the speaker the fact that τότε... ἀσχόλως εἶχεν περὶ ἀναγωγὴν ὤν. It is noticeable that the speaker does not refute this alleged reason of Apaturius by saying that it involved an impossibility. Instead he refutes the statement by saying that Apaturius had lost all his possessions and had sold his ship. If it were impossible for Apaturius to be busy περὶ ἀναγωγήν the speaker would no doubt have taken great delight in saying so. Yet what is said is not inconsistent with the manuscript reading. In the first place, traders could be sailing both early and late in the season. Thus Nicobulus says that he set out on what was probably a trading voyage (see on 37.6) immediately after he had concluded a financial transaction in Elaphebolion, the month before Munichion. Cf. also 35.13. In the second place, to say that a man was busy περὶ ἀναγωγὴν ὤν does not necessarily mean that he was actually sailing. To carry out repairs on a ship which had been beached for the winter, to arrange loans to finance trading, to arrange a cargo, to contract cargo space to other merchants must have been activities which took time and which must have been begun some time before the beginning of the sailing season. Someone engaged in these activities could be described by the words at 33.25.[74] In the face of the unanimity of the manuscript tradition and of the fact that 33.23 and 25 can readily be seen to be consistent with that tradition, Paoli's transposition of the months should be rejected.[75]

[74] Other passages which have been thought to have a bearing on the question of the transposition of the months are discussed by Cohen 46ff. None provides cogent evidence either way for the procedure in δίκαι ἐμπορικαί in the later fourth century.

[75] Dem. 56.30 shows that a merchant might winter abroad by making his last voyage of the season an outward trip. Cf. 34.8 (of an agent). Cf. also Ar. Birds 1047 with schol., ATL II, A9 6f. (IG I² 63) as restored. These last texts show that in the fifth century foreigners could be expected to come to Athens in the winter.

INDEXES

1 English

'ab urbe condita' construction, 85

accusative: absolute, 97, 103, 177, 179; adverbial, 79, 173; double, 127; internal, 77; of respect, 104; of part affected, 98

actions: classification of, 4, 90, withdrawal of, 146

agon; *atimetos*, 2, 147; *timetos*, 2, 133, 220

anakrisis, 4, 74, 120

Anthesteria, 180

anticipation of opponent's argument, 15f., 155, 186

Apaturia, 166, 172

arbitration, 4, 93ff., 218

Archebiades, 96f.

archon, 151f., 174f.

article, 94

association, blackening opponent by, 9, 100, 211

authenticity, 17f., 203f.

bankers, 200f., 217

Basileus, 174f.

bastards, 94, 169f., 182

Brauron, 93

brevity, promise of, 77, 186

Cammys, 160

captatio benevolentiae, 77, 120

character, 8f., 73, 76, 78, 96, 100, 104, 155f., 177f., 191, 214f.

challenges, 95, 102, 127, 137, 146, 170, 219

children, acknowledgement of, 166, 182f.

choregus, 173, 180

chorus, 180

citizenship, 169, 172

Cleomenes, 201f., 211

clubs, 98

cock-fighting, 84

compendious expression, 173

conditional clauses, negative in, 96, 97

contracts, 200f., 210, 215, 220, 224, 228

corn: crisis, 204f.; laws, 197; sources, 212

court fees, 148

cross-examination, 188

dance, 184

dead, offerings to, 190

debtors to state, 134f., 179

deme, enrolment, 161, 172, 187

Demosthenes, 18ff.

depositions, 5

discipline, military, 80f.

dithyramb, 173, 184

documents in speeches, 134, 228

dokimasia, see scrutiny

double standards, 78, 100, 147f., 151, 180, 191

drinking, 78

eisagogeis, 142

election of military officers, 182

emotion, appeals to, 10, 77, 189, 211, *see also* pity

ephebe training, 69, 78

ethopoiia, see character

evidence, 4f.; of slaves, 137

family, 182, 190

filial piety, *see* parents

flattery of jury, 179

genitive: of articular infinitive, 90; characterizing, 87, 98; of

comparison, 179; defining, 176;
partitive, 188; with ἐγκαλέω, 76,
131; with ἐυπορέω, 136; with
κρίνω, 76
gymnasiarch, 174

help, appeals for, 77
homicide, 92, 157ff.; pardon for,
158
horoi, 106 n. 8, 124
humour, 86

imperative, third person, 229
imperfect in narrative, 91
impiety, 88f., 101
imprisonment, 209
inheritance, 173, 190
interest rates, 196
irony, 156
irrelevance, 8ff.

juries, 1ff., 77, 96, 100, 182

kleteres, 4
knowledge, appeal to jurors', 96, 97,
169

Laurion, 105, 120
litigiousness, Athenian dislike of, 89,
168, 217
liturgies, 104, 173f.
logographer *see* speechwriter
lungs, 85

Mantias, 160ff.
maritime loans, 195f.
Maroneia, 120
mines: tenure and payment, 134;
boundaries, 145
money, value of, 1, 206
moneylenders, prejudice against, 155

name: full formula, 173; of
grandfather, 186; pet names, 175
negative: in conditional clauses, 96,
97; with participle, 97, 124, 136,
183, 191; repeated, 104f.; after

verbs of asseveration, 98; after
verbs of denying etc., 118
Niceratus, 97

oaths, 94, 99f., 103, 170, 191, 194
optative of indefinite frequency, 78,
79
oral nature of Athenian society, 183
ore processing, 120

Pamphilus (father of Plangon), 160
Panactum, 69
Panathenaea, 175
paragraphe, 111f., 208
parents, treatment/rights of, 92, 188,
193
participle: conditional, 97, 124, 136,
183; expressing main idea, 102f.;
substantival, 82
penalties for prosecutors, 76, 208f.
periphrasis with ποιεῖσθαι, 182
Phocion, 179
phratry, 161f., 169, 171f., 189
physical appearance, 155f.
pity, appeals for, 103, 153, 190
Plutarchus, 179
politics in litigation, 170f.
pollution, 158f.
Polyaratus, 160
Pontus, 122
precedents in Greek trials, 93
present infinitive/participle
representing imperfect of direct
statement, 178
prosecutors, 3f.
prudential arguments, 10, 104, 232
purification, 101, 159
Pythodorus, 82

quotations, 175

relative, connective, 176
ring-composition, 85f., 172, 232

sale with right of redemption, 105ff.,
121ff., 129, 139f.
scrutiny of deme members, 172

shops, 82
slaves: cost of, 133; assault on, 80;
    evidence of, 137, 147f.;
    prosecution of, 154
speechwriters, 13ff.
Spintharus, 83
stick as a sign of character, 156
strategus, 80f., 175f.
summons, 4, 148
suppression of indecency, 83f., 89
sycophant, 168f.
symmories, 145f., 174
synegoros, 7f., 198 n. 47

Tamynae, 179
taxiarch, 79, 180
Theophilus, 105
thesmothetae, 142
Thrasymus, 135

torch-races, 174
Triballians, 69, 100f.
trierarchy, 104, 174f.

vagueness, deliberate, 93, 143
variety, 79
voice as a sign of character, 155f.
voting: in lawcourt 2f.; for military
    officers, 182

walk as a sign of character, 155
water clock, 6, 99, 105
witnesses, 5, 137, 200f., 216; to
    δεκάτη, 183; to marriage, 183
women, seclusion of, 151, 175f.

youth: indulgence towards, 91;
    modesty expected from, 76

2 Greek

ἀγὼν ἀτίμητος, τιμητός see agon
    atimetos, timetos
ἀδικέω, 190
ἀθλοθέται, 175
αἰτιάομαι, 127f.
ἀκαριαῖος, 226
ἀκέραιος, 226
ἀλλά…γε, 214, ἀλλὰ νὴ Δία, 97
ἀμφιδρόμια, 152
ἀναιρέομαι, 217
ἀναμείγνυμι, 83
ἀνίσταμαι, 96
ἀντιλαγχάνω, 142, 192
ἀντιπροκαλέομαι, 150
ἀπάγω, 190
ἀπαγωγή, 74f., 76, 178
ἀπαλλαγή, 117f.; ἀπαλλάττω,
    117f., 130, 132
ἁπλᾶ, 98
ἀποδέχομαι, 227
ἀποδιαιτάω, 192
ἀποδίδομαι, 108f.
ἀποδιδότωσαν, 229
ἀποκηρύττω, 193
ἀποκεκλεῖσθαι τῶν σιτίων, 85

ἀπολαμβάνω, 122, 216
ἀποπέμπομαι, 79
ἀπορέομαι, 85
ἀπὸ ταὐτομάτου, 97, 216
ἀπράγμων, 92
ἀρχιτέκτων, 214
ἀσέλγεια, 86
αὐτολήκυθος, 87
ἄφεσις, 117f., 228; ἀφίημι, 117f.,
    131, 132, 154
ἀφίσταμαι, 124

βακτηρία, 155f.
βούλομαι, 78

γε, 136, 153
γνώμηι τῆι δικαιοτάτηι, 194
γραμματείδιον, 99, 206
γραφή: ἀστρατείας, 179; λιποταξίου,
    180; ξενίας, 181; τραύματος, 90;
    ὕβρεως, 74ff., 80, 142
γυμνασίαρχος, see gymnasiarch
γυμνός, 84

δέ, apodotic 222
δεῖνα, ὁ, 157, 232
δεινότης, 178
δεκάτη, 182
δή, 186
διηγησις, 77, 168
δίκη: αἰκείας, 75f., 142; βλάβης, 134,
    166, 172, 199; βιαίων, 141;
    βουλεύσεως, 93; ἐξούλης, 122,
    144, 179, 190; κακηγορίας, 89f.;
    φόνου, 92, 157ff.;
    ψευδομαρτυρίων, 5 n. 11, 181;
    δίκαι ἔμμηνοι, 113, 119f., 234;
    δίκαι ἐμπορικαί, 201, 203, 209,
    233f.
δοκιμασία see scrutiny

ἔγκλημα, 134
εἰσαγγελία, 152
εἰσάγειν: δίκην, 180; εἰς τούς
    φράτερας, 171f.
εἰσαγωγεύς, 142f.
εἰσβιάζομαι, 189
εἰσπηδάω, 79
εἰσφορά, 145, 174, 179
εἶτα, 90
Ἑκαταῖα, 101
ἐκπίπτω, 122, 159
ἕλκω, 149f.
ἔμμηνοι, 119
ἔμπορος, 212, 233 n. 68
ἔμπνος, 85
ἔνδειξις, 178
ἐξαλείφω, 193
ἐξανίστημι, 83
ἐξαπατάω, 100
ἐξίλλω, 144
ἐξίστασθαι τῶν ὄντων, 153
ἐπαγγέλλω, 129
ἐπεί + imperative, 189
ἐπιβάτης, 214
ἐπιβουλεύω, 134
ἐπὶ δυοῖν ἀγκύραιν ὁρμεῖν, 231
ἐπικατατέμνειν τῶν μέτρων ἐντός,
    145
ἐπίκληρος, 111, 113, 151f.
ἐπίλογος, 74, 105

ἐπιμελεῖσθαι, 151f.
ἐπιτάττω, 219
ἐπιτείνω, 216, 222
ἐπωβελία, 208f.
ἔρανος, ἐρανίζω, 181
ἐργασία, 205
ἐργαστήριον, 120, 168
ἑταιρεῖαι, see clubs
ἔχειν καὶ κρατεῖν, 124
ἐχῖνος, 95, 181

ζυγομαχέω, 173

ἦ μήν, 102

θαυμαστῶς ὡς, 124

ἱερὰ καὶ ὅσια, 190
ἰθύφαλλος, 86

καθάπαξ, 140, 153
κάθαρσις, 85
καὶ δή, 174
κακοδαιμονισταί, 86
κακοῦργοι, 75
καλὸς κἀγαθός, 86
κάπηλος, 212
καταγιγνώσκω, 191
καταδιαιτάω, 192
καταλαμβάνω, 124
καταπλάττω, 150
κατασκευάζω, 87
κατεπιορκέομαι, 102
κεγχρεών, 136f.
κλεψύδρα, see water clock
κληροῦν: τὰς δίκας, 74; ἀρχήν, 176
κουρεῖον, 172

λαγχάνειν δίκην, 74
λέγειν τι, 178
Λεωκόριον, 81f.
λῃτουργίαι, see liturgies
ληξιαρχικὸν γραμματεῖον, 172
λωποδύτης, 74f.

μά, 131
μάλιστα, 190

μεῖον, 172
Μελίτη, 82
μέν, 104, 205f.
μέτρα, 145
μή with participle, with verbs of
  asseveration, with verbs of
  denying etc., see negatives; μή τί
  γε (δή), 89; μή ὅτι...ἀλλά, 89

νή Δία, 138, 188

οἴχομαι, 71, 84
ὁμόσε πορεύομαι, 217
ὁ καὶ ὁ, 94
οὐ in conditional clauses, see
  negatives; οὐ μὴν ἀλλά, 135
οὐδὲ πολλοῦ δεῖ, 102
ὅρκον διδόναι, 171

παθεῖν τι, 92
πάθος, 77, 91, see also emotion, pity
παλιγκαπηλεύω, παλιγκάπηλος, 212
πάνυ, 74; πάνυ γε, 177
παρά, 120, 185, 228
παραγραφή, see paragraphe
παραγράφειν, 188; παραγράφεσθαι,
  117
παρακαταβολή, 148
παράστασις, 148
παρασυγγραφέω, 200 n. 50, 224
παρεῖναι, 94
πάροινος, 87
πατρόθεν, 180
πίστεις, 86, 173
πλημμελέω, 136
πλύνω, 177
ποιεῖσθαι, 172, 181, 190
ποῖος, 176
πρᾶσις ἐπὶ λύσει, see sale with right
  of redemption
πρατήρ, 108f.
προάγω, 92
προεισφορά, 145f
προΐεμαι, 206
πρόκλησις, see challenges
προξενέω, 125f.
προοίμιον, 74, 168

προσκρούω, 130
προσπαραγράφω, 175
πρυτανεῖα, 148
πῦρ, 102

ῥήγνυμι, 221

σκυθρωπάζω, 97
συγγραφή, συγγράφομαι, 200 n. 50;
  see also contracts
συκοφάντης, συκοφαντέω, 129, 168f.
συμβουλεύω/-ομαι, 74
συνήγορος, see synegoros
συντετραίνω, 146
συντιμάω, 212
σώιζω, σώιζομαι, 221, 227

τιμάω, τιμάομαι, 2, 123, 212
τίς = ὅστις, 222
τοιχωρύχοι, 99
τρέπεσθαι εἰς κεφαλήν, etc., 88
τρίβων, 98
τύφω, 144f.

ὕβρις, 75ff., 77
ὑπεύθυνος, 154
ὑπογράφω, 135
ὑποστέλλομαι, 153
ὑποτίθημι, 207f.

φαίνομαι + participle, 184, 222
φάσις, 145, 178
Φερρεφάττιον, 83
φιλοπραγμοσύνη, 168
φοιτάω, 184
φόνος ἀκούσιος, ἑκούσιος, 157f.

χαλκοῦς, 206
χειροτονέω, 182
Χοεῖς, 180
χορηγός, see choregus
χράομαι, 178
χρόνος, 182

ὠνεῖσθαι: of πρασις ἐπὶ λύσει, 108;
  of lease of mines, 134
ὥρα, 207

DATE DUE